DATE DUE

D1376950

(THE) JOHNS HOPKINS UNIVERSITY, STUDIES IN
HISTORICAL AND POLITICAL SCIENCE

Under the direction of the Departments of History,
Political Economy, and Political Science

SERIES LXXXIII   NUMBER 2
(1965)

A BARONIAL FAMILY IN MEDIEVAL ENGLAND:
THE CLARES, 1217–1314

A BARONIAL FAMILY IN MEDIEVAL ENGLAND: THE CLARES, 1217-1314

By

MICHAEL ALTSCHUL

BALTIMORE
THE JOHNS HOPKINS PRESS
1965

TO MARIAN

PREFACE

This study is based on a doctoral dissertation completed at The Johns Hopkins University in 1962. I am grateful to the supervisors of the dissertation, Professor John W. Baldwin of The Johns Hopkins University and Professor Fred A. Cazel, Jr., of the University of Connecticut for their unfailing aid and encouragement, both then and since. I owe a special debt of gratitude to Professor Sylvia L. Thrupp of the University of Michigan, who read the entire manuscript and made numerous suggestions for its improvement. I should also like to thank Dr. E. B. Fryde of University College, Aberystwyth, Dr. C. H. Lawrence of the University of London, Mr. T. B. Pugh of Southampton University, and Mr. W. Rhys Robinson for their valuable suggestions and criticisms. Portions of Chapters II, IV, and VIII, in somewhat altered form, were originally written for Volume III of *The County History of Glamorgan* (to be published by the University of Wales Press). I am indebted to the editor of Volume III, Mr. T. B. Pugh, and to the General Editor, Professor Glanmor Williams of University College, Swansea, for their kind permission to use this material again.

Much of the research for this book was done in 1960–61 at the Public Record Office and the Department of Manuscripts of the British Museum. I am permanently indebted to the staffs of these bodies for their kindness and patience, and to the Fulbright Program and the United States Educational Commission in the United Kingdom for the opportunity to avail myself of those facilities. My thanks are also due to the staffs of the libraries at the following institutions: The Johns Hopkins University, the Peabody Institute of Baltimore, the Library of Congress, the University of Michigan, the British Museum, and the Institute of Historical Research, London University. The study was assisted in its final stages by a grant from the Faculty Research Fund of the Horace H. Rackham School of Graduate Studies of the University of Michigan. I am most grateful to Mrs. Dorothy Foster for her expert typing of the manuscript.

9

There are two special debts which, for different reasons, I can never fully repay.

The first is to the late Professor Sidney Painter, who originally suggested a study of the Clare family and gave cheerfully and unstintingly of his knowledge and advice before his untimely death in January, 1960.

The second is to my wife.

MICHAEL ALTSCHUL

Ann Arbor, Michigan
May, 1965

TABLE OF CONTENTS

11

PART II: THE ESTATES

LIST OF ABBREVIATIONS

Brit. Mus.	British Museum
Cal. Chart. Rolls	Calendar of Charter Rolls 1226– (London: H. M. Stationery Office, 1903–)
Cal. Close Rolls	Calendar of Close Rolls 1272– (H. M. Stationery Office, 1900–)
Cal. Docs. Ireland	Calendar of Documents relating to Ireland 1171–1307 (H. M. Stationery Office, 1875–86)
Cal. Fine Rolls	Calendar of Fine Rolls 1272– (H. M. Stationery Office, 1911–)
Cal. Inq. Post Mortem	Calendar of Inquisitions Post Mortem, Henry III– (H. M. Stationery Office, 1904–)
Cal. Liberate Rolls	Calendar of Liberate Rolls 1226– (H. M. Stationery Office, 1917–)
Cal. Pat. Rolls	Calendar of Patent Rolls 1232– (H. M. Stationery Office, 1906–)
Cartae de Glamorgan	Cartae et alia munimenta quae ad dominium de Glamorgancia pertinent (6 vols.; 2nd ed.; ed. G. T. Clark; Cardiff, 1910)
Close Rolls	Close Rolls, Henry III [1227–72] (H. M. Stationery Office, 1902–38)
Curia Regis Rolls	Curia Regis Rolls, Richard I– (H. M. Stationery Office, 1922–)
G. E.C.	G. E. C[okayne], The Complete Peerage . . . of the United Kingdom . . . (12 vols.; new ed., ed. Vicary Gibbs et al., London, 1910–59)
KR	PRO, Exchequer, King's Remembrancer
LTR	PRO, Exchequer, Lord Treasurer's Remembrancer
PRO	Public Record Office, London
Rolls Series	Chronicles and Memorials of Great Britain and Ireland during the Middle Ages (99 vols.; London, 1858–97)
Tewkesbury	Annales de Theokesberia, ed. H. R. Luard (Annales Monastici, vol. I, Rolls Series XXXVI, 1864)

13

PART I: THE FAMILY

CHAPTER I

THE FAMILY AS A SOCIAL UNIT IN THE
THIRTEENTH CENTURY

Introductory. The Inheritance, 1066–1217

The Clares came to England with the Conqueror. Like many other great families settled on English soil after the Conquest, they were related to the dukes of Normandy and had established themselves as important members of the Norman feudal aristocracy in the late tenth and early eleventh centuries. The origin of the family can be traced to Godfrey, eldest of the illegitimate children of Duke Richard I (the Fearless), the Conqueror's great-grandfather. Godfrey's relations with Duke Richard and his successor, Duke Richard II, are obscure. The chronicler Orderic Vitalis states that Duke Richard I gave the *comté* of Brionne to Godfrey, and that Brionne then passed, on Godfrey's death about 1015, to his son Gilbert.[1] Recent investigation, however, indicates that while the duke granted Brionne to Godfrey, he did not make him a count, and that Godfrey's comital title actually derives from the grant of the county of Eu made to him sometime after 996 by his half brother, Duke Richard II.[2] After Godfrey's death, Eu was given to William, another of Duke Richard I's bastard sons, and Gilbert, the son of Godfrey, was left with only the lordship of Brionne. Under Duke Robert I, the father of William the Conqueror, Gilbert became a figure of considerable importance, and he seems to have assumed the title of count of Brionne, while at the same time never relinquishing his claim to Eu.[3] When Count

[1] Orderic Vitalis, *Historia Ecclesiastica,* ed. Auguste Le Prévost (Société de l'Histoire de France, 1838–55), III, 340.
[2] David Douglas, "The Earliest Norman Counts," *English Historical Review,* LXI (1946), 134, 140.
[3] *Ibid.,* p. 140 and note 4.

17

William of Eu died shortly before 1040, Gilbert did assume the
land and title, but he was assassinated in 1040 [4] and his young
sons, Richard and Baldwin, were forced to flee Normandy, finding
safety at the court of Baldwin V, count of Flanders. When
William the Conqueror married Count Baldwin's daughter, he
restored Gilbert's sons to Normandy, although he did not invest
them with either Brionne or Eu or a comital title. William granted
the lordships of Bienfaite and Orbec to Richard fitz Gilbert, and
Le Sap and Meules to Baldwin. Although Gilbert's descendants
later pressed a claim for Brionne, it was never restored.[5]

Richard and Baldwin fitz Gilbert took part in the Norman con-
quest of England, and both assumed important positions in the
Conqueror's reign. Baldwin was made guardian of Exeter in 1068,
and appears in Domesday Book as sheriff of Devon, lord of
Okehampton and numerous other estates in Devon, Dorset, and
Somerset. His sons William and Richard were also sheriffs of
Devon and participated in the abortive Norman penetration of
Carmarthen in the early twelfth century.[6]

The lasting position of the family in England, however, must be
credited to Baldwin's brother, Richard fitz Gilbert I. He was
regent of England jointly with William de Warenne during the
Conqueror's absence in 1075, and he served in various other
important capacities for the king.[7] King William rewarded his
cousin well, granting him one of the largest fiefs in the territorial
settlement. The lordship centered on Clare, Suffolk, which had
been an important stronghold in Anglo-Saxon times. The bulk
of Richard fitz Gilbert's estates lay in Suffolk, Essex, Surrey, and
Kent, but comprised holdings in various other counties in the
southern and eastern parts of the kingdom as well. In addition,
William arranged for his marriage with Rohese, sister of Walter

[4] Oderic Vitalis, *Historia Ecclesiastica*, II, 369.
[5] *G. E. C.*, III, 242; Orderic Vitalis, *Historia Ecclesiastica*, III, 343. See also
note 11 below.
[6] *Liber Censualis vocatus Domesday-Book*, eds. A. Farley and Sir Henry Ellis
(Record Commission, 1783–1816), I, 81, 93, 105–6 (hereafter cited as *Domesday
Book*); J. Horace Round, *Feudal England* (London, 1895), pp. 329, 472; J. Horace
Round, *Studies in Peerage and Family History* (Westminster, 1901), pp. 212–4;
Sir John E. Lloyd, *A History of Wales to the Edwardian Conquest* (2 vols.;
3rd ed.; London, 1939), II, 401, 406, 427.
[7] Sir Frank Stenton, *Anglo-Saxon England* (2nd ed.; Oxford, 1947), pp. 623–25,
641.

Giffard, later earl of Buckingham, and her dowry, consisting of lands in Huntingdon and Hertford, became absorbed in the family inheritance.[8] The composition of the honor of Clare changed considerably in the early twelfth century through subinfeudation, exchange, and alienation to religious foundations such as the abbey of Bec, of which the early members of the family were important patrons,[9] but paucity of evidence makes it impossible to trace the process in much detail. In 1166 the honor of Clare was assessed for 127 ¼ fees, created before the death of King Henry I in 1135, and 7 ⅝ fees *de novo*, although scutage was later charged on 132 ½ fees.[10] In addition to the honor of Clare, Richard held the manor and castle of Tonbridge and associated manors in Kent as a fief of the archbishop of Canterbury.[11] Through his marriage with Rohese Giffard, his descendants a century later were to inherit half the Giffard estates. Richard fitz Gilbert I prospered from his close associations with his kinsman William the Conqueror, and by the time of his death in 1090 he had laid secure territorial foundations for the future greatness of his house.

After Richard's death, his extensive properties in Normandy and England were divided between his two older sons. The Norman fiefs of Bienfaite and Orbec passed to Roger, while Gilbert, who was probably the younger of the two, inherited the English honors of Clare and Tonbridge.[12] Gilbert fitz Richard I found himself at odds with the Conqueror's successor, William Rufus,[13] but he and the other members of the family in England enjoyed great favor with King Henry I. It has been suggested by Round and Painter, among others, that Henry's largesse stemmed from the fact that Walter Tirel, the husband of Richard fitz Gilbert's daughter Adelize, shot the arrow which slew Rufus. The proof of a definite connection between the death of Rufus and Henry's

---

[8] *Domesday Book*, I, 14 (Kent), 34b–35b (Surrey), 72 (Wilts), 113 (Devon), 130 (Middlesex), 142b (Hertford), 196b (Cambridge), 207 (Huntingdon), 216 (Bedford); II, 38b–39 (Essex), 263 (Norfolk), 389b, 447b–448 (Suffolk).

[9] Marjorie Morgan, *English Lands of the Abbey of Bec* (Oxford, 1946).

[10] *Red Book of the Exchequer*, ed. Hubert Hall (Rolls Series XCIX, 1896), I, 139, 403–6; I. J. Sanders, *English Baronies* (Oxford, 1960), p. 35 note 2.

[11] *Domesday Book*, I, 4–6. It is possible that Richard accepted Tonbridge in return for relinquishing the family claim to the lordship of Brionne in Normandy. Douglas, "Earliest Norman Counts," p. 135 note 1.

[12] *G. E. C.*, III, 243 and note (a).

[13] Austin Lane Poole, *Domesday Book to Magna Carta* (2nd ed.; Oxford, 1955), p. 109.

favor to the Clares is lacking, and all that can be said with certainty is that the wealth and position of the family increased rapidly in his reign.[14] The king employed all the rights and techniques of patronage and favor at his disposal to promote the family. Walter Tirel and Eudo Dapifer, the husbands of Richard fitz Gilbert's daughters Adelize and Rohese, were close friends of the king. One of Rohese Giffard's brothers was made earl of Buckingham and another bishop of Winchester. In addition, Gilbert fitz Richard's younger brothers were handsomely provided for. Richard, a monk of Bec, was made abbot of Ely in 1100, shortly after Henry I assumed the throne.[15] Another brother, Robert, was granted the forfeited manors of Ralph Baynard in East Anglia, while Walter, who founded Tintern Abbey in 1131, was given the great lordship of Netherwent with the castle of Striguil in the southern march, territories previously held by Roger, son of William fitz Osbern, earl of Hereford, who had forfeited them in 1075.[16] Gilbert fitz Richard himself was married to Adeliz, daughter of Hugh, count of Clermont. In 1110 he was granted the lordship of Ceredigion (Cardigan) in southwestern Wales, and immediately embarked upon an intensive campaign to subjugate the area.[17]

Gilbert fitz Richard I died in 1117, but his children continued to profit from royal generosity and favorable connections. His three daughters were married to important barons, William de Montfichet, lord of Stansted in Essex, the marcher lord Baderon de Monmouth, and Aubrey de Vere, lord of Hedingham in Essex and father of the first Vere earl of Oxford. Gilbert also left five sons. Little is known of two of them, Hervey, whom King Stephen sent on an expedition to Cardigan around 1140, and a certain Walter, who participated in the Second Crusade of 1147.[18] The

[14] Round, *Feudal England*, pp. 468–79; Sidney Painter, "The Family and the Feudal System in Twelfth Century England," *Speculum*, XXXV (1960), 6. The most recent treatment of these events is in Christopher Brooke, *The Saxon and Norman Kings* (London, 1963), pp. 179–80, 186, 189–92.

[15] Eadmer, *Historia Novorum*, ed. Rev. M. Rule (Rolls Series LXXXI, 1884), pp. 143, 185.

[16] Sanders, *English Baronies*, pp. 110–11, 129–30.

[17] Lloyd, *Hist. Wales*, II, 426–27; Sir J. Goronwy Edwards, "The Normans and the Welsh March," *Proceedings of the British Academy*, XLII (1956), 162–68. Cardigan had originally been invaded by Roger, earl of Shrewsbury, but his son Robert of Bellême forfeited the lands in 1102.

[18] Sanders, *English Baronies*, pp, 52, 65, 83; Round, *Feudal England*, p. 472;

youngest son, Baldwin, established himself as an important member of the lesser baronage by obtaining the Lincolnshire barony of Bourne through marriage.[19] The eldest son and heir, Richard fitz Gilbert II, was allowed to marry Adeliz, sister of Ranulf des Gernons, earl of Chester, acquiring lands in Lincoln and Northampton as her marriage portion.[20] Probably of greater importance from King Henry's point of view was the fact that Richard II's ties of kinship with the earl of Chester and Baderon de Monmouth provided added social cohesiveness to the small group of marcher lords campaigning against the Welsh. Richard—in a manner reminiscent of his thirteenth century descendants—was mainly occupied with marcher affairs. His efforts to consolidate the gains made by his father in Cardigan were at first largely successful, but he was killed in an ambush in 1136 and the lordship was soon recovered by the Welsh.[21]

Of Gilbert fitz Richard I's sons, only one, Gilbert, achieved any great prominence in the middle decades of the twelfth century. Gilbert was the founder of the great cadet branch of the family, and the father of one of the most famous men in English history. He seems to have been far more powerful and important than even his brother Richard, and the fortunes of his line deserve separate consideration.

Gilbert fitz Gilbert de Clare seems to have stood high in the favor of Henry I, perhaps because his wife Isabella, daughter of Robert de Beaumont, count of Meulan and earl of Leicester, was one of Henry's favorite mistresses. When Gilbert's uncle Roger, brother of Gilbert fitz Richard I, died without heirs, Henry granted him the lordships of Bienfaite and Orbec in Normandy. Gilbert served King Stephen more or less faithfully in the civil wars that followed Henry I's death, and he received many important grants from the king. When another uncle, Walter, lord of Netherwent in South Wales, died without issue in 1138, Gilbert was given his lordship as well.[22] Shortly before, the king had granted him the

---

J. Horace Round, *Geoffrey de Mandeville* (London, 1892), pp. 389–92; Lloyd, *Hist. Wales*, II, 474.
[19] Sanders, *English Baronies*, p. 107.
[20] William Farrer, *Honors and Knights' Fees* (3 vols.; London, 1923–25), II, 183, 210–11.
[21] Lloyd, *Hist. Wales*, II, 471–75.
[22] *G.E.C.*, X, 348–49 and note (d).

lordship of Pembroke, which had been forfeited by Arnulf of
Montgomery in 1102, and in 1138, about the time he obtained
Netherwent, Gilbert was created earl of Pembroke.[23] He generally styled himself thereafter as earl of Striguil, deriving the name
from the *caput* of his lordship of Netherwent.[24] At his death in
1148, he was succeeded by his son Richard fitz Gilbert, more commonly known as " Strongbow," who led the Norman invasion of
Ireland and obtained the great lordship of Leinster in 1171.[25] In
two generations, the cadet branch of the Clares thus established
itself among the most important noble families of the realm and
developed a vast territorial endowment. Strongbow, as earl of
Pembroke, lord of Netherwent and lord of Leinster, was the most
powerful of the marcher and Anglo-Irish magnates under King
Henry II. The exact details are obscure, but his control over the
family lordships in Normandy was not continuous, for Orbec was
held by a cousin, Robert de Montfort, in 1172, although Strongbow apparently regained it later.[26] Strongbow died in 1176, leaving a son Gilbert who died about 1185.[27] Four years later, the
inheritance passed to Strongbow's daughter Isabel and her husband, William Marshal (d. 1219), who somewhat later assumed
the title of earl of Pembroke.[28]

While the cadet branch of the family became extinct in the
male line, the senior branch continued to prosper under Stephen
and Henry II, despite the loss of Cardigan following the death of

[23] *Ibid.*, X, 349–51.
[24] Round, *Geoffrey de Mandeville*, pp. 320–21. On occasion, however, he employed the proper title, witnessing a charter of his nephew *ca.* 1148 as " Comes
Gillebertus de Penbroc." PRO, Duchy of Lancaster, Ancient Deeds, Series LS,
DL 27/47, printed from a later copy in *Sir Christopher Hatton's Book of Seals*,
eds. Lewis C. Loyd and Doris M. Stenton (Northamptonshire Record Society,
vol. XV, 1950), no. 84.
[25] For a detailed account of the Norman conquest of Ireland, see Goddard H.
Orpen, *Ireland under the Normans 1169–1333* (4 vols.; Oxford, 1911–20), vol. I
passim. A shorter version, based on Orpen, is given in Poole, *Domesday Book to
Magna Carta*, pp. 302–10. Strongbow's career and the early history of Leinster
are discussed more fully below in Chapter IX.
[26] F. M. Powicke, *The Loss of Normandy 1189–1204* (2nd ed.; Manchester,
1961), p. 350.
[27] *G. E. C.*, X, 357–58.
[28] Sidney Painter, *William Marshal* (Baltimore, 1933), pp. 66–67, 76–79. William and his descendants were in continuous possession of the Norman lands,
despite Philip Augustus' conquest of Normandy in 1204. *Ibid.*, pp. 136–40;
G. E. C., X, 368.

Richard fitz Gilbert II in 1136. After his death, the honors of
Clare and Tonbridge and the other estates passed to his elder
son Gilbert fitz Richard II, who was created earl of Hertford by
King Stephen. The exact date of the granting of the comital title
is unknown, but it probably dates from 1138, the year in which
his uncle, Strongbow's father, was created earl of Pembroke. Gilbert II was certainly earl by 1141, when he witnessed a charter
of Stephen as " Comes Gislebertus de heortford." [29] Henceforth
the earls used this title interchangeably with that of " Comes de
Clare." It should be noted, however, that Gilbert, like some other
earls created at this time, for example Aubrey de Vere, earl of
Oxford, held few lands in the county from which he assumed the
proper title.[30] Earl Gilbert seems to have deserted Stephen and
sided with the Empress Matilda in the civil wars of the mid-
twelfth century, although his activities were not especially noteworthy. He was probably unmarried, and died in 1152, when his
younger brother Roger inherited the estates and the comital title.
Roger's major activity was to resume the campaigns against the
Welsh in Cardigan which had occupied his grandfather and father,
but which his brother had neglected. After eight years of warfare
he was finally defeated in 1165 and abandoned the effort.[31] Earl
Roger was thus unable to re-establish the senior branch of the
Clare family in the Welsh march, but he did manage to add some
lands and nine additional knights' fees to the inheritance in England through his marriage to Maud, daughter and heir of the
Norfolk baron James de St. Hilary. Earl Roger died in 1173 and
his widow conveyed the remainder of the St. Hilary barony to her
second husband, William de Aubigny, earl of Arundel.[32] The
Clare estates themselves, along with the earldom, passed to Roger's
son, Richard.[33]

For over four decades until his death in 1217, Richard, earl of
Hertford, was the head of the great house of Clare. He does not

---

[29] *G. E. C.*, VI, 498–9; Round, *Geoffrey de Mandeville*, p. 173.

[30] " Comes de Clare " is used e. g. in the charter *ca.* 1148 cited above, note 24.
I am grateful to Professor Fred A. Cazel, Jr., for pointing out the analogy with
the earl of Oxford. A full discussion of this point is contained in Sir Frank
Stenton, *The First Century of English Feudalism 1066–1166* (2nd ed.; Oxford,
1961), pp. 232–34.

[31] Lloyd, *Hist. Wales*, II, 506, 513–14.

[32] *Red Book of the Exchequer*, I, 406–7; Sanders, *English Baronies*, p. 44.

[33] *G. E. C.*, VI, 501.

seem, however, to have played a part in national politics com-
mensurate with his standing or potential importance. He was not
active in the later years of Henry II's reign and took little part
in politics during the absentee reign of Richard I. He did emerge
as a leading figure in the opposition to King John, which culminated in Magna Carta, and was one of the twenty-five barons
charged with enforcing its provisions; but as Painter has stated,
Earl Richard's " position rather than his activity gave him importance in the baronial party." [34]

Richard de Clare's major importance was the fact that he added
immensely to the wealth, prestige, and landed endowment of his
line. In 1189 he acquired half of the former honor of Giffard.
Walter Giffard, earl of Buckingham, died in 1164 and his extensive lands in England and Normandy escheated to the Crown.
King Richard I, in need of money for the Third Crusade, agreed
to divide the estates between Earl Richard and his cousin Isabel,
Strongbow's daughter and wife of William Marshal. Both the
earl and Isabel based their claims on the fact that they were
descendants of Rohese Giffard, Walter's aunt and wife of Richard
fitz Gilbert I, the companion of the Conqueror. Both the English
and Norman lands were divided equally. Longueville, the chief
seat in Normandy, passed to the Marshals, while Earl Richard
obtained Long Crendon in Buckingham, the *caput* of the Giffard
honor in England, associated manors in Buckingham, Cambridge
and Bedfordshire, and 43 knights' fees.[35] Long Crendon, however,
must have been sold or alienated to William Marshal about this
time, for it was in the possession of his heirs in 1229 and passed
to the Mortimer family when the Marshal inheritance itself was
partitioned in 1246.[36] In addition, Earl Richard acquired some of
the former Giffard lands in Normandy, thus becoming the first
head of the senior branch of the Clares to hold estates on both

[34] Sidney Painter, "The Earl of Clare," in *Feudalism and Liberty*, ed. Fred A.
Cazel, Jr. (Baltimore, 1961), p. 225. The earl's career is briefly outlined in
ibid., pp. 220, 222–25.

[35] *Pipe Roll 2 Richard I*, ed. Doris M. Stenton (Pipe Roll Society, vol. XXXIX,
new ser. I, 1925), pp. 102, 145; *Cartae Antiquae* (*Rolls 11–20*), ed. J. Conway
Davies (Pipe Roll Society, vol. LXXI, new ser. XXXIII, 1957), pp. 165–6. Each
party offered 2,000 marks, but Richard had paid only about half the amount by
1200. See *Pipe Roll 1 John* and *3 John*, ed. Doris M. Stenton (Pipe Roll Society,
vols. XLVIII, LII, new ser. X, XIV, 1933, 1936), pp. 265, 64.

[36] *Cal. Chart. Rolls 1226–57*, p. 142; PRO, Chancery Miscellanea, C 47/9/20.

sides of the Channel since Richard fitz Gilbert I in the late eleventh century. His position in Normandy was brief, however, for the estates were seized by Philip Augustus in 1204 and never restored.[37] In 1195 the earl made another substantial, although less important, addition to the Clare inheritance by obtaining the honor of St. Hilary on the death of his mother Maud, widow of Earl Roger. Maud's second husband, William de Aubigny, earl of Arundel, who had held St. Hilary *jure uxoris*, died in 1193, and despite the fact that he had a son and heir, the honor reverted to Maud and after her death escheated to the Crown. Earl Richard offered £360, in all probability far more than it was actually worth, to acquire it. The honor, which later became thoroughly absorbed in the honor of Clare and lost its separate identity, included lands in Norfolk and Northampton.[38]

By far the most important act of Earl Richard, insofar as the future position of the family was concerned, was his marriage to Amicia, second daughter and eventual sole heir of William, earl of Gloucester. Possession of the vast Gloucester inheritance, which comprised the earldom and honor of Gloucester with over 260 knights' fees in England, along with the important marcher lordships of Glamorgan and Gwynllwg, represented great political as well as territorial power, and its descent was complicated by this fact.

William, earl of Gloucester, died in 1183, leaving three daughters. The eldest, Mabel, had married Amaury de Montfort, count of Evreux, while the second daughter Amicia was married to Earl Richard de Clare. Henry II arranged the marriage of the youngest, Isabel, to his son John, count of Mortain. They were married in 1189, and Isabel conveyed the inheritance to him. When John became king in 1199, he divorced her to marry Isabelle of Angoulême.[39] King John kept Isabel of Gloucester in his own custody however. In 1200, he created Mabel's son Amaury earl of Gloucester, granting him the normal comital privilege of the third penny of the pleas of the shire, but only the revenues of four

---

[37] Powicke, *Loss of Normandy*, p. 336.

[38] *Pipe Roll 7 Richard I*, ed. Doris M. Stenton (Pipe Roll Society, vol. XLIV, new ser. VI, 1929), p. 225; Sanders, *English Baronies*, p. 44.

[39] *G. E. C.*, V, 689; Sidney Painter and Fred A. Cazel, Jr., "The Marriage of Isabelle of Angoulême," *English Historical Review*, LXIII (1948), 83–89; LXVII (1952), 233–35.

demesne manors in England. In addition, Earl Richard de Clare and his son Gilbert were given a few estates and 10 fees of the honor of Gloucester in Kent; otherwise John kept the bulk of the honor, along with the great lordships of Glamorgan and Gwynllwg, in his own hands.[40] Amaury died without issue in 1213, and the following January John gave Isabel of Gloucester in marriage to Geoffrey de Mandeville, earl of Essex. Shortly thereafter, Geoffrey was also created earl of Gloucester. Unlike Amaury de Montfort, he did obtain possession of most of the English estates and the marcher lordships, but John retained the valuable town and castle of Bristol, which had formed the *caput* of the honor of Gloucester in the twelfth century. The king also imposed a fine of 20,000 marks on Geoffrey for the marriage and the estates.[41] John's exercises in financial extortion are well known and were a major cause of the baronial revolt in the last years of his reign, but although this fine was the largest he ever imposed on any of his barons, Earl Geoffrey managed to pay about two-thirds of it before his death in February 1216.[42] After Geoffrey de Mandeville's death, custody of the inheritance was assigned to Hubert de Burgh, the justiciar in the last years of John's reign and for most of the minority of Henry III. Hubert married the Countess Isabel shortly before her death in October 1217.[43] He did not retain the estates, however, for with Isabel's death they passed to her sister Amicia, now recognized as countess of Gloucester, and her husband, Richard, earl of Hertford, despite the fact that Richard and Amicia had been separated since 1200.[44] Earl Richard himself did not live long

[40] G. E. C., V, 692–93; *Chancellor's Roll 8 Richard I*, ed. Doris M. Stenton (Pipe Roll Society, vol. XLV, new ser. VII, 1930), p. 288; *Liberate Roll 2 John*, ed. H. G. Richardson, in *Memoranda Roll 1 John* (Pipe Roll Society, vol. LIX, new ser. XXI, 1943), p. 89; *Pipe Roll 2 John*, ed. Doris M. Stenton (Pipe Roll Society, vol. L, new ser. XII, 1934), pp. 126–27. Cf. also Painter, "The Earl of Clare," p. 223.
[41] Sidney Painter, *The Reign of King John* (Baltimore, 1949), pp. 283–84.
[42] See PRO, Pipe Roll 9 Henry III, E 372/69 r. 8–8d. I am indebted for this information to Professor Cazel.
[43] Matthew Paris, *Chronica Majora*, ed. H. R. Luard (Rolls Series LVII, 1872–84), VI, 71–72.
[44] G. E. C., VI, 502 and note (1). The reason for the separation is unclear. Amicia claimed they were separated "per lineam consanguinitatis per preceptum summi pontificis." Both were related to the royal family (Amicia's grandfather Robert was the most important of Henry I's numerous illegitimate children), but no stigma was attached to the children of this marriage.

enough to obtain formal seisin of the estates and title, only out-
living Isabel by about six weeks. By November 28, 1217, he was
dead, leaving his elder son Gilbert, who was about thirty-eight
years old, as the sole heir to both the Clare and Gloucester
inheritances.[45]

Shortly after his father's death, Gilbert de Clare assumed the
title of earl of Gloucester and Hertford and obtained livery and
seisin of his great patrimony. He was charged with £350 relief
for the honors of Clare, Gloucester, and St. Hilary and his half
of the old Giffard barony.[46] The addition of over 260 knights'
fees appurtenant to the honor of Gloucester gave him control of
some 456 fees, a total far greater than that of any other magnate
of his day, and the figure does not include about 50 fees in
Glamorgan and Gwynllwg as these were not liable to scutage or
service to the Crown.[47] Gilbert's only failure was his inability to
recover Bristol. The town and castle, having been separated from
the honor of Gloucester by King John, were never restored to the
Clares despite claims to them made by Gilbert's descendants later
in the century.[48] As compensation, the regents for the young
Henry III intended to give him the hundred of Barton-juxta-
Bristol, but the constable of the castle, Hugh de Vivonne, resisted
all orders to surrender it.[49] King Henry must have decided to

[45] *Rotuli Litterarum Clausarum 1204–1227*, ed. T. D. Hardy (Record Commission, 1833–44), I, 344b. Cited hereafter as *Rot. Claus.*

[46] PRO, Pipe Roll 2 Henry III, E 372/62 r. 7d.; PRO, Exchequer, KR Memoranda Roll 4 Henry III, E 159/3 m. 2d. No relief was charged for Tonbridge,
as it was not held in chief of the Crown. Gilbert paid the sums for Clare, Gloucester, and Giffard, but there is no evidence that he paid anything for St. Hilary.
PRO, Pipe Rolls 3 and 6 Henry III, E 372/63 r. 9, E 372/66 r. 15d. I owe these
latter references to the kindness of Professor Cazel.

[47] The 456 figure is made up as follows: honor of Clare, 141 ½ (including the
9 St. Hilary fees); honor of Gloucester, 261 ½; honor of Gloucester in Kent,
10; and moiety of Giffard honor, 43. The next largest number of fees controlled
by a single baron of Earl Gilbert's generation seems to be about 370, held by
Ranulph de Blundeville, earl of Chester (d. 1232). See Sanders, *English Baronies*,
pp. 18, 32, 61, 127, 140. The Marshals had over 80 fees in England (about half
derived from their share of the Giffard honor), about 40 in Pembroke, 100 in
Leinster, and over 65 in Netherwent. PRO, Chancery Miscellanea, C 47/9/20. No
other magnates seem to have approached these totals: e. g., the Bigods, earls of
Norfolk, had some 160 fees in England, and the Bohuns, earls of Hereford and
Essex, almost 100 in 1245.

[48] Below, pp. 77, 127.

[49] *Rot. Claus.*, I, 211b, 305, 344, 350, 360b, 387, 405b, 429b, 448, 543b; *Patent
Rolls 1216–25* (H. M. Stationery Office, 1901), pp. 275, 277, 306.

ignore the regents' action as well, for Barton remained in royal keeping until 1254, when he gave it, along with the town and castle, to his own son, the future King Edward I. In return, however, the Clares did receive an annual sum of £40 19s. 5d. for the farm of the hundred—or more precisely, had this amount credited against their numerous debts to the royal exchequer.[50]

By a remarkable series of fortuitous marriages and rapid deaths, the Clares were left in 1217 in possession of an inheritance which in terms of social prestige, potential revenues, knights' fees, and a lasting position of great importance among the marcher lords of Wales, far exceeded the original East Anglian endowment they themselves had acquired and expanded since the days of Richard fitz Gilbert I. Painter, in discussing the fortunes of both the senior and cadet branches, has stated that "the Clares were the most successful family in developing their lands and power" in the twelfth century.[51] But it was as earls of Gloucester and lords of Glamorgan that the members of the senior branch of the family were to achieve a prominence and importance that despite all the resources of royal favor and personal initiative, they had never enjoyed as lords of Clare or earls of Hertford alone. The failure to obtain the town and castle of Bristol was more than offset by what they did acquire. The addition of the earldom and honor of Gloucester and the lordships of Glamorgan and Gwynllwg to their already substantial inheritance made the Clares in many ways the most powerful noble family in thirteenth century England.

The Family, 1217–1317

In 1217, the acquisition of Gloucester and Glamorgan raised the Clares to a position of pre-eminence in the ranks of the English aristocracy. Almost exactly a century later, the male line of the family became extinct and the inheritance was partitioned. Between these dates, there were four generations of Clares. Relatively abundant information has survived to provide at least some

---

[50] PRO, Pipe Rolls 6 and 8 Henry III, E 372/66 r. 15d., E 372/68 r. 9; *Close Rolls 1227–31*, p. 427; *Cal. Liberate Rolls 1240–45*, p. 267; *ibid. 1251–60*, pp. 332, 450; PRO, Exchequer, KR Memoranda Roll 24–25 Edward I, E 159/70 mm. 14–14d.

[51] Painter, "The Family and the Feudal System," p. 6.

indication of the careers of all the various members of the family. In addition, there is sufficient evidence to adduce specific examples of family co-operation and cohesion over the course of this century as well. In their concern for the solidarity and promotion of the family, the Clares were of course by no means unique, and both the motives for and methods of co-operation are to be found in their contemporaries on all levels of society. Apart from anti-quarian or genealogical studies of individual families, however, there has been little or no investigation of the great baronial or comital houses along these lines, and it cannot always be readily determined if the activities of the Clares were in any way excep-tional or if comparable patterns can be discerned elsewhere. After a summary of what is known about the members of each genera-tion, the entire family will be treated more generally on a com-parative basis.[52]

In addition to his eldest son and heir (Gilbert, born around 1180) Richard, earl of Hertford, left by his wife Amicia, who died in 1225, a younger son Richard or Roger, who was unmarried, and a daughter Matilda. This Richard accompanied Henry III's brother, Richard of Cornwall, to Gascony in 1225–26, but nothing further is known of him beyond the report of his death in the Tewkesbury chronicle, the best-informed source for matters con-cerning the earls of Gloucester and their families from the twelfth to the mid-thirteenth century. The young Richard was apparently murdered in London in May, 1228, but the circumstances sur-rounding this act are obscure. The chronicler remarks cryptically that "in revenge many of the king's servants were slaughtered," but there is simply no other information to add anything further to the story.[53] The earl's daughter Matilda was married to William de Braose (d. 1210), eldest son of the great marcher baron

---

[52] For a general discussion of this question for the twelfth century, along some-what different lines, see *ibid.*, pp. 1–16.

[53] Tewkesbury, p. 70: "in cujus vindictam plures de servientibus domini regis trucidati sunt." The chronicle gives his name as "Richard," and this is followed in *G. E. C.*, VI, 503 note (d). The chancery documents recording his stay in Gascony mention sums allowed to the earl of Gloucester "ad opus Rogeri de Clar' fratris sui." *Rot. Claus.*, II, 16b, 98. There was another Roger de Clare or Clere in royal service at this time. He held lands of the first Earl Gilbert, but he was married and lived until 1241. *Ibid.*, II, 214b; *Cal. Liberate Rolls 1226–40*, pp. 1, 105, 177, 225; *Cal. Pat. Rolls 1232–47*, p. 38; *Excerpta e Rotulis Finium 1216–1272*, ed. Charles Roberts (Record Commission, 1835–6), I, 350, 361–62, 364. Henceforth cited as *Rot. Fin.*

William de Braose (d. 1211), lord of Brecknock, Abergavenny, Builth, Radnor, and Gower, who was exiled by King John. In 1210, the younger William and his mother were starved to death by John, and Painter has suggested that this atrocity may have been the major reason for the earl of Hertford's opposition to the king.[54] In any event, Matilda returned to her father after the younger William's death. In 1219 she and her eldest son John sued Reginald de Braose, second son and heir of the elder William, for the family lands. They only succeeded in recovering Gower and the Sussex barony of Bramber, while the other marcher lordships remained in Reginald's family.[55]

Matilda seems to have been married a second time. According to the two printed versions of the Welsh "Chronicle of the Princes" (*Brut Y Tywysogyon*), the daughter of the "earl of Clare" was married in 1219 to Rhys Gryg, a son of Rhys ap Gruffydd of Deheubarth and a major figure in the Welsh wars of the early thirteenth century. Rhys Gryg died in 1233, and no further mention is made of his wife.[56] There is some uncertainty as to her proper identity. Earl Richard and Amicia of Gloucester were separated in 1200, and somewhat later the earl paid a certain Beatrice de Langele £10 per year "pro servicio suo."[57] If this Beatrice was his mistress, it is possible that the entries in the two versions of the *Brut* may actually refer to a different daughter, born illegitimately sometime shortly after 1200. Furthermore, if Matilda were intended, it is difficult to understand why the compilers of the *Brut* neglected to give her name or to mention her first marriage. On the other hand, it is also possible that Beatrice was employed as Matilda's companion when she returned to her father's household after 1210; and an argument *ex silentio*

---

[54] Painter, *The Reign of King John*, pp. 242–50; Painter, "The Earl of Clare," p. 224.

[55] *Rot. Claus.*, I, 405; *Royal Letters, Henry III*, ed. Walter W. Shirley (Rolls Series XXVII, 1862–6), I, 136; Sanders, *English Baronies*, pp. 7–8, 21–22, 108. For Gower, see also note 58 below.

[56] *Brut Y Tywysogyon: Red Book of Hergest Version*, ed. and trans. Thomas Jones (Board of Celtic Studies, History and Law Series, no. XVI, Cardiff, 1955), pp. 219, 233; *Brut Y Tywysogyon: Peniarth MS. 20 Version* [translation], ed. Thomas Jones (Board of Celtic Studies, History and Law Series, no. XI, Cardiff, 1952), pp. 97, 103. These two versions of the chronicle will henceforth be cited as *Brut Hergest* and *Peniarth*. They supersede the inferior edition by J. Williams ap Ithel (Rolls Series XVII, 1860).

[57] *Curia Regis Rolls 1219–20*, p. 62.

from a chronicle is always dangerous. On the whole, the wording of the passages, and Matilda's prior connections with the marchers and Wales, suggest with reasonable assurance that Rhys Gryg did in fact marry the widow of William de Braose the younger.[58]

Earl Richard's widow Amicia lived out her life in retirement. She made no effort to rejoin the earl after 1200, and seems to have had little contact with her children. Her activities were not remarkable. Like most other great countesses she engaged in charitable acts during her widowhood, founding a hospital at Sudbury in Suffolk and making other gifts to the priory of Stoke by Clare, a cell of the Benedictine abbey of Bec. She died in January 1225, and it was only at this time that her son Earl Gilbert received the third penny of the pleas of the shire for his Gloucester earldom.[59]

Gilbert de Clare, earl of Gloucester and Hertford from 1217 to 1230, was married in October, 1214, to his cousin Isabel, second daughter and eventual coheiress of William Marshal, earl of Pembroke (d. 1219).[60] By Isabel, he left three sons and two daughters. The eldest son and heir, Richard, was born on August 4, 1222, and was only eight years old when his father died. Richard came of age and obtained livery and seisin of the estates and titles in 1243. He died at the age of forty, on July 15, 1262.[61] The second son, William, was born in 1228.[62] He was unmarried, and his career is linked with that of his brother. He held lands of Earl Richard in Hampshire and Norfolk for the service of a knight's fee, and he seems to have discharged this service by direct

[58] The career of Rhys Gryg is discussed in Lloyd, *Hist. Wales*, II, 577, 633–63 *passim*, 674, 680, but Lloyd does not mention this marriage. The *G.E.C.* is also silent on the matter. J. Beverly Smith, " The ' Chronica de Wallia ' and the Dynasty of Dinefwr," *Bulletin of the Board of Celtic Studies*, XX (1962–64), 266 note 4, mentions the marriage but hazards no opinion as to the precise identity of Rhys Gryg's wife. It should be noted that Matilda's eldest son John de Braose was also married in 1219, to Margaret, daughter of Llywelyn ap Iorwerth of Gwynedd (d. 1240). It was through Llywelyn that John recovered *de facto* as well as *de jure* control of Gower in 1220–21. From 1217 until that time, it was controlled by Rhys Gryg himself. *Brut Hergest*, pp. 217, 219, 223, *Peniarth*, pp. 95, 97, 99; *Royal Letters*, I, 176; Lloyd, *Hist. Wales*, II, 658.
[59] Brit. Mus., Cotton MS Appendix xxi (Register of Stoke by Clare Priory), fols. 28–31; *Rot. Claus.*, II, 10b.
[60] Tewkesbury, p. 61.
[61] *Ibid.*, pp. 66, 130–31, 169. His career will be discussed in detail below in Chapter II.
[62] *Ibid.*, p. 70.

activity in his brother's retinue both overseas and in the Welsh campaigns of the middle decades of the century. In June, 1258, as part of the baronial reform program, William was granted custody of Winchester castle, undoubtedly through Earl Richard's influence. The following month he died, reportedly of poison administered by the earl's seneschal, Walter de Scoteny, acting in collusion with Henry III's Poitevin half brothers, who strongly opposed the baronial program and Earl Richard's participation in it.[63] The third son, Gilbert, was born in 1229, and had an ecclesiastical career.[64] In 1242 the abbot of Tewkesbury asked Robert Grosseteste, bishop of Lincoln, if he should admit Gilbert, still a minor, as rector of the church of Great Marlowe, Buckingham, a Clare advowson. The bishop suggested that Gilbert be granted 26 marks a year as a stipend in lieu of the benefice, and that someone else be instituted. Neither the bishop nor the abbot was legally bound to provide for the young cleric, but since he was presented either by Earl Richard (himself still a minor) or by Richard of Cornwall, Henry III's brother and second husband of Earl Gilbert's widow Isabel Marshal, they obviously felt that some sort of provision was both expedient and expected.[65] In 1244 Richard of Cornwall obtained a papal dispensation for the young Gilbert to hold benefices with care of souls to the annual value of 300 marks, and his career in the Church was thus assured.[66]

Earl Gilbert's daughters were similarly well placed. Amicia, born in 1220,[67] was betrothed in 1226 to Baldwin de Reviers, grandson and heir of William de Reviers, earl of Devon (d. 1217). Baldwin was only one or two years older than Amicia, and Earl Gilbert offered 2,000 marks to the king for the marriage and custody of some of the Reviers estates during Baldwin's minority.[68] The marriage must have been consummated around

[63] Cal. Pat. Rolls 1247–58, pp. 12, 638; Cal. Chart. Rolls 1226–57, p. 334; Tewkesbury, pp. 165, 167; Matthew Paris, Chronica Majora, V, 702–4, 709, 747–8. For Earl Richard and the baronial reform movement, see below, "The Movement for Reform, 1258–1262," in Chapter II.

[64] Tewkesbury, pp. 72–73.

[65] Ibid., pp. 122–24; Rotuli Roberti Grosseteste, episcopi Lincolniensis, 1235–1253, ed. F. N. Davis (Lincoln Record Society, vol. XI, 1914), pp. 362, 363–64; Susan Wood, English Monasteries and their Patrons in the Thirteenth Century (Oxford, 1955), p. 113.

[66] Calendar of Papal Letters 1198– (H. M. Stationery Office, 1894–), I, 207.

[67] Tewkesbury, p. 64.

[68] Ibid., p. 68; Patent Rolls 1225–32 (H. M. Stationery Office, 1903), pp. 87,

1235, for Baldwin's son and heir was born the following year. After her husband's death in 1245, Amicia controlled the lands of her son Baldwin (d. 1262) for a time, and was given permission to marry a minor English baron, Robert de Guines or Gynes, uncle of Arnold III, count of Guines. The countess spent much of her later life engaged in an interminable lawsuit with her daughter, Isabella de Fortibus, countess of Aumale and Devon. She frequently went overseas on pilgrimages, and perhaps to visit her second husband's relatives as well, and died in 1283.[69] Earl Gilbert's other daughter, Isabel, was born in 1226.[70] In 1240 she married the Scots baron Robert Bruce, lord of Annandale (d. 1295), and by him was the grandmother of the hero of Bannockburn. Since her father Earl Gilbert was dead and her brother Richard was a minor, the marriage must have been arranged by her mother Isabel and her uncle Gilbert Marshal, Isabel's brother, for it was Gilbert Marshal who gave her the Sussex manor of Ripe as a marriage portion.[71]

Isabel Marshal outlived Earl Gilbert de Clare by ten years, but she was not destined to spend her widowhood in obscurity. In 1231 she was married to Richard of Cornwall, apparently to the displeasure of Henry III, who was trying to arrange another match for his brother.[72] By the time of her death in 1240 she had borne Richard of Cornwall four children, only one of whom, Henry, lived past infancy.[73] Unlike Amicia of Gloucester, Isabel was

---

133–4; *Rot. Claus.*, II, 157, 171. Gilbert owed about half the amount at the time of his death. His widow was regularly charged £684 for the marriage fine, but she insisted that her second husband, Richard of Cornwall, pay it instead. In 1297, King Edward I was still demanding this sum from the executors of Earl Gilbert's grandson. PRO, Exchequer, KR Memoranda Roll 24–25 Edward I, E 159/70 m. 14.

[69] *Cal. Pat. Rolls 1247–58*, pp. 5, 39, 408, 630; *G. E. C.*, VI, 224 and note (c). Robert was the younger brother of Baldwin III, count of Guines, but the bulk of his own lands were in England. Cf. Sanders, *English Baronies*, p. 142, and *Sir Christopher Hatton's Book of Seals*, nos. 85, 135. For the lawsuit between Amicia and her daughter, see F. M. Powicke, *King Henry III and the Lord Edward* (2 vols.; Oxford, 1948), II, 707–8, 712 note.

[70] Tewkesbury, p. 68.

[71] *Ibid.*, p. 115; *Cal. Chart. Rolls 1226–57*, p. 252; Sanders, *English Baronies*, p. 102.

[72] Tewkesbury, p. 78; N. Denholm-Young, *Richard of Cornwall* (Oxford, 1947), p. 18.

[73] *Ibid.*, 18 and note 7. Henry was murdered at Viterbo in 1271, and Richard of Cornwall's heir was thus Edmund, born in 1249 to the earl and his second wife, Sanchia of Provence.

strongly attached to the house of Clare, as her numerous gifts to Tewkesbury Abbey and her arrangments for her daughter Isabel attest. According to the Tewkesbury chronicle, she wished to be buried at the abbey next to her first husband, but Richard of Cornwall had her buried at Beaulieu Abbey in Hampshire, although as a pious gesture he allowed her heart to be sent to Tewkesbury.[74] With the next generation, the Clare family reached the height of its prominence in the thirteenth century. Earl Richard de Clare was twice married, secretly in 1232 to Meggotta, daughter of the justiciar Hubert de Burgh, who had Richard's custody during his minority after 1230,[75] and in 1237 to Maud, daughter of John de Lacy, earl of Lincoln (d. 1240).[76] There was no issue by the ill-fated first marriage, but by Maud de Lacy Richard had three sons and four daughters. The eldest son and heir, Gilbert, was born on September 2, 1243, and was called Gilbert Goch ("the Red") after the fiery color of his hair. The Red Earl had seisin of his estates in 1263–64 and was undoubtedly the single most powerful magnate of the realm, in the later years of Henry III's reign and under King Edward I, until his death on December 7, 1295.[77] The second son, Thomas, born sometime between 1244 and 1247, and the youngest, Bogo, born in 1248,[78] had remarkably dissimilar but equally significant careers. Thomas, who died in 1287, was a close friend of Edward I and one of the most important members of the lesser baronage in his reign. He entered royal service and in a manner reminiscent of his ancestor Strongbow a century earlier, succeeded in establishing himself among the great Anglo-Irish magnates in the late thirteenth century by conquering the lordship of Thomond (modern County Clare). He left two legitimate sons who succeeded him, Gilbert (d. 1308) and Richard (d. 1318), a bastard son Master Richard, who died in 1338, and two daughters, Maud, the wife of Robert de Clifford

[74] Tewkesbury, pp. 113–14. Cf. also Denholm-Young, *Richard of Cornwall*, pp. 18–19, and Wood, *English Monasteries*, pp. 130, 136.

[75] *Patent Rolls 1225–32*, p. 412.

[76] These marriages and their political importance will be discussed in more detail below, pp. 60–62.

[77] Tewkesbury, p. 130; *Monasticon Anglicanum*, ed. William Dugdale; new ed., ed. J. Caley *et al.* (London, 1817–30), II, 61. His career is discussed below, Chapters III–IV.

[78] Tewkesbury, p. 136. The exact date of Thomas' birth is unknown, but the *G. E. C.*, V, 701, regards him as the elder of the two.

of Westmoreland (d. 1314) and Robert de Welle, and Margaret, the wife of Gilbert de Umphraville (d. 1307), son of the earl of Angus, and Bartholomew de Badlesmere (d. 1322). Thomas' brother Bogo, on the other hand, had what might conservatively be described as a colorful ecclesiastical career, and by the time of his death in 1294 had made himself the most successful and notorious pluralist in the English Church. The careers of Earl Gilbert the Red's two brothers are well documented, and are good examples of the ways in which such men could profit from family influence and power; more importantly, they provide excellent illustrations of the kinds of opportunities available in contemporary society to younger members of great baronial houses. For these reasons, a detailed examination of their careers has been reserved for a separate chapter (Chapter VI).

Of Earl Richard's four daughters, three married well, the fourth, Eglentina, dying in infancy in 1257.[79] The eldest, Isabel, born in 1240, was married in June 1258 to an important nobleman, William, marquis de Montferrat. Earl Richard paid the marquis 4,000 marks to secure the marriage, and allowed him a choice of brides in addition. Since Isabel was about eighteen and her surviving sisters each less than eight years old, the choice must have been easy.[80] They were married at Lyons, and Isabel seems never to have returned to England. Montferrat was a lordship in northern Italy, technically a member of the Empire but subject to Provençal and Angevin influences. The marquis was a prominent figure on the Ghibelline side in thirteenth century Mediterranean politics, but nothing further is known of Isabel. She probably died sometime before 1271, since the marquis married a daughter of King Alfonso X of Castile in that year.[81] The second daughter, Margaret, was born in 1250 and was unmarried at the time of her father's death in 1262. In 1272, probably by arrangement with her mother Maud and her brothers Bogo and Earl Gilbert, she was married to Edmund, son and heir of Richard of Cornwall by his second marriage.[82] Margaret's marriage, however, was an unhappy

---

[79] Tewkesbury, p. 159.

[80] Ibid., pp. 117, 162; Cal. Chart. Rolls 1257–1300, pp. 3–5; Cal. Pat. Rolls 1247–58, p. 662.

[81] Sir Steven Runciman, The Sicilian Vespers (Cambridge, 1958), p. 123. Some of the marquis' activities are discussed in ibid., pp. 84, 100, 107, 121, 209–10, 233.

[82] Tewkesbury, p. 139; Annales Prioratus de Dunstaplia, ed. H. R. Luard

one. She seems to have been pregnant in 1285, but either miscarried or had a stillborn child. Perhaps because she was unable
to have children thereafter, Edmund left her in 1289. For the
next two or three years, efforts were made by such people as John
Peckham, archbishop of Canterbury, and Bogo de Clare, to reconcile them, but they were unsuccessful and the marriage was formally annulled in 1294.[83] In 1300 Edmund died and Margaret was
assigned dower by Edward I. She did not remarry and lived in
seclusion until her own death in 1312.[84] The third daughter,
Rohese, born in 1252, was married in 1270 to a member of the
lesser baronage, Roger de Mowbray, lord of the Yorkshire barony
of Thirsk (d. 1297). Again, the marriage was arranged by her
mother, the dowager Countess Maud, and her brother Bogo.[85]

Maud de Lacy, widow of Richard, earl of Gloucester, outlived
her husband by more than a quarter of a century, dying in March
1289. From 1262 until her death she held one-third of the Clare
inheritance in dower, although her son Earl Gilbert the Red did
successfully challenge the original composition of her dower
portion, which was readjusted in 1267.[86] Maud did not remarry,
preferring to spend her long widowhood living off the revenues
of her estates, contributing handsomely to ecclesiastical foundations, and helping to promote her children. Her activities on
behalf of her daughters Margaret and Rohese have been noted,
and she also attempted, with less success, to present her son Bogo
to the church of Adlingfleet in Yorkshire.[87] Her gifts to religious
houses were numerous. In 1248 Earl Richard founded Clare Priory,

---

(Annales Monastici, vol. III, Rolls Series XXXVI, 1866), p. 253. Hereafter cited
as Dunstable.

[83] Registrum Johannis de Pontissara, episcopi Wintoniensis, 1282–1304, ed. Cecil
Deedes (Canterbury and York Society, vols. XIX, XXX, 1915–24), I, 300;
Registrum Epistolarum Johannis Peckham, ed. C. T. Martin (Rolls Series LXXVII,
1882–86), III, 969; Rolls and Register of Bishop Oliver Sutton (1280–1299), ed.
Rosalind M. T. Hill (Lincoln Record Society, vols. XXXIX, XLIII, XLVIII,
1948–54), III, 33–36, 96; Rotuli Parliamentorum (Record Commission, 1783–
1832), I, 17; Cal. Pat. Rolls 1292–1301, p. 63.

[84] Cal. Close Rolls 1296–1302, pp. 426, 435–39; T. F. Tout, Chapters in the
Administrative History of Medieval England (6 vols.; Manchester, 1920–33), II,
323, 351.

[85] Tewkesbury, p. 150; Close Rolls 1268–72, pp. 284–85. Rohese was still living
in 1299. Catalogue of Ancient Deeds (H. M. Stationery Office, 1890–1915), II, 223.

[86] See below, pp. 95–96, 99–100, 117.

[87] Below, pp. 183–84.

the first house of Austin Friars in England, and after his death
the countess continued his generosity with several grants of land
to the priory.[88] In addition, a scheme to found an Augustinian
nunnery attracted her. In 1284 she refounded the priory of Canonsleigh in Devon. Canonsleigh was originally established for seven
Augustinian canons by Walter de Clavill, a mesne tenant of the
honor of Gloucester, but in 1284 Maud provided an annual gift
of £200 for the support of an abbess and 40 canonesses of that
order.[89] She had originally had the idea of doing this for Sandle-
ford Priory in Berkshire, but for some reason the plan fell through
in 1274, and a decade later she refounded Canonsleigh instead.
By 1286 the new nunnery was in existence, and the dispossessed
canons were under royal protection.[90]

Like his father Richard, Earl Gilbert the Red was married twice.
In 1253 Richard arranged for the marriage of his son, then about
ten years old, to Henry III's niece Alice, daughter of Hugh de
Lusignan, count of La Marche and Angoulême. Although she
had two daughters, the match proved to be both a personal and a
political failure; Gilbert and Alice were formally separated in
1271 and the marriage was finally annulled in 1285. Even before
the annulment, Earl Gilbert and King Edward I had discussed the
possibility of a marriage into the royal family. In May 1290,
after a long delay pending the annulment and the necessity for
a subsequent papal dispensation, Gilbert married Edward's fifth
child and second surviving daughter Joan, who had been born at
Acre in Palestine in 1272. Joan of Acre was to outlive the Red
Earl by some twelve years, but between 1290 and his death in
1295 they had a son and heir, the last Earl Gilbert, and three
daughters, the eventual coheiresses of the Clare inheritance.[91]

The children of Earl Gilbert the Red by his two marriages
comprised the last generation of the Clare family. Before discussing their fortunes and the descent of the estates in the late
Middle Ages, however, mention should be made of the Red Earl's
two wives. Their activities stand in sharp contrast. Beyond the

[88] Brit. Mus., Harleian MS 4835 (Register of Clare Priory), fols. 4–6. Cf.
also K. W. Barnardiston, *Clare Priory* (Cambridge, 1962).
[89] *Cal. Papal Letters*, I, 478; Wood, *English Monasteries*, p. 27.
[90] *Cal. Papal Letters*, I, 448, 485; Wood, *English Monasteries*, p. 27 and note 7.
[91] These marriages and their political importance will be discussed more fully
below, pp. 102–3, 148–49.

fact that she was supported by Henry III and presumably by Edward I,[92] nothing is known of Alice de Lusignan from the time of the separation in 1271 to the formal annulment in 1285. At that time, Gilbert settled some manors on her for life " in consideration of the nobility of her kin and because he did not wish to cause her grief for lack of suitable maintenance." Alice's activities after 1285 are unknown, and it is possible that she spent most of her time on the Continent with her relatives. She died in May 1290 and the estates reverted to the earl.[93]

Joan of Acre, on the other hand, was a remarkably active woman in the dozen years following the Red Earl's death. By the terms of the marriage agreement of 1290, the entire inheritance was enfeoffed jointly on Gilbert and Joan. This meant that it would not be possible for her father Edward I to grant her only a third of the estates in dower and control the rest himself during the long minority of her son Gilbert. Joan was thus sole mistress of the inheritance, and she controlled it with marked ability. In 1297, much to Edward's displeasure, she secretly married an otherwise obscure knight in her *familia*, Ralph de Monthermer (d. 1325). Ralph was styled earl of Gloucester *jure uxoris* and for the next decade administered the estates with the king's daughter.[94] After Joan's death, his rights to the estates and title lapsed, and he was thenceforth treated as an ordinary baron. His children by Joan of Acre were likewise excluded from the inheritance, and had no future connection with the Clares, aside from a daughter, Mary, who was married in 1307 to Duncan, son and heir of Duncan, earl of Fife, and Joan, the Red Earl's daughter by his first marriage to Alice de Lusignan.[95] Joan of Acre died in April, 1307, but during her tenure of the inheritance important modifications were introduced in its administrative structure. After Isabella de Forti-

[92] See *Cal. Liberate Rolls 1267–72*, p. 234 (October, 1272).

[93] *Foedera, Conventiones, Litterae*, ed. Thomas Rymer; new ed., ed. A. Clark et al. (Record Commission, 1816–69), I, 654.

[94] *G. E. C.*, V, 709–12; below, pp. 157–59.

[95] *G. E. C.*, V, 374, IX, 143–45. This Duncan's marriage was first granted to Earl Gilbert the Red in 1292. After his death it was given to his daughter Isabella, the sister of Countess Joan of Fife. She in turn sold it before 1302 to Edmund Mortimer of Wigmore. The marriage took place in November 1307, after a papal dispensation had been granted. *Sir Christopher Hatton's Book of Seals*, no. 102; *Calendar of Documents Relating to Scotland 1108–1509*, ed. J. Bain (Edinburgh, 1881–88), II, no. 1311; *Cal. Papal Letters*, II, 30; *Foedera*, II, 5.

bus, dowager countess of Devon and Aumale (1262–93), Countess Joan stands as perhaps the best example in thirteenth century English history of the ability of a widow to run the estates and otherwise manage the complex affairs of a great comital house.[96]

Earl Gilbert the Red left a son and five daughters. Of his two daughters by Alice de Lusignan, the elder, Isabella, was born in 1263. In 1297 she was betrothed to Guy, son and heir of William de Beauchamp, earl of Warwick. Guy de Beauchamp succeeded his father as earl in 1298, but the projected marriage, although still pending, never took place. Not until 1316 was Isabella married, at the advanced age of fifty-three, to the Gloucestershire baron Maurice de Berkeley, and she died without issue in 1338.[97] The other daughter, Joan, probably born sometime between 1264 and 1271, was married in 1284 to Duncan, earl of Fife, who died in 1288. The marriage of their son Duncan (d. 1353) to Mary, daughter of Joan of Acre and Ralph de Monthermer, has already been mentioned. In 1302 or shortly thereafter, Joan married another Scots baron, Gervase Avenel. They entered the fealty of her kinsman Robert Bruce and were declared rebels by King Edward II. Her estates in England, which her father had given as a marriage portion at the time of her betrothal to the earl of Fife, were forfeited, and later granted to Hugh Despenser, husband of Joan's half sister Eleanor, the eldest daughter of Earl Gilbert the Red and Joan of Acre.[98]

When the Red Earl married King Edward's daughter, the inheritance was entailed on their issue; Gilbert's daughters by Alice de Lusignan were excluded as potential heiresses in the event of the failure of the male line. Ironically, the king's proviso became operative, with serious political consequences for Edward II. The earl's only son Gilbert, born in 1291, was styled earl of Gloucester in 1307, shortly after the death of his mother and the consequent reversion of his stepfather, Ralph de Monthermer, to ordinary baronial status. The young Earl Gilbert was also the last. His

[96] Joan's administration of the inheritance after 1295 will be treated in Part II of this work, *passim*. Isabella de Fortibus and her inheritance is the main subject of N. Denholm-Young, *Seignorial Administration in England* (Oxford, 1937).

[97] Tewkesbury, p. 169; *Cal. Papal Letters*, I, 570; *Registrum Roberti Winchelsey 1294–1313*, ed. Rose Graham (Canterbury and York Society, vols. LI–LII, 1952–56), II, 271; *G. E. C.*, V, 707 note (j).

[98] *G. E. C.*, V, 373–74; *Cal. Docs. Scotland*, II, nos. 602, 1066, 1104, 1108, 1299, III, no. 492, IV, no. 36.

tenure of the inheritance was brief. On June 24, 1314, he was killed at the battle of Bannockburn, and with his death the male line of the senior branch of the family became extinct.[99] In 1308 Gilbert had married Maud, daughter of Richard de Burgh, earl of Ulster, but they had no children, or at least no surviving issue. According to the compiler of the *Flores Historiarum*, there was a son John who was born in April 1312 and who died before the end of the year. The accuracy of the chronicle on matters of this sort is often suspect, but the authenticity of the statement has been accepted by modern peerage writers.[100] In December, 1314, Maud de Burgh was granted dower, but this was intended only as a temporary and precautionary measure, since she claimed to be pregnant. For nearly three years thereafter, the countess continued to insist on her pregnancy, but in 1317 Edward II, who had hoped that the birth of a child would preserve the inheritance intact, reluctantly concluded that her claims were spurious. In November of that year, the great Clare inheritance was partitioned among the husbands of the last Earl Gilbert's full sisters, and after the countess' death in 1320, her dower portion was likewise divided.[101]

In 1317 the Clare inheritance, which had been slowly built up over the course of the preceding two and a half centuries, was suddenly and irreparably shattered. The fate of the three heiresses was of the utmost political importance. The eldest, Eleanor, probably born in 1292, was married in 1306 to Hugh Despenser the younger, who became the most powerful individual in the kingdom in the last years of Edward II's reign. Hugh was executed in 1326, shortly before Edward's deposition and imprisonment. The following year, Eleanor was married to William la Zouche. Both died in 1337, and her share of the inheritance passed to her descendants by the first marriage. In the fifteenth century, the estates passed from the Despensers to the Beauchamp and Neville earls of Warwick, and ultimately to George, duke of Clarence, brother of King Edward IV, and Richard, duke of Gloucester, later King Richard III.[102] The second heiress, Margaret, was born

[99] His career will be treated below, Chapter V.
[100] *Flores Historiarum*, ed. H. R. Luard (Rolls Series XCV, 1890), III, 335; *G. E. C.*, V, 715.
[101] See below, " The Partition," in Chapter V.
[102] *G. E. C.*, IV, 274–82, XII (pt. II), 383–94.

around 1293. In 1307 she was married to Edward II's favorite, Peter Gaveston, earl of Cornwall, who was murdered in 1312 by the king's opponents. In 1317, shortly before the partition, Edward arranged her marriage to a political associate, Hugh D'Audley, who was created earl of Gloucester by Edward III in 1337. Margaret died in 1342 and Hugh D'Audley in 1347; the estates passed to their daughter and her husband Ralph Stafford, and continued in the Stafford family until the early sixteenth century.[103]

The youngest heiress, Elizabeth, is also the best known. She was born around 1295, and by the time she was twenty-seven had been married and widowed three times. Her first marriage, on September 30, 1308, to John, son of Richard de Burgh, earl of Ulster, was undoubtedly arranged by her brother, the last Earl Gilbert, who had married Richard's daughter Maud the previous day. John de Burgh died in 1313 and three years later Elizabeth was abducted by the marcher lord Theobald Verdun, who was obviously attracted by the opportunity to gain her expected share of the Clare estates for himself. Shortly after the marriage, however, Theobald died, and in 1317 Edward II married the heiress to still another associate among the lesser baronage, Roger Damory, who was executed for treason in 1322. Understandably enough, Elizabeth never remarried. In contrast to her turbulent youth, she lived out a long and peaceful widowhood. From 1322 until her death in 1360 she was content to manage her various dower lands and her portion of her brother's estates, spending much of her time and money on charitable acts, such as the founding of Clare College, Cambridge. At her death the estates passed to her granddaughter's husband Lionel, duke of Clarence, the third son of King Edward III. Lionel died in 1368 and the lands then passed to his daughter Philippa (d. 1394) and her husband Edmund Mortimer, earl of March, and finally in 1425 to the House of York.[104]

Taken as a whole, the Clare family represents what might be termed one of the most successful joint enterprises in medieval English history. More than two centuries of steady territorial growth raised the family to a position of pre-eminence in the

---

[103] *Ibid.*, V, 715–19, XII (pt. I), 174–81.
[104] *Ibid.*, VIII, 445–53, XII (pt. II), 177–80, 905–10. A list of the estates acquired by each sister in 1317 is given in Appendix II.

ranks of the higher nobility. The major factors in this development in the twelfth century were undoubtedly royal favor and
shrewdly chosen marriages. The Clares prospered from their
intimate connections with successive rulers of England, and the
male members of the house were rewarded with a series of important fiefs and well-placed ladies. The power and prestige of
the family reached their highest level in the thirteenth century,
and the fortunes of its members help illuminate almost every
aspect of the social and political life of the English baronage in
this period.

The marriages of the sons and daughters of the earls of Gloucester exemplify the importance of personal and territorial considerations in the small and relatively homogeneous upper levels
of society, and the network of social relationships that were both
created and exploited in this way. The four successors of Richard,
earl of Hertford were all married to the daughters of English
earls, with the exception of Earl Gilbert the Red, who married
first the daughter of a French count and then the daughter of the
king himself. Many of the families thus married into, especially
the Marshals, were already related to the Clares. Isabel Marshal,
the wife of the first Earl Gilbert, was Strongbow's granddaughter
and thus the earl's cousin, and her sister Eve was married to the
marcher lord William de Braose (d. 1230), nephew of Earl
Gilbert's sister Matilda. Maud de Lacy, the second wife of
Richard, earl of Gloucester, was the daughter of the earl of
Lincoln, whose own wife Margaret later married William Marshal's fourth son, Walter (d. 1245).[105] Whenever possible, the
marriages of the heirs were arranged by their fathers, although
Henry III and Edward I determined some. Richard, earl of Hertford married his son Gilbert to Isabel Marshal, and in 1253, Earl
Richard of Gloucester arranged his son's marriage to Alice de
Lusignan.[106] The Red Earl's second marriage to Joan of Acre
may have originally been his own suggestion, but the terms of the
marriage settlement of 1290 leave no doubt that King Edward
was in full command of the arrangements. The minority of the
young Earl Richard after 1230 created special circumstances in
which Henry III in effect set aside the heir's secret marriage to

[105] Sanders, *English Baronies*, pp. 18, 63.
[106] Tewkesbury, pp. 61, 153–54; Matthew Paris, *Chronica Majora*, V, 364, 366.

the daughter of Hubert de Burgh, and then married him to the daughter of the highest bidder, the earl of Lincoln. According to Matthew Paris, Henry at first desired to marry Richard to a Lusignan. He abandoned the effort, but the marriage of Gilbert the Red in 1253 was largely undertaken at the king's prompting. Henry's efforts to secure a Clare–Lusignan alliance were thus rewarded, although the match eventually had a political effect contrary to the king's original intention.[107]

In contrast to the earls themselves, almost all of their younger brothers were unmarried. The first earl's brother Richard (Roger), who was murdered in 1228, Earl Richard's brothers William and Gilbert, and the Red Earl's brother Bogo, did not marry. With the exception of Bogo and his brother Thomas, they were of little prominence in national affairs, but their varied careers as ecclesiastics, royal officials, and political associates of the earls do illustrate the opportunities available to men in their position. Only one younger brother, Thomas de Clare, established a cadet branch of the family in the thirteenth century. Probably by arrangement with Earl Gilbert the Red and King Edward I, Thomas married Juliana, daughter of Maurice fitz Maurice of Offaly (d. 1286), a leading Anglo-Irish baron and former justiciar of Ireland. Thomas' two legitimate sons, Gilbert and Richard, were themselves married and succeeded in turn to their father's lands, but this Richard's son died at the age of three in 1321. The estates were divided between Thomas' daughters and abandoned to the Irish, and the cadet branch thus died out less than a decade after the extinction of the senior branch of the family.[108]

Younger brothers in some other great comital houses followed a somewhat different pattern, at least insofar as marriages were concerned. The four younger sons of William Marshal might be taken as representative, despite the special circumstances of their father's career and the exceptional fact that each in turn became earl of Pembroke upon the death of his elder brother and died without issue. The eldest of William Marshal's sons, William, who succeeded his father in 1219 and died in 1231, was married first to the daughter of a count of Aumale and then, in 1224, to King John's daughter Eleanor, later the wife of Simon de

[107] Matthew Paris, *ibid.*, III, 386, V, 514.
[108] See below, pp. 195–97.

Montfort, earl of Leicester. Of the other sons, one, Richard
(d. 1234) married the daughter and heir of a minor French nobleman, Alan, lord of Dinan. The third, Gilbert, who died in 1241,
was originally a clerk. He renounced his ecclesiastical positions
when he succeeded Richard as earl of Pembroke, and married
a daughter of William I, king of Scots (d. 1214). The marriage
of the fourth son Walter to Margaret, cousin of the earl of Winchester and herself widow of John de Lacy, earl of Lincoln, has
already been mentioned. Finally, the last son Anselm (d. 1245)
was married to Maud, daughter of Humphrey de Bohun, earl of
Hereford (d. 1275).[109] Most of William Marshal's sons were
married before they assumed the family estates and title, and their
marriages may be regarded as more typical of the activities of
younger brothers than their counterparts among the Clares. The
fact that Bogo, Earl Richard's brother Gilbert, and Thomas'
illegitimate son Master Richard were churchmen is in itself representative of the careers chosen by many younger brothers in
baronial families, but there is no evidence to indicate that the
first Earl Gilbert and Earl Richard tried to arrange marriages for
their brothers Richard and William before their deaths in 1228
and 1258 respectively.[110]

Richard, earl of Hertford and his successors left a number of
daughters whose marriage connections were more typical than
those of the younger sons. There were thirteen such daughters
in the period of this study, counting the two daughters of Thomas
de Clare and omitting the Eglentina who died a few weeks after
her birth in 1257.[111] Five were married once, seven twice, and
one, Elizabeth (d. 1360), three times, for a total of twenty-two
marriages. Of these daughters, six married as their first or only
husband an earl or another member of comital houses: Baldwin,
earl of Devon, Edmund, the successor to Richard of Cornwall,
Peter Gaveston, created earl of Cornwall in 1307, John de Burgh,
son of the earl of Ulster, and two Scotsmen, Duncan, earl of Fife,

[109] *G. E. C.*, X, 365–77.

[110] The silence of the Tewkesbury chronicle and other sources such as Matthew
Paris on this point suggests that these brothers may have preferred to remain
unmarried. Any marriage projects would otherwise surely have been mentioned.

[111] The following paragraphs are based on the foregoing discussion of the
daughters and the genealogical tables, and the specific references need not be
repeated.

and Gilbert de Umphraville, son of the earl of Angus. In addition, Earl Gilbert the Red's sister Isabel was married to the marquis de Montferrat, and his daughter Isabella was originally betrothed to Guy de Beauchamp, earl of Warwick, although they did not marry. Most of the others married English barons (Roger de Mowbray, Hugh Despenser the younger, Maurice de Berkeley and Robert de Clifford), although one married the marcher baron William de Braose the younger and another the Scots lord Robert Bruce. Of the eight daughters who had a second husband, five married relatively minor English barons, Robert de Guines (who was however related to the French counts of Guines), Robert de Welle, Bartholomew de Badlesmere, William la Zouche, and Hugh D'Audley, created earl of Gloucester in 1337, twenty years after his marriage. One daughter married the Scots knight Gervase Avenel and another the Welshman Rhys Gryg, while Elizabeth de Burgh was married to Theobald Verdun, an important baron with lands in the Welsh march and Ireland, and after his death to the English baron Roger Damory. It is interesting to note that in every case of remarriage, the daughters were widows; their first husbands either died a natural death or else were killed in battle, such as Robert de Clifford at Bannockburn, or were executed for political reasons, for example Hugh Despenser the younger. Furthermore, all except Hugh D'Audley's wife Margaret (d. 1342) outlived their second husbands, at least by a few months, and Elizabeth de Burgh died almost forty years after her third husband Roger Damory was executed in 1322.

In most instances, these marriages were dictated by political and territorial considerations and were arranged by the earls, other members of the family, or in some cases solely by the king. A surprisingly large number, however, reveal a personal initiative on the part of the daughter or her husband. The earls of Gloucester were obviously interested in extending the network of personal relationships based on marriage ties to Ireland, Scotland and the Welsh march in addition to England proper, as the geographical distribution of the family estates and fees, and their own marriage connections with the Marshal and de Burgh families attest. Six daughters, almost half the total, married as their first or second husband men from these regions. Two others were married to barons whose major interests lay in northern England,

Roger de Mowbray and Robert de Clifford, while the rest, with the exception of Isabel, wife of the marquis de Montferrat, married earls or barons whose lands were in southern England, in close proximity to the great family honors of Clare, Gloucester and Tonbridge.

Of the twenty-two marriages, only four, those with the younger William de Braose, Baldwin de Reviers, earl of Devon, the marquis de Montferrat, and Duncan, earl of Fife, can be attributed directly to the girls' fathers. Six seem to have been arranged by other members of the family, and most concern daughters who were still unmarried when their fathers died. Isabel Marshal, the widow of the first Earl Gilbert, and Maud de Lacy, widow of Earl Richard, married their daughters to Robert Bruce, Edmund of Cornwall and Roger de Mowbray. In all three instances the widows acted in conjunction with male relatives, Gilbert Marshal, Countess Isabel's brother, and Bogo de Clare, Maud's youngest son.[112] The two marriages of Thomas de Clare's daughter Margaret to the son of the earl of Angus and Bartholomew de Badlesmere were arranged after her father's death by her uncle, Earl Gilbert the Red, and her cousin, the last Earl Gilbert. The last earl also married his sister Elizabeth to John de Burgh, son of Richard, earl of Ulster, at the same time as his own marriage to the earl's daughter Maud. Both marriages may have been urged by Earl Gilbert's cousin Richard, the second son of Thomas de Clare, who had just succeeded his brother as lord of Thomond and who perhaps wished in this way to solidify his own position in the ranks of the Anglo-Irish baronage.[113] Instances in which the kings acted directly are few. Edward II married the last earl's sisters Margaret and Elizabeth to Hugh D'Audley and Roger Damory in 1317, but these were conditioned by the special circumstances attendant upon the last earl's death. Edward and Gilbert probably

---

[112] G. E. C., V, 373–74; Patent Rolls 1225–32, p. 87; Close Rolls 1268–72, pp. 284–85; Tewkesbury, pp. 115, 162; Dunstable, p. 253.

[113] In 1289, the Red Earl gave the earl of Angus 1,200 marks to have the marriage of his son for Thomas' daughter. PRO, Coram Rege Roll Easter 17 Edward I, KB 27/118 m. 21. The earl of Angus' son was heir apparent, but died before his father. Margaret married Badlesmere around 1312. G. E. C., I, 149, 372, III, 246–47. For the marriages of the last Earl Gilbert and his sister to the children of the earl of Ulster, see Chronica Maiorum et Vicecomitum Londoniarum, ed. Thomas Stapleton (Camden Society, old ser., vol. XXXIV, 1846), Appendix, p. 251.

acted jointly in this Margaret's first marriage to Peter Gaveston. The marriage of the earl's third full sister, Eleanor, to the younger Hugh Despenser was arranged by Edward I, possibly in association with his daughter Joan of Acre, Eleanor's mother.[114]

The other eight marriages, more than a third of the total, took place under exceptional or unknown circumstances. The conditions under which the earl of Hertford's daughter married Rhys Gryg in 1219, and under which Thomas de Clare's elder daughter Maud was married first to Robert de Clifford in 1295 and to Robert de Welle after 1314, are obscure. In most other instances, however, the daughters married on their own initiative. The first earl's daughter Amicia, widow of Baldwin de Reviers and dowager countess of Devon, secured the king's license in 1247 to marry Robert de Guines " if she will," and she did in fact marry Robert shortly thereafter. The daughters of Earl Gilbert the Red by Alice de Lusignan, Joan, widow of Duncan, earl of Fife, and Isabella, originally betrothed to Guy de Beauchamp, apparently married Gervase Avenel and Maurice de Berkeley entirely of their own accord. Finally, the circumstances surrounding the extinction of the male line of the family in 1314 and the partition of the inheritance induced two barons, Theobald Verdun and William la Zouche, to take matters into their own hands. Theobald abducted and married Elizabeth de Burgh in 1316, and in 1327 William, undoubtedly inspired by this example, abducted Hugh Despenser's widow Eleanor. Theobald's plans were nullified by his death, but William la Zouche did manage to control his wife's share of the inheritance until his own death in 1337, despite objections raised at the Roman Curia by another knight, John Grey, who claimed he had the idea of abducting Eleanor first.[115]

For the most part, the marriages of the daughters correspond closely to the patterns discernable for other baronial families. Of William Marshal's five daughters, for example, two were married twice, in each instance to an earl, while the third, Sibyl, also married an earl and the remaining two a marcher lord and an

[114] G. E. C., V, 715; Flores Historiarum, III, 139, 194; Vita Edwardi Secundi, ed. N. Denholm-Young (London and Edinburgh, 1957), p. 2; Cal. Pat. Rolls 1301–07, p. 443.

[115] G. E. C., V, 373 note (c), 707 note (j); Rot. Parl., I, 352–53; Cal. Pat. Rolls 1247–58, p. 5; ibid. 1327–30, p. 422; Cal. Papal Letters, II, 394; Cal. Inq. Post Mortem, VIII, nos. 112, 132.

English baron respectively.[116] Of the seven daughters of Sibyl
Marshal and William de Ferrers, earl of Derby (d. 1254), three
married barons with interests in the march and northern England.
Most of the other four, two of whom were married twice and two
three times each, were married to English knights, although one
had as her second husband Roger de Quincy, earl of Winchester
(d. 1262), and another as her third husband the French nobleman
Amaury, vicomte de Rochechouart.[117] Full information on the
families of the three Bigod earls of Norfolk and the four Bohun
earls of Hereford and Essex in the thirteenth and early fourteenth
centuries is lacking, but the marriages of their daughters seem to
have followed a similar pattern. Most were married to English
barons, but a daughter of the Humphrey de Bohun who died in
1265 married Robert de Ferrers, earl of Derby (d. 1279), and as
noted earlier, a daughter of Earl Humphrey (d. 1275) was married
to William Marshal's fifth son, Anselm. Over the course of the
century, the Clares seem to have been somewhat more successful
in marrying their daughters and sisters into comital houses and
in establishing marriage ties among the Irish, Scots and marcher
baronage, but in general the differences were not pronounced.[118]

   The marriages of the various members of the family and the
instances of co-operation or service in any given generation served
to widen the range of political and territorial associations or to
strengthen existing ones. The promotion of family interests was
of concern not only to the earls themselves, but also to their
brothers and sisters, wives and in-laws. Instances have already
been cited of the ways in which the earls' widows and sons secured
favorable marriages for their daughters, sisters and cousins in the
thirteenth and early fourteenth centuries. Examples of co-operation extended to relatives by marriage as well. Gilbert Marshal
provided a marriage portion for his niece Isabel when she married
Robert Bruce. Bogo de Clare helped arrange the marriage of his

---

[116] In addition to Isabel, who married the first Earl Gilbert and Richard of
Cornwall, William Marshal's daughters included: Maud, wife of Hugh Bigod,
earl of Norfolk (d. 1225) and William de Warenne, earl of Surrey (d. 1240);
Sibyl, wife of William de Ferrers, earl of Derby (d. 1254); Eve, wife of William
de Braose (d. 1230); and Joan, wife of Warin de Mountchesney, lord of Swanscombe in Kent (d. 1255).

[117] A convenient list is given in Sanders, *English Baronies*, p. 63 note 5.

[118] *G. E. C.*, VI, 459–69; Sanders, *English Baronies*, pp. 63, 80, 95, 149.

sister Rohese to Roger de Mowbray in 1270, and in return Roger participated in some complicated maneuvers to enable Bogo to obtain the rectorship of Melton Mowbray in 1284. Around 1320 Maud de Burgh, widow of the last Earl Gilbert, lent £600 to her brother-in-law Hugh D'Audley, husband of the earl's sister Margaret.[119]

The brothers were often of considerable political assistance to each other. William de Clare served in the retinue of Earl Richard in military campaigns and on social occasions such as tournaments. When William was defeated in a tournament in France in 1252, the earl went abroad to restore his brother's lost prestige. Richard not only recovered the horses and armor William had lost, but in the words of the Tewkesbury chronicler, returned "with the greatest honor to his own land, having almost annihilated his adversaries."[120] Thomas and Bogo de Clare served a number of useful and important functions for their brother, Earl Gilbert the Red. Thomas aided the earl in 1265, when he broke with Simon de Montfort and rejoined the royalist side in the Barons' War, and they fought together at the battle of Evesham in which Earl Simon was killed.[121] Bogo was often active in marcher affairs on the earl's behalf. In 1285 Gilbert became involved in a jurisdictional dispute with the abbot of St. Augustine, Bristol, and Bogo helped imprison the abbot in the earl's jail at Cardiff.[122] He also used his authority as chancellor of the diocese of Llandaff, a position he probably acquired through Gilbert's patronage in 1287, to block the election of Philip de Staunton, whose nomination as bishop by the cathedral chapter had been approved by King Edward I. Bogo must have had a double motive. Since Earl Gilbert had various fiscal and judicial rights in the bishopric *sede*

---

[119] *Cal. Chart. Rolls 1226–57*, p. 252; *Close Rolls 1268–72*, pp. 284–85; "Wardrobe and Household Accounts of Bogo de Clare, 1284–1286," ed. M. S. Giuseppi, *Archaeologia*, LXX (1918–20), Introduction, pp. 13–16; *Cal. Close Rolls 1318–23*, p. 323.

[120] Tewkesbury, p. 151; "cum maximo honore repatrians ad patria, omnibus adversariis suis in nihilum fere redactis." The translation is that of Doris M. Stenton, *English Society in the Early Middle Ages (1066–1307)* (Harmondsworth, 1952), p. 85.

[121] Below, pp. 108, 188.

[122] *Cal. Pat. Rolls 1281–92*, p. 212. The dispute seems to have involved the abbot's claims to exemption from services for the lands held by the abbey in Gilbert's lordship of Glamorgan, but the records of the affair have not survived.

vacante, Bogo was obviously desirous of keeping the see vacant as long as possible for his brother's exploitation. Later, when Edward challenged Gilbert's rights, Bogo continued to obstruct matters, probably in the hope that the king would ease his pressure on the earl in return for the orderly nomination and election of a new bishop.[123]

Finally, the earls made direct use of their estates to promote or provide for the other members of the family. Most of the younger brothers were given estates to help support themselves. William de Clare held lands—in Petersfield and Mapledurham (Hants), and in Walsingham, Wells, and Warham (Norfolk)— of Earl Richard for a knight's fee. Bogo de Clare held some manors for life in the lordship in Usk [124] of Earl Gilbert the Red. Similarly, Thomas held Tarrant Rushton and the hundred of Coombsditch (Dorset) and lands in Standon (Hertford) of his brother's enfeoffment, and his sons continued to hold them under Joan of Acre and the last Earl Gilbert.[125] Other estates served a variety of social purposes, and were used especially as marriage portions. After their marriage was annulled in 1285, the Red Earl granted Alice de Lusignan a life interest in the manors of Thaxted (Essex), Burford (Oxford), Spenhamland (Berkshire), and Wells and Warham (Norfolk), the latter two previously held by William de Clare from 1248 to 1258.[126] When Alice died in 1290, the estates reverted to the earl, but in 1297 Burford was demised by Joan of Acre to her stepdaughter Isabella for the minority of the young Earl Gilbert. When he gained seisin of the inheritance in 1307, he gave the manor, along with Skipton, another Oxford estate, to Isabella for life, and in 1314 he granted her some additional properties as well. The earl's half sister was still unmarried in 1314, and Gilbert undoubtedly intended the

---

[123] See, in general, W. Greenway, "The Election of John de Monmouth, Bishop of Llandaff, 1287–97," *Morgannwg*, V (1961), 3–8; Glanmor Williams, *The Welsh Church from Conquest to Reformation* (Cardiff, 1962), p. 68. The dispute between Gilbert and King Edward over Llandaff will be treated in detail below, pp. 273–75.

[124] Usk was acquired by Earl Richard in 1246 as part of the partition of the Marshal inheritance. PRO, Chancery Miscellanea, C 47/9/20. See below, pp. 75–76.

[125] *Cal. Chart. Rolls 1226–57*, p. 334; *Cal. Inq. Post Mortem*, IV, no. 435, V, no. 44.

[126] *Foedera*, I, 654.

grants for a dual purpose. She could use the revenues from the estates to support herself, even if she remained single. If and when she did marry, they would then serve the added function of a marriage portion.[127] Some other estates were regarded as expendable commodities and were in effect reserved for these and related purposes. In 1259 Earl Richard granted Carlton in Lincoln with some other properties to Nigel de Amundeville in exchange for a third of the barony of Southoe. When Nigel died somewhat later, Carlton reverted to Earl Gilbert the Red, who gave it along with Glapthorne (Northants) to his daughter Joan when she married Duncan, earl of Fife in 1284.[128] The Bedfordshire manor of Sundon is the best example of an estate often used as a marriage portion. When Richard of Cornwall married the first earl's widow Isabel Marshal, the manor came into his possession. Richard died in April 1272 and Sundon reverted to Gilbert the Red, who promptly gave it to his sister Margaret when she married Richard's heir Edmund six months later. From 1300 Margaret held Sundon as part of the dower assigned to her after Edmund's death. When she died in 1312, it reverted again to the head of the Clare family, and this time the last Earl Gilbert gave it, along with Thaxted, to his cousin, another Margaret, daughter of Thomas de Clare, when she married the earl's friend and political associate, the Kentish baron Bartholomew de Badlesmere. Grants such as these not only served to create or strengthen tenurial ties with other members of the English baronage, but also gave the earls concrete means of providing for the social and personal needs of the other members of the family.[129]

The fortunes of the Clare family over the course of the hundred years from the acquisition of the Gloucester inheritance in 1217 to the partition of 1317 were conditioned not only by their vastly increased wealth and power, but by other factors, either nonexistent or poorly documented for the twelfth century. For example, each

[127] Cal. Fine Rolls 1272–1307, p. 521; Cal. Pat. Rolls 1313–17, p. 223.

[128] Sanders, English Baronies, pp. 80–81; Final Concords of the County of Lincoln, 1242–1272, ed. C. W. Foster (Lincoln Record Society, vol. XVII, 1920), II, 286–87; Cal. Docs. Scotland, II, no. 1108, IV, no. 36. Nigel appears as a witness to a charter of Earl Gilbert the Red ca. 1263–70. Brit. Mus., Add. Ch. 20398.

[129] Denholm-Young, Richard of Cornwall, p. 169; Dunstable, p. 253; cf. Cal. Pat. Rolls 1313–17, p. 131.

of the three Clare earls of Gloucester following the first Earl Gilbert was a minor at the time of his father's death. In addition, all four earls left widows whose activities present some interesting contrasts. None of the twelfth century lords of Clare or earls of Hertford was a minor at the time of his succession, and very little is known about any of their widows. The facts of minority and widowhood were thus new, or newly important, in the thirteenth-century history of the family. They created special circumstances in which the Crown exercised its powers of wardship and related rights, and as the subsequent chapters will show, these often proved to be of considerable political importance in the affairs of the kingdom at large. Finally, each earl except the last left, in addition to his eldest son and heir, daughters and younger sons, whose welfare and connections were of prime importance to the rest of the family. Their careers and marriages afford excellent examples not only of the opportunities open to them in the contemporary social structure, but also of the ways in which the various members of any given generation or generations could co-operate with each other in providing mutual services, support and advancement. The careers of the earls themselves are of course the dominant aspects of family history in the thirteenth century, and they will be treated in detail in the following chapters. But more is involved than the story of the earls alone. In many ways, the entire family was the real unit of social behavior and interest.

CHAPTER II

THE EARLS OF GLOUCESTER AND HENRY III, 1217–1262

The First Earl and the Minority

The first representative of the Clare family to assume the title of earl of Gloucester is also the least known, and, insofar as his public career is concerned, the least prominent. Before succeeding to the inheritance, Gilbert de Clare was associated with his father, Richard, earl of Hertford, in the baronial rebellion against King John. With Earl Richard he was among the twenty-five barons entrusted with the task of enforcing Magna Carta in 1215.[1] Despite sentences of excommunication issued against them by Innocent III in December,[2] both Richard and Gilbert remained in open opposition to the royalists, and the following March the king declared the earl's estates forfeited. After John's death in October, 1216, Richard and Gilbert were numbered among the supporters of Prince Louis of France, the son and eventual heir of King Philip Augustus, whom the rebels called over to England as the rival to the young Henry III. Efforts by the new regent William Marshal to reconcile the Clares to the royalists in March, 1217, proved fruitless, and in May Gilbert sided with Louis at the battle of Lincoln, which culminated in a royalist victory and effectively ended French intervention.[3]

After the battle of Lincoln, the Clares did return to the royalist side. In September, 1217, William Marshal, acting on behalf of Henry III, concluded a treaty at Lambeth with Prince Louis. The

[1] Matthew Paris, Chronica Majora, II, 604–5. Cf. also Painter, The Reign of King John, pp. 291–92, and J. C. Holt, The Northerners (Oxford, 1961), pp. 83, 110.
[2] Matthew Paris, Chronica Majora, II, 643; Foedera, I, 139.
[3] Rot. Claus., I, 251; Patent Rolls 1216–25, p. 48. For the defeat of Louis, see Powicke, King Henry III, I, 10–17.

previous July Gilbert had conferred with the regent at Gloucester, undoubtedly to secure promises that he and his father would not be penalized for their allegiance to the prince.[4] Shortly after the peace treaty, both Earl Richard and Gilbert were formally received into the king's peace, and the estates were restored.[5] Gilbert's motives were both personal and political. He was willing to work with the new government in its efforts to rid the administration of John's foreign favorites, such as Faulkes de Breauté, who were still attempting to maintain their former positions of power.[6] Furthermore, the ties of kinship with William Marshal, who was Earl Richard's cousin and Gilbert's father-in-law, must have proved major personal factors in the reconciliation. The most important reasons, however, were probably the advanced age of his father, who was at least sixty-five, and the death of Isabel, countess of Gloucester, in mid-October. Gilbert suddenly stood to inherit both the Clare and Gloucester estates, and he certainly did not wish to jeopardize his prospects by continued resistance. After his father's death in November, Gilbert obtained both inheritances and the comital titles and was quickly restored to royal favor. In January, 1218, he was one of the " dilecti et fideles " of the realm charged with ensuring the good conduct of the sons of William de Braose the younger, who had just been released from custody.[7]

The first Earl Gilbert was a major figure in the government of the kingdom during the minority of Henry III, but he did not assume the prominence or importance of such men as William Marshal, the papal legates Guala Biachieri and Padulph, or the justiciar, Hubert de Burgh. His own activities correspond closely to those of most of the other great magnates. In 1228 he was summoned for the campaign in Wales against Llywelyn ap Iorwerth, prince of Gwynedd, but there is little to indicate the actual part he played in the fighting.[8] He also participated in various ceremonial functions, serving on diplomatic expeditions to Ger-

---

[4] Cf. *Patent Rolls 1216–25*, p. 79. The text of the treaty is printed in *Foedera*, I, 148.

[5] *Rot. Claus.*, I, 327b.

[6] Cf. the remarks of Holt, *The Northerners*, pp. 251–52.

[7] *Patent Rolls 1216–25*, p. 134. They were Gilbert's nephews. Their mother, Matilda, was the new earl's sister.

[8] *Close Rolls 1227–31*, p. 115; Lloyd, *Hist. Wales*, II, 667–69. Llywelyn and Henry III had concluded a peace treaty in 1218, shortly after the treaty of Lambeth, but it was often disturbed in the following decade. Lloyd, *Hist. Wales*, II, 653–67.

many in 1227 and Brittany in 1230.[9] He acted only infrequently in the administration. In the years 1224–26 he attested a number of writs and letters dealing with routine matters, usually in conjunction with the justiciar or other officials but occasionally by himself. Somewhat more significantly, he aided the government in 1224 in its efforts to rid the kingdom of the last of Faulkes de Breauté's adherents, and in 1225 he was one of the witnesses to the reissue of Magna Carta and the Charter of the Forest.[10]

Such functions as Earl Gilbert did assume in the affairs of the realm were of little consequence, both to the kingdom at large and to himself. His activities were of the kind to be excepted of a man of his standing, and in no way were they decisive. Of far greater importance were his personal affairs. Gilbert was already close to forty when his father died, and he controlled the estates for only about a dozen years before his own death in 1230. His major concern during this period was to provide for the continuity of the inheritance and to promote the fortunes of his family. He had married William Marshal's daughter Isabel in 1214, but had no children when he succeeded to the estates and titles in 1217. His first child, Amicia, was not born until 1220, but by 1229 there were also three sons and another daughter. Gilbert married Amicia to Baldwin de Reviers, the future earl of Devon, in 1225, and although he died before he could arrange for the other children, his eldest son and heir Richard, his widow Isabel Marshal, and Isabel's relatives, did provide for them.[11]

Apart from ensuring an adequate number of children, Earl Gilbert's prime task was to consolidate and implement his authority in his great new inheritance in England and Wales. Little is known of the economic or administrative organization of the English estates during the period of his tenure. He apparently enjoyed the revenues from the estates and exercised his authority over them with little difficulty, although the available evidence indicates that they achieved a greater profitability and efficiency of control under his descendants.[12] A far different set of conditions, however, con-

[9] *Patent Rolls 1225–32*, pp. 161–62, 357–60, 410; Tewkesbury, p. 76.

[10] *Patent Rolls 1216–25*, pp. 445, 458, 465, 485; *ibid. 1225–32*, p. 48; *Rot. Claus.*, II, 62, 65b; *Annales de Burton*, ed. H. R. Luard (*Annales Monastici*, vol. I, Rolls Series XXXVI, 1864), pp. 232, 236.

[11] *Patent Rolls 1225–82*, p. 87; above, pp. 31–33.

[12] See below, Chapter VII *passim*.

fronted Earl Gilbert in the great lordship of Glamorgan. Formal title to the lordship did not automatically assure him or his successors of effective political and military control of the area. Indeed, Gilbert was opposed in 1218 by a number of Welsh chieftains who claimed virtual independence of their new overlord, much as his own marcher status conferred upon Gilbert a freedom from most of the limitations the Crown had imposed upon the English baronage in the decades following the Conquest.[13] The situation in Glamorgan was the most immediate and serious problem facing the Clares, and Earl Gilbert's efforts to strengthen his position began a process that was completed only by his son and grandson, Earl Richard and Earl Gilbert the Red. Marcher politics proved to be the main focus of attention of the Clares for the bulk of the thirteenth century, and they often assumed a significance that transcended their apparently localized interest.[14]

Glamorgan was the largest and strategically the most important of the great marcher lordships of Wales. The original Norman conquerors in the late eleventh and early twelfth centuries, led by Robert fitz Hamon and his successor, Robert, earl of Gloucester (d. 1147), had occupied only the lowlands and coastal areas, leaving the local chieftains in the outlying mountainous regions with almost complete autonomy. In the twelfth century these chieftains allied themselves with the rulers of Deheubarth in southern Wales, but in the early thirteenth century they began to transfer their allegiance to the great northern dynasty of Gwynedd, which under the leadership of Llywelyn ap Iorwerth replaced the house of Deheubarth as the dominant political power in Wales. These alliances thus posed a threat not only to the Clares, but to the Crown as well, for the lordship of Glamorgan was the key to the political stability of the southern march.[15]

The chieftains who confronted Earl Gilbert represented local dynasties long established in Glamorgan. The cantred of Seng-

---

[13] See, in general, J. Otway-Ruthven, "The Constitutional Position of the Great Lordships of South Wales," *Transactions of the Royal Historical Society*, 5th ser. VIII (1958), 1–18; Edwards, "The Normans and the Welsh March," pp. 155–77; William Rees, *South Wales and the March 1284–1415* (Oxford, 1924), pp. 43–46.

[14] For much of the structure and argumentation of what follows on Glamorgan in this chapter, I am indebted to J. Beverly Smith, "The Lordship of Glamorgan," *Morgannwg*, II (1958), 9–37.

[15] *Ibid.*, pp. 13–25; for the rise of Llywelyn ap Iorwerth to 1218, Lloyd, *Hist. Wales*, II, 612–54.

henydd, situated between the Rhymny and the Taf Rivers, was divided into three commotes, the southernmost of which, Cibwr, had been converted into the lordship of Cardiff by Robert fitz Hamon to serve as the *caput* of the entire lordship. The two out-lying commotes, Uwch– (*Trans*) and Is– (*Cis*) Caiach[16] were held by the descendants of Ifor ap Meurig (Ifor Bach), who in 1158 had come into serious conflict with the then lord of Glamor-gan, William, earl of Gloucester.[17] After 1211 the commotes were held by Ifor Bach's grandson, Rhys ap Gruffydd (d. 1256).[18] There is no evidence that any friction developed between Rhys and his new overlord; but further west, in the broad uplands between the Taf and the Nedd, Earl Gilbert came into continual conflict with the other great commotal lords, notably Morgan Gam of Afan, Hywel ap Maredudd of Meisgyn, and Morgan ap Cadwallon of Glynrhondda. These three chieftains were cousins, and were descended from Iestyn ap Gwrgant, the "king" of Glamorgan (Morgannwg) ousted by fitz Hamon.[19] There is some evidence to suggest that in the late twelfth century the eldest of Iestyn's four grandsons, Morgan ap Caradog, lord of Afan, exercised some sort of overlordship over his brothers, Maredudd, lord of Meisgyn, and Cadwallon, lord of Glynrhondda.[20] In the early years of the thirteenth century, Hywel ap Maredudd succeeded his father in Meisgyn and Morgan ap Cadwallon assumed control over Glyn-rhondda. It is not certain whether Morgan ap Caradog maintained his suzerainty over the new chieftains; in any event he died shortly before 1217 and was succeeded by his son, Morgan Gam. The details of the process by which control of Afan was vested in Morgan Gam are obscure, for it seems that initially his brothers and at least one sister had some share of the territory. By 1217, however, it is clear that Morgan Gam was in sole possession of Afan.[21] The most important problem facing the new Earl Gilbert, therefore, was the effort of Morgan Gam, on the one hand to assert his own independence of the earl's authority, and on the

[16] For the use of *trans* and *cis* in place of the more usual translations *supra* and *subtus*, see Melville Richards, "The Significance of *Is* and *Uwch* in Welsh Commote and Cantref Names," *Welsh History Review*, II (1964–), 9–18.
[17] Lloyd, *Hist. Wales*, II, 507–8.
[18] *Ibid.*, II, 545, 674 and note 109, and the genealogical table, II, 770.
[19] *Ibid.*, II, 771.
[20] Smith, "The Lordship of Glamorgan," pp. 25–27.
[21] *Cartae de Glamorgan*, II, 328–29, III, 925–26, 931–32.

other, to regain that position of supremacy over the other commotes between the Taf and the Nedd, Meisgyn and Glynrhondda,
which his father Morgan ap Caradog had enjoyed.[22]

The entire period of Earl Gilbert's rule was filled with sporadic
warfare against these chieftains. In 1224 Morgan Gam's cousin,
Morgan ap Owain, attacked the great Cistercian abbey of Margam,
and in succeeding years numerous raids were made on other abbey
lands, including Newcastle, which had formed part of Morgan
ap Caradog's patrimony, but which after his death was separated
from it and not granted to Morgan Gam.[23] It is clear that the
lord of Afan was the instigator of these attacks. He wished to
regain Newcastle, and there is evidence that he attempted not only
to maintain his independence of Earl Gilbert, but also to bring
Margam Abbey itself completely under his own domination. One
of the first acts of the new earl was to issue a charter asserting
the traditional right of the lord of Glamorgan to custody and
protection of the abbey and exclusive control over all jurisdictional
matters pertaining to its lands. In so doing, Earl Gilbert apparently sought to confront Morgan Gam squarely on this issue, for
Morgan, in an undated but contemporary charter, claimed his own
right to cognizance of disputes involving Margam without men-
tioning the superior jurisdiction of the earl or any right of appeal
to the comital courts.[24]

Morgan Gam's policies do not seem to have been entirely
successful, but his resistance to Earl Gilbert increased the possibility that Llywelyn ap Iorwerth might be able to extend his own
power into Glamorgan. In 1228 Gilbert participated in the Kerry
campaign against the prince of Gwynedd, and he took advantage
of the situation to assert his military strength in Glamorgan. The
number of knights proffered for his English estates in the campaign, which ended in October, is unknown; but about the same
time, according to the Tewkesbury chronicle, the earl undertook
a concerted attack " cum exercitu magno " on the Welsh. The
wording of the passage suggests that this was a separate contingent, directed against Morgan Gam and his allies, and that
the force consisted of the earl's Norman tenants in Glamorgan,

[22] Cf. the remarks of Smith, " The Lordship of Glamorgan," pp. 26–27.
[23] *Annales de Margam*, ed. H. R. Luard (*Annales Monastici*, vol. I, Rolls Series
XXXVI, 1864), pp. 34–35; Smith, " The Lordship of Glamorgan," pp. 25, 27.
[24] *Cartae de Glamorgan*, II, 359–61, III, 925, 926.

who were undoubtedly as anxious as their overlord to end the Welsh raids. These assumptions are confirmed by the account in the Margam chronicle, which records the fact that Gilbert did capture the lord of Afan, and sent him off to one of his English jails, possibly Clare, for safekeeping.[25]

Earl Gilbert's campaign was designed to remove the chief threat to the security of the lordship. But Hywel ap Maredudd, lord of Meisgyn, immediately replaced his cousin as leader of the Welsh resistance. In 1228 Hywel captured and mutilated Morgan ap Cadwallon and annexed his lordship of Glynrhondda.[26] In the following year he attacked the Norman fees of St. Nicholas and St. Hilary, and the Clare stronghold of Kenfig in the south-western part of the lordship.[27] Hywel ap Maredudd clearly intended by these actions to sustain the policies of Morgan Gam. The exact sequence of events in 1228 is obscure, but it seems likely that the seizure of Glynrhondda took place shortly after Morgan Gam's capture, and that it signified Hywel's own attempt to effect the reintegration of the commotes between the Taf and Nedd under a single hegemony, which the lord of Afan had thus far been unable to bring about. Furthermore, it is possible that Hywel assumed *de facto* control of the latter commote as well, following Morgan's imprisonment. The attacks on Kenfig, the demesne castle closest to Afan, and on the Norman fees such as St. Nicholas, were similarly part of a continued effort to remind Earl Gilbert that Morgan Gam's allies and relatives would not readily submit to Norman overlordship. Finally, Hywel's activities meant that the opportunities for Llywelyn ap Iorwerth in Glamorgan were not diminished. Large portions of the lordship thus remained in control of forces openly hostile to the earl of Gloucester. In short, the efforts of the first Earl Gilbert to assert his authority in Glamorgan, while forceful, and from his own point of view necessary, merely served to sharpen, not resolve, the underlying conflict.

In the fall of 1230, Earl Gilbert de Clare went to France on a diplomatic mission for Henry III. On October 25, he died at Penros in the duchy of Brittany, and was brought home for

[25] *Annales de Margam*, p. 36; Tewkesbury, p. 70.
[26] *Annales de Margam*, p. 36.
[27] *Ibid.*, pp. 36, 37.

burial at Tewkesbury Abbey.[28] The first earl is a somewhat obscure figure. He spent much of his adult life in the background, associated with his father, Richard, earl of Hertford. Nothing is known of his personality, and there are few distinguishing marks to his public career after 1217. His activities and interests in the march, however, do foreshadow the policy consciously pursued and finally realized by his descendants. But the immediate results of his death were additional problems and difficulties, both for his heir and for the Crown. The earl left as his eldest son and heir Richard, a boy of eight. For the first time in the long history of the Clare family, the inheritance now passed to a minor, and for the next decade both he and the estates came under royal custody. Control of the young heir was a valuable commodity, and his fortunes are intimately connected with the political crises involving King Henry and the justiciar, Hubert de Burgh. In addition, the Crown was now forced to assume direct responsibility for the struggle to impose the authority of the lord of Glamorgan over the Welsh chieftains, a struggle exacerbated by the overt intervention of Llywelyn ap Iorwerth, prince of Gwynedd.

On November 1, 1230, a few days after hearing of Earl Gilbert's death, King Henry III granted custody of the Clare estates along with the right to Richard's marriage to Hubert de Burgh for 7,000 marks.[29] Hubert had established himself as the dominant force in the government, and custody of the estates and heir did nothing to detract from his position. For almost two years the young Richard de Clare remained a ward in Hubert's household. In the summer of 1232, however, the justiciar was suddenly dismissed from office, deprived of his own lands and privileges, and subsequently outlawed.[30] The crisis in Hubert's fortunes was precipitated by the king's growing resentment of his domination, and by the return to power of Hubert's former rival, Peter des Roches, bishop of Winchester. Hubert's downfall was swift and severe, and as part of the governmental reorganization attendant upon it, Henry assigned custody of the ward to Peter des Roches, and

---

[28] Tewkesbury, pp. 76–77.

[29] *Patent Rolls 1225–32*, p. 412; *Pipe Roll 14 Henry III*, ed. Chalfant Robinson (Pipe Roll Society, vol. XLII, new ser. IV, 1927), p. 96; *Rot. Fin.*, I, 205. See also note 38 below.

[30] For a brief account of Hubert's career, see Powicke, *King Henry III*, I, 68–83.

granted control of the Clare inheritance itself to the bishop's nephew, Peter de Rivaux.[31]

Unknown to the king, Richard de Clare was already married by this time to Hubert's daughter Meggotta (Margaret).[32] In the fall of 1232 Hubert's wife, Margaret of Scotland, had taken refuge at Bury St. Edmund's, and without his knowledge, married their daughter to Earl Gilbert's heir. Both children were about ten years old. Margaret must have been prompted by the hope of securing her daughter's future despite Hubert's disgrace, and she may have been prepared to defend her act on the basis of the original grant of November 1, 1230.[33] The marriage went undetected for a number of years. Neither the king nor, apparently, Hubert himself, knew of it in 1234, when Henry restored the former justiciar to favor following the downfall of des Roches and de Rivaux. Rumors of the marriage began circulating in 1236, and it was formally disclosed in the fall of that year, when Hubert was again brought to trial and deprived of some of the positions which he had been granted two years earlier following his reconciliation with the king.[34]

It is doubtful that the marriage was ever consummated, despite statements by Margaret de Burgh which suggested as much. The young Richard was apparently in the custody of Peter des Roches and then Peter de Rivaux until the summer of 1234. King Henry kept him in his own household thereafter. He specifically forbade Hubert from resuming custody in 1234, granting the heir 200 marks a year for expenses and entrusting him to the new keeper of the honors of Gloucester and Clare, Richard de la Lade.[35] Furthermore, it is highly unlikely that Richard and Meggotta were allowed to live together when their marriage was publicly

[31] Tewkesbury, p. 86; *Patent Rolls 1225–32*, pp. 500–501.

[32] The following paragraphs are based on F. M. Powicke, "The Oath of Bromholm," *English Historical Review*, LVI (1941), 539–48, reprinted in his *King Henry III*, II, 760–68. References will be to this reprint.

[33] *Ibid.*, II, 760–62, 767.

[34] *Ibid.*, II, 761–63; Matthew Paris, *Chronica Majora*, III, 386; Tewkesbury, p. 102; *Cal. Pat. Rolls 1232–47*, p. 48. For the fall of Peter des Roches and Peter de Rivaux, see Powicke, *King Henry III*, I, 135–38.

[35] Tewkesbury, p. 86; *Close Rolls 1231–34*, p. 218; *Cal. Pat. Rolls 1232–47*, p. 54; *Cal. Liberate Rolls 1226–40*, pp. 275, 360, 369–70; *ibid. 1240–45*, pp. 35, 97. Richard de la Lade had been an official of the first Earl Gilbert. *Close Rolls 1227–31*, p. 252; *Curia Regis Rolls 1227–30*, p. 175. Tonbridge was released to the archbishop of Canterbury in May 1235. *Cal. Pat. Rolls 1232–47*, p. 104.

disclosed in 1236, and the girl seems in fact to have remained with her mother during the entire time. In 1239, Henry raised the issue again, but forgave Hubert and Margaret for the marriage and other alleged offenses against the king. He could afford to pardon them; by this time Meggotta was dead, and the king himself had arranged another marriage for Richard de Clare.[36]

Negotiations for the second marriage began even before Meggotta de Burgh's death in November, 1237. As early as 1236, before the original match was publicly revealed, King Henry had entertained notions of marrying the heir to one of his French relatives. The plan apparently fell through, perhaps when news of the first marriage came out. In the fall of 1237, while Meggotta was still alive, John de Lacy, earl of Lincoln, offered 5,000 marks, a sum roughly equivalent to the gross annual value of the Clare inheritance,[37] to have Richard's marriage for his own daughter Maud. The earl was undoubtedly moved by many of the same considerations that had prompted the wife of Hubert de Burgh, although he had no need to resort to the drastic actions she had taken in 1232. He was the highest, and perhaps the only, bidder, but Henry still desired to marry Richard to a foreign kinsman. Through the efforts of his brother Richard of Cornwall, the step-father of the young heir, a compromise was effected. On October 26, 1237, Henry offered the marriage to Hugh de Lusignan, count of La Marche, for one of his daughters, with the proviso that if the count did not agree to the proposal by the following January, the earl of Lincoln could have it for 3,000 marks. Hugh de Lusignan did not agree, and on January 25, 1238, Richard de Clare was married to Maud de Lacy.[38]

By the time of his second marriage, Richard was almost sixteen.

[36] Powicke, *King Henry III*, II, 764–68.

[37] The earls of Gloucester had an annual income of some £3,000 to £4,000 in the mid-thirteenth century. See below, pp. 203–5.

[38] *Cal. Pat. Rolls 1232–47*, pp. 199–200, 208; Tewkesbury, p. 106; Matthew Paris, *Chronica Majora*, III, 386, 476; *G. E. C.*, V, 700 and notes; Powicke, *King Henry III*, II, 764–65. John de Lacy paid at least 500 and possibly 1,000 marks of the marriage fine before his death in 1240. *Cal. Liberate Rolls 1226–40*, pp. 348, 421. In 1242, Hubert de Burgh owed 4,000 marks for his original custody of the estates and heir. *Pipe Roll 26 Henry III*, ed. H. L. Cannon (New Haven, 1927), p. 196. His original fine was 7,000 marks, but it is not likely that he had paid anything. The king probably pardoned him 3,000 marks, the amount to be collected from the earl of Lincoln, in 1239. Cf. *Cal. Chart. Rolls 1226–57*, p. 148. Hubert died in 1243.

He was to remain a ward of the king until 1243, when he came of age and was formally granted seisin of his inheritance. His fortunes shed a grim light on the political and financial manipulations of the rights of wardship and marriage, and on the impact of those rights on national politics. His own attitudes and personal feelings never emerge during this entire period. As Powicke has remarked, " one would like to know how Richard de Clare felt about it all." [39]

The personal difficulties experienced by Richard de Clare after his father's death in 1230 were paralleled by the political and military difficulties of the Crown in the lordship of Glamorgan. When the king granted custody of the estates to Hubert de Burgh in November, 1230, he reminded the Welsh commotal lords, including Hywel ap Maredudd of Meisgyn, Rhys ap Gruffydd of Senghenydd, and Morgan ap Hywel of Caerleon, lord of Machen in Gwynllwg,[40] of the fealty and allegiance they owed to the royal appointee as representative of the lord of Glamorgan.[41] The order had no effect. Led by Morgan Gam of Afan, who had secured his release in 1229,[42] the chieftains openly allied themselves with Llywelyn ap Iorwerth. The inclusion of the lords of Senghenydd and Machen in their ranks meant that the situation was even more dangerous after 1230 than before, when only the descendants of Iestyn ap Gwrgant confronted the first earl. As part of a major assault on southern Wales, in which he overran Brecknock, Cardigan and Caerleon, Llywelyn marched on the western part of Glamorgan, where with the aid of Morgan Gam he destroyed the castle of Neath in 1231. In the following year, he and Morgan Gam led still another attack, this time on Kenfig. According to the Margam chronicler, Llywelyn's allies included " most of the noblest princes of Wales, acting under his command." This statement undoubtedly includes the commotal lords

[39] Powicke, King Henry III, II, 764.
[40] Morgan, who died in 1248, was the son of Hywel ap Iorwerth (d. 1211). In 1217, William Marshal had taken Caerleon from Morgan ap Hywel, and it remained in the Marshal family to 1245. Although Morgan never recovered it, he did hold other territories in the Marshal lordship of Netherwent, as well as the commote of Machen in the Clare lordship of Gwynllwg. Brut Hergest, p. 217, Peniarth, p. 96; Close Rolls 1247–51, p. 233; Lloyd, Hist. Wales, II, 653, 674 note 108, 712–13 and note 113, 771.
[41] Patent Rolls 1225–32, p. 412.
[42] Annales de Margam, p. 37.

of Glamorgan, and as such indicates clearly that their transfer of allegiance to the dynasty of Gwynedd was an accomplished fact.[43]

In September, 1232, Peter de Rivaux replaced Hubert de Burgh as guardian of the " castles and honors of Cardiff, Newport and Glamorgan." But Peter was as unsuccessful as his predecessor in asserting royal authority; and the rising baronial opposition to the king and his new favorites, led by the young Richard Marshal, who had succeeded his brother William as earl of Pembroke in 1231, added yet another complication to the already difficult situation.[44] In the king's name, Peter de Rivaux controlled, in addition to Glamorgan and Gwynllwg, the great lordships of Cardigan and Carmarthen and other strongholds in the southern march. This brought him into direct conflict with Richard Marshal, who based his opposition to King Henry on the political and military importance of his own marcher dominions of Pembroke and Netherwent. The support of Llywelyn ap Iorwerth and the chieftains under his command was of paramount importance in the warfare that followed. Richard apparently came to an understanding with the prince in 1233, promising certain Clare lands in Glamorgan to Morgan Gam, Hywel ap Maredudd and Rhys ap Gruffydd in return for their support. Unfortunately, the available evidence does not name the territories so promised, but it seems likely that the lord of Afan, at least, was destined to recover Newcastle, which his father Morgan ap Caradog had controlled before 1217.[45]

Immediately after the new alliance had been formed, open hostilities ensued. Richard broke a conditional truce he had previously reached with the king. He attacked Glamorgan and the neighboring lordships, undoubtedly in conjunction with the local commotal chieftains, and succeeded in capturing the vital strongholds of Newport in Gwynllwg and Cardiff itself. Richard Mar-

---

[43] Lloyd, *Hist. Wales*, II, 673–75; *Annales de Margam*, pp. 38–39; *Brut Hergest*, p. 229, *Peniarth*, p. 102; *Annales Cambriae*, ed. J. Williams ap Ithel (Rolls Series XX, 1860), p. 78; " Chronicle of the Thirteenth Century," *Archæologia Cambrensis*, 3rd ser., VIII (1862), 278; " Chronica de Wallia," ed. Thomas Jones, *Bulletin of the Board of Celtic Studies*, XII (1946–48), 37.

[44] For these events, see Powicke, *King Henry III*, I, 123–35, and for de Rivaux and his deputies, *Patent Rolls 1225–32*, pp. 500–501; *Close Rolls 1231–34*, p. 222; *Cal. Pat. Rolls 1232–47*, pp. 6, 27.

[45] *Close Rolls 1232–37*, pp. 590–91, 594–95; Smith, " The Lordship of Glamorgan," p. 29.

shal thus replaced Peter de Rivaux as effective ruler of Glamorgan. It is clear that his attacks were aimed both at the king and at Peter, and the conquest of the lordship, combined with Llywelyn ap Iorwerth's renewed assaults on Brecknock and Carmarthen, assured the antiroyalist forces of an almost unassailable position. Richard Marshal's promises of lands to Morgan Gam and the others were probably predicated upon the success of the campaign; the support of the commotal lords was secured in defiance of the royal authority, not on behalf of it.[46]

Whatever the precise conditions of the alliance between Richard and the Welsh chieftains may have been, they did not remain in effect for long. Full-scale civil war in England and Wales was averted in 1234 by the downfall of Peter des Roches and his protege, Peter de Rivaux, and by the death of Richard Marshal himself in Ireland.[47] The earl was succeeded by his brother Gilbert, and the quarrel with the king subsided. On June 3, 1234, as part of the reconciliation, Henry granted custody of Glamorgan to Richard Siward, who held Llanbleddian and other important fees within the lordship. Gilbert Marshal seems to have assumed control of Glamorgan when his brother sailed to Ireland, for in the grant to Siward, the king directed the earl to surrender seisin to the new keeper. Siward, who was a member of Gilbert Marshal's *familia* and had been one of Richard's leading allies in the revolt of 1233–34, retained custody until February, 1235, when Gilbert himself was formally appointed keeper.[48] Of equal significance, peace was restored with Llywelyn ap Iorwerth as well. The lands granted or promised to Morgan Gam and his allies were to be surrendered, and when the commotal lords balked, their compliance was secured by the prince of Gwynedd himself.[49]

For the next few years there were no serious internal disturbances in the lordship, but the conflict between the house of Gwynedd and the Crown for the allegiance of the local chieftains remained unresolved. Llywelyn pressed his claims for the homage of Morgan ap Hywel of Caerleon, as part of his policy to effect stable relationships with the Welsh lords beyond the boundaries

---

[46] *Brut Hargest*, pp. 231, 233, *Peniarth*, p. 103; Tewkesbury, pp. 90–91; *Annales Cambriae*, p. 79; "Chronica de Wallia," p. 37.

[47] See Powicke, *King Henry III*, I, 135–38.

[48] *Cal. Pat. Rolls 1232–47*, pp. 53, 96.

[49] *Close Rolls 1231–34*, pp. 594–95.

of his own patrimony of Gwynedd.[50] In 1238 he summoned the chieftains of southern Wales to the Cistercian abbey of Strata Florida in Cardigan to give their allegiance to his son and designated heir, Dafydd. It is probable that the commotal lords of Glamorgan were among those who attended, for the Crown specifically forbade Rhys ap Gruffydd of Senghenydd, Hywel ap Maredudd of Meisgyn and Glynrhondda, and the son of Morgan Gam of Afan, whose name is not given, from swearing their homage and fealty. Henry III recognized the explicit repudiation of marcher and royal authority that such an oath to Llywelyn's heir would entail, but he could do little to prevent the formalization of the allegiance of these chieftains to the ruling house of Gwynedd.[51]

This situation, however, was drastically altered in the opening years of the new decade. Llywelyn ap Iorwerth died in 1240, and the bonds of personal allegiance and loyalty he had developed were too fragile and unstable to maintain the strength of the dynasty under the less capable leadership of his sons Dafydd and Gruffydd; and about the same time, Richard de Clare finally assumed direct control over the lordship of Glamorgan. The conflict of authority, challenged but not resolved by the first Earl Gilbert and by King Henry III after 1230, was shortly to be decided in favor of the house of Clare.

Earl Richard and Glamorgan

Richard de Clare came of age in August, 1243, and was granted formal livery and seisin of his English estates at Michaelmas for a fine of 1,200 marks.[52] He was not knighted, however, until

[50] *Close Rolls 1234–37*, pp. 369–70. The significance of this policy has recently been emphasized by Ceri Lewis, " The Treaty of Woodstock, 1247," *Welsh History Review*, II (1964–), 37–41, although the analogies with the Hohenstaufen kings of Germany and the Capetian kings of France seem rather forced.

[51] *Close Rolls 1237–42*, pp. 123–24. Cf. Lloyd, *Hist. Wales*, II, 692–93.

[52] Tewkesbury, pp. 130–31; *Close Rolls 1242–47*, p. 44; *Rotulorum Originalium in Curia Scaccarii Abbreviatio*, ed. H. Playford (Record Commission, 1805–10), I, 5. It is not stated whether this fine included relief. According to the Tewkesbury account, Richard sought to recover his estates on August 4, the date of his twenty-first birthday, but since King Henry was in Gascony and did not return to England until September, formal seisin was delayed until Michaelmas.

June, 1245, and the earliest references to him as earl of Gloucester and Hertford date from the summer of that year.[53] Immediately after assuming control of the inheritance, Earl Richard became one of the leading magnates of the realm, although until 1258 the nature of his activities resembled that of his father, the first Earl Gilbert. Perhaps the most distinguishing feature of his personality was his cosmopolitanism. Earl Richard traveled frequently and widely. He was especially attracted by such largely ceremonial ventures as tournaments and pilgrimages. He often participated in tournaments on the Continent, usually in conjunction with Henry III's half brothers, the Valences, and his own brother William de Clare, and he made pilgrimages in 1248 and 1249 to Pontigny in France and to the famous shrine of St. James at Compostella in Spain in 1250.[54] In addition, he occasionally went abroad on behalf of the king and Richard of Cornwall. He spent most of 1254 in France in the company of King Henry and Queen Eleanor, and attended the marriage of the Lord Edward and Eleanor of Castile, daughter of Ferdinand III, king of Castile and Leon, which took place at the Castilian capital of Burgos in October.[55] In 1250, before going to Compostella, he accompanied Richard of Cornwall on a diplomatic mission to Pope Innocent IV at Lyons, and on two separate occasions in 1256–57 he acted as an envoy in Germany in the tortuous negotiations preceding the famous but specious double election of Richard of Cornwall and Alfonso X of Castile as king of the Romans in 1257.[56] Little is known of Earl Richard's actual participation in

[53] Matthew Paris, Chronica Majora, IV, 418; Rot. Fin., I, 436; Close Rolls 1242–47, p. 337.

[54] Matthew Paris, IV, 633, 649, V, 83, 367; Tewkesbury, pp. 137–38, 140–41, 151, 152–53; Cal. Pat. Rolls 1247–58, pp. 12, 61. His sister Amicia, dowager countess of Devon and wife of Robert de Guines, went to Pontigny in 1255. Ibid., p. 408. The shrine of Edmund of Canterbury (canonized in 1246) was located there. C. H. Lawrence, St. Edmund of Abingdon (Oxford, 1960), pp. 4–5.

[55] Tewkesbury, p. 155; Annales de Burton, p. 323; Cal. Pat. Rolls 1247–58, pp. 377, 390.

[56] Matthew Paris, Chronica Majora, V, 111, 117, 604, 622, 625; Cal. Pat. Rolls 1247–58, pp. 481, 486; Close Rolls 1256–59, p. 124. For the journey to Lyons, see Denholm-Young, Richard of Cornwall, pp. 73–74, and for the double election, ibid., pp. 86–97; Charles C. Bayley, The Formation of the German College of Electors in the Mid-Thirteenth Century (Toronto, 1949). Richard had also accompanied Cornwall to France while still the king's ward in the fall of 1242. Denholm-Young, Richard of Cornwall, p. 50 and note 7.

these affairs, but for the most part he seems to have played a conventional role, much like his father on similar occasions earlier in the century. Combined, however, with the fact that he carefully arranged the marriage of his son and heir Gilbert to the daughter of Hugh de Lusignan in 1252–53, and of his daughter Isabel to the marquis de Montferrat five years later,[57] they illustrate his familiarity with the nobility of western Europe and the ease with which he moved in its circles. Much more than any of the other earls of Gloucester in the thirteenth century, Richard de Clare participated fully in the institutional forms and customs of feudal society.

For all of Earl Richard's interest in tournaments and other social and diplomatic functions, his major concern was Wales and marcher politics. He remained a ward of King Henry until the fall of 1243, and there is no evidence that he sought to obtain the English estates until August, when he attained his majority. According to the usually reliable Tewkesbury account, however, Richard paid his uncle, Gilbert Marshal, earl of Pembroke, 500 marks to have seisin of the lordship of Glamorgan on August 5, 1240.[58] By this time Richard was eighteen, and his recovery of the lordship a full three years before obtaining the rest of the inheritance attests both to his interest in its affairs and to his belief in his own ability to control it. There is some evidence that the Crown did not officially recognize his action. When a dispute over the bishopric of Llandaff arose in the fall of 1240, Gilbert Marshal was summoned to the king's court to answer on behalf of the heir.[59] Gilbert died in 1241, and an entry on the Close Roll dated July 1, 1242 seems to regard Richard Siward of Llanbleddian, who had been keeper of Glamorgan in 1234–35, as once again *custos* of the entire lordship.[60] Regardless of the formal

[57] Above, pp. 35, 42, below, pp. 102–3.

[58] Tewkesbury, p. 117. This was the same amount that Gilbert Marshal had paid the king in 1236 for the custody of Glamorgan in place of Richard Siward. *Cal. Liberate Rolls 1226–40*, p. 248.

[59] PRO, Curia Regis Roll Michaelmas 25 Henry III, KB 26/121 m. 17d. On this matter, see below, p. 273.

[60] *Close Rolls 1237–42*, p. 448. A writ attested by Walter de Gray, archbishop of Canterbury, ordered Roger Pichard to go " ad ballivos Ricardi Syward de Clammorgan" to receive from them the heir of a certain William le Gros and take him to Bristol. Such matters would normally be handled by the officials of the lord of Glamorgan, i. e., Richard de Clare himself. Both the king and Siward were in Gascony at this time. *Cal. Pat. Rolls 1232–47*, p. 296.

position of the Crown, however, it is clear that Richard de Clare was exercising his authority in Glamorgan, at least in an unofficial capacity, by the summer of 1242.[61]

Unlike his father, Earl Richard did not encounter his greatest opposition from the lords of Afan. In the period of royal custody after 1230, Morgan Gam had taken advantage of the political disturbances and of his alliances with Richard Marshal and Llywelyn ap Iorwerth to stage a number of raids on the Norman fees within Glamorgan and to revive his claims to Newcastle. Furthermore, he had restated his claims to custody and protection of Margam Abbey, and even abrogated to himself the right of confirming the charters and deeds of his nominal overlord, the first Earl Gilbert, to the abbey.[62] Morgan Gam died in February, 1241, leaving Afan to his elder son Lleision.[63] The new chieftain was either unwilling or unable to sustain the policies of his father. Although he pressed unsuccessfully for the return of Newcastle in 1246,[64] in other respects he resigned himself to Earl Richard's overlordship. In 1247 and 1249, he answered writs of *novel disseisin* brought by the earl in pleas involving Margam and her sister abbey of Neath. By answering these writs in the earl's court at Cardiff, Lleision ap Morgan Gam clearly abandoned the claims to his own judicial independence and control over Margam which his father Morgan Gam had championed. Henceforth the lords of Afan caused no serious trouble to the Clares, and later in the century they tended to identify themselves more closely with the Norman tenants-in-chief of the lordship than with the other Welsh commotal lords.[65]

The center of conflict shifted after Morgan Gam's death to the relations between the Clares and the other chieftains, notably Hywel ap Maredudd. Hywel, who was lord of Meisgyn by inheritance, had also been lord of Glynrhondda by conquest since

[61] Tewkesbury, p. 124 (late July–August, 1242). The events of this year will be discussed below. Richard was in France in September and October 1242 (see above, note 56), and in his absence the lordship was controlled by his sheriff. Cf. *ibid.*, pp. 125–26.

[62] For Margam, see *Cartae de Glamorgan*, III, 927.

[63] Tewkesbury, p. 116; Lloyd, *Hist. Wales*, II, 712 note 112.

[64] Cf. *Annales Cambriae*, p. 86. It remained in the possession of Margam Abbey, and somewhat later Lleision and his allies made restitution for damages. *Cartae de Glamorgan*, II, 532–33, 534–36, 544–46.

[65] *Cartae de Glamorgan*, II, 543, 561–62; below, p. 134.

1228, and he came naturally to the forefront of the Welsh resistance to Earl Richard. In 1242, according to the Tewkesbury chronicle, Hywel ap Maredudd and Rhys ap Gruffydd of Senghenydd were waging war on Gilbert de Turberville, lord of Coety. The precise cause of the conflict is not stated, but the fighting in itself is indicative of the chronic state of warfare between the Welsh and Normans which had plagued the lordship since the days of Robert fitz Hamon. The young Richard de Clare, acting through the abbot of Tewkesbury " et alios de specialibus amicis suis," managed to arrange a truce at a meeting of the Cardiff county court. Rhys surrendered his son to the earl's representatives as a hostage, and Hywel found a number of pledges for his good conduct.[66]

Shortly thereafter, the truce was broken by Richard Siward, who as lord of Llanbleddian, Talyfan, and Rhuthun, occupied the strategic tract of land between the earl's demesne and the southern boundary of Hywel's lordships of Meisgyn and Glynrhondda. In all probability, border disputes or similar questions had created friction between the two, and Siward seems to have been the instigator of the hostilities. At this point Earl Richard intervened, and a detailed consideration of the subsequent events reveals fully the nature of his policy and his ability to enforce it.

An almost complete record of the events of 1242 and the following years is contained in an appeal brought by Richard Siward to the court of King Henry III in 1247.[67] In November, 1242, Siward was summoned to Cardiff to re-establish the truce arranged with Hywel's consent in late July. A panel of jurors, acting on the earl's behalf, was appointed to conclude a separate truce between the contending parties, but Siward refused to co-operate. Hywel ap Maredudd, apparently impatient with the delay, then

[66] Tewkesbury, pp. 124–25.
[67] A full record of the case is contained in PRO, Curia Regis Roll 31–42 Henry III, KB 26/159 m. 2 (Easter 31 Henry III), mm. 10–11 (Michaelmas 31–32 Henry III). The Michaelmas portion is printed from a somewhat inaccurate transcript (by Sir Robert Cotton) in Cartae de Glamorgan, II, 547–55. Curia Regis Roll 159 was compiled under Edward I, and contains the proceedings of cases relating to Wales between 1247 and 1258. See J. Conway Davies, Introduction to The Welsh Assize Roll, 1277–1284 (Board of Celtic Studies, History and Law Series, no. VII, Cardiff, 1940), pp. 27–30. The original rolls for 31–32 Henry III have not survived.

chose to break his original armistice with Earl Richard, and renewed hostilities against the earl himself. This time Siward resolved his own difficulties with Hywel and joined forces with him; the lord of Llanbleddian, no less than the lord of Meisgyn, resented all efforts by his suzerain to impose checks on his behavior, and saw here an opportunity to assert his independence. Unfortunately, no details of the actual fighting survive beyond the fact that Hywel staged a major assault against the Clare castle of Kenfig in 1243, but Earl Richard eventually managed to defeat him and seize the commotes of Meisgyn and Glynrhondda. In 1245 he then brought his own suit in the county court against Richard Siward, charging him with felonious breach of the peace. Unable to find pledges for his attendance, Siward was forced to surrender his lordships, including Talyfan castle, to Earl Richard's keeping. When he failed to appear at the three subsequent meetings of the court to answer the charges, he was formally outlawed and his estates declared forfeited " secundum consuetudinem et usagium patrie de Glamorgan." [68]

It was at this point that Siward appealed to the *curia regis*. He complained of irregularities in the proceedings against him, and further charged that the earl had unjustly exacted homage and fealty from his own tenants when he assumed temporary control of Llanbleddian and the other fiefs as surety for his attendance. In addition, he claimed default of justice in that he was serving in the king's army at Degannwy (in modern Denbighshire) in the campaign of 1245 against the prince of Gwynedd, Dafydd ap Llywelyn ap Iorwerth, and thus could not appear at the meetings of the Cardiff court. [69]

When summoned to respond to the suit, Earl Richard did not bother to answer this latter charge, for he was much more active in the Degannwy campaign than Siward could have been. Siward's name does not seem to appear on the Scutage Roll for 1245 or in other chancery documents, while that of Earl Richard does. [70]

---

[68] PRO, Curia Regis Roll 159, m. 2. Hywel's attack on Kenfig is mentioned in " Chronicle of the Thirteenth Century," p. 279. For his ouster, see *Brut Hergest*, p. 241, *Peniarth*, p. 107.

[69] For the campaign, see Lloyd, *Hist. Wales*, II, 701–5. Siward would be serving for his English, not marcher, estates. He was lord of one third of the Oxfordshire barony of Headington in right of his wife Philippa, widow of Henry de Newburgh, earl of Warwick (d. 1229). Sanders, *English Baronies*, p. 52.

[70] PRO, Chancery, Scutage Roll 29 Henry III, C 72/7 m. 1; *Cal. Pat. Rolls*

Furthermore, the earl's retinue included such prominent tenants as Stephen Baucen, who was sheriff of Glamorgan on three separate occasions between 1243 and 1247 and who acted on Earl Richard's behalf in the litigation against Siward; Walter de Sully, who held four fees of the earl within the lordship and who was to be sheriff in 1262; and Gilbert de Umphraville, lord of Penmark, a fee in southern Glamorgan midway between Llanbleddian and the Bristol Channel.[71] The names of both Sully and Umphraville also appear in the judicial records of 1245. Like Siward, they were summoned for their English estates, but Henry III specifically ordered the sheriff of Somerset and Dorset not to distrain them for service in those counties, since they were in Earl Richard's contingent "de licencia regis," an arrangement that was to become much more prominent in the Welsh wars of King Edward I after 1276.[72] In short, both Earl Richard and tenants who participated in the judicial proceedings of 1245 at Cardiff also managed to serve in the Degannwy campaign, and the earl must have felt that Richard Siward's defense in this regard was sufficiently weak for him to disregard it.

Richard de Clare's actual answers to the suit brought by Siward in 1247 contain a number of significant points which foreshadow the arguments advanced by Earl Gilbert the Red on similar occasions under Edward I later in the century. The earl claimed that since the warfare involving Hywel ap Maredudd, Richard Siward, and himself had occurred entirely within the lordship of Glamorgan, he alone, by virtue of his regality, had full cognizance of the matter. He argued in general terms that the nature of his lordship was such that "none of his own men or the men of any others ought to plead any case elsewhere than within his liberty,"[73] and

1232–47, p. 460. Earl Richard had also served in the campaign of 1244. *Ibid.*, pp. 431, 447; *Close Rolls 1242–47*, pp. 246, 256, 258.

[71] *Close Rolls 1242–47*, pp. 326–27, 337. For Baucen and Sully as sheriffs of Glamorgan, see *Cartae de Glamorgan*, II, 521–22, 533, 535, 543; *Calendar of Ancient Correspondence Concerning Wales*, ed. J. G. Edwards (Board of Celtic Studies, History and Law Series, no. II, Cardiff, 1935), p. 38. Baucen was seneschal of Gascony under the Lord Edward in 1255. *Royal Letters, Henry III*, II, 400.

[72] See below, "The Welsh Wars," in Chapter IV. Both were serving "in partibus de Glammorgan," undoubtedly to secure the lordship while Earl Richard was in the north. *Close Rolls 1242–47*, p. 337. For their English lands, see Sanders, *English Baronies*, p. 49, and for their Glamorgan fees, *Cartae de Glamorgan*, II, 650.

[73] PRO, Curia Regis Roll 159, mm. 2, 10–10d.; *Cartae de Glamorgan*, II, 548:

then offered to let a commission from the king's council examine
the records of the county court to determine if justice had been
done " according to the custom of the march " (*secundum consuetudinem patrie*).[74] Earl Richard thus claimed judicial autonomy
for his lordship, in much the same conventional manner as other
marcher lords engaged in similar cases; but his willingness and
even eagerness to have the king examine his conduct of the affair
suggests a desire for an even wider and more explicit acceptance
of the freedom his marcher status conferred. Richard, in short,
sought not only the right to complete cognizance and authority
over all pleas within his lordship, but also the acknowledgment,
on the part of the Crown itself, that the body of law and custom
within it was totally independent of the English common law, and
could be shaped and determined only by the lord of Glamorgan
himself.[75] The essential quality of kingship, the right and duty
to declare the law and to decide cases arising from it, was confined
to the boundaries of England; for the lordship of Glamorgan, at
least, the king had his counterpart in Richard de Clare. Richard
Siward, for his part, in effect admitted as much. When he appealed
to King Henry, he claimed he could not obtain justice against Earl
Richard in the latter's own court, where the lord of Glamorgan
" fuit dominus et quasi rex et justiciarius." [76]

It is clear that Earl Richard was successful on all counts, although the final ruling of the *curia regis* is unfortunately lacking.[77]
Within a short space of time, the earl had incorporated into his
own demesne not only the commotes of Meisgyn and Glynrhondda,
but also the Norman lordships of Llanbleddian, Talyfan and
Rhuthun. Both Hywel ap Maredudd and Richard Siward were
permanently dispossessed, and their turbulent marcher careers
ended. Sometime before 1246 Hywel fled to the court of Llywelyn
and Owain ap Gruffydd, the grandsons of Llywelyn ap Iorwerth,

---

" nullus de hominibus suis nec aliis debent de aliquo placito placitare alibi infra
libertatem suam de Glamorgan."

[74] PRO, Curia Regis Roll 159, mm. 2, 10–11; *Cartae de Glamorgan*, II, 549.

[75] Cf. the remarks of Smith, " The Lordship of Glamorgan," pp. 33–34.

[76] PRO, Curia Regis Roll 159, m. 11; *Cartae de Glamorgan*, II, 554.

[77] Since Curia Regis Roll 159 was compiled for Edward I (see note 67 above),
it is possible that the royal justices and clerks deliberately omitted the final decision
of the court. Unlike his father, Edward was not of a mind to tolerate from the
marchers such sweeping privileges as Earl Richard claimed. Cf. below, Chapters IV,
VIII, for his dealings with Earl Gilbert the Red and others.

in Gwynedd. He appears as an ally of Llywelyn ap Gruffydd in 1258 and 1277, and in 1279 either he or a descendant, perhaps a grandson, seems to have held some minor properties within Meisgyn.[78] By 1249 Earl Richard had granted half of Glynrhondda to the sons of Morgan ap Cadwallon, the chieftain whom Hywel had dispossessed in 1228, and they held it until at least 1262.[79] Richard Siward died in 1248, and his family held some small territories within Glamorgan under the Clares.[80] The bulk of the commotes and fiefs, however, remained with Earl Richard and his successors. Henceforth the Clares controlled directly that wide tract of land between Senghenydd and Afan, and Richard constructed a new castle at Llantrisant in southern Meisgyn to serve as both the administrative and military nucleus of his new territories. Richard de Clare had thus gone far towards effecting the unity and territorial integration of the lordship which his father had been unable to bring about; by the same token, he was able to limit effectively the fragmentation and endemic warfare which had characterized Glamorgan in the century and a half prior to his rule.[81]

By his vigorous actions, Earl Richard succeeded in reducing the areas of Welsh autonomy and potential resistance to the commotal lordships of Senghenydd and Afan in Glamorgan and Machen in Gwynllwg. Isolated from each other, and with their old ties to the house of Gwynedd broken or severely attenuated, the lords of these areas caused little trouble in subsequent years. The acceptance of Richard's suzerainty by Lleision ap Morgan Gam of Afan has already been noted, and it was not until the revival of Gwynedd under Llywelyn ap Gruffydd after 1255 that the Welsh of Senghenydd and the neighboring commotes again posed a challenge to his authority. Richard's ability to establish his own control and impose peace in Glamorgan left him free to attend to other matters. It is surely more than coincidental that the frequency with which he engaged in pilgrimages, tournaments,

---

[78] *Brut Hergest*, p. 241, *Peniarth*, p. 107; *Littere Wallie*, ed. J. G. Edwards (Board of Celtic Studies, History and Law Series, no. V, Cardiff, 1940), pp. 44, 184–85; *Cal. Pat. Rolls 1272–81*, p. 300.
[79] *Cartae de Glamorgan*, II, 565, 651.
[80] Rice Lewis, "A Breviat of Glamorgan, 1596–1600," ed. William Rees (South Wales and Monmouth Record Society, vol. III, 1954), pp. 103–4.
[81] For the castle, see Lloyd, *Hist. Wales*, II, 712 note 111.

and other festivities increased sharply after 1247, when he had incorporated the lordships formerly held by Hywel ap Maredudd and Richard Siward into his own demesne, and when he had successfully defended his actions before King Henry III.[82]

Of greater importance than his public activities, Richard was able to add substantially to the Clare inheritance in other ways at this time. His major territorial gain resulted from the extinction of the male line of the Marshal family in 1245 and the subsequent partition of its great dominions in England, W̵les, and Ireland. A large portion of the endowment originally established by Gilbert fitz Gilbert de Clare, earl of Pembroke, and his successor Strongbow in the twelfth century thus came back to the senior branch of the family in the mid-thirteenth century.

William Marshal died in 1219, leaving five sons and five daughters. The fourth son, Walter, died without issue on November 24, 1245. A month later, his brother and heir, Anselm, also died, before he could obtain livery and seisin of the estates and comital title. The Marshal lands in England, the lordships of Pembroke and Netherwent in Wales and Leinster in Ireland, thus escheated to the Crown,[83] and the immense properties were partitioned among the families of the five daughters in 1246–47.[84] The Marshal's second daughter Isabel had died in 1240, and her share of the inheritance passed to Earl Richard as heir of her first husband, Earl Gilbert de Clare. In July, 1246, the marcher estates were partitioned. Richard obtained the lordship of Usk in Netherwent, a compact block of territory between the Wye and Usk Rivers to the north of Chepstow (Striguil) and Caerleon,

---

[82] See above, pp. 67–68.

[83] *G. E. C.*, X, 377; *Rot. Fin.*, I, 444.

[84] Numerous versions of the partition exist. The most nearly contemporary are in PRO, Chancery Miscellanea, C 47/9/20, and PRO, Rentals and Surveys, General Series, SC 11/22. They seem to date from 1248–49, for they include the arrangements for the future partition of the estates held in dower by Eleanor de Montfort (d. 1275), widow of William Marshal the younger (d. 1231); Henry III ordered such provisions made in November 1248. In 1365, an *inspeximus* of the partition was made at the request of Lawrence Hastings, earl of Pembroke. It appears on *Cal. Pat. Rolls 1364–67*, pp. 263–75. The original writs and returns for this later inquisition survive as PRO, Chanc. Misc., C 47/88/4 no. 70, mm. 1–13. Still another version is in Chanc. Misc., C 47/9/21. The handwriting seems to date from the second half of the fourteenth century, and it may represent a transcript of the original version of 1248–49 made for the purpose of comparison with the inquisition of 1365, or perhaps a later copy of the version on the Patent Roll.

plus the barony of Castle Walwyn on the western coast of Pembrokeshire, although he did not add the latter to his own demesne possessions.[85] Because of special difficulties involved in arranging an equitable division of the great lordship of Leinster in Ireland, it was not partitioned until the spring of 1247. Earl Richard's share was the liberty of Kilkenny.[86] Eleanor de Montfort, dowager countess of Pembroke and Leicester, died in 1275, and the lands she held in dower were also partitioned. By this time, Earl Richard himself was dead, and his heir Earl Gilbert the Red obtained an additional twenty-seven knights' fees along with estates in Berkshire, Oxford and Wiltshire, some of them originally acquired by William Marshal in 1189 from the old honor of Giffard.[87] The partition of the Marshal inheritance thus contributed materially to the landed wealth of the Clares. By obtaining Usk, Earl Richard increased his holdings in the southern march, and the extinction of the Marshals left him unquestionably as the most powerful and important of the marcher lords. The acquisition of Kilkenny further increased the range of family influence and interests and established the earls in the leading ranks of the Anglo–Irish baronage. Finally, the acquisition of 36 additional fees in 1272–75 gave the earls of Gloucester a total of almost 500 knights' fees in England, a figure more than double that of their nearest competitor. The failure of the cadet branch of the Clares after the death of Strongbow's only son in 1185 was thus partially redeemed by the senior branch less than a century later.[88]

---

[85] PRO, C 47/9/20; *Cal. Pat. Rolls 1232–47*, p. 484. Earl Richard, along with the other heirs who received lordships within Pembrokeshire, agreed to let this barony remain under the jurisdiction of the Pembroke county court. Castle Walwyn was held by the de Brian family of the Clares for $1\frac{1}{3}$ fees. PRO, Curia Regis Roll Easter 36 Henry III, KB 26/146 m. 8d.; *Cal. Anc. Correspondence, Wales*, pp. 210–12; *Cal. Inq. Post Mortem*, V, no. 64. Pembroke passed to William de Valence. For the shares of the other coparceners in the march, see Lloyd, *Hist. Wales*, II, 711–12. Lloyd's statement, followed by other writers, that Earl Richard also acquired the lordship of Caerleon at this time is erroneous. See below, p. 126.

[86] Full details are given in Chapter IX below.

[87] PRO, Chanc. Misc., C 47/9/20. For these estates, see Chapter VII. In 1272, after the death of Richard of Cornwall, the Clares also obtained 9 fees, representing one-fifth of the Marshal half of the old honor of Giffard. Sanders, *English Baronies*, p. 63.

[88] A total of 492 fees is reached by adding the 36 to the 456 controlled by the first Earl Gilbert in 1218 (see above, Chapter I, note 47). Additional acquisitions

The partition of the Marshal estates represents the last major instance in which the Clares acquired lands and fees through marriage connections. Thenceforth there was a marked tendency to accumulate estates through exchange and purchase. In 1258, as part of the baronial reform movement, Richard gained control of the Dorset manors of Portland and Wyke and the borough of Weymouth, and he obtained full title to them by exchange with the priory of St. Swithun's.[89] In two separate transactions in 1259 he acquired two-thirds of the barony of Southoe Lovetot, Huntingdonshire.[90] In 1254, when Henry III gave the town and castle of Bristol to the Lord Edward, Earl Richard even attempted to revive the family claims to them. His efforts were unsuccessful, however, and a similar attempt by Earl Gilbert the Red to regain Bristol somewhat later was eventually quashed by Edward I in 1276.[91] Despite this failure, the Clares did add a number of important new territories to their holdings. Finally, this policy of gradual accumulation included the purchase of small properties appurtenant to estates already in demesne. Both Richard and his successors, especially Gilbert the Red, were remarkably active in this respect as well.[92]

By 1255, Richard de Clare had not only increased the size and wealth of his landed endowment, but had also established his authority in the lordship of Glamorgan. Moreover, as the construction of Llantrisant castle attests, he had begun a process of administrative reorganization designed to implement that authority

---

and enfeoffments raised the total to 520 by the early fourteenth century. See below, p. 221 and note 70. These figures do not include some 100 additional fees in Kilkenny and the marcher lordships. The death of Ranulph de Blundeville in 1232 and the absorption of Chester and other honors by the Lord Edward in 1254 left the Bigods, earls of Norfolk, as the magnates with the next greatest number of English fees after the Clares in the mid-thirteenth century. They already controlled over 160 fees as lords of the barony of Framlingham and other estates, and additional fees acquired by virtue of the Marshal partition brought their total to about 200, not including almost 100 fees in Striguil and Leinster. PRO, C 47/9/20; Sanders, *English Baronies*, pp. 47, 63, 111.

[89] *Cal. Pat. Rolls 1247–58*, pp. 640, 654; *Cal. Chart. Rolls 1257–1300*, p. 16.

[90] Sanders, *English Baronies*, pp. 90–91.

[91] Tewkesbury, p. 155, and for Gilbert, see below, p. 127 and notes 16–17. Bristol formed the center of Edward's English estates, and he organized his exchequer there. PRO, Ministers' Accounts, SC 6/1094/11. Edward also acquired the lordships of Ireland, Chester, Gascony, and other properties at this time.

[92] Below, pp. 210–13.

and improve its enforcement. This program, however, was by no means completed during his lifetime, and the major steps towards realizing it were taken only later in the century. Of more immediate importance, a number of territories, including the two northern commotes of the cantred of Senghenydd, were still in potentially hostile hands. The relations of the Clares with the lords of Senghenydd form an integral part of the wider political scene, characterized by the inability of King Henry III to check the resurgence of the house of Gwynedd under Llywelyn ap Gruffydd.

The new ruler of Gwynedd posed an even greater threat to the authority of the Clares in Glamorgan than had his grandfather, Llywelyn ap Iorwerth, before 1240. For the most part, Henry III had been able to counter Dafydd ap Llywelyn,[93] but similar efforts to reduce Llywelyn ap Gruffydd were uniformly unsuccessful. Between 1246 and 1255, Llywelyn eliminated all rivals to his hegemony in Gwynedd and revitalized the strength of the dynasty.[94] Immediately thereafter, he embarked upon an ambitious program of establishing his superiority beyond its borders by forging ties of personal allegiance and homage with the other Welsh princes. These policies, designed to offset the inherent weaknesses in the Welsh political and social structure,[95] had been anticipated by his predecessors, notably Llywelyn ap Iorwerth, but Llywelyn ap Gruffydd was by far the most successful ruler of Gwynedd in achieving them. In 1258, as a conscious symbol of his accomplishment, he abrogated to himself the title " prince of Wales." [96]

By this time Llywelyn had extended his authority over northern and central Wales and was threatening the great marcher dominions of the south, including Glamorgan. As early as 1257, he attacked Richard's demesne lordship of Tiriarll (" The Earl's Land "), situated to the southwest of the newly incorporated commote of Glynrhondda, and destroyed Llangynwyd castle.[97]

---

[93] See, in general, Lloyd, *Hist. Wales*, II, 694–706.
[94] The weakness of the house of Gwynedd in its relations with Henry III in 1247 is discussed in Lewis. " The Treaty of Woodstock," pp. 46–53, 58–59, 64–65. For Llywelyn's elimination of opposition to his rule, see Lloyd, *Hist. Wales*, II, 706–15; Edwards, *Littere Wallie*, Introduction, pp. xxxviii-xli.
[95] Cf. the remarks of J. G. Edwards, *ibid.*, pp. xxxvi–xxxviii.
[96] Lloyd, *Hist. Wales*, II, 723–24.
[97] *Brut Hergest*, p. 249, *Peniarth*, p. 111; Matthew Paris, *Chronica Majora*, V, 642.

A sustained invasion of Glamorgan did not materialize thereafter, but the situation was regarded as sufficiently dangerous for Henry III to appoint Earl Richard as captain of the English forces in South Wales and put him in charge of the operations for Glamorgan, Pembroke and the neighboring lordships. The campaign of 1257 centered, however, in northern and central Wales, and ended in a disastrous defeat for the king.[98]

Llywelyn's allies in the raid of 1257 seem to have been drawn largely from Deheubarth and Gwynedd, but he soon won new support from the Welsh in the Glamorgan commotes of Meisgyn, Glynrhondda, and most importantly, Uwch-Caiach in the cantred of Senghenydd. Rhys ap Gruffydd, lord of the cantred since the early thirteenth century, died in 1256, and was succeeded by his son, Gruffydd ap Rhys. The new ruler immediately allied himself with Llywelyn, and seems by this action to have attracted the Welsh of the neighboring commotes to side with the prince as well.[99] A full-scale invasion of Glamorgan via Senghenydd had suddenly become a distinct possibility. The tradition of Welsh resistance to Norman overlordship had not been entirely eliminated with the ouster of Hywel ap Maredudd and the quiescent behavior of Rhys ap Gruffydd and the sons of Morgan Gam; and through the support given to the new prince of Wales by Gruffydd ap Rhys and others, that tradition now seemed to have its greatest prospect of success since the days of Llywelyn ap Iorwerth. In 1258, Earl Richard's entire program and policy was in serious danger of being overthrown.

It was at this point that the attention of Richard de Clare and indeed the entire baronage turned to an event of national political and constitutional importance: the formation of an antiroyalist movement which culminated in the promulgation of the Provisions of Oxford and the establishment of baronial control of the government. In this movement, Earl Richard and his successor, Earl

[98] Lloyd, *Hist. Wales*, II, 719–22, provides a full account of the campaign. For Earl Richard, see Matthew Paris, *Chronica Majora* V, 633; Dunstable, pp. 203–4; *Close Rolls 1256–59*, pp. 90–91, 141; *Cal. Pat. Rolls 1247–58*, p. 577; Smith, " The ' Chronica de Wallia ' and the Dynasty of Dinefwr," p. 270.

[99] Cf. Smith, " The Lordship of Glamorgan," p. 35. Precise details and documentation are lacking, but that this situation had materialized by 1258 is clear from later evidence on the relations between Llywelyn ap Gruffydd and Earl Gilbert the Red after 1266. See below, Chapter IV.

Gilbert the Red, were to play significant and often decisive roles; but the emphasis on Glamorgan and Welsh politics in general in this chapter is justified by their interests and behavior, both before and after the summer of 1258. Like the first Earl Gilbert, both Richard and, as the succeeding chapters will show, his son Gilbert the Red, regarded themselves primarily as lords of the march rather than English earls, and they acted accordingly, even on the wider scene of national politics. Their political conduct clearly reveals that Cardiff, much more than Clare, was the focus of their attention and the real source of their power.

The Movement for Reform, 1258–1262

In 1258, baronial opposition to King Henry III crystallized in a full-scale movement for reform. The basic causes of disaffection are well known. To the barons, Henry was ruling by secretive and arbitrary means, disregarding their rightful claims as his natural counselors and relying instead on a small group of professional ministers directly subject to his wishes. Of more practical significance was their feeling that he was ruling badly as well. They complained of his abuse of the rights of wardship and marriage and of other feudal incidents. He had thus far been unable to check Llewelyn ap Gruffydd, who in three years had established his hegemony in Wales and was now posing a serious threat to the great marcher lordships. He showed an untoward generosity to his Savoyard and Poitevin friends and relatives, notably the Lusignans and Valences, who had become highly influential at court after 1247. Finally, his vain hopes of securing the kingdom of Sicily for his son Edmund had committed the king far beyond his financial means and had brought his government perilously close to bankruptcy. From the baronial point of view, the king was hopelessly entangled in Mediterranean politics, which left him abjectly subservient to the wishes of the papacy.[100] The reform movement did not challenge the existing machinery of government, but rather the exclusive control over it exercised

---

[100] See, in general, Powicke, *King Henry III*, I, 290–98, 343–92. Runciman, *The Sicilian Vespers*, pp. 56–64, places Edmund's candidacy within the broader context of papal-Hohenstaufen relations.

by the king and the ways in which he was managing it. The measures taken by the baronage indicate the degree to which its political ideas and consciousness had expanded since the days of Magna Carta. In 1215 the barons sought only the proper means to coerce the king if he violated the Charter; in 1258 they demanded a thoroughgoing reform of the central government and were prepared to assume the responsibility for it in the king's name.

At the meeting of the Great Council in London in April 1258, Henry put forward proposals to enable him to carry out a campaign against Llywelyn and to meet the terms set by the pope for the Sicilian expedition. His demands aroused angry protest, and led a small group of powerful men to embark upon a plan for the reform of the realm. On April 12 an oath of mutual assistance was sworn by Earl Richard de Clare, Roger Bigod, earl of Norfolk, his brother Hugh Bigod, Simon de Montfort, earl of Leicester, Peter of Savoy, the queen's uncle, and two close friends of Simon, John fitz Geoffrey, a former justiciar of Ireland and son of Geoffrey fitz Peter, earl of Essex (d. 1213), and Peter de Montfort.[101] The composition of this group is interesting. On the surface at least there was relatively little social homogeneity and even less to suggest a common base of political interests. Simon de Montfort's personal enmity to King Henry is well known, but there is no evidence of major personal friction between the king and the others. In terms of wealth and landed endowment, the earls of Gloucester and Norfolk far exceeded the rest, ranking below only the king, the Lord Edward, and Richard of Cornwall as the wealthiest men in the kingdom.[102] In addition, each had important lordships in Wales that were threatened by Llywelyn ap Gruffydd, and aside from John fitz Geoffrey, who controlled the relatively small lordship of Ewyas Lacy on the Herefordshire border, none of the other parties to the oath had such tangible grounds for dissatisfaction with King Henry's military leadership. No reliable estimate of Simon de Montfort's wealth has been made, but he had substantial landed

---

[101] A transcript of the oath from a nineteenth century copy in the Bibliothèque Nationale, Paris, is printed in Charles Bémont, *Simon de Montfort* (Paris, 1884), pp. 327–28. Future references to Bémont will be to the new edition (Oxford, 1930, trans. E. F. Jacob) unless otherwise specified.

[102] Denholm-Young, *Seignorial Administration*, p. 22, and below, pp. 205–6.

interests on the continent not shared by the other earls. John fitz Geoffrey and Peter de Montfort were relatively minor barons, not of comital rank, and they lacked the direct family connection that characterized Hugh Bigod.[103] The presence of Peter of Savoy indicates that in his case political considerations outweighed ties of kinship to the king, but it also reveals that initially at least, the xenophobia which later strongly marked the baronial movement was absent. In short, the only major factor which could link these disparate men together was a common feeling of opposition to the policies of the royal government; and it is possible to surmise that this very heterogeneity of social interests and standing was deliberately designed, so as to attract as much support as possible from the varied ranks of the English baronage.

Perhaps the most remarkable feature of this grouping, however, is the emergence of Richard de Clare to a position of leadership in the ranks of the nobility. Hitherto the Clares, for all their wealth and territorial connections, had not assumed an overt, major role in national politics. It is true that his grandfather, Richard, earl of Hertford, was an important figure in the baronial opposition to King John, but his importance consisted more in being the focus of a complex pattern of marriage and tenurial ties among the barons than in any direct political or military actions of his own.[104] Earl Richard, however, was from the very beginning of the antiroyalist movement of 1258 among the very few great individuals whose activities shaped the course of the movement and determined its very success or failure. His motives are not immediately apparent. His presence might well indicate the widening of his own political experience, but too much should not be made of this. Richard was not the sort of man to engage in speculation on the theory or practice of government, and the grounds for his opposition must be sought in concrete personal or territorial considerations.[105] He certainly had his differences

---

[103] Earl Richard and John fitz Geoffrey were cousins. John's mother, Aveline, was the sister of Richard, earl of Hertford. *G. E. C.*, V, 433 and note (e). For the descent of the earldom of Essex to the Bohun family, see *ibid.*, pp. 124–35.

[104] Painter, " The Earl of Clare," pp. 220–25; *The Reign of King John*, pp. 287–99.

[105] For a somewhat different assessment, cf. R. F. Treharne, *The Baronial Plan of Reform 1258–1263* (Manchester, 1932), p. 71, and F. M. Powicke, " Some Observations on the Baronial Council (1258–1260) and the Provisions of West-

with King Henry, as his demands in 1254 for the restoration of Bristol attest,[106] but for the most part he seems to have been quite friendly with the king and his French relatives. At the instigation of Henry and his half brothers William and Aymer de Valence, he had married his eldest son and heir to their niece Alice de Lusignan; and in the decade preceding the outbreak of the baronial movement he frequently engaged in tournaments on both sides of the Channel with men such as William de Valence.[107] It is true that the baronial program aroused strong opposition on the part of Henry's relatives, and this in turn led to a break between Earl Richard and the Valences: Matthew Paris relates that in July, 1258, William de Valence bribed Walter de Scoteny, Richard's seneschal, to poison both the earl and his brother William de Clare. There is probably little truth to this story, although it is indicative of what contemporaries might imagine; more importantly, however, it does not in itself explain or contribute to our understanding of Earl Richard's actions and motivations in the spring of that year. Personal enmity to the king or his relatives, such as largely motivated Simon de Montfort, does not seem to have been a major factor in Richard's behavior.[108]

Other features of Richard's previous career and interests reveal more concrete and compelling reasons for his actions at this point. Prior to 1258, his main concern, the one to which he devoted his energy and attention above all else, was the establishment and expansion of his authority in the lordship of Glamorgan. In this he was vigorous and highly successful; but despite this fact—or more accurately, precisely because of it—there is no reason to think that marcher affairs did not occupy the center of his thoughts. They may well have been the primary factors which brought him to wider political prominence. His control over Glamorgan was by no means entirely certain. Llwelyn ap Gruffydd's recent attack

---

minster," in *Essays in Medieval History Presented to Thomas Frederick Tout* (Manchester, 1925), pp. 121–22.

[106] Tewkesbury, p. 155.

[107] Matthew Paris, *Chronica Majora*, IV, 649, V, 17–18, 83, 265, 364, 514; Tewkesbury, pp. 152, 154–55; Lady Stenton, *English Society in the Early Middle Ages*, pp. 84–85.

[108] Matthew Paris, *Chronica Majora*, V, 747; cf. Tewkesbury, pp. 165, 167. Treharne (*Baronial Plan of Reform*, pp. 80–81) regards Williams's death and Richard's serious illness as actually caused by an epidemic. But Scoteny was tried and hanged.

on Llangynwyd and his growing support among the Welsh in Meisgyn and Senghenydd were serious challenges to Earl Richard's position, and indeed it was only some two decades later that his heir finally secured the political stability of the lordship.[109] In these circumstances, it is probable that Richard desired effective action on the part of the central government itself as the best means available to eliminate the threat of Llywelyn completely, and that Henry's repeated failures drove him into the ranks of the opposition. His concern over Llywelyn, as later events were to prove, was exaggerated, for an open attack on Glamorgan did not occur; and Richard may also have been motivated in part by a desire to see reforms effected in the judicial and administrative organization of the royal government and in the king's exercise of his rights of feudal overlordship. But the situation in the march was in all probability the decisive element in the spring of 1258. Initially at least, it may be suggested, " reform " for Earl Richard meant primarily reform of the military capabilities of the kingdom. His own interests may have been overshadowed by the motives and plans of others, who were more concerned with changes in the structure of the government than fighting the prince of Wales, but Richard's wealth, prestige and territorial standing were welcome assets to the antiroyalist side, and they both prompted and enabled him to act in the vanguard of the movement.

Events moved rapidly following the formation of the confederation. The unpopularity of Henry's regime is attested by the ease with which the confederate leaders attracted the support of almost the entire baronage. The barons, who never again were to be so united or decisive in their actions as in the summer of 1258, petitioned Henry and the Lord Edward to abide by proposals to be drafted by a committee of twenty-four and to be presented at a parliament at Oxford in June. In addition, they urged the king to press Pope Alexander IV for a modification of his terms; in return, they agreed to a general aid to help the king meet the costs of the planned expedition against the Welsh.[110]

The baronial petition and the subsequent Provisions of Oxford outlined a comprehensive scheme which in practice firmly placed

[109] Below, Chapter IV.
[110] Tewkesbury, pp. 163–64; Foedera, I, 370. The twenty-four included Earl Richard and the other parties to the original oath.

the government under baronial initiative and direction. A Council of Fifteen was organized, with power to compel the king to follow its advice on all matters of government. While the Council deliberately included royal partisans such as Boniface of Savoy, archbishop of Canterbury, John du Plessis, earl of Warwick, and Henry's trusted household clerk, the pluralist John Mansel, its composition was decidedly weighted in favor of the baronage. The baronial members included the earls of Norfolk and Hereford, three of the original confederate leaders (Peter of Savoy, Peter de Montfort, and John fitz Geoffrey), two important marcher lords (Roger Mortimer of Wigmore and James de Audley), and Walter de Cantilupe, bishop of Worcester. But the leadership rested with the earls of Gloucester and Leicester.[111]

The Council went immediately to work. The chancery documents not only record the changes in the administrative personnel of the government, but more significantly reveal the degree of initiative and co-operation exemplified by the baronial leaders. The royal castles were redistributed to new keepers sworn to obey the commands of the Council, and the chancellor and treasurer were also made responsible to it. The office of justiciar was revived and given to Hugh Bigod, the brother of the earl of Norfolk. In addition, the Provisions stipulated that three meetings of the Great Council, or parliaments, were to be held each year on February 2 (Candlemas), June 1, and September 29 (Michaelmas), to treat the great affairs of state. A legislative Committee of Twelve was appointed to act as a liaison between the Council of Fifteen and the barons assembled in parliament.[112]

The transfer of executive power from the king to the Council of Fifteen was complete. The original agreement entered into by Richard de Clare, Simon de Montfort, and their associates had expanded into a sworn confederation of almost the entire baronage. For the next eighteen months, the Council of Fifteen was the real ruler of England. Almost immediately, it resolved the two major issues which had given impetus to the formation of the movement. The Sicilian adventure was abandoned, leaving Pope

[111] The various articles which form the Provisions are printed in *Select Charters*, ed. William Stubbs (9th ed., ed. H. W. C. Davis, Oxford, 1921), pp. 373–84.

[112] For a detailed summary of the changes made in accordance with the Provisions, see Treharne, *Baronial Plan of Reform*, pp. 83–95.

Alexander and his successor, Urban IV, free to begin negotiations with Charles of Anjou, brother of King Louis of France. In addition, a truce was arranged with Llywelyn ap Gruffyd in June. The Council also participated in the negotiations between Henry III and Louis IX which culminated in the Treaty of Paris of December, 1259, and controlled the difficult proceedings involving the various disputes between King Henry, his sister Eleanor, and her husband, Earl Simon.[113] In most of these matters, Richard de Clare played an active role. It may be surmised that he only reluctantly agreed to the truce with Llywelyn, and it is impossible to determine exactly how much of the Council's other actions were attributable to his own initiative and authority.[114]

The settlement of these affairs left the Council free to deal with domestic business. Henry's Poitevin half brothers objected to the Provisions and were expelled from England in July, 1258. The Council made few changes of any importance in the personnel of the royal household and exchequer, but their operations were brought under close scrutiny.[115] Earl Richard's name appears frequently on the entries in the chancery documents authorizing routine matters of administration. For the most part he acted in conjunction with other members of the Council, both baronial associates such as the justiciar Hugh Bigod and Earl Simon de Montfort, and royalists such as John Mansel. Occasionally, however, writs were issued solely on his own authorization. In general, Earl Richard seems to have played an important but not determinative role in the activities of the Council. He was only one of a number of baronial leaders, and the power to shape the scope and direction of the Council's authority tended to reside more in the hands of the justiciar, and somewhat later, in the hands of the earl of Leicester.[116]

Of far greater importance and significance than the changes in the personnel of the central government was the attention paid to the complaints of the middle strata of society, the lesser free-

[113] Runciman, *Sicilian Vespers*, pp. 63–77; Lloyd, *Hist. Wales*, II, 722–24; Powicke, *King Henry III*, I, 245–54. See also note 137 below.
[114] *Cal. Pat. Rolls 1258–66*, pp. 14, 17, 18, 24–27; Matthew Paris, *Chronica Majora*, V, 741, 744–45.
[115] See Treharne, *Baronial Plan of Reform*, pp. 95–101.
[116] *Cal. Pat. Rolls 1258–66*, pp. 7–8, 11, 15, 21–22, 42, 60, and for instances in which the earl acted alone, *ibid.*, p. 24; *Cal. Liberate Rolls 1251–60*, p. 463.

holders, burgesses and mesne tenants, men of local standing and substance who did not as yet have corresponding political influence or representation. The opposition of the magnates to the central government had its counterpart in local groups and associations who wished to correct abuses in administration and justice on the levels of the shire and hundred. The baronage tried to win their support by heeding their grievances. Indeed, the most valuable work of the baronial government was the hearing and redressing of complaints against both royal and seigneurial officials, and the men most active in these matters were the justiciar Hugh Bigod, his successor Hugh Despenser, and the judges and justices associated with them.[117] Legislative proposals designed to implement the judicial findings were contained in the Provisions of Westminster, issued in the fall of 1259, which attempted a comprehensive program of local reform and sought to impose limitations on the conduct and jurisdictional powers both of royal sheriffs and of other officials, and—what was even more striking and novel—of bailiffs of the great baronial franchises as well.[118]

The initial stages of the movement for reform had been carried out with efficiency and unity of purpose, and much necessary work had been accomplished. But ominous signs of discontent and rivalry were already beginning to appear. The basic causes of trouble were King Henry's active opposition to the movement and the investigation into local misgovernment and the abuse of franchisal privileges. With the abandonment of his son's Sicilian candidacy in December, 1258, Henry was no longer a willing accomplice to the baronial program and sought to free himself from the domination of the Council. He felt, with considerable justification, that the movement in large part was little more than the fragmentation of monarchical authority among fifteen other men. His efforts at reasserting his personal power were enhanced by the fact that enthusiasm for the movement had begun to cool within the ranks of the baronage itself. Men such as Richard de Clare, Peter of Savoy, and ultimately even Hugh Bigod as well, did not share the zeal which seemed to characterize Simon

---

[117] E. F. Jacob, *Studies in the Period of Baronial Reform and Rebellion, 1258–1267* (Oxford, 1925), pp. 36–70, 96–121; Treharne, *Baronial Plan of Reform*, pp. 111-15, 144–56, 246–50.

[118] The Provisions of Westminster are printed in *Select Charters*, pp. 390–94.

de Montfort. Simon's reforming fervor, combined with the investigation into the seigneurial franchises, tended to alienate the more
conservative of the original baronial leaders, who now began to
view the movement as a threat to their own privileges and interests
and who also wished by this time to restore, at least to some
degree, the traditional structure of monarchal rule.[119]

These elements of dissension enabled King Henry to break
what hitherto had been the united antiroyalist forces, and to
establish a new community of political interests favorable to his
own cause. On November 14, 1259, accompanied by Richard
de Clare and John Mansel, he crossed over to France and on
December 4 did homage to King Louis and ratified the Treaty
of Paris. Henry delayed his return home, partly because of further
arbitration necessitated by the terms of the Treaty, and partly
because of illness. At this point the impending crisis was precipitated by Llywelyn ap Gruffydd, who took advantage of the
king's absence to break the truce and attack Edward's stronghold
of Builth in the southern march. On January 16, 1260, Henry
wrote the justiciar to suspend the Candlemas meeting of parliament and gather a force to relieve the castle.[120] At about the
same time Simon de Montfort, who had been in France since
October, returned to England and immediately challenged Henry's
right to suspend the meeting of parliament duly stipulated in the
Provisions of Oxford. Simon was prepared at all costs to stand
by the measures to which he had sworn a solemn oath. He revived
the xenophobia attendant upon the expulsion of the Lusignans
and Valences by forcing Peter of Savoy from the Council; he
engaged retainers and enlisted the support of the Lord Edward.[121]
At the end of March, Henry countered by writing Hugh Bigod and
Richard de Clare, who had returned from France earlier that
month, for assistance, and ordered an armed force to gather at
London on April 25. The movement for reform had suddenly
narrowed to a struggle for supremacy between Simon de Montfort
and Henry III, and in this struggle Earl Richard and other baronial
leaders had joined the king's side.[122]

----

[119] Powicke, *King Henry III*, I, 394–407; Jacob, *Studies*, pp. 84–86; B. Wilkinson,
The Constitutional History of England 1216–1399 (3 vols.; London, 1948–56),
I, 134–35, 142–43.

[120] *Royal Letters*, II, 148–50.

[121] See Bémont, *Simon de Montfort*, p. 186.

[122] *Close Rolls 1259–61*, pp. 283–84.

King Henry reached London, which was being held by Earl Richard and Philip Basset, on April 30, 1260. His actions and the growing support afforded him by men such as the earl of Gloucester dissuaded Edward and Simon from armed rebellion, and the threat of war subsided. Henry leveled bitter accusations at Simon and intended to bring him to trial, but moderate counsel effected a superficial reconciliation. Writs were issued to raise a levy against Llywelyn, with the earls of Gloucester and Leicester as leaders of the forces. Before the armies could start, however, the truce was renewed at Montgomery. In the meantime, through the efforts of Earl Richard and John Mansel, Edward was completely reconciled with his father. He entrusted Bristol, which formed the administrative center of his estates, to Philip Basset, and departed for Gascony in October.[123]

Henry III regained the initiative in 1260, and the baronial government, torn by dissension and disagreement, soon collapsed: the Council of Fifteen ceased to operate in December, 1260.[124] The king won over to his side many of the original supporters of the baronial movement of 1258, the most powerful of whom was Richard de Clare. The earl's motives were mixed. The apparent reluctance of Llywelyn ap Gruffydd to invade Glamorgan must have eased his apprehensions on that score. The only serious uprising in Glamorgan was an attack on Neath castle in September, 1259, but there is no evidence that it was instigated by the prince of Wales; otherwise the lordship seems to have remained quiet.[125] Of far greater significance by this time, however, was the fact that Richard had developed an antipathy to Simon de Montfort's rigid adherence to the Provisions and the readiness with which Simon had resorted to the threat of arms to assert his position; and he certainly did not intend to deny permanently Henry's place in the government of the realm, as Montfort now seemed to be contemplating. Moreover, Richard's ardor must have cooled. It was one thing to sign oaths and encourage plans of reform, and quite another actually to come to grips with the hard tasks of assuming executive power and supervising the complex

---

[123] Foedera, I, 398–400, for the truce, and for Edward, Dunstable, pp. 215–17; Cal. Pat. Rolls 1258–66, p. 126.
[124] Cf. Treharne, Baronial Plan of Reform, pp. 235–50 passim.
[125] Tewkesbury, p. 167. For Llywelyn's activities from 1258 to 1260, see Lloyd, Hist. Wales, II, 722–28.

administrative machinery. He also felt that the zeal shown on behalf of the lesser freeholders had perhaps been too great, and constituted a direct threat to his control over his own estates and franchises. Indeed, he may have made the extension of his jurisdictional powers a condition of his support for the king. On March 18, 1260, a writ attested by the justiciar appointed Henry de Bathonia to inquire " of the counties of Norfolk, Suffolk, Cambridge, Huntingdon, Essex, Hertford, Kent, Surrey and Sussex, how much the king would lose of the farm of these counties if he granted to Richard de Clare, earl of Gloucester and Hertford, the return of all the king's writs, and the execution thereof in all his fees of the honor of Clare in those counties." [126] Nothing further seems to have come of this inquiry, if indeed it was held at all. But this combination of desire for private gains and disaffection for the reforming energies displayed by the earl of Leicester and his followers induced Richard and many others to side with Henry and goes far to explain the resurgence of royal power after 1259. There is no need, however, to characterize Richard's actions as mere reactionary jealousy and hatred of the selfless idealism of Simon de Montfort. [127] The real hero of the early stages of the baronial movement was not the earl of Leicester but Hugh Bigod, and it was Simon's rash actions and personal enmity toward Henry which alienated less intransigent or precipitous men and brought about the disruption of the unity enjoyed by the reformers in the early stages of the movement.

The king emerged fully triumphant in the first half of 1261. In the spring, he announced his opposition to the entire baronial program and reasserted the traditional prerogatives of monarchy. [128] Backed by Richard de Clare and most of the other baronial leaders, Henry took complete command of the government. He obtained from Pope Alexander IV a bull absolving him from his oath to maintain the Provisions of Oxford and Westminster. [129] He recalled his Poitevin relatives, named Philip Basset as justiciar, and ap-

[126] Cal. Pat. Rolls 1258–66, p. 99.
[127] A position argued at length by Treharne, Baronial Plan of Reform, pp. 139–41, 216–17, 378–79.
[128] The document is printed by E. F. Jacob, "The Complaints of Henry III against the Baronial Council in 1261," English Historical Review, XLI (1926), 559–71; for a summary, see Bémont, Simon de Montfort, pp. 189–90.
[129] Foedera, I, 405–6.

pointed his favorites to the other major offices of state. Finally, he brought in foreign mercenaries, took control of the City and Tower of London from Hugh Despenser, and resumed control of Dover castle and the Cinque Ports from Hugh Bigod.[130]

Henry's sense of triumphant vindication was not necessarily shared by his new allies among the magnates. He overplayed his hand. His actions, especially the recruitment of soldiers from his friends and kinsmen in France, could only be interpreted as preparation for open war on his enemies. They merely served to arouse fresh opposition from the same men who had opposed the king once before. Richard de Clare and Simon de Montfort reconciled their differences and rejoined forces; the bishop of Worcester, the Bigods, and the earls of Hereford and Surrey became their allies.[131] The king spurned their offer to refer the question to King Louis of France for arbitration and publicly opposed all efforts by the baronage to impose any sort of restraint upon his authority. The magnates, led by the bishop of Worcester and the earls of Gloucester and Leicester, attempted to form a rival government and to retain the support of the freeholders. They summoned three knights from each shire south of Trent to deliberate with them at St. Albans; but Henry countered by ordering his sheriffs to have them assemble at Windsor to treat of the "honor and common profit of the realm" on the same day,[132] and he summoned additional military aid from the Continent. But the barons, except perhaps for Simon, were not prepared to fight. Men such as Earl Richard preferred to reach a settlement by peaceful means and they were certainly not of a mind to elevate the reform program and the Provisions into the cause and symbol of open civil war. Once again Earl Richard, Hugh Bigod and Humphrey de Bohun, earl of Hereford, deserted Montfort's side. Richard of Cornwall was back in England after a brief trip to what was left of his kingdom of Germany, and he was always willing to arbitrate a dispute. In anger and disgust, Simon left England and returned to France.[133]

---

[130] Cal. Pat. Rolls 1258–66, pp. 151, 152, 172; Tout, Chapters, I, 296–300.

[131] Flores Historiarum, II, 467; Bémont, Simon de Montfort, p. 192; Powicke, King Henry III, II, 422.

[132] Select Charters, pp. 394–95.

[133] Dunstable, p. 217, which regards Richard's defection as a "betrayal" of Simon's cause.

An agreement between Henry and the barons was reached in December, 1261. The king regained undisputed right to nominate his own sheriffs and other officials, and ordered new eyres to be made by the itinerant justices.[134] On February 25, 1262, he obtained a bull from the new pope, Urban IV, confirming Pope Alexander's declaration releasing him from his oaths to observe the Oxford Provisions.[135] On May 2 the king issued a public proclamation which formally annulled the Provisions, at the same time reaffirming his adherence to Magna Carta.[136] But Henry still felt that his triumph was incomplete. He was determined to crush Simon de Montfort, who refused to recognize the validity of the settlement. On July 14, 1262, Henry crossed over to France, and in the court of King Louis attempted to revive all the grievances he held against the earl. Efforts by Louis to reconcile the two failed completely, but negotiations were still being conducted when the king finally returned to England on December 20.[137]

On July 15, 1262, the day after the king sailed to France, Earl Richard de Clare died. Two weeks later he was buried at Tewkesbury Abbey.[138] The earl had not played a conspicuous role in the baronial movement since the settlement of 1261; he had been in ill health for some months before his death, and rumors circulated that he had been poisoned.[139] Despite his later inaction, Richard's activities in the early stages of the reform movement were unquestionably of the greatest importance. His emergence on the wider scene of political activity contrasts sharply with his earlier preoccupation with marcher affairs, and yet it is likely that these marcher affairs first encouraged him to play that wider role. Richard may not have had the personal magnetism of other

---

[134] The agreement, published on January 29, 1262, is in *Foedera*, I, 415. For Cornwall's activities, see Denholm-Young, *Richard of Cornwall*, pp. 108–13.

[135] *Foedera*, I, 416.

[136] *Close Rolls 1261–64*, p. 123.

[137] The story is told in detail by Bémont, *Simon de Montfort*, pp. 196–97. The conflict included, in addition to the clash over the Provisions, charges against Simon while seneschal of Gascony from 1248 to 1252, and the suit brought by the earl and his wife Eleanor over the assignment of dower to her from the Marshal estates. This dispute had already had serious repercussions which delayed the negotiations over the Treaty of Paris: Powicke, *King Henry III*, I, 252–54, 408.

[138] Tewkesbury, p. 169.

[139] E.g., Dunstable, p. 219; *Annales Cambriae*, pp. 99–100, where "Gilbert" is wrongly given for "Richard." These chronicles have probably confused the earl's natural death with the alleged poison plot of 1258.

baronial leaders such as Simon de Montfort, but his early support for the Provisions of Oxford surely had as much or perhaps even more practical impact than the support of the earl of Leicester. It was, moreover, the rise of Earl Simon and his adherents which largely explains Richard's subsequent defection from the ranks of the baronial opposition; the Provisions of Westminster and the ensuing investigation into the seigneurial franchises, and the personality of Earl Simon himself, contributed more to Richard's later actions than the reluctance of Llywelyn ap Gruffydd to resume hostilities in Glamorgan. Richard de Clare seems to have been quite friendly with King Henry and, by returning to the royal side, he implicitly approved the king's repudiation of the program embodied in the Provisions; but he did so with few qualms. His apparent inconsistency is characteristic of most of the great baronial leaders, who either championed or opposed their own program, not on the basis of some vague commitment to some even vaguer principles of constitutional government, but rather on the basis of whether or not it contributed to their own personal power, influence, and interests. Earl Richard is perhaps the prime example of such a man.

CHAPTER III

EARL GILBERT THE RED AND THE BARONS' WAR

Gilbert de Clare, the "Red Earl" of Gloucester and Hertford, was after Simon de Montfort the single most important figure in the later stages of the baronial opposition to Henry III. From his father Earl Richard he inherited not only the great Clare estates and lordships in England, Wales, and Ireland, but also a position of leadership among the magnates of the realm; and he was destined to play an even more decisive role in the civil wars which determined the fate of the struggle between king and baronage than his father had played in the initial stages of the movement for reform.

From July to December, 1262, King Henry was in France, attempting to crush Simon de Montfort and cap his apparent triumph over the antiroyalist forces. But his long sojourn abroad was a foolish mistake; the political situation in England rapidly deteriorated in his absence. Once again, Llywelyn ap Gruffydd was threatening the marches, and instead of consolidating his position at home, the king whiled away his time in pursuing his claims against Earl Simon. These circumstances alienated the barons, many of whom viewed the king's complete repudiation of the Provisions with suspicion, and allowed them time to rally their forces. The idea of "reform" still attracted much support, and it had become identified with Simon de Montfort. The situation had developed in such a way by the beginning of 1263 that the only practical choice now lay between total acquiescence to the king or armed rebellion. The only spark needed to touch off full civil war was the return of Simon to England. He would have the support of many great men, but none more powerful than Earl Richard's heir, Gilbert de Clare.

94

Amiens, Lewes, and Evesham

The death of Richard de Clare on July 15, 1262 was a serious blow to King Henry in his struggle against Simon. Of more immediate importance, however, was the fear that Llywelyn ap Gruffydd might finally be encouraged to attack the Clare lordships in the southern march, a step he had so far avoided taking. The king ordered the estates taken into custody and, to safeguard the march, on July 18 appointed Humphrey de Bohun, earl of Hereford, as keeper of Glamorgan and Usk.[1] Earl Richard's heir Gilbert, an impetuous and headstrong youth who was not quite nineteen years of age,[2] sailed at once to Boulogne in hopes of gaining seisin of his father's properties. The king, always punctilious in such matters, refused to accommodate him. The entire inheritance, both from financial and military considerations, was of great value to Henry, and he was not of a mind to relinquish his rights of wardship. Moreover, he treated the young heir in such a way as to incur his enmity. Despite the intervention of the king's half brother, William de Valence, lord of Pembroke, Gilbert found it difficult to obtain even an interview, and was forced to return home empty-handed.[3] The king then initiated an inquisition *post mortem*, and ordered a detailed investigation into all the lands, liberties and acquisitions of the late earl for the purpose of recovering all the rights of the Crown which Richard allegedly had usurped. He also began to utilize the issues and resources of the estates for his own purposes.[4] In all these measures Henry acted well within his rights and while Gilbert might grumble, he had no legitimate grounds for hostility. But when the king assigned dower to Richard's widow Maud, he drove Gilbert into open rebellion.

On August 4, 1262, Henry settled some manors on the countess

---

[1] Earl Humphrey remained as *custos* until February, 1263, when he was replaced by Walter de Sully. *Close Rolls 1261–64*, pp. 212–13. The other lands were assigned to various keepers and the honor of Tonbridge was released to the archbishop of Canterbury. *Ibid.*, p. 141; PRO, Fine Roll 46 Henry III, C 60/59 m. 7.

[2] Gilbert was born on September 2, 1243. Tewkesbury, p. 130.

[3] Gervase of Canterbury, *Historical Works*, ed. William Stubbs (Rolls Series LXXIII, 1879–80), II, 215–16.

[4] *Close Rolls 1261–64*, pp. 141–42, 171–72, 184, 187–88; *Cal. Pat. Rolls 1258–66*, pp. 235–36, 268; *Cal. Liberate Rolls 1260–67*, pp. 113, 114.

as a temporary measure until he could assign her a " reasonable
dower." [5] By the end of the year, the inquisition *post mortem*
had been completed, and when the returns were sent to the
chancery, the lands were divided into groups of equal value from
which the king could choose the dower portions.[6] At the beginning
of 1263, Henry made a final settlement which clearly violated
accepted feudal custom and law. Among other things, he assigned
Maud the third penny of the county of Hertford, the castle, manor,
and honor court of Clare with other manors, and the castles of
Usk and Trellech. The young heir was embittered by these actions;
the king had not only rebuffed his efforts to recover the estates,
but had also assigned the symbol of his comital standing, the
center of the English lands, and a number of strategic manors
and castles in Wales to his mother. The barons had previously
complained that Henry abused his rights of feudal overlordship.
Gilbert could not but feel that these grievances were justified, and
might well have been tempted to join any antiroyalist movement.[7]

He did not have long to wait. The Welsh march was already
in a state of confusion and unrest. As early as August, 1262, the
earl of Hereford had written the chancellor, expressing apprehen-
sion over a possible invasion of Glamorgan.[8] Moreover, Lord
Edward had quarreled with his seneschal, the Kentish baron Roger
Leyburn, who turned for aid to his friends among the younger
marcher lords, led by Roger Clifford, lord of Eardisley in Herefordshire, and John Giffard of Brimpsfield.[9] Llywelyn did not
invade the Clare lordships, but began hostilities in November by

[5] PRO, Fine Roll 46 Henry III, C 60/59 m. 6: " donec eidem Matildae racion-
abilem dotem assignetur."

[6] PRO, Chancery Inquisitions Post Mortem (Henry III), C 132/27/5 mm. 41–47;
cf. *Cal. Inq. Post Mortem,* I, no. 530 (pp. 155–61). This arrangement, which is incomplete and somewhat inaccurate in its figures, was enrolled on the Close Roll in
February 1263: *Close Rolls 1261–64,* pp. 284–93. See also note 85 below.

[7] *Close Rolls 1261–64,* pp. 204, 218–19, 286–88; *Cal. Pat. Rolls 1258–66,* pp. 242,
243; PRO, Min. Accts., SC 6/1202/1 m. 2. It is laid down in Bracton that a
widow was not to be endowed with the *caput* of an honor. Sir Frederick Pollock
and Frederick William Maitland, *History of English Law* (2 vols.; 2nd ed.;
Cambridge, 1898), I, 280.

[8] *Royal Letters,* II, 217–18; *Cal. Anc. Corr., Wales,* p. 38.

[9] *Cal. Pat. Rolls 1266–72,* Appendix, p. 727 (July 25, 1262); Treharne, *Baronial
Plan of Reform,* p. 302; Powicke, *King Henry III,* II, 435–36. The story of the
role played by the marchers in the whole period is well told by T. F. Tout, " Wales
and the March during the Barons' War," *Collected Papers of Thomas Frederick
Tout* (3 vols.; Manchester, 1934), II, 47–100.

attacking Roger Mortimer's castle of Cefnllys in Maelienydd near the Herefordshire border. By the end of the year he had conquered the rest of the territory and even subdued the younger Humphrey de Bohun's lordship of Brecknock. He attacked Abergavenny, which was in the Lord Edward's hands during the minority of George Cantilupe, but a valiant effort by Peter de Montfort repelled him.[10] While Roger Mortimer and some others came to Montfort's aid, the majority of the marchers had no interest in helping to defend Edward's castles because of Edward's quarrel with Leyburn. Their discontent spilled over into opposition to the king. It sparked disturbances in Kent and other areas in eastern England among the lesser freeholders who had never accepted Henry's annulment of the Provisions.[11]

On his return to England, the king tried to deal with the unrest. At the end of January, 1263, he reissued the Provisions of Westminster in a feeble effort to placate the lesser freeholders, and attempted to rally the marchers against Llywelyn by issuing writs on May 25 for a feudal levy to gather at Worcester on August 1.[12] But it was too late. The confederation formed by Leyburn and Clifford had begun to attract many great men, such as Henry of Almain, son of Richard of Cornwall, John de Warenne, earl of Surrey, and most important of all, Gilbert de Clare. The king sought a display of allegiance by having the barons assemble at Westminster in March to do homage and fealty to Edward. Gilbert refused and placed himself firmly in the opposing camp.[13]

The barons turned to Simon de Montfort as their leader and urged his return from France. Simon landed in England on April 25, 1263, and his arrival " turned a faction born of restlessness and self-interest into a party with a policy." [14] The old reforming zeal was apparently revived. A parliament was held at Oxford on May 20 under the leadership of Simon, Gilbert, and John de Warenne. The barons demanded that the king observe the Pro-

---

[10] Lloyd, *Hist. Wales*, II, 730–31.

[11] Powicke, *King Henry III*, II, 436–37.

[12] *Ibid.*, II, 437. Henry ordered troops raised from the Clare estates as well. *Close Rolls 1261–64*, pp. 305–6. He also made free use of Cardiff and the other manors and castles in Wales still in his hands. *Ibid.*, pp. 212, 223, 225–26.

[13] *Foedera*, I, 425; Dunstable, p. 220.

[14] F. M. Powicke, *The Thirteenth Century* (Oxford, 1953), p. 174; *Chronicon Thomae Wykes*, ed. H. R. Luard (*Annales Monastici*, vol. IV, Rolls Series XXXVI, 1869), p. 133 (cited hereafter as Wykes) ; *Flores Historiarum*, II, 431.

visions of Oxford and declare all who oppose them enemies of the state.[15] Henry refused, and widespread plundering broke out in the marches and the bordering countries. A force led by Gilbert, Roger de Clifford, and their associates, disregarding the writs of summons against Llywelyn, attacked the manors of the Savoyard bishop of Hereford, Peter of Aigueblanche. The bishop was captured and dispatched to Clifford's castle at Eardisley. The rebels then seized Gloucester castle, which gave them full control of the Severn valley. Simon de Montfort assumed command and entered into an alliance with Llywelyn ap Gruffydd. Under the earl's skillful leadership, the army moved to the east, where it secured the Cinque Ports. The royalist forces were no match for Simon's military prowess, and efforts by Richard of Cornwall to negotiate proved fruitless.[16] In the middle of July, Simon forced King Henry to agree to what amounted to a full re-establishment of the original program of reform, and an extensive reshaping of the administration was begun. The clergy, led by Walter de Cantilupe, bishop of Worcester, one of the members of the old Council of Fifteen, gave its support to the earl, who crushed Edward's final attempts at resistance. Finally, on September 9, the king publicly announced his willingness to abide by the terms of the settlement and to observe the Oxford Provisions.[17]

Simon seemed to be the master of England, but in fact his position rapidly deteriorated during the following months. Although his actions commanded a wide base of approval among the middle elements in society, they did not enjoy the support of a united baronage. Powerful men such as the earls of Norfolk and Hereford and Roger Mortimer remained royalist. A few of Simon's friends, especially Peter de Montfort and Hugh Despenser, joined him out of loyalty; but the bulk of his followers consisted of the troublesome and volatile marcher lords, who had opposed Henry and Edward out of discontent and personal grievances. As the initial flush of enthusiasm faded, they began to view with disenchantment the earl's passionate commitment to the

---

[15] Dunstable, p. 221: "omnes venientes contra statuta Oxoniae haberentur pro inimicis capitalibus." Wykes, p. 133, wrongly names London as the meeting place.

[16] Wykes, pp. 134–35; Dunstable, pp. 222–24; *Chronica Maiorum*, pp. 53–54; *Royal Letters*, II, 247, 248.

[17] *Cal. Pat. Rolls 1258–66*, pp. 269–74, 278–80; Treharne, *Baronial Plan of Reform*, pp. 310–19.

Provisions—and his alliance with Llywelyn. The suspicion grew that a regime headed by Simon might be no better, and perhaps worse, than one led by the king. They began to waver, and Edward played on their doubts. In August, he reconciled himself to Leyburn and his followers [18] and actively sought to detach them from Simon's side. His success was remarkable. By October fully half the earl's supporters had deserted him.[19]

Earl Gilbert's activities during the fall and winter of 1263–64 are obscure. It is possible that he was reconciled to Henry and Edward. He gained at least part of his initial objectives for supporting Simon when he was allowed seisin of his estates in July and August, 1263, for a fine of £1,000, even though he had not yet attained his majority.[20] According to Bémont, a dispute then developed between Gilbert and Simon in September.[21] This might refer to the castles and other lands in the Clare marcher lordships assigned in dower to Countess Maud. Humphrey de Bohun, the *custos* of the marcher estates, had released the manors and castles of Usk and Trellech to the countess on February 8, 1263.[22] By August, Earl Simon was in effective control of the

---

[18] *Foedera*, I, 430.

[19] In addition to Gilbert de Clare, Earl Simon's chief supporters in the spring of 1263 included Earl Warenne, Henry of Almain, Henry de Hastings, John fitz John, Roger Leyburn, Nicholas Segrave, Geoffrey de Lucy (Dunstable, pp. 221–22); John fitz Alan, William de Munchensy (Wykes, p. 133); Roger Clifford, John Giffard, John Vaux, Hamo L'Estrange (Treharne, *Baronial Plan of Reform*, p. 302); James Audley, Reginald fitz Peter, William de Braose (Lloyd, *Hist. Wales*, II, 733); and two northern barons related to Clifford and Leyburn, John de Vescy of Alnwick and Robert de Vipont of Appelby (see Sanders, *English Baronies*, pp. 63, 103–4). By the end of the year the following had been won over to Edward's side: Warenne, Henry of Almain, Leyburn, Clifford, Vaux, L'Estrange (Dunstable, p. 225); fitz Alan, fitz Peter, Audley and Braose (Lloyd, *Hist. Wales*, II, 733). Segrave, fitz John, Hastings, and presumably the others remained loyal to Simon, and were joined by Robert de Ferrers, earl of Derby, Robert de Vere, earl of Oxford, and Humphrey de Bohun the younger (Gervase of Canterbury, II, 226).

[20] PRO, Pipe Roll 48 Henry III, E 372/108 r. 5d.; *Rot. Fin.*, II, 402–3; *Cal. Pat. Rolls 1258–66*, p. 273. Formal livery was granted in September, 1264, when Gilbert had come of age. Gilbert paid £100 of the fine and was pardoned the rest in February 1266. *Cal. Pat. Rolls 1258–66*, pp. 350, 354, 553.

[21] Bémont, *Simon de Montfort*, p. 202 (English trans.), pp. 201–2 (French ed.). Bémont gives no details, however, and the references cited are erroneous (*Chronica Maiorum*, p. 59, in the English translation; *Chroniques de London*, ed. G. Aungier [Camden Society, old ser., vol. XXVIII, 1846], p. 59, in the French ed.). I have been unable to find the correct reference.

[22] PRO, Min. Accts., SC 6/1202/1 m. 2.

government, and he undoubtedly rewarded the young heir for his support by allowing him to fine for his other estates at this time. Gilbert recovered his Welsh lands on August 10. It is possible that he also demanded the castles assigned in dower, but that Simon, perhaps at the instigation of his ally, Llywelyn ap Gruffydd, overrode his claims and allowed the countess to retain seisin. If these conjectures are true, they lend substance to Wykes' statement that Gilbert was on the royalist side at the beginning of 1264.[23] In any case, the countess held the castles until 1266–67, when the earl successfully brought suit for their recovery.[24]

There is other evidence, however, to suggest that the reasons for Gilbert's detachment were more complex. An anonymous letter, probably written by a member of his circle early in 1264, indicates that the earl was still attracted to the antiroyalist movement as a whole, but that he had doubts about Simon's motives and behavior. The letter unfortunately is couched in rather vague and ambiguous terms, but many of its statements are consistent with motives later professed by Gilbert when he broke completely with the Montfortian position. The writer complains about Earl Simon's inconsistent treatment of the aliens: he had opposed some, but he continued to favor others; such actions were thought to jeopardize the baronial cause; moreover, the writer felt, the earl was getting old, and the reformers ought to have a successor in mind. The letter thus implied that if Simon were not forceful enough in his actions, Gilbert might be prepared to assume the lead. Too much, perhaps, should not be made of this letter; but it does provide some insight into Gilbert's thinking at this time. He still favored the baronial movement. If he held himself aloof at this point, it was because of personal animosity to Earl Simon, occasioned by the question of the aliens, and quite probably also by the matter of his mother's dower lands in the march. Similarly, his reconciliation with Henry and Edward was superficial and temporary, and did not indicate support for the royalist position. It was not the only time that Earl Gilbert the Red was to distinguish between the cause of reform and the cause of Simon de Montfort himself.[25]

[23] Wykes, p. 140.
[24] Below, p. 117.
[25] The letter is printed in Tewkesbury, pp. 179–80, and is briefly discussed in Powicke, *King Henry III*, II, 444 note 2.

By April, 1264, however, the earl of Gloucester was once more fighting on Montfort's side. In October, 1263, seriously weakened by the many defections to the royalists, Simon agreed to submit to arbitration by King Louis IX of France. He could hardly have expected Louis to effect a compromise in which the basic features of the baronial program would be accepted in both the theory and practice of government; indeed, the award, issued at Amiens on January 23, 1264, was a complete and unequivocal repudiation of the Provisions of Oxford. It immediately overthrew all that the baronial forces had accomplished or envisioned since 1258; but this may not have been entirely unwelcome to Simon. It gave him the opportunity to regroup and strengthen his forces—in particular, to win back to his side such men as Earl Gilbert—and to impose, by renewed armed rebellion, not only the Provisions, but his own personal mastery. As his previous actions had demonstrated, the earl of Leicester was not adverse to such a course.[26]

The Mise of Amiens thus marked the renewal of civil war. Simon rallied his followers and formed a fresh alliance with Llywelyn ap Gruffydd.[27] At first, however, the fighting went against the Montfortians. Edward and the marcher lords led a successful expedition to capture the strongholds of Huntingdon and Hay and the lordship of Brecknock. They then took Gloucester castle, securing their control over the Severn valley, and marched east, capturing Northampton on April 7.[28] These military successes of the royalists together with the award at Amiens forced Earl Gilbert to make a decision. For all his suspicions about Simon, he chose the Montfortian side.

Gilbert's decision to rejoin Earl Simon was prompted by a number of considerations which shed light on his character and the general pattern of his behavior throughout the entire period

[26] The award is printed in *Foedera*, I, 433–44. The baronial case is printed from documents in the Archives Nationales, Paris, by P. Walne in "The Barons' Argument at Amiens, January 1264," *English Historical Review*, LXIX (1954), 418–25; LXXIII (1958), 453–59.

[27] He also found support among the Londoners and "fere omnis communa mediocris populi regni Angliae, qui vero non posuerunt se super regem Francie." *Chronica Maiorum*, p. 61. This does not necessarily imply a communal movement of the lesser burgesses and craft guildsmen against the municipal aristocracies, and indeed too much should not be made of Simon's appeal to "democratic" sentiments. Cf. Powicke, *King Henry III*, II, 445–49.

[28] Wykes, pp. 140–45; *Chronica Maiorum*, pp. 61–62.

of the Barons' War. Wykes, usually a well-informed source, declares that Gilbert's mother persuaded him to join Simon after Amiens,[29] but he gives no details, and since the countess held Clare, Usk castle, and some other important estates in dower, it seems highly unlikely that the young earl would succumb readily to maternal entreaties. The truth seems to lie deeper. The basic fact is that the Red Earl did not share his father's willingness to acquiesce in the overthrow of the Provisions, whether by Henry III of England or Louis IX of France. The anonymous letter from Gilbert's circle shows that he had become more committed to their principles than the marcher lords, and in particular to the xenophobia which the movement aroused. He tended to identify the " aliens," Henry's French relatives and their associates, as the " evil counselors " responsible for royal misgovernment. He constantly sought their elimination from court, and indeed their expulsion from the kingdom. His opposition to the aliens may not have been carefully thought out, but it was a major feature of his motivation and behavior all the same.

At least part of this feeling stemmed from personal enmity to Henry III's half brothers and their families. Unlike his father, Earl Gilbert displayed no interest in tournaments or other social festivities on the Continent; whenever possible, he remained on his own estates in England and Wales, and had little to do with the king's relatives. The precise causes of this disaffection are somewhat uncertain. It is not likely, however, that Gilbert believed the rumor that the Valences were behind a plot to poison Earl Richard and his brother William de Clare in 1258; the fact that William de Valence had interceded with King Henry on Gilbert's behalf in 1262, and that the two were allied against Simon de Montfort in later years, clearly indicate that Gilbert's hostility was not directed against the lord of Pembroke.[30]

The Red Earl's marriage to Alice de Lusignan was another matter entirely. In 1252 his father Earl Richard had agreed with the Valences to the marriage of the young Gilbert, then about nine years old, with their niece. According to Matthew Paris, King Henry promised Richard 5,000 marks, the same amount stipulated

[29] Wykes, p. 140.
[30] Above, pp. 83, 95; below, p. 108. William's brother, Aymer de Valence, bishop of Winchester, died in December, 1260.

in the marriage contract to be paid to Count Hugh, if he would consent to the match, and that the earl, an avaricious man, readily agreed. In the spring of 1253, Richard and William de Valence took Gilbert with them to Poitou, and the marriage was completed.[31] Matthew Paris claims that it was designed by the king to ally the Clares and the aliens, but after Earl Richard's death, at least, it had the exact opposite effect. While aristocratic marriages seldom if ever contained much semblance of affection, much less love, this match bred deep antagonisms, both personally and politically. Alice in particular seems to have become almost morbidly depressed about it; as his political activities suggest, Gilbert was not an easy man to get along with. In 1267 she broke openly with her husband, and supported the king against him. Shortly thereafter, she was rumored to have transferred her affections to the Lord Edward. Regardless of the truth of the latter story, the marriage ended in separation in 1271.[32] There is no direct evidence of trouble between them in 1264, but in view of these later developments, it is entirely possible that it existed by this time. Personal animosities of this kind contributed to the Red Earl's actions during the entire period, and did much to attract him to the reform movement as a whole. Gilbert was later to direct his xenophobia against Earl Simon himself and his family. For the present, however, it served, along with Louis' award at Amiens, to turn him against the royalists.

By the spring of 1264, therefore, Gilbert was firmly on the side of the reformers. He had not taken part in the early stages of the fighting, but remained in Tonbridge castle watching developments. The royalist successes, culminating at Northampton, prompted him to action. There is no indication of the size or composition of his force, but his support for Earl Simon turned the scales. Together they took the city of Rochester and began to besiege the castle on April 18. Edward hurried to relieve it, and the earls fell back to London. The royalists captured Gilbert's stronghold

[31] Matthew Paris, *Chronica Majora*, V, 362–64, 366–67, 514; Tewkesbury, pp. 151, 153–54. The contract with Hugh de Lusignan is in *Cal. Chart. Rolls 1226–57*, pp. 438–39. See also *Cal. Pat. Rolls 1247–58*, pp. 174–75.

[32] *G. E. C.*, V, 707 and note (i); Dunstable, pp. 245–46; *The Chronicle of Bury St. Edmunds 1212–1301*, ed. Antonia Gransden (London and Edinburgh, 1964), p. 45; PRO, Exchequer, KR Ecclesiastical Documents, E 135/7/1; below, pp. 118, 127.

at Tonbridge, and the baronial forces marched south, encountering
Henry's army at Lewes, the Sussex estate of Earl Warenne, on
May 12. In the negotiations immediately preceding the battle,
Simon and Gilbert were declared enemies of the king's person by
Henry, Edward, and Richard of Cornwall. They in turn renounced
their homage to the king by a formal act of *diffidatio*. Just before
the battle was joined on May 14, Simon knighted his younger
followers, including Earl Gilbert. The battle of Lewes ended
in a complete triumph for Simon's forces, and the royalist army
was crushed. In the actual warfare Richard of Cornwall was
forced to surrender by John Giffard, and declared himself Gilbert's
prisoner. The earl is even credited by some chroniclers with having
captured King Henry himself.[33]

The victory at Lewes marked the high point of Simon de Montfort's fortunes. For the second time in less than a year, the earl
of Leicester imposed a revolutionary regime on the kingdom. He
took the Lord Edward, Henry of Almain, and others into custody
to ensure the co-operation of the marchers, who were released.
The king was forced to submit to Simon's dictates. Once again
the old conditions were imposed. Henry swore to observe the
Provisions, which were to be subject, however, to certain future
modifications. The administrative personnel was reorganized.
Complete amnesty was given to Simon, Gilbert, and their followers. On May 15 Simon forced Henry to order the garrisons of
the castles still in royalist hands to end all resistance, and on
June 4 orders were issued for the re-establishment of *custodes
pacis* in each shire. At the same time Simon did not forget his
following among the lesser freeholders. Four knights from each
shire were to come to London at the end of June to treat with
the magnates and prelates on the state of the realm.[34]

The victors in the meantime reaped the spoils. While Earl

[33] Wykes, pp. 149–51; Dunstable, pp. 230–32; Gervase Cant., II, 235–37; *Flores
Hist.*, II, 496; *Annales Monasterii de Waverleia*, ed. H. R. Luard (*Annales
Monastici*, vol. II, 1865), p. 357; *Annales Prioratus de Wigornia*, ed. H. R. Luard
(*Annales Monastici*, vol. IV, 1869), p. 451. The correspondence between the
opposing leaders is given in *Foedera*, I, 440, and William de Rishanger, *Chronica
et Annales*, ed. H. R. Luard, in *Chronica Monasterii S. Albani* (vol. II, Rolls Series
XXVIII, 1865), pp. 22–24.

[34] Full details of the settlement are given in Bémont, *Simon de Montfort*, pp.
214–15, and in Powicke, *King Henry III*, II, 467–73. For the administrative
changes, see Tout, *Chapters*, I, 309–12.

Simon's sons received some important, and lucrative, positions,[35] Gilbert and his followers were also handsomely rewarded. Gilbert himself was appointed governor of Boston on June 15 and until July 8 had temporary custody of the lands of the bishopric of Hereford.[36] Simon de Pattishull, a military tenant and household knight, was named sheriff of Bedford and Buckingham, while another retainer, Brian de Gouiz, was made keeper of Sherborne castle in Dorset. In addition, Hervey de Borham, who had been Earl Richard's seneschal in 1259, was given custody of several royal honors.[37] At the same time, important Montfortian leaders were given strategic lands in England and Wales to conquer, in an attempt to reduce the continued power of the great royalist magnates. On June 20, Gilbert obtained custody of Earl Warenne's lands, except for the castles of Reigate and Lewes. On July 10, he gained possession of Richmond castle and the lands of Peter of Savoy. Most important, however, was the grant, dated June 6, of custody of the Valence lordship and castle of Pembroke. Simon could not be sure the marchers would behave, and Valence was at large. The lordship was therefore entrusted to a man who had a personal interest in the tranquillity of the region, and the ability to enforce it.[38]

The assembly of June 23 effected a considerable modification of the scheme of government organized in 1258.[39] The old Councils of Twenty-four, Fifteen, and Twelve were not revived. Instead, a Committee of Three, consisting of Earl Simon, Earl Gilbert, and Stephen de Berksted, bishop of Chichester, were given power to elect a Council of Nine, whose " advice " the king was constrained to follow in the exercise of executive authority. The functions of the Nine, however, were vague, and until recently even their identities were not fully established. In fact, the existence of the Nine did not preclude the independent action of Earl Simon or the justiciar or any other important person acting in a capacity as counselor to the king. Actual power, therefore, rested with the Three, or more precisely, with Simon de Mont-

[35] See Bémont, *Simon de Montfort*, p. 215.
[36] *Cal. Pat. Rolls 1258–66*, pp. 325, 332.
[37] *Ibid.*, pp. 327, 346, 385.
[38] *Ibid.*, pp. 322, 326, 333.
[39] The text of the settlement is printed in *Foedera*, I, 443–44.

fort.[40] Moreover, this form of government was not meant to be permanent. The letters patent formally empowering the Three to nominate the Council of Nine specifically stated that the king would rule with their counsel " until the Mise lately made between the king and his barons at Lewes, or another form, if a better can be provided, be completed." [41] In fact, another system was never found. The government formed at the London parliament remained in effect for the duration of Simon's revolutionary regime.

For the third time since 1258, a baronial government had been formed. For the third time the king promised to observe the principles of the Provisions. And for the third time the reform movement ended in disaster. The reasons for the decline of the Montfortian government were numerous. The kingdom was not at peace. Important men such as William de Valence and John de Warenne were at large and ready to reopen fighting. Henry also had powerful support in France, as well as the backing of the papacy and the majority of the English clergy. In addition, the objectives which had solidified the baronial forces behind Simon had been won, and there was nothing to prevent internal dissension over such questions as the division of spoils, the control of prisoners, the problem of the aliens, or the personal power of Earl Simon himself. Simon's undisputed qualities of leadership and military ability could not obscure the fact that the provisional government was little more than a disguised form of autocracy. For all the support the earl enjoyed among the middle elements of society, it was the opinion of the great men that counted. Personal antipathies to Simon, especially those displayed by the earl of Gloucester, contributed materially to his defeat and death scarcely a year after his triumph.

The immediate danger, however, was the renewed warfare on the marches. Simon and Gilbert found a useful ally in Llywelyn who joined with them in capturing a number of important castles. The success of the campaign forced the marchers to sue for peace at Montgomery on August 25. They agreed to surrender the other castles still in their hands, notably Bristol, and to appear in the king's court to release the prisoners they still held.[42] But they

---

[40] Cf. Bémont, Simon de Montfort, pp. 216–17, and Powicke, King Henry III, II, 474.

[41] Cal. Pat. Rolls 1258–66, p. 326; Foedera, I, 443.

[42] Lloyd, Hist. Wales, II, 735; Cal. Pat. Rolls 1258–66, p. 344.

had no intention of complying. As soon as they regrouped their forces, they repudiated the agreement and took to the field again. An attempt to rescue Lord Edward from his prison at Wallingford was repulsed by Simon's youngest son, Guy de Montfort. A second campaign by the Montfortians produced a second capitulation at Worcester in December. It is probable that Earl Gilbert joined forces with Simon and Llywelyn, but there is no direct evidence of this. At any rate, Simon imposed terms which would make him master of the west. Edward was forced to surrender the palatine county of Chester and the castle and town of Bristol in return for lands of equal value elsewhere in England. Mortimer, Clifford, and their allies were to leave the country and retire to Ireland for a year and a day. On January 5, 1265, Simon recognized the aid afforded him by Llywelyn and granted that any marcher castles and lands he had captured would remain in his possession. Edward's surrender of Chester was confirmed in a charter issued on March 20, a few days after Simon had formally freed him from captivity. At the same time King Henry swore to observe the provisional government established the previous June.[43]

Simon's supremacy was short-lived. Henry's proclamation was in reality an admission that no advance had been made on the precarious settlement after Lewes. Simon's enemies were more determined than ever to end his regime by force. The marchers continually postponed their departure on various pretexts, and the earl was unable to enforce his orders.[44] More ominously, a number of Simon's supporters now deserted him, including the earl of Gloucester.

Gilbert's defection proved the decisive factor in the situation. The chroniclers record a long list of grievances, and the chancery records bear at least some of them out. He had become increasingly dissatisfied with Simon's regime and reproached the earl for his supposed autocratic rule.[45] He was jealous of the high position the earl's sons held in the government.[46] He quarreled

---

[43] *Cal. Pat. Rolls 1258–66*, pp. 396–97; *Cal. Chart. Rolls 1257–1300*, p. 54; *Foedera*, I, 453.

[44] *Cal. Pat. Rolls 1258–66*, pp. 410, 415, 418 (March 2, March 17, April 8, 1265).

[45] Rishanger, *Chronica*, p. 32; Gilbert protested that " hic alienigena (Simon) praesumebat sibi totius regni dominium subjugare."

[46] Bémont, *Simon de Montfort*, pp. 236–37; cf. Dunstable, p. 238. Gilbert had

with Simon over the control of royalist castles and manors, and the exchange of prisoners.[47] He objected to the use of foreign knights in important castles [48] and the failure to expel all the aliens from court.[49] His support for Simon had not been unqualified, as the letter written in the winter of 1263–64 had shown. A combination of grievances thus drove him into opposition. Hardly had the king's proclamation been issued when he retired to his Welsh lordships. The alliance of Simon with Llywelyn began to rankle; Gilbert's interests demanded a reconciliation with the marchers. According to Wykes, he came to terms with John Giffard, and then the others. He harbored the marchers on his estates, and refused to attend a tournament at Northampton arranged for April 20, fearing Earl Simon's wrath.[50] Simon ordered him to remove the marchers from his keeping so that the sentence of exile could be carried out, but Gilbert refused. Letters issued by Simon on May 20 denying all rumors of discord deceived no one.[51] At the beginning of May, John de Warenne and William de Valence landed in Pembroke and were received by Gilbert's men. The resumption of hostilities seemed inevitable.[52] Simon took Edward and an unwilling Henry with him to the west, and encamped at Hereford until May 24. Attempted negotiations proved fruitless, for Gilbert had already worked out a plan with Edward and Roger Mortimer which would seal Simon's fate.[53] On May 28, with the assistance of Thomas de Clare, Earl Gilbert's younger brother, Edward managed an escape. He joined forces with Mortimer at Wigmore, and the next day Gilbert joined them in Ludlow.[54] Wykes, perhaps the best in-

---

arranged for a tournament at Dunstable in February against Simon's sons. Cal. Pat. Rolls 1258–66, p. 406.

[47] Cal. Pat. Rolls 1258–66, p. 479; Close Rolls 1264–68, pp. 33–34, 41–44; Chronica Maiorum, p. 73; cf. Powicke, King Henry III, II, 493–94, 496.

[48] Rishanger, Chronica, p. 32.

[49] Brit. Mus., Cotton MS Nero A IV (Chronicon Laudunense), fol. 46.

[50] Wykes, pp. 160–62; Dunstable, p. 238. This was the tournament postponed from Dunstable on February 16 (see above, note 46).

[51] Foedera, I, 455.

[52] Cal. Pat. Rolls 1258–66, pp. 423–24.

[53] Chronica Maiorum, p. 73.

[54] The story is told with numerous variations in all the chronicles. See Powicke, King Henry III, II, 497–98, and Bémont, Simon de Montfort, pp. 238–39. Thomas was in Edward's household at this time, and had been an aide of Simon prior to his brother's defection. Wykes, p. 162; Cal. Pat. Rolls 1258–66, pp. 344, 419; below, p. 188.

formed chronicler of this period, records an important set of conditions that Earl Gilbert demanded as the price of his support. The earl made Edward swear a solemn oath that, if victorious, he would cause the " good old laws " of the realm to be observed; evil customs would be abolished, aliens banished from the king's council and administration; and the king would rule with the counsel of his faithful subjects. If Wykes' account of the oath is substantially correct, it clearly shows that Gilbert remained firmly attracted to the principles of the Provisions, however vaguely envisioned and conventionally expressed, and to the xenophobia which the movement engendered. If he withdrew his support from Simon, it was not because he was willing, like his father Earl Richard in 1260, to repudiate the Provisions, but because he felt that Simon did not distinguish between the baronial ideals and his personal ambition. The cause of reform, in short, was not the exclusive prerogative of the earl of Leicester.[55]

The military operations are quickly told. Under the leadership of Edward and Earl Gilbert, the royalists gathered at Gloucester, cutting off Simon's retreat across the Severn at that point. Boldly making his way into the march, Simon renewed his alliance with Llywelyn in the middle of June. He then went through Monmouth to the borough of Newport in the Clare lordship of Gwynllwg and attempted to cross over to Bristol, but this plan was foiled when Earl Gilbert destroyed the convoy sent for that purpose. Simon managed to return to Hereford, and tried to join forces with an army led by his son. Edward and Gilbert, however, surprised the younger Simon at Kenilworth in Warwick on August 1, routed his forces, and immediately doubled back to intercept Earl Simon. The earl reached the Worcester manor of Evesham on August 3, but was surrounded by the royalists. The next day battle was joined. As Simon advanced on a troop led by Roger Mortimer, Earl Gilbert, who commanded the second line, suddenly attacked from the rear. The outcome was less a battle than

---

[55] Wykes, pp. 164–65; Gilbert began to raise troops, " recepto a domino Edwardo prius apud Lodelawe corporali sacramento, quod si eo juvante posset obtinere victoriam, antiquas leges bonas et approbatas faceret observari, pravas consuetudines quae in regno inoleverunt abrogari, et quod regem induceret ut alienigenas a regno et a consilio suo amoveat, nec permitteret eos habere custodiam castrorum, vel aliquid genus administrationis in regno, et quod rex indigenarum sibi fidelium consilio regeretur. . . ."

a slaughter. The only important marcher who fought with Simon, Humphrey de Bohun the younger, was captured and imprisoned at Beeston castle in Cheshire, where he died on October 27. Two other men with marcher affiliations, Henry de Hastings and John fitz John, were also imprisoned. Otherwise the royalists showed no mercy. Simon de Montfort, his son Henry, his loyal friend Peter de Montfort the elder, the justiciar Hugh Despenser and many others were slain. King Henry himself was rescued by Roger Leyburn. The Montfortian experiment was ended.[56]

The Disinherited

The death of Simon de Montfort did not produce peace. The ferocity with which the royalists had crushed their enemies carried over into a period of widespread seizures of rebel lands and indiscriminate plundering which produced further turmoil and unrest. In addition, the territorial policy adopted by the restored royal government provoked those supporters of Earl Simon still at large into guerilla operations which turned into full-scale warfare and prevented a final pacification of the kingdom until the end of 1267. In this period the actions of Gilbert de Clare again proved decisive. His support for the disinherited rebels was a major factor in the establishment of internal order following the two years of continued civil strife which constituted the aftermath of the battle of Evesham.

The immediate task facing Henry and Edward was the re-establishment of royal authority. Bristol and the other castles still held by Montfortian adherents were quickly forced to surrender. On October 1 Henry annulled all measures taken while he was in the "keeping and power" of Earl Simon after Lewes.[57] A parliamentary assembly gathered at Winchester in the middle of September to deal with the defeated Montfortians. The flush of royalist triumph, however, led to renewed resistance. There had

---

[56] The best chronicle account is that of Wykes, pp. 165–74. Standard secondary accounts are contained in Bémont, *Simon de Montfort*, pp. 239–44, Powicke, *King Henry III*, II, 498–502, and Sir Charles Oman, *History of the Art of War in the Middle Ages* (2 vols.; 2nd ed.; London, 1924), I, 431–41. For Llywelyn, see Lloyd, *Hist. Wales*, II, 736–37.

[57] *Cal. Pat. Rolls 1258–66*, p. 549.

been much usurpation of rebel properties immediately after Evesham, in which men such as Gilbert de Clare, John de Warenne, and even the Lord Edward had participated. The parliament decided that all rebel lands, including those already seized by the royalists, and the Michaelmas rents from them were to be taken into the king's hands. Juries were empaneled in each hundred to assist the sheriffs and royal *seisitores* in this task.[58] At the same time, all goods and chattels taken by the royalists were to remain in their possession.[59] Henry used the confiscations made in his name as a means of curbing the excesses of private individuals acting without royal authorization; but he still had to reward his followers. The result was a process of territorial redistribution to royal favorites which produced wide-scale protest and upheaval. The only recourse of the Disinherited was to form bands of roving brigands and engage in acts of pillage and local warfare. Wykes, who alone among the chroniclers had been unfavorable to Simon de Montfort, blames the royalists' actions for the continued unrest which gripped the kingdom in the two years following Evesham.[60] This period witnessed a more general breakdown of local administration and dislocation of economic activity than at any other time in the entire reform movement.[61]

The returns of the *seisitores* reveal the ubiquity of the initial seizures and the thoroughness with which they were carried out.[62] Although most of the great royalist barons engaged in usurpations, Gilbert de Clare was certainly the most vigorous and probably the most successful in the scramble for territory. On August 6, two days after the battle, he ordered his tenants to aid his officials

---

[58] *Ibid.*, pp. 490–91.

[59] *Ibid.*, p. 493. In a dispute between Gilbert de Clare and Roger Leyburn over rebel properties in Kent, it was stated that "by consent of the magnates lately after the conflict at Evesham, it was granted that to the first occupiers of the lands late of the favorers of Simon de Monte Forti, earl of Leicester, the king's enemy, the goods and chattels then found in such lands should remain. . . ."

[60] Wykes, pp. 183–84. Cf. the remarks of Jacob, *Studies*, pp. 167–70.

[61] Jacob, *Studies*, pp. 248–75.

[62] The returns are preserved in PRO, Inquisitions Miscellaneous (Chancery), C 145/files 25–30, and are summarized in *Calendar of Inquisitions Miscellaneous* (H. M. Stationery Office, 1916–), vol. I, (1219–1307), nos. 609–940. Various other documents relating to the seizures are printed in *Rotuli Selecti*, ed. Joseph Hunter (Record Commission, 1834). There is other information scattered through the chancery and legal records. The whole question is discussed in detail by Jacob, *Studies*, pp. 223–48.

in seizing the lands of the king's enemies, and they seem to have pursued their task with efficiency and dispatch.[63] The lands of the Montfortian leaders attracted the earl's attention, and the returns are full of references to seizures of lands formerly held by such men as John fitz John, Robert de Vere, earl of Oxford, and especially Simon and his sons.[64] In addition Gilbert occupied lands which belonged to members of his *familia* who had remained loyal to Simon, for example the manors of Simon de Pattishull, Brian de Gouiz and Hamo Hautein.[65]

Gilbert's actions were often quite arbitrary. On occasion, lands seized at his order were surrendered to the king for redistribution, but not before the earl kept not only the movables but also the rents for himself.[66] Sometimes Gilbert seized lands to reward his followers. He captured Henry de Hasting's manor of Lidgate in Essex and gave it to his brother Thomas.[67] He took properties of John de St. Elena in Wottenham, Berkshire, and William de Elmsberry in Finchingfield, Essex, giving them to Emery de St. Amando and Thomas de Ispania. He also seized Earl Simon's tenements in Nailsea in Suffolk, later enfeoffing William de Munchensy with them.[68] Nor did he feel obliged to limit his confiscations to rebel lands. Properties were seized in Kent and Oxford, although their owners were " never against the king." Gilbert eventually restored the manors to the owners, but not before pocketing the rents.[69]

There is no evidence, however, that Earl Gilbert added any of the confiscated estates to his demesne. He seems to have been

---

[63] PRO, Assize Rolls, JI 1/59 m. 8, printed in Jacob, *Studies*, p. 406.

[64] *Cal. Inq. Misc.*, nos. 631, 661, 700, 707, 723, 833, 843, 878, 898; *Rotuli Selecti*, pp. 131, 139, 141.

[65] *Cal. Inq. Misc.*, nos. 632, 656, 829.

[66] E.g., *Cal. Inq. Misc.*, nos. 611, 753, 910; *Rotuli Selecti*, pp. 134–35, 141. Gilbert had already begun seizing lands after the battle of Kenilworth. Towcester manor in Northampton was taken from William de Munchensy on August 2 and surrendered to the king on October 2. *Cal. Inq. Misc.*, no. 845.

[67] *Cal. Inq. Misc.*, no. 895. The seizure was formally confirmed by the king in August, 1266, although no mention is made of Thomas de Clare. *Cal. Pat. Rolls 1258–66*, p. 621.

[68] *Cal. Inq. Misc.*, nos. 625, 665 (p. 206), 888; *Cal. Inq. Post Mortem*, IV, no. 98.

[69] *Cal. Inq. Misc.*, nos. 727, 855. He even seized Richard of Cornwall's manor of Harwell in Berkshire, carried off some oxen, and then surrendered the manor in mid-September. *Ibid.*, no. 622.

primarily interested in keeping the rents, probably as a reward for his services to the royal cause at Evesham, and as late as 1297 his executors were charged with £160 owing to the king from such rents.[70] Moreover, he was at least equally desirous of taking advantage of the confused situation to usurp franchisal and juris-dictional privileges within his own holdings, both as a means of increasing his revenues and of consolidating control over his tenants. The *quo warranto* inquests of Edward I reveal that he was highly active in this endeavor.[71]

Personal gain was by no means the only motive for the earl's disobedience of royal orders. The most striking point in the findings of the *seisitores* is that in numerous instances the manors of the rebels were restored to their original owners.[72] Earl Gilbert had deserted the baronial forces out of personal animosity to Simon de Montfort, and retained a strong measure of sympathy for the disherisoned rebels, many of whom were his own tenants. It is indicative of the kind of support enjoyed by the Montfortian forces that many of Gilbert's associates and household knights deserted their master to stand with Simon in the civil war; but it is equally significant that Gilbert was willing to accept them back into his graces. A partial list of his household in the summer of 1267 shows that a number of men who had adhered to Simon were back with Gilbert. They included mesne tenants and ad-ministrators such as Simon de Pattishull, Hamo and Bartholomew Hautein, Roger Tailard, John de Bruton, Brian de Gouiz, and John de Neville, and there were doubtless many others whose names do not appear in connection with the inquests relating to the *terrae rebellium*.[73] In a similar fashion, John fitz John and William de Munchensy, who had been Gilbert's allies at Lewes and enemies at Evesham, were also in his household by 1267.[74]

---

[70] PRO, Exchequer, KR Mem. Roll 24–25 Edward I, E 159/70 m. 14. In 1337 Edward III was still demanding rents seized after Evesham from Gilbert's heir, Hugh D'Audley. PRO, KR Mem. Roll 10 Edward III, E 159/112 (Mich. recorda). I owe this latter reference to the kindness of Dr. E. B. Fryde.

[71] *Placita de Quo Warranto*, ed. W. Illingsworth (Record Commission, 1818), pp. 183, 253, 339, 703–4, 774–76. See also Donald W. Sutherland, *Quo Warranto Proceedings in the Reign of Edward I 1278–1294* (Oxford, 1963), pp. 146–47 and *passim*.

[72] *Cal. Inq. Misc.*, nos. 667, 731, 736, 738, 743, 835.

[73] The members of the *familia* are given in *Cal. Pat. Rolls 1266–72*, pp. 145–47. For these men, see *Cal. Inq. Misc.*, nos. 632, 829, 835, 839, 877, 903.

[74] *Cal. Pat. Rolls 1266–72*, p. 143; Wykes, p. 198. John fitz John was the son

Throughout the remainder of Henry III's reign, Gilbert was busy securing pardons for his followers for their previous allegiance to Simon.[75]

By the end of 1265, Gilbert turned his attention to the plight of the Disinherited as a whole. He strongly opposed King Henry's redistribution of confiscated lands, and at the time of the inquests resisted as often as possible attempts to make him surrender the lands into the king's hands.[76] It is at least possible that the earl's seizures of lands held by Pattishull, Gouiz and others were actually designed to protect their holdings from the rapacity of barons such as Roger Mortimer and Roger Clifford, who favored a harsh policy of total disherison; and it is also probable that he quickly restored their lands to them whenever possible.[77] Gilbert's support for the king was no less qualified than it had been for Simon, as his actions on behalf of the Disinherited were to prove.

Throughout the spring and summer of 1266, efforts were made by Edward, Gilbert, and above all the papal legate, Ottobuono Fiechi, to secure permanent terms for dealing with the rebels. Earl Simon's surviving sons and his widow had either fled or been forced to leave England by the beginning of 1266. Edward conciliated the barons of the Cinque Ports and ended the piracy which had disrupted coastal trade. Along with Roger Leyburn, he managed to capture some of the rebels in East Anglia, but Henry de Hastings, who had escaped from prison, occupied Kenilworth castle, while others, led by John d'Eyville, took refuge on the Isle of Ely. Kenilworth was besieged and the holdouts forced to submit to terms. The legate, Edward, Gilbert, and Richard of

of John fitz Geoffrey, one of the original baronial leaders of 1258. In January, 1266, Earl Gilbert was given custody of his lands, and restored them in 1267. In July, 1268, Henry ordered the lands seized again, on the grounds that John had given his homage to Gilbert, not the king. *Rot. Fin.*, II, 472–73.

[75] *Cal. Pat. Rolls 1258–66*, pp. 472–73, 500, 509, 535, 550, 552, 626; *Close Rolls 1264–68*, pp. 138–39, 140, 237; *Cal. Pat. Rolls 1266–72*, pp. 240, 268, 315, 429, 446–47, 531–32, 617. Gilbert himself, along with his brother Thomas, John Giffard, and others, was formally pardoned on October 6 by the king for having adhered to Simon at Lewes. *Foedera*, I, 464.

[76] E.g., *Cal. Inq. Misc.*, nos. 857, 888, 936.

[77] E.g., *ibid.*, no. 877 (Brian de Gouiz's manor of Kingston in Somerset). By January, 1266, however, Henry had already granted numerous manors held by Earl Gilbert's tenants. For example, Munchensy's lands were granted to William de Valence, and were only redeemed in December 1267. *Cal. Pat. Rolls 1258–66*, p. 532; *ibid. 1266–72*, p. 481.

Cornwall took the lead. A committee of twelve was organized to draft a program, which was submitted to a parliament at Northampton, formally ratified and published by the king on October 31. The document, known as the Dictum de Kenilworth, provided for a comprehensive settlement. All measures drawn up at the instigation of Simon de Montfort were annulled, and the king was to exercise his full power and authority according to the " established laws and customs " of the realm. Amnesty was promised to all rebels who submitted within forty days. They could repurchase their lands for a sum set at five times the annual value. All those unwilling to abide by these terms were to appear at the king's court to hear judgment; if they refused, their lands and goods would be declared permanently forfeit.[78]

In fact, however, the Dictum did not bring peace. The garrisons at Kenilworth and Ely refused to assent. They felt the conditions were still too harsh. Many lacked the financial resources to comply with the terms of repurchase, and most probably felt suspicious of the king's assurances of good will. They had fought with Earl Simon, and entertained hopes that his son might return from France to lead them again. Their hopes were in vain, for the younger Simon de Montfort never returned to England. The Kenilworth garrison was forced to capitulate by December 14, but Henry de Hastings managed to join forces with the Ely rebels, who were in a stronger military position and determined to hold out to the last.[79] Their ranks were swollen by the addition of many other dissidents, and they found a leader in Gilbert de Clare.

Earl Gilbert had ample reason to come to their support. He had substantial landed interests in East Anglia, and many of his tenants and associates were among the rebels. Although he had served on the committee which framed the Dictum, he found many of its features unsatisfactory. It left many questions unanswered, especially in regard to the lands seized after Evesham and still held by the royalists. Gilbert doubted the willingness of men such as Roger Mortimer, or even Edward, to restore the lands to their owners as he had done, and he desired restoration as a preliminary to the enforcement of the terms of the Dictum.

[78] Select Charters, pp. 407–11.
[79] Cf. Cal. Pat. Rolls 1266–72, pp. 17, 152.

He also doubted the eagerness of the king to expel his alien relatives and friends. The earl's franchisal usurpations did not imply
that he felt no attachment to the demands of the lesser freeholders
for reform of local royal government. In short, his *volte-face* was
based on the fact that he still felt a strong attraction to the reform
movement. There is no reason to believe with Wykes that his
professed motives were merely propaganda to cloak his territorial
designs; [80] as early as January, 1266, Henry had been obliged to
deny rumors of discord and dissatisfaction between Gilbert and
the Lord Edward, presumably on these scores. The Red Earl
had not forgotten the oaths he compelled Edward to take at
Ludlow.[81]

Gilbert's actions, of course, were not based solely on these
motives. Personal animosities and ambition also contributed in
large measure to his stand. Henry had granted away many of the
manors held by Gilbert's tenants, and his rights of wardship,
reliefs, and suit of court were bound to be adversely affected.
In September the king ordered an investigation into the earl's
actions after Evesham, thus revoking a promise he had made the
previous January not to molest him in any way regarding his
seizures of rebel properties.[82] Moreover, a personal quarrel had
arisen between the earl and Roger Mortimer over control of the
lands and castles of Humphrey de Bohun the younger. The lordship of Brecknock was nominally committed to Mortimer after
Evesham, although Llywelyn ap Gruffydd was in effective control
of it. On October 29, 1265, two days after Humphrey's death,
Gilbert was granted custody of the lordship with the marriage of
his heir. Mortimer refused to assent to this arrangement. In May,
1266, he made an unsuccessful attempt to take Brecknock from
Llywelyn, and as late as December of that year had not yet
released his claims. In addition, the castles of Hay in Brecknock
and Huntingdon in Herefordshire were also transferred to Gilbert
in the fall of 1266, and Mortimer did not receive compensation
until the following April. These disputes involved not only a
question of prestige, but also concrete military and territorial

[80] Wykes, pp. 199–200.
[81] *Foedera*, I, 467. Cf. Dunstable, p. 245, and the remarks of Jacob, *Studies*,
pp. 172–74.
[82] *Cal. Pat. Rolls 1258–66*, pp. 532, 533, 676.

considerations in the march. They sparked further dissensions between the two men, who were already at odds over the treatment of the Disinherited.[83]

Of even greater importance, Earl Gilbert did not have possession of his own marcher lordships. In the spring of 1266, he brought suit against his mother, the dowager Countess Maud, for the castles of Usk and Trellech, which she had held in dower since 1262–63. King Henry ordered both Glamorgan and Usk taken into royal custody pending a new inquest and the settlement of the suit. On April 30, 1266, he appointed the elder Humphrey de Bohun, earl of Hereford, as keeper.[84] Objections raised by the countess as to the validity of the king's writ in the march delayed the proceedings until well into the fall. Gilbert only regained Glamorgan and his other lands on November 8, and finally on January 25, 1267, recovered the castles from his mother, while the manors of Usk and Trellech and the other estates she held in the lordship remained in her possession.[85]

The difficulties and delays experienced by the earl in these matters must have added to his impatience and indignation. In 1266, his base of strength in the march was seriously weakened. The disputed custody of Brecknock brought him into conflict with a fellow marcher lord who favored a policy concerning the Disinherited almost exactly opposite his own. That King Henry had deemed it necessary to take Glamorgan as well as Usk into royal keeping despite the fact that Gilbert sought only to recover castles in the latter lordship further angered the earl. In a writ

[83] *Ibid.*, p. 495; *ibid.* 1266–72, pp. 56, 127; *Cal. Liberate Rolls 1260–67*, pp. 245, 272–73; Rishanger, *Chronica*, pp. 45–46. For the descent of Brecknock to the Bohun family, see Sanders, *English Baronies*, pp. 6–8.

[84] *Cal. Pat. Rolls 1258–66*, pp. 588, 592, 662–63. Humphrey had also been keeper of the lordships in 1262 after Earl Richard's death. The preliminary stages of the action are given in PRO, Curia Regis Roll Michaelmas 50–51 Henry III, KB 26/177 m. 3. They are discussed in E. F. Jacob, "The Reign of Henry III: Some Suggestions," *Transactions of the Royal Historical Society*, 4th ser., X (1927), 25–28, but the case is misdated 49–50 Henry III.

[85] *Close Rolls 1264–68*, p. 264; PRO, KB 26/177 mm. 13–13d. In addition to the manor and borough of Usk and the manor of Trellech, Maud held the manors of Troy and Cwmcarvan, and Rhymny in the lordship of Gwynllwg. The new dower settlement is contained in PRO, Rentals and Surveys, General Series, SC 11/610 m. 1. An amplified and corrected version of the valuations of the English estates made in 1262 and printed in *Close Rolls 1261–64*, pp. 284–93, appears on mm. 2–7 of this document.

dated August 20, 1266, Henry granted Gilbert the full possession of any lands of the Welsh supporters of Simon de Montfort and Llywelyn ap Gruffydd which he could conquer; but without Glamorgan as his base of operations, Gilbert could hardly have taken advantage of the grant at this time, and he must have viewed the king's offer as a feeble and transparent attempt to soothe his ruffled feelings.[86] Personal grievances of this kind, combined with an underlying feeling of support for the cause of the Disinherited, drove the Red Earl once more into open opposition to the king.

Gilbert's intervention on behalf of the rebels proved decisive. Efforts by the Lord Edward to negotiate at a parliament at Bury St. Edmunds in February, 1267, accomplished nothing. Gilbert withdrew to the march, both to consolidate his authority in his newly recovered lordships and to gather an armed force. He sent envoys to King Henry to demand the immediate restoration of their estates to the Disinherited. When the king refused to heed his request, Gilbert acted swiftly. While Henry delayed at Canterbury, the earl sent three of his advisers, William de Munchensy, Robert of Leicester, and Hervey de Borham to enlist the support of the Londoners.[87] He also reached an agreement with John d'Eyville and the other Ely leaders. At the beginning of April, d'Eyville slipped out of Ely and made for London. Although the king was warned of his movements by Gilbert's wife, Alice de Lusignan, he was unable to contain him. On April 8 Gilbert entered the city, joined forces with the rebels, and began to raise fortifications. The *populus minutus* of the city overthrew the merchant oligarchy and established a popularly elected commune. Gilbert's actions rallied the Disinherited, who gathered in London under his protection. Preparations were made for a prolonged siege.[88]

The earl of Gloucester had succeeded Simon de Montfort as the hero of the reform movement. But he did not contemplate a *coup d'état*. Rather, he desired by vigorous action to bring the entire matter to a head and to secure more favorable terms for the Disinherited. He probably felt that a show of force was the

[86] *Cal. Pat. Rolls 1258–66*, p. 674.

[87] Dunstable, pp. 244–45; Wykes, pp. 198–99.

[88] Dunstable, pp. 245–46; *Chronica Maiorum*, pp. 90–91. For a full account of the events in London during the 1260's, see Gwyn A. Williams, *Medieval London* (London, 1963), pp. 214–42.

only means which would achieve these ends. The king was finally stirred into action. He reached Windsor on May 5 and four days later settled down with his army at Stratford in Essex, where he remained for several weeks. He seemed at first determined to put down the uprising by force, and sent Roger Leyburn to France to enlist further armed support.[89] But more moderate counsel prevailed. Neither side was fully prepared for war. On April 20 Gilbert had been given safe-conduct to begin negotiations with Richard of Cornwall and Philip Basset, who had also opposed the policy of total disherison adopted at Winchester.[90] Under the auspices of Cardinal Ottobuono, a peaceful settlement was soon reached. On May 13 Gilbert and his followers agreed to withdraw from London to Southwark.[91] On June 4 safe-conducts were issued to six of his men, including John fitz John, Hamo Hautein, and Hervey de Borham, acting as the earl's envoys to discuss terms with the king, Richard of Cornwall, his son Henry, Philip Basset, and the Lord Edward.[92] A final settlement was reached in mid-June. Gilbert gave sureties for his good behavior, offering 10,000 marks, a sum later doubled by the pope. A general amnesty was offered to all who had adhered to his cause and the clergy was induced to grant an aid which was applied to the repurchase of rebel lands. The Disinherited thus got what they wanted: immediate restoration of their lands if they came into the king's peace and better financial terms toward their full redemption. During the next few weeks almost all the rebels agreed to these terms. The danger of civil war was averted, and judicial commissions were sent out in the fall to settle all territorial disputes in accordance with the terms of the Dictum.[93]

[89] PRO, Exchequer, KR Miscellanea, E 163/1/41 no. 11; Jacob, *Studies*, p. 259. For Leyburn's career, see Alun Lewis, "Roger Leyburn and the Pacification of England, 1265–1267," *English Historical Review*, LIV (1939), 193–210.

[90] *Cal. Pat. Rolls 1266–72*, p. 55.

[91] PRO, Chanc. Miscellanea, C 47/14/6 no. 4. The agreement was drawn up by the legate for the king and his sons Edward and Edmund, and was witnessed by William de Valence, Roger Bigod, John de Warenne, Humphrey de Bohun, John Balliol, and Philip Basset.

[92] *Cal. Pat. Rolls 1266–72*, p. 143. The other three were Robert de Munteny, Robert de Montfort (no relation to Simon), and Master Robert de Trillawe.

[93] *Ibid.*, pp. 70–74, 114–15, and Powicke, *King Henry III*, II, 545–46, 561, for the settlement. Gilbert's letters announcing his acceptance of the terms are preserved in PRO, Chanc. Misc., C 47/14/6 no. 5. Clement IV raised the sum to 20,000 marks, and added that as surety either Tonbridge castle was to be handed over

The Barons' War was at an end, due mainly to the patient efforts of the legate Ottobuono to secure a peaceful settlement and the energy displayed by Gilbert de Clare in forcing the issue to a head. The earl's actions had brought better terms for the rebels, and it was only after his rising that the machinery of the Dictum was put into full effect. Gilbert hastened, rather than prevented, the pacification of the realm. The widespread unrest and turmoil which had beset the eastern half of the kingdom subsided, and the application of legal and peaceful means of settling disputes was once again enforced. For the first time since 1263, something like internal order and unity were slowly restored. Moreover, the principles underlying the Provisions of Westminster were not forgotten. They were incorporated into the Statute of Marlborough, issued in November 1267, and became part of the law of the land. The demands of the lesser freeholders for reform in local government were finally heeded. The most profound effect of the movement, however, was the one least apparent to contemporaries. King Henry was by now an old and weak man, and Edward was the real ruler of England after 1267. He did not forget the lessons of ten bitter years of constitutional conflict and open warfare, and he was to rule in such a way that the great questions which had convulsed the kingdom from 1258 to 1267 were not reopened until the last years of his reign.[94] Edward had, in short, learned the lessons of kingship, and the movement led by Gilbert de Clare contributed materially to that education.

The most striking feature of Gilbert de Clare's role in the later stages of the baronial movement is its consistency. The Red Earl's shifting allegiance was a sign not of vacillation but of independence. He was the moderating force against the extremes of both the royalist and the Montfortian sides. He was attracted to the baronial movement as a whole, but even more than his father Earl Richard, he drew the crucial distinction between its policies and the great earl whose name is inseparably associated with that movement. Earl Gilbert was not convinced that Simon

---

to Henry of Almain, or Gilbert's daughter Isabella to the queen. The king later remitted this latter condition. *Foedera*, I, 472. For the individual letters of pardon, see *Cal. Pat. Rolls 1266–72*, pp. 72–73, 113, 145–49 and *passim*. The judicial eyres made in accordance with the Dictum are analyzed in Jacob, *Studies*, pp. 176–221.

[94] Cf. the remarks of Powicke, *King Henry III*, II, 694–95, who perhaps overestimates Edward's qualities and capabilities.

de Montfort's actions were always and indisputably right, and he withdrew his support when he felt that Simon's regime was no better in its way than King Henry's had been. His adherence to the royalists, however, was no less qualified. When two years of continued resistance to the restored government of Henry III produced further social and political unrest, Earl Gilbert's rising proved the decisive factor in restoring unity and tranquillity to the realm. Unlike Earl Richard, Gilbert had not accepted Henry's repudiation of the principles which underlay the Provisions of Oxford and Westminster. His activities, while strongly colored by personal animosities and conditioned by personal interests, nevertheless reveal a continuity of purpose which did much in helping to incorporate those principles into the fabric of the common law and the conduct of monarchy.

CHAPTER IV

EARL GILBERT THE RED AND EDWARD I

Caerphilly Castle

The end of the Barons' War was followed by renewed negotiations with Llywelyn ap Gruffydd, whose power had not been
affected by the defeat of the Montfortian party at Evesham. A
temporary truce had been arranged in February, 1267, but the
king recognized the need for a lasting settlement. Under the
auspices of the legate Ottobuono, a formal treaty was drawn up
and ratified at Montgomery on September 29.[1] The Treaty of
Montgomery was seemingly a complete triumph for Llywelyn.
The title prince of Wales, which he had assumed in 1258, was
now formally recognized by the Crown. It carried with it overlordship over the other Welsh chieftains with the exception of
Maredudd ap Rhys Gryg, lord of Ystrad Tywi, who was allowed
to remain a direct vassal of the king. The territorial gains made
by the prince since 1256 were confirmed. This left him in control
of substantial Crown properties in Cardiganshire and southern
Powys, as well as numerous marcher lordships, the most important
of which was Brecknock. It also gave him claims to Roger Mortimer's lordship of Maelienydd, and the cantred of Senghenydd and
other territories in Glamorgan. His efforts to assert his position
in these areas and others brought him into open conflict with the
most formidable lords of the march, and were a major cause of the
renewal of warfare between England and Wales under Edward I.[2]

With the settlement of the Disinherited crisis and the final end
of the Barons' War, Earl Gilbert de Clare once again turned his

[1] *Littere Wallie*, pp. 1–4; *Foedera*, I, 474.
[2] For the Treaty, see Lloyd, *Hist. Wales*, II, 739–41, and Edwards, Introduction
to *Littere Wallie*, pp. xlviii–l.

major attention to marcher politics, and indeed he was to remain preoccupied with affairs in Wales for the remainder of his life. He recognized the threat which the Treaty of Montgomery posed to his supremacy in the southern march. Until 1267 Llywelyn ap Gruffydd had been more interested in consolidating and maintaining his authority in northern and central Wales, and had let pass numerous opportunities to renew those attacks on Glamorgan in which he had been engaged before 1258. An attack had been feared by the royal *custos* of the lordship in 1262, but failed to materialize, while in 1263 and 1264, of course, Llywelyn was at least nominally allied to Earl Gilbert and Simon de Montfort. Indeed, if the evidence of the *Brut* may be believed, he even formed a temporary alliance, or at least agreed to a truce, with Gilbert early in 1267, just before the earl's occupation of London. But the passages in the two versions of the chronicle obscure a crisis which, combined with the Treaty of Montgomery, at last brought the prince of Wales and the young lord of Glamorgan into open conflict.[3]

The strategic cantred of Senghenydd was the focus of contention. By 1264 Llywelyn controlled the neighboring Bohun lordship of Brecknock, and in the struggle to retain it against the rival claims of Roger Mortimer and Gilbert de Clare, both of whom claimed custody of the lordship during the minority of the heir,[4] the prince strengthened his support among the Welsh of Meisgyn and the adjacent northern commotes of Senghenydd, Uwch– and Is–Caiach. From 1256 the two commotes were controlled by Gruffydd ap Rhys, who had shifted his allegiance to Llywelyn from Gilbert's father Earl Richard shortly after this date. There is no direct evidence that Gruffydd was engaged in any actions openly hostile to Gilbert, but on January 9, 1267, the earl suddenly raided the commotes and captured the chieftain, imprisoning him at Cardiff and later transporting him to Kilkenny castle in Ireland.[5] The timing of Gilbert's raid and the subsequent agreement with Llywelyn are significant. In November, 1266, two months before the capture of Gruffydd, he had recovered Glamor-

---

[3] Lloyd, *Hist. Wales*, II, 728–38, and above, Chapter III *passim*. The alliance in 1267 is mentioned in *Brut Hergest*, p. 259, *Peniarth*, p. 114.

[4] Above, p. 116.

[5] " Chronicle of the Thirteenth Century," p. 282. There is no mention of this in the two versions of the *Brut*.

gan and his other lordships, which had been in royal custody pending the settlement of the suit he had brought against his mother. Gilbert was obviously attempting to expand and consolidate his own position in Glamorgan after a long period of royal control, but the fate of the Disinherited still occupied his attentions, and this factor must have prompted him to seek some sort of accord with the prince. For his own part, Llywelyn, to judge from his later actions, was probably content to agree, for it gave him additional time to enlarge his own forces and begin preparations for an invasion of the newly conquered commote of Is-Caiach. In view of these circumstances, the " pact " between Earl Gilbert and Llywelyn ap Gruffydd described in the *Brut* should be regarded as a fragile and temporary armed truce.[6]

The truce was not designed to last, and in effect the terms of the Treaty of Montgomery assured that it would not. To Llywelyn, it appeared that the Treaty gave royal sanction to his claims over Senghenydd and Meisgyn, claims buttressed by the adherence of Hywel ap Maredudd, who was at his court from 1246 to at least 1277,[7] and now by the allegiance of the newly dispossessed chieftain, Gruffydd ap Rhys. Furthermore, Gilbert's control over Senghenydd was not complete despite his capture of Gruffydd. A commission dated September 29, 1267, to ensure the enforcement of the Treaty in South Wales provided that " the king's peace be observed to the said Llywelyn . . . as well within the lands of the earl of Gloucester as elsewhere in those parts." This statement indicates that the prince remained in *de facto* possession of considerable portions of northern Glamorgan, probably including the whole of Uwch–Caiach, and that the Crown, recognizing this fact, realized the dangers it involved.[8]

Llywelyn ap Gruffydd could now use the terms of the Treaty of Montgomery to appeal for support from the king in the matter of Gruffydd ap Rhys. In the fall he lodged a formal protest against Gilbert's actions, claiming Gruffydd as his *fidelis* and the two commotes of Senghenydd as subject to his own authority. Henry III, beset with numerous problems of this kind arising from

---

[6] *Close Rolls 1264–68*, p. 264; PRO, Curia Regis Roll Mich. 50–51 Henry III, KB 26/177 m. 13; *Brut Hergest*, p. 259, *Peniarth*, p. 114.
[7] *Brut Hergest*, p. 241, *Peniarth*, p. 107; *Littere Wallie*, pp. 44, 184–85.
[8] *Cal. Pat. Rolls 1266–72*, p. 114.

the Treaty, urged litigation to settle the dispute. On January 1, 1268, he answered the prince, stating that the question of Gruffydd's release should be determined in the royal courts. In fact, however, nothing seems to have been done. Gilbert also had grounds for his action in the royal grant of August 20, 1266, which had authorized him to hold any lands of the supporters of Llywelyn he could capture. It is not known whether the earl actually appealed to this grant, for there seems to be no mention of the affair in the contemporary judicial records. In any event, nothing further is heard of Gruffydd ap Rhys, and he undoubtedly languished in Kilkenny castle.[9]

Earl Gilbert's apparent success in keeping Gruffydd ap Rhys imprisoned did not, however, end the contention. Llywelyn still controlled northern Meisgyn and Uwch–Caiach, and the situation was further complicated in 1270 by the prince's claims to the allegiance of a certain Maredudd ap Rhys, who was probably a brother of Gruffydd and hence nominal successor to the chieftain as lord of Senghenydd.[10] Of more tangible importance was the fact that in April, 1268, Earl Gilbert began the construction of a great new castle at Caerphilly in Is–Caiach, designed to secure the commote and to improve his own military and territorial position by guarding the Rhymny valley and the approach to Cardiff. The building of Caerphilly, combined with Llywelyn's inability to secure the release of Gruffydd ap Rhys, finally produced open warfare. A brief but sharp encounter between the prince and Gilbert's Norman tenants in Glamorgan resulted in the deaths of a number of foot soldiers and the capture, among others, of Gilbert de Umphraville, son of the lord of Penmark.[11] In March, the Lord Edward had taken the lead in initiating discussions between Gilbert and Llywelyn, but the construction of Caerphilly and the subsequent warfare nullified his efforts. The royal government, however, continued to press for a settlement, and finally in September, 1268, a commission led by the bishop of Exeter

[9] *Close Rolls 1264–68*, p. 497; *Cal. Pat. Rolls 1258–66*, p. 674.

[10] *Close Rolls 1268–72*, p. 234. Sir John E. Lloyd, "Llywelyn ap Gruffydd and the Lordship of Glamorgan," *Archaeologia Cambrensis*, 6th ser., XIII (1913), 61, hazards no opinion as to this Maredudd ap Rhys. He is clearly not to be identified with the lord of Ystrad Tywi, but there is simply no further mention of him.

[11] "Chronicle of the Thirteenth Century," p. 282. Neither the exact date of the fighting nor the eventual fate of the captives is given.

got the two parties to agree to negotiations. Each named four arbiters. If they could not reach an accord, the matter would be referred to the king's court for final adjudication. In the meantime, Llywelyn was to retain control of the men and castles of northern Meisgyn and the commote of Uwch–Caiach.[12]

For the next eight months no progress was made, and it is probable that both parties merely wanted to use the time to consolidate their forces. On May 21, 1269, the king sent Edward to Montgomery on a general commission to hear grievances between the prince and the marchers.[13] Far from solving the dispute involving Earl Gilbert, Edward merely created further difficulties which embittered his own relations with the earl. In 1268–69, to round off his territories in the southern march, Gilbert acquired the lordship of Caerleon and its members. Caerleon, a part of the old Marshal lordship of Netherwent, had passed in 1246 to Agnes de Vescy and Maud de Kyme, daughters of Sibyl Marshal and William de Ferrers, earl of Derby (d. 1254). In 1268–69 Gilbert exchanged some estates in England with Maud and her third husband, Amaury de Rochechouart, in return for Caerleon manor. In a separate but probably simultaneous transaction, he purchased Agnes' share of the lordship.[14] By acquiring Caerleon, Gilbert extended his nominal overlordship over Maredudd ap Gruffydd, the grandson and successor of Morgan ap Hywel of Caerleon (d. 1248). Maredudd already held the commote of Machen in the lordship of Gwynllwg of Earl Gilbert, but he was also lord of Edelegan and Llefnydd bedelries, territories juridically dependent on Caerleon. Maredudd had previously allied himself with Llywelyn, and under Edward's sanction, he now gave formal homage at Montgomery to the prince. Earl Gilbert's acquisition of Caerleon, designed to establish a solid block of territory by linking the lordships of Gwynllwg and Usk,

[12] The agreement is printed in *Cartae de Glamorgan*, II, 693–94, and *Littere Wallie*, pp. 101–3. Gilbert's nominees were the former Montfortian leader John fitz John, John de Breuse or Braose, lord of Glasbury (near Brecon), Hervey de Borham, a former seneschal of Clare, and Master Roger de Leicester, papal chaplain. For Edward's earlier commission, see *Cartae de Glamorgan*, II, 636–37 (misdated 1267).

[13] *Foedera*, I, 479.

[14] *Close Rolls 1242–47*, p. 447; PRO, Chanc. Misc., C 47/9/20; *Feet of Fines for the County of Somerset 1196–1307*, ed. E. Green (Somerset Record Society, vol. VI, 1892), pp. 377–78; Brit. Mus., Add. MS 6041, fol. 78.

served instead to strengthen the influence of the prince of Wales in his dominions with the explicit approval of the royal government.[15]

Edward's action created additional friction between Earl Gilbert and himself. The two men were already at odds over other matters. At the end of October, 1268, Gilbert revived the family claims to Bristol, and was given permission to sue, but on condition that even if successful, Edward would still retain the town and castle and the earl would be compensated with lands of equal value elsewhere in England. These conditions must have been a source of great annoyance, and the situation was further aggravated by rumors that Edward was paying too much attention to Gilbert's wife, Alice de Lusignan. There was probably little truth to this latter story, but in any event Gilbert and Alice were formally separated shortly thereafter, in July, 1271.[16] The case involving Bristol only came *coram rege* in 1276, when Edward had succeeded his father as king. Earl Gilbert's claims were dismissed on the grounds that John and Henry III had had continuous seisin of the castle and town and that Gilbert's arguments were therefore without basis.[17] Finally, Gilbert was engaged in still another dispute in 1269, this one directly with King Henry. On May 4, Henry demanded the restoration of Wyke and the Isle of Portland in Dorset, which Earl Richard had obtained by exchange with the priory of St. Swithun's in 1258.[18] Gilbert defied the orders to surrender them. The case came before the justices at Westminster in October, 1269. The justices denied the validity of the letters and charter by which Richard had gained title to the estates, claiming that the king's acquiescence to the transactions

---

[15] *Cal. Pat. Rolls 1266–72*, p. 385. Maredudd also held the commote of Hirfryn in Cantref Bychan, Carmarthenshire. See Lloyd, *Hist. Wales*, II, 712–13 and note 113; *Brut Hergest*, p. 259, *Peniarth*, p. 115, and for Machen, Lloyd, *Hist. Wales*, and *Cartae de Glamorgan*, II, 651.

[16] For Bristol, see *Close Rolls 1268–72*, p. 7; *Cal. Pat. Rolls 1266–72*, p. 373. The rumors concerning Edward and Alice are reported in *The Chronicle of Bury St. Edmunds*, p. 45. The text of the separation is in PRO, Exchequer, KR Ecclesiastical Documents, E 135/7/1.

[17] The decision is printed from the Coram Rege roll in *Parliamentary Writs and Writs of Military Summons*, ed. Sir Francis Palgrave (Record Commission, 1827–34), I, 6.

[18] *Close Rolls 1268–72*, pp. 44–45, and for Earl Richard, *Cal. Pat. Rolls 1247–58*, pp. 640, 654; *Cal. Chart. Rolls 1257–1300*, p. 16.

was made "tempore inoportune." [19] Gilbert raised numerous objections to the suit, and managed to retain at least *de facto* control of the manors. The case was still pending in 1270, and Gilbert must have upheld his claims successfully. Edward I revived the affair in 1279, but the earl and his successors remained in control of the estates.[20]

This complex pattern of legal and personal quarrels threatened yet another matter, the projected crusade which the legate Otto-buono had first organized in 1267–68 as part of a general recon-ciliation following the end of the Barons' War. In June, 1268, Earl Gilbert agreed to accompany Edward on crusade,[21] but he now began to make difficulties on this score as well. He was obviously reluctant to go abroad while Llywelyn was threatening his Welsh lands, but the strained relations with Edward and Henry III also contributed to his recalcitrance. In October, 1269, dis-cussions were held with the envoys of the king of France, but must have proved fruitless, for the following February Gilbert and Edward crossed to Paris to put the matter before Louis. The king urged the earl to fulfill his vows for the sake of the enter-prise, but Gilbert refused to listen. He sailed home and returned to his Welsh estates.[22] The affair was turned over to Richard of Cornwall at the Easter parliament for arbitration, and an agree-ment was reached in May, 1270.[23] Edward was planning to sail in the late summer, and Gilbert was to follow six months later. King Henry would give him a warship and 8,000 marks toward his expenses if on his arrival in the Holy Land he co-operated with Edward; if he wished to act independently, he would receive only 2,000 marks. As surety for his departure Richard of Cornwall was to control the Clare castles of Tonbridge and Hanley until the earl was at sea. During Gilbert's absence the disputes with Llywelyn would be dealt with by the king " according to the

[19] PRO, Curia Regis Roll Michaelmas 53–54 Henry III, KB 26/191 m. 9.

[20] *Close Rolls 1268–72*, pp. 271, 292; *Cal. Inq. Post Mortem*, III, no. 371, V, no. 538; *Select Cases in the Court of King's Bench under Edward I*, ed. G. O. Sayles (Selden Society, vols. LV, LVII–LVIII, 1936–39), I, nos. 41–42. Henceforth cited as Sayles, *Select Cases*.

[21] Wykes, pp. 217–18.

[22] *Cal. Pat. Rolls 1266–72*, pp. 369, 410; Gervase of Canterbury, II, 249–50.

[23] See Wykes, pp. 228–33. The text is given in full in *Letters from Northern Registers*, ed. J. Raine (Rolls Series LXI, 1873), pp. 27–30, from the register of Walter Giffard, archbishop of York.

laws and customs of the march."[24] Violation of any of the terms would mean a fine of 20,000 marks and possible excommunication.[25]

Edward departed on August 20, 1270, but Gilbert never sailed. Various commissions had failed to bring peace on the march, and in the fall Llywelyn resumed open hostilities. On October 13 he seized and destroyed Caerphilly castle.[26] Earl Gilbert's crusading vow was forgotten. He did not surrender his English castles, and he was neither fined nor excommunicated. The entire matter was simply dropped, and the earl concentrated all his energies on defending his marcher lordships. He was apparently dissuaded from attacking Llywelyn in northern Meisgyn and Uwch–Caiach by Henry and the council, who sent out another commission; but he did seize Machen, Edelegan, and Llefnydd from the prince's ally, Maredudd ap Gruffydd. The precise sequence of events is somewhat uncertain. It was stated in an inquisition of 1278 that Gilbert dispossessed Maredudd "while (Edward) was in the Holy Land." Since Edward left England on August 20, 1270, and Maredudd died on either October 18 or December 13 of that year, the seizure of Machen, Edelegan, and Llefnydd must be dated between late August and mid-December 1270. In all likelihood it occurred in the fall, just after Llywelyn's attack on Caerphilly on October 13.[27]

Regardless of the exact date, the seizure allowed Gilbert to incorporate these territories into his personal demesne. At the same time he regained control over Is–Caiach and immediately began to rebuild Caerphilly. King Henry could not interfere with the construction of the stronghold, but he continued to call for a peaceful settlement of the dispute. Numerous commissions were

[24] *Letters from Northern Registers*, p. 29: "En droit del article des terres le cunte purprises par Lewelin en la Marche, diums ke pro ceo il sont ambedeus les homes le roy de Engleterre, ke le roy face droit a ambedeus les parties solum costumes e usages de la Marche si hastmement com leiu pora sans delay."

[25] On the award, see also Denholm-Young, *Richard of Cornwall*, pp. 146–47.

[26] *Brut Hergest*, p. 259, *Peniarth*, p. 115, mention the seizure; the destruction of the castle is recorded in "Chronicle of the Thirteenth Century," p. 282 (misdated 1269).

[27] *Cal. Inq. Post Mortem*, II, no. 289; *Brut Hergest*, p. 259, *Peniarth*, p. 115. For the commission, see *Foedera*, I, 486. The two versions of the *Brut* record different dates for Maredudd's death, and it cannot be determined which is correct. See *Brut Peniarth*, p. 213.

appointed in the spring and summer of 1271, but without effect. Llywelyn was again preparing to attack, and refused to heed the king's exhortations.[28] Earl Gilbert, however, offered to surrender the castle into royal custody. He probably did not wish to engage in full-scale warfare until it was completed, and it is also possible that he wanted to appear as the aggrieved party. In late October, 1271, the king sent Roger Longespee, bishop of Coventry–Lichfield, and Godfrey Giffard, bishop of Worcester, to take control of the castle and secure the withdrawal of Llywelyn's troops from the surrounding countryside. Arrangements were completed at the beginning of November.[29] But Gilbert immediately capitalized on the fact that Llywelyn had relaxed his guard. By a simple ruse, the earl soon regained control of the stronghold. According to a letter Henry wrote to his brother, Richard of Cornwall, sometime before February, 1272, Gilbert sent his constable of Cardiff with forty men to Caerphilly, ostensibly to make an inventory of the arms stored within the castle. When they were granted admission, they immediately seized the castle and forced the bishops' men to retire. The earl cloaked his action in a legalism which Henry was forced to accept, for on February 22 he wrote Llywelyn in a feeble effort to explain away the seizure.[30] Gilbert once again professed his willingness to surrender the castle at the Easter parliament, but in fact he never did.[31]

The matter had ended in Gilbert's favor, and work on the castle resumed. Caerphilly was rebuilt as a massive stone fortress with an intricate series of defenses. A great inner keep was erected on a mound of gravel, surrounded by a middle ward and a low curtain-wall. The structure was encircled by an artificial lake, and the only access was by causeways on the eastern and western fronts. Each approach was guarded by two separate works which comprised the outer ward, and which in turn were surrounded by moats. In all likelihood, however, the castle did not assume its final form in 1271–72. Some of its most impressive features, such as the spurred towers of the gatehouse on the eastern outer ward, probably date from the first quarter of the fourteenth

[28] *Cartae de Glamorgan*, II, 757–60; *Cal. Pat. Rolls 1266–72*, pp. 591, 596.
[29] The commission and the agreement between Llywelyn and the bishops are printed in *Cartae de Glamorgan*, II, 760–65.
[30] *Ibid.*, III, 888–89; *Royal Letters*, II, 342–43.
[31] *Royal Letters*, II, 343–44; *Close Rolls 1268–72*, p. 474.

century, when Hugh Despenser was lord of Glamorgan. It has often been assumed that the concentric features of Caerphilly served as the model for Edward I's great series of castles in northern Wales, but more recent investigation indicates that the concentricity was developed only gradually, and was probably inspired by Edward's example at Harlech, which was completed after 1286. At any rate, the castle as it stood in 1272 was a remarkable achievement, the greatest baronial stronghold yet built, and a symbol of the power of Gilbert de Clare in the march.[32]

Earl Gilbert had thus secured control of Is–Caiach, but Llywelyn still remained in possession of the rest of Senghenydd and large parts of Meisgyn. The basic cause of friction had not been settled. These circumstances drew the earl into closer alliance with Henry and the council, and in particular with the men Edward had named as the guardians for his English affairs, including Walter Giffard, archbishop of York, and Roger Mortimer.[33] The earl made his peace with the king,[34] who was dangerously ill at this time, and with Mortimer. He assumed an active role as a counselor and immediately after the king's death helped quell a disturbance in London occasioned by the election of an unpopular mayor.[35] On November 16, 1272, the day of Henry's death, Earl Gilbert was summoned to the old king's bedside. He swore to uphold the peace and guard the kingdom for Edward. On November 23 the bishops and magnates sent letters to Edward, who was in Sicily, informing him of his father's death and of

[32] A. J. Taylor, "Military Architecture," in *Medieval England*, new ed., ed. A. L. Poole (Oxford, 1958), I, 119; A. J. Taylor, "Building at Caerphilly in 1326," *Bulletin of the Board of Celtic Studies*, XIV (1950–52), 299–300; Peter Brieger, *English Art 1216–1307* (Oxford, 1957), pp. 262–64. A description of the castle, with plans and photographs, is contained in William Rees, *Caerphilly Castle* (Cardiff, 1937).

[33] Edward had also appointed Philip Basset, who died in October, 1271, and Richard of Cornwall, who died on April 2, 1272. *Foedera*, I, 484. Another appointee, Robert Walerand (d. February, 1273), had already been replaced by Robert Burnell, archdeacon of York, by February, 1272. *Cal. Pat. Rolls 1266–72*, p. 650.

[34] In May, 1272, Henry ordered the sheriff of Cambridge to raise £523 and let Gilbert have it "without fail." This sum was due Earl Gilbert for the third penny of the earldom of Gloucester and the Barton of Bristol; the king's action suggests an effort at reconciliation following the end of the dispute over Caerphilly. *Cal. Liberate Rolls 1267–72*, p. 215.

[35] *Close Rolls 1268–72*, p. 462; *Rot. Fin.*, II, 574; *Chronica Maiorum*, pp. 148–53.

his own accession. The same day the new king's peace was proclaimed throughout the realm. The solemn document was witnessed by Archbishop Giffard, Edmund, earl of Cornwall, and Gilbert, earl of Gloucester. The old feuds with Henry and his son were over.[36]

Edward I was absent from England for two more years. In the meantime Earl Gilbert co-operated with the regents, who included Archbishop Giffard, Edmund of Cornwall, Robert Burnell, and the new chancellor, Walter de Merton. Gilbert was on good terms with Edmund, who married his sister Margaret in October, 1272, and they occasionally acted together on routine matters of administration.[37] In the summer of 1274 he went overseas, probably to visit his Irish lordship of Kilkenny for the first time.[38] When Edward returned to England in August, 1274, the earl entertained him at Tonbridge castle, and in June, 1275, he went to France as the king's envoy to bring Gaston de Béarn, who was disputing Edward's rights in Gascony, back to Westminster for negotiations.[39]

The major problem confronting the regents for Edward I was the sudden intransigence of Llywelyn ap Gruffydd. Prior to Henry's death, the relations between the prince and the English government seem to have been cordial. Llywelyn had performed homage and fealty to Henry, and regularly paid the installments on the fine of 25,000 marks set by the Treaty of Montgomery for his privileges. In addition, he had been allowed to purchase the homage of Maredudd ap Rhys of Ystrad Tywi in 1270.[40] After 1272, however, his attitude changed. He refused to give fealty to the new king in January 1273 and began to default on his payments.[41] The continued friction in the march largely accounts for his behavior. Roger Mortimer had begun to rebuild the castle of Cefnllys in Maelienydd, the lordship to which Llywelyn laid claims in 1267.[42] Moreover, Humphrey de Bohun,

[36] Foedera, I, 497; Chronica Maiorum, p. 155.
[37] E.g. Cal. Close Rolls 1272–79, p. 9.
[38] Cal. Pat. Rolls 1272–81, pp. 48, 53.
[39] Flores Hist., III, 43; Cal. Pat. Rolls 1272–81, p. 94; Gervase of Canterbury, II, 280. On the dispute, see Powicke, Thirteenth Century, pp. 284–87.
[40] For the payments before 1273, see Littere Wallie, pp. 140–53 passim, and Introduction, p. li, note.
[41] Foedera, I, 498, 505; Cal. Pat. Rolls 1272–81, p. 72.
[42] Cal. Anc. Correspondence, Wales, p. 94.

grandson of the earl of Hereford and son of the Montfortian leader captured at Evesham, was able to retake his lordship of Brecknock from the prince. Gilbert de Clare, who had nominally held Brecknock in custody since 1265, surrendered it to Humphrey when the latter came of age in the fall of 1270.[43] Humphrey managed to recapture large areas in Brecknock from Llywelyn in 1272–73, and two years later, when he succeeded his grandfather in the earldom, he had evidently reconquered almost the entire lordship.[44]

Of greater importance from the point of view of this study, Gilbert de Clare was also strengthening his position at Llywelyn's expense. He had already taken Is–Caiach in Senghenydd from Gruffydd ap Rhys in 1267, and Machen in Gwynllwg and the Caerleon lordships of Edelegan and Llefnydd from Maredudd ap Gruffydd in 1270;[45] he was now able to take advantage of Llywelyn's preoccupation with Humphrey de Bohun and Brecknock to reassert his authority in northern Meisgyn and Uwch–Caiach as well. In the fall of 1272, Llywelyn complained to Henry III of " excesses and transgressions " committed against him by both Humphrey and Gilbert. In February, 1274, he wrote King Edward, who was in Gascony, that he would pay the next installment only when and if Edward compelled " the earl of Gloucester, Humphrey de Bohun, and the rest of the marchers to restore the lands by them unjustly occupied and more unjustly detained." The references to Earl Gilbert indicate that between these dates he recaptured all the lands in northern Glamorgan to which Llywelyn had laid claim in one form or another ever since 1256. There is no specific mention of Gruffydd ap Rhys or Maredudd ap Gruffydd and his lordships in Gwynllwg and Caerleon, and since Meisgyn and Uwch–Caiach bordered directly on Brecknock, it seems clear that by 1274 the Red Earl had succeeded in taking control of these latter territories.[46]

[43] *Close Rolls 1268–72*, pp. 205–6.
[44] *Cal. Anc. Corr., Wales*, pp. 57–58, 109–10; *Cal. Pat. Rolls 1272–81*, pp. 116–17; Lloyd, *Hist. Wales*, II, 751–52; William Rees, " The Medieval Lordship of Brecon," *Transactions of the Honourable Society of Cymmrodorion* (Session 1915–16), pp. 197–99.
[45] In 1278, Maredudd's son Morgan brought suit against the earl for these lands, but by an error in procedure the case was dismissed in Gilbert's favor. *The Welsh Assize Roll*, pp. 268, 276.
[46] Henry III's reply to Llywelyn, dated October 30, 1272, is in *Cartae de*

Thus in the period 1267–74, Earl Gilbert the Red completed that process of territorial integration undertaken by his father Earl Richard. A few Welsh families, such as the descendants of Gruffydd ap Rhys in Senghenydd, continued to hold small and scattered properties in their ancient patrimonies. The only chieftains of any importance still retaining substantial commotal lands in the later thirteenth century were the lords of Afan, the descendants of Morgan Gam. But they had already accommodated themselves to Norman overlordship, and in 1276 Morgan Fychan (d. 1288), who had succeeded his brother Lleision as lord of Afan, moved directly into the circle of the Norman tenantry by marrying a daughter of Walter de Sully. Morgan Fychan and his descendants adopted the Normanized surname " de Avene " and rapidly became indistinguishable from the Anglo–Norman aristocracy within the lordship.[47] Henceforth the power of the old commotal lords was permanently broken, and the danger of their forming effective alliances with the house of Gwynedd ended. The personal demesne of the Clares as lords of Glamorgan was far greater than that of their twelfth century predecessors, and both the Welsh and Anglo–Norman tenantry were subject to a centralized and well-organized administrative bureaucracy, whose structure can be clearly discerned in the late thirteenth- and early fourteenth-century sources which have survived. The process, in short, involved much more than a mere continuation of the policies and activities of Robert fitz Hamon and the twelfth-century earls of Gloucester. In the thirteenth century, the Clares undertook and successfully completed the second Norman conquest of Glamorgan.[48]

The Welsh Wars

In 1274, Llywelyn ap Gruffydd was forced to abandon his *de facto* gains in Glamorgan and Brecknock. Their loss signaled the beginning of a process which ended in the extinction of Welsh

---

Glamorgan, III, 765–67. The letter to Edward I is in *Cal. Anc. Corr., Wales*, pp. 92–93.

[47] PRO, Chanc. Misc., C 47/9/24; *Cartae de Glamorgan*, III, 923–24, 1052, 1055; " Chronicle of the Thirteenth Century," p. 282.

[48] Cf. Smith, " The Lordship of Glamorgan," pp. 30–31, 37, and for the administration of the lordship, see below, Chapter VIII.

independence itself a decade later. The personal and political relations between the king of England and the prince of Wales deteriorated completely after Edward's return to England in August, 1274, and the actions of both men made full-scale warfare almost inevitable. Llywelyn refused to attend the coronation, and spurned repeated demands to pay homage to the king.[49] At the beginning of 1274, Llywelyn's brother Dafydd, along with Gruffydd ap Gwenwynwyn, lord of southern Powys, conspired to assassinate the prince and secure his dominions for themselves. The plot failed, but when Llywelyn overran Powys in December, both conspirators escaped to Edward's safekeeping.[50] By the fall of 1276, the situation had reached a breaking point, and it is quite likely that Edward, although not directly associated with the attempted assassination two years earlier, was deliberately trying to provoke open warfare. Llywelyn's position was grave. His relations with the marchers had steadily worsened, and the prince bitterly resented Edward's reception of Dafydd and Gruffydd ap Gwenwynwyn, as well as the fact that the king was also detaining Llywelyn's wife, Eleanor de Montfort.[51] Under these circumstances Llywelyn understandably refused to pay homage and fealty to Edward and in October demanded an immediate redress of all grievances.[52] Edward's response this time was to prepare for war. He had the support of a united baronage, and a number of marchers were quick to take advantage of the formal declarations of hostilities to regain lands still held by Llywelyn.[53] On December 12, 1276, Edward, having ordered troops raised from the shires, issued writs for a formal feudal levy to gather at Worcester on July 1 following.[54]

In less than a year the military operation was complete. Even before the gathering of the feudal host, Edward invaded southern Wales. In April, 1277, Rhys ap Maredudd, who had succeeded

---

[49] *Littere Wallie*, Introduction, p. lvi and references.

[50] *Ibid.*, pp. liii–lv, and Lloyd, *Hist. Wales*, II, 748–50.

[51] See Lloyd, *ibid.*, II, 755–57. Eleanor was Earl Simon's sister.

[52] Cf. his letter to Pope Gregory X in September, 1275: *Littere Wallie*, pp. 114–16; *Foedera*, I, 528.

[53] Lloyd, *Hist. Wales*, II, 758, who mentions Ralph Tony, lord of Elfael, which lay between Maelienydd and Brecknock; Peter Corbet, lord of Gorddwr on the Shropshire march, and Earl Humphrey de Bohun in the westernmost areas of Brecknock.

[54] *Parl. Writs*, I, 193–95.

his father as lord of Ystrad Tywi in 1271, surrendered, and the other chieftains quickly followed suit. Gruffydd ap Gwenwynwyn was restored in Powys, and Llywelyn was completely cut off from his supporters in southern Wales.[55] In July Edward moved with the main army to Chester and began what amounted to a siege of Llywelyn in Gwynedd. A fleet from the Cinque Ports secured Anglesey and cut off Llywelyn's supplies, and in November, 1277, the prince was forced to capitulate.[56]

On November 9 a treaty was signed at Conway.[57] Edward was not bent on a full conquest of Wales, but he imposed harsh terms. Llywelyn was allowed to retain the title of prince of Wales, but was shorn of all his territories in central and southern Wales, and was left with only Gwynedd west of the Conway River (modern Caernarvon and Merioneth). Two of the Four Cantreds of eastern Gwynedd (in modern Denbigh and Flint) were given to his brother Dafydd, while the others were annexed to the Crown. Cardigan and Carmarthen were reorganized as royal shires and placed under the jurisdiction of a justiciar of West Wales in 1280. In addition, Llywelyn lost the right to suzerainty over the Welsh chieftains except for a few minor instances and at Christmas was finally forced to pay his long-deferred homage to the king.[58]

Gilbert de Clare's activities in the campaign of 1277 were not especially remarkable. He seems to have accompanied the king in the expedition against Llywelyn in northern Wales, but there is almost nothing in the chronicles or the government records to indicate the actual part he played in military operations. Edward I was so thoroughly the master of the situation that the earl could not play the decisive role he had assumed at the time of the Barons' War. Moreover, the effectiveness and importance of the normal feudal levy had steadily diminished in the thirteenth century due to the reduction in the quotas proffered by the military tenants-in-chief.[59] By the beginning of the century the Crown had come

[55] Lloyd, Hist. Wales, II, 758.

[56] The campaign is described in detail in John E. Morris, The Welsh Wars of Edward I (Oxford, 1901), pp. 126–41.

[57] Text in Foedera, I, 545.

[58] Lloyd, Hist. Wales, II, 759–60.

[59] On this whole question, see I. J. Sanders, Feudal Military Service in England (Oxford, 1956), pp. 50–91; Michael Powicke, Military Obligation in Medieval England (Oxford, 1962), pp. 63–81.

to accept small contingents from the magnates, and the cavalry raised by Edward in 1277 was found to be wholly inadequate for the prolonged campaigns and tactical operations necessitated by conditions in northern Wales. Under these circumstances Edward placed increasing reliance on paid squadrons of infantry and household knights. Building upon changes introduced and fostered by Henry III, he recruited contingents of foot soldiers, archers, and workmen, not only from the English shires and Crown properties in Wales, but from the marcher lordships, including Glamorgan, as well.[60] He utilized his household troops as the core of a standing army, serving under wages. While Earl Gilbert and the men under his command served beyond the normal forty-day period, without pay, lesser barons were recruited into paid squadrons when their traditional period of service had expired.[61] The development of a system of paid troops (as distinct from mercenaries) and the combination of infantry and cavalry in open battle, while only perfected in campaigns subsequent to 1277, were the chief factors in the strength of the Edwardian army; but of equal importance, Edward had those qualities of military ability and leadership Henry III had lacked.[62]

The organization of the force raised by the normal feudal levy has been analyzed in detail by Morris.[63] Earl Gilbert was charged with scutage on more than 450 fees, but he proffered the service of only ten knights for his English estates, and there is little evidence as to the identity of his soldiers.[64] In July, 1277, two knights, Philip de Colevill and Richard de Grenvill, are stated to have gone to Wales on the king's service in Gilbert's contingent.[65] Colevill, who went on crusade with Edward in 1270, may have been related to Walter de Colevill, a member of Gilbert's

[60] Morris, *Welsh Wars*, pp. 92–95.

[61] *Ibid.*, pp. 68–70, 84–86.

[62] Cf. the remarks of Morris, *ibid.*, pp. 68, 104–5, and Powicke, *Military Obligation*, pp. 96–133 *passim*.

[63] Morris, *Welsh Wars*, pp. 35–66.

[64] *Parl. Writs*, I, 198; Morris, *Welsh Wars*, p. 39; PRO, Exchequer, LTR Miscellanea, E 370/1/14 mm. 1, 1d., 3, 5d. (extracts from the Pipe Rolls of 7 Edward I and 15 Edward II relating to scutage exacted for the campaigns of 1277 and 1282). In 1218 and 1229 Gilbert's grandfather, the first Clare earl of Gloucester, had led contingents of twenty knights. PRO, Chancery, Scutage Roll 2–15 Henry III, C 72/2 mm. 21, 22, printed in Sanders, *Feudal Service*, pp. 111, 121.

[65] *Cal. Pat. Rolls 1272–81*, pp. 220, 221.

familia in 1267. Grenvill held Kilkhampton manor in Cornwall and lands in Devon of the earl for 4 ½ fees.[66] Neither appears on the muster roll for the campaign as an independent tenant-in-chief, although Grenvill was summoned in 1282 for service in southern Wales.[67] The names of the other eight knights are unknown. In addition, Earl Gilbert may have had under him a force composed of his own tenants in Glamorgan, whose service, since it was not owed to the Crown, would not be recorded in the government records.

An important, although not new, feature of the organization of the feudal host in 1277 was the appearance of barons serving in the retinue (*comitiva*) of other great lords. A number of tenants-in-chief served, apparently without pay, under the earl of Gloucester. John de Horbury, lord of one-ninth of the barony of Beauchamp in Bedford, and John de Bosco, who acknowledged the service of one-half fee for lands in Suffolk, went to Wales with Earl Gilbert.[68] There is no evidence that those men had any close connections with Gilbert in other respects, although Bosco must have been related to a certain William de Bosco, who held the manor and hundred of Halberton in Devon of the earl.[69] In addition, the retinue included Baldwin Wake, lord of the baronies of Bourne, Cottingham and Liddel, and a former leader of the Disinherited. Baldwin, who proffered the service of four knights for his baronies and also recognized the service of one-fifth of a knight's fee for the properties which he had inherited from William de Briwerre, stated that he was " de familia Comitis Gloucestriae. Et supplicat Regi quod possit facere servicium in ii. quarentena." [70] It seems likely that Baldwin performed the service demanded for his lands by serving with three other knights in Earl Gilbert's *comitiva* for the first forty days of the campaign, and then discharged his fractional service by remaining with the

[66] *Ibid. 1266–72*, pp. 146, 480; *Cal. Inq. Post Mortem*, III, no. 371 (p. 250).

[67] *Parl. Writs*, I, 244. He was also summoned for the Gascon expedition in 1297 and the Scottish campaign of 1301 under the new conditions of distraint of knighthood imposed by Edward I. *Ibid.*, I, 214, 285, 351.

[68] *Cal. Pat. Rolls 1272–81*, pp. 220, 221; *Parl. Writs*, I, 203; Sanders, *English Baronies*, p. 11.

[69] *Cal. Inq. Post Mortem*, III, no. 371 (p. 235).

[70] *Parl. Writs*, I, 200. For his lands, see Sanders, *English Baronies*, pp. 37, 107–8, 123, 129. He was Horbury's father-in-law. *Ibid.*, p. 11.

earl for at least part of the second forty-day period.[71] Some other instances of men serving in the company of another baron can be found in the campaign, and the practice became more widespread in subsequent wars. It was probably encouraged by Edward I for the purpose of improving organization and discipline, and royal license seems to have been required to enter into such an arrangement. Combined, however, with a series of detailed contractual agreements and a scale of wages, the practice could easily have served as a basis for the development of the system of indentured retainers.[72] The most important aspects of Gilbert's participation in the war of 1277, then, lie in the fact that they illustrate some of the major modifications introduced into the structure of the army in the later thirteenth century.

In 1282 warfare erupted again.[73] The truce was broken by the treacherous behavior of Dafydd, who on March 21 seized the castle of Hawarden on the Dee by a surprise attack and laid siege to Edward's newly constructed castles of Flint and Rhuddlan. His action touched off a widespread revolt in central and south-western Wales. The Welsh chieftains, with the important exception of Rhys ap Maredudd, joined the revolt, and by June Llewelyn, who was reconciled to his brother, had also renewed hostilities in Carmarthen. On March 25 King Edward appointed commanders in Wales to direct operations until a full levy could be summoned. On April 10 the king named Gilbert de Clare captain in southern Wales, and on May 24 summoned a formal feudal host to meet at Rhuddlan on August 2.[74] In the meantime, squadrons of paid cavalry and household knights were gathered under the various captains.[75] At the end of April a paid force of 96 men was put at Gilbert's disposal. He may have brought a considerable troop

[71] For the baronies, Baldwin proffered the service of himself, his brother Hugh, Gerard de Insula, and John de Rippinghale. On July 1, 1277, Rippinghale is noted as going to Wales in Wake's train. Insula seems to have served directly with the king, and his place was taken by Robert de Willoughby and Simon Basset. Cal. Pat. Rolls 1272–81, pp. 217, 220, 221. Cf. Morris, Welsh Wars, p. 70.

[72] On this point see Morris, Welsh Wars, pp. 70–71, and Sanders, Feudal Service, pp. 94–95. For an indenture of 1297 between two Clare tenants in Wales, see below, pp. 279–80.

[73] For the underlying causes, see Morris, Welsh Wars, pp. 149–53, and Edwards, Littere Wallie, Introduction, pp. lxi–lxix.

[74] Parl. Writs, I, 222, 224, 225–27. Gilbert replaced the original captain, Robert de Tibetot, justiciar of West Wales, who had been appointed on March 25.

[75] Morris, Welsh Wars, pp. 155–56, 158–63, for details.

of unpaid knights from his Welsh estates as well, but no mention of them is contained in the documents. The force was strengthened by levies of foot from the march and cavalry contingents from William de Valence, lord of Pembroke, his son William, other marchers such as Patrick de Chaworth, lord of Kidwelly, and Rhys ap Maredudd.[76] A contingent of 300 footmen was raised by Reginald fitz Peter, lord of Blaenllyfni (adjacent to Brecknock) and put under Earl Gilbert's command. Footmen were also raised from Hereford and the Forest of Dean at the beginning of June.[77] Gilbert was to pacify Carmarthen and bring the English settlers in that area to Llanbadarn near Aberystwyth for safe-keeping. In addition the king granted John Giffard of Brimps-field the castle of Llandovery, which had belonged to the rebellious Welsh chieftain Rhys Fychan, and ordered Gilbert to conquer it for him.[78]

Earl Gilbert's preliminary campaigns seem to have met with little success, and on June 17 his force was surprised by the Welsh at Llandeilo Fawr, a small outpost on the Tywi about a mile from Dinefwr castle. The English were completely routed. William de Valence the younger was killed, and the troops led by Reginald fitz Peter deserted. Llywelyn took advantage of the English defeat to overrun Carmarthen and penetrate into Cardigan. On July 2, Edward ordered the tenants-in-chief of southwestern England to concentrate in southern Wales instead of coming to Rhuddlan, and four days later appointed the elder William de Valence as captain of the force in place of Earl Gilbert. The earl seems to have been thoroughly discredited by his defeat, and retired to defend his Glamorgan estates.[79]

The force led by Valence was soon able to reassert its power in southern and southwestern Wales. Valence and Robert Tibetot recovered Cardigan and Carmarthen, and to the east Humphrey de Bohun quelled uprisings in his lordship of Brecknock, while

[76] Morris, Welsh Wars, pp. 163–64. Chaworth also held Ogmore in Glamorgan of Earl Gilbert.

[77] Cal. Anc. Corr., Wales, pp. 116–17; Calendar of Welsh Rolls 1277–1294, in Calendar of Chancery Rolls, Various, 1277–1326 (H. M. Stationery Office, 1912), p. 251.

[78] Cal. Welsh Rolls, pp. 213–14, 221–22.

[79] Annales Cambriae, p. 106; Cal. Anc. Corr., Wales, p. 114; Rishanger, Chronica, p. 100; Parl. Writs, I, 227, 244; Morris, Welsh Wars, pp. 166–67.

Roger L'Estrange secured Builth and Roger Mortimer subdued Radnor and the upper Severn area. By October the southern and central parts of Wales had been rewon by the English, and Edward was able to concentrate his forces on Gwynedd.[80] The main offensive followed the same lines as the first campaign of 1277. Edward marched inland from Rhuddlan and quickly secured eastern Gwynedd. In mid-October the Four Cantreds and lands to the south were granted as marcher lordships to a few magnates who had served the king well: John de Warenne, earl of Surrey, Henry de Lacy, earl of Lincoln, and Reginald Grey, justiciar of Chester.[81] The Welsh, however, were not completely subdued. They secured Anglesey, and Llywelyn went south in an attempt to rally his followers in Brecknock and Builth. On December 11 the prince was intercepted unattended at Orewin bridge and slain.[82] Llywelyn's death was a military and psychological blow from which his followers were unable to recover. Edward, sensing this fact, pressed his advantage hard, calling up crossbowmen and mercenaries from Gascony to complement his paid force. He marched into the mountainous areas of Snowdonia in western Gwynedd, conducting a campaign throughout the winter of 1282–83 to starve Dafydd ap Gruffydd into submission. Finally in June, 1283, Dafydd was captured, taken to Shrewsbury at Michaelmas, tried as a traitor and hanged. The great dynasty of Gwynedd was destroyed.[83]

The role played by Gilbert de Clare in the campaign of 1282–83 is obscure. He proffered ten knights for the muster at Rhuddlan, but does not seem to have served in person before the death of Llywelyn.[84] At least four tenants-in-chief, however, Richard fitz John, John de Bosco, John de St. John, and Thomas de Berkeley, are stated to have served in his *comitiva*, probably for an eighty-day period beginning August 2, 1282.[85] Earl Gilbert does not

[80] Full details are given in Morris, *Welsh Wars*, pp. 168–73.
[81] *Cal. Welsh Rolls*, pp. 240, 241, 243; *Cal. Chart. Rolls 1257–1300*, p. 262.
[82] For the story of his death, see Morris, *Welsh Wars*, pp. 182–83, 306–8, and Lloyd, *Hist. Wales*, II, 763.
[83] Morris, *Welsh Wars*, pp. 184–95.
[84] *Parl. Writs*, I, 236. His proffer was marked on the muster roll with the notation "respicuatur."
[85] *Ibid.*, I, 231, 234, 242; *Cal. Anc. Corr., Wales*, p. 115. Bosco was the same man who served under Gilbert in 1277. Fitz John (brother of the Montfortian leader John fitz John), who was in the earl's contingent "de licencia regis,"

appear as a witness to the charters by which Edward created the marcher lordships for Warenne, Lacy, and Grey in October, and since Llywelyn was threatening Brecknock in the fall of 1282, it is probable that the earl remained in Glamorgan whence he had retired after his defeat at Llandeilo in June. After Llywelyn's death, however, he brought his contingent to Edward's army. In January, 1283, he was with the king at the siege of Dolwyddelan, and in February witnessed royal charters issued at Rhuddlan.[86] On March 14 he and the other tenants-in-chief were again summoned to gather their forces at Montgomery on May 2,[87] and the earl appears as a witness to charters issued on May 10 and 26.[88] On June 30 he was ordered to appear at Shrewsbury at Michaelmas to give counsel to the king concerning Dafydd, and on November 18 witnessed the king's charter at Hereford by which John Giffard was given the commote of Isgenen in Cantref Bychan.[89]

Gilbert seems to have been on good terms with Edward in the ensuing period of peace. On March 19, 1284, the king issued the Statute of Wales, by which Gwynedd was annexed to the Crown and reorganized into the royal shires of Anglesey, Caernarvon and Merioneth.[90] The king then made a tour of his new dominions, and visited Cardigan and Carmarthen in November. In December he passed over into Glamorgan where he was received by Earl Gilbert "cum honore maximo." The earl then conducted him at his own expense to Bristol, where the two men celebrated Christmas.[91] In May 1286 Edward went overseas to do

held lands in chief in Wilts and Bucks. He also held the manor of Shalford, Surrey, of the honor of Tonbridge, and the Barony of Islands in Thomond of Thomas de Clare. *Cal. Inq. Post Mortem*, III, nos. 422, 507. Earl Gilbert held the manor of Corhampton of St. John, who was lord of the barony of Basing, Hants. *Cal. Inq. Post Mortem*, III, no. 371 (p. 235); Sanders, *English Baronies*, p. 9. For Berkeley, see Sanders, *ibid.*, p. 13.

[86] *Parl. Writs*, I, 12; Morris, *Welsh Wars*, p. 190; *Cal. Welsh Rolls*, pp. 264, 265.

[87] *Parl. Writs*, I, 246.

[88] *Cal. Welsh Rolls*, pp. 271, 272; *Cal. Chart. Rolls 1257–1300*, p. 266.

[89] *Parl. Writs*, I, 15; *Cal. Welsh Rolls*, p. 283.

[90] The introduction of English law and administration into this area as a result of the Statute is best discussed in W. H. Waters, *The Edwardian Settlement of North Wales* (Cardiff, 1935). For a summary, see Powicke, *Thirteenth Century*, pp. 435–38.

[91] Rishanger, *Chronica*, p. 107. Edward was at Cardiff on December 15 (*Cal. Close Rolls 1279–88*, p. 345), and Gilbert appears as a witness to a charter issued at Bristol on December 27 (*Cal. Welsh Rolls*, p. 297).

homage to Philip IV and attend to affairs in Gascony, leaving his cousin Edmund of Cornwall as regent. Earl Gilbert was among those accompanying the king to France, and was with him in July. Gilbert seems to have returned to England by the end of October, while Edward went on to Gascony where he stayed until 1289.[92]

During the king's absence, a new revolt, led by Rhys ap Mare-dudd, lord of Ystrad Tywi, erupted in Wales. Rhys, who had remained loyal to Edward in 1282–83, was engaged in a bitter dispute with John Giffard over Isgenen, which had been granted Giffard in 1283. In the spring of 1287 Rhys was summoned to the county court of Carmarthen by the justiciar, Robert Tibetot, and when he failed to appear, was outlawed.[93] On June 8, he opened hostilities by overrunning Isgenen and seizing Dinefwr and Llandovery castles. The regent summoned the Crown tenants to gather at Gloucester on July 21, and in the meantime appointed various commanders to raise levies of foot soldiers from Wales and the adjoining English shires.[94] Edmund of Cornwall assumed command of the entire force and a siege of Dryslwyn was begun in late August. The castle was taken in early September, and by the end of the month the lands overrun by Rhys had been pacified. According to Wykes, a truce was then arranged by Gilbert and some other prominent marchers (unnamed), who supposedly sympathized with Rhys' resistance to the use of English common law procedure as a means of settling territorial disputes. At any rate, the army was disbanded.[95] Fighting broke out again in November, but the insurrection was quickly put down by Tibetot, and Rhys was forced to flee. It was rumored that Gilbert offered him refuge in Kilkenny, but nothing is known of his whereabouts until 1292, when he was finally captured and hanged.[96]

[92] Gilbert witnessed charters at Dover on May 13 and at Paris on July 1 and July 26. He does not appear as a witness to a charter issued by the king at Libourne, near Bordeaux, on October 23. *Cal. Chart. Rolls 1427–1516*, Appendix (1215–88), pp. 291, 292.

[93] Morris, *Welsh Wars*, pp. 205–6; *Cal. Welsh Rolls*, p. 306.

[94] *Parl. Writs*, I, 250–52.

[95] Wykes, pp. 310, 311; Morris, *Welsh Wars*, pp. 212–13. The marchers' actions, however, may have been based on personal relationships. See note 96.

[96] Wykes, p. 311; *Brut Peniarth*, p. 121; Morris, *Welsh Wars*, pp. 213–18. Rhys had important marriage ties with some of the marchers. His uncle had married one of the daughters of William de Braose (d. 1230). He himself was married to the sister of John de Hastings, and through his mother was related to the Earl Warenne and Roger Bigod, earl of Norfolk and lord of Striguil. Cf.

The interest of the campaign lies chiefly in the remarkable speed and ease with which great numbers of cavalry and foot were raised and deployed. The methods employed by Edward I in the wars of 1277 and 1282 were applied on an even broader scale, and provided the key to the overwhelming strength and superiority displayed by the royal forces. By August, 1287, Cornwall had under his command some 11,000 foot, most of them Welsh, and 500 paid knights composed of the contingents brought up by the tenants-in-chief.[97] No attempt was made to exact the feudal *servitium debitum* from the Crown tenants; such troops as they brought up were organized into paid units led by the earls or other prominent captains. There is no evidence that the personal retinues of the earls of Gloucester and Hereford or of Cornwall himself were paid, but the other earls and lesser barons received wages, as did the foot soldiers and workmen recruited from the marcher lordships.[98]

These changes are clearly reflected in Earl Gilbert's operations during the campaign. Rhys' uprising had touched off revolts in the Bohun lordship of Brecknock, and on July 23 Gilbert was appointed captain of that area to subdue the uprising and clear the path for Cornwall's army, which was marching from Hereford to Dryslwyn. Gilbert raised over 5,000 footmen from Glamorgan alone, and the forces brought by the other marcher lords of the area and put under his command brought the total to 12,500. By the end of August, the force, which was put on the payroll at the beginning of the month, had completed its work, and was disbanded.[99] The marchers were able to join Cornwall at Dryslwyn with unpaid contingents of cavalry drawn from their mesne tenants, but Earl Gilbert also brought up a force of 3,500 paid foot

---

Cal. Anc. Corr., Wales, pp. 138–39, and the genealogical table in Lloyd, *Hist. Wales,* II, 768. Rhys was also related to the Clares through his grandfather, Rhys Gryg. See above, pp. 30–31, and cf. *Cal. Anc. Corr., Wales,* p. 139.

[97] Morris, *Welsh Wars,* pp. 208–9.

[98] Morris estimates that the unpaid units amounted to no more than 200 knights. *Ibid.,* p. 210.

[99] *Parl. Writs,* I, 252; Morris, *Welsh Wars,* pp. 211–12. Edmund de Mortimer of Wigmore raised 3,000 foot, John de Hastings of Abergavenny 600, John Giffard of Builth 800, Ralph Tony of Elfael 360, John fitz Reginald (son of Reginald fitz Peter) of Blaenllyfni 300, and Humphrey de Bohun 2,000 from Brecknock and Hay.

from his Welsh estates to aid in the siege.[100] Earl Gilbert's activities in the campaign of 1287 thus reveal, to an even more striking degree than his role in the first two Welsh wars, the extent to which the Crown had profoundly modified the traditional structure of military service by developing the system of a national levy recruited from the shires and liberties and serving with pay.

Trouble on the March

The Edwardian conquest and settlement of Wales brought into sharp focus another matter of the greatest importance, that of the relation between the Crown and the lords of the march themselves. From the Welsh chieftains whom they displaced, the marchers had inherited and for two centuries successfully maintained powers and privileges not enjoyed by the other members of the baronage. Within their liberties they exercised an all-embracing jurisdiction, which had developed independently of English common law and which excluded the king's writ. Edward I proclaimed that a suit involving marcher lords who were also tenants-in-chief of the Crown could ultimately be appealed to the king as feudal over-lord; [101] but the " custom of the march," based on an amalgamation of Norman and Welsh tribal law, recognized the prior right of the marchers to try disputes by friendly agreement among themselves, at a " day of the march," a point eloquently argued by Gilbert de Clare in 1291.[102] The most distinctive and cherished

---

[100] Morris, *Welsh Wars*, p. 213. Gilbert's soldiers included Philip de Colevill, who had served with him in 1277; Nicholas de la Huse, who held lands in chief in Wiltshire and Gloucestershire; and John Bigod, brother of the earl of Norfolk. *Cal. Pat. Rolls 1281–92*, pp. 269, 272.

[101] That the case could in the last resort be appealed to the king was laid down in 1275 by the Statute of Westminster I, c. 17: if disputes arose " in the marches of Wales, or any other place where the lord king's writ does not run, then the king, who is sovereign lord over all, shall do right therein unto all such as will complain." *Statutes of the Realm*, ed. A. Luders *et al.* (Record Commission, 1810–28), I, 31. See also T. F. T. Plucknett, *Legislation of Edward I* (Oxford, 1949), p. 30; Otway-Ruthven, " The Great Lordships of South Wales," pp. 11–12.

[102] He maintained " quod consuetudo Wallie diu optenta talis est quod in casibus ubi contentiones emerserunt inter magnates Wallie qui tenent de rege in capite, quod antequam querela fiat in curia Regis de predictis contencionibus, capi debet quidam dies amoris sivi parliamenti quidem dies vocatur dies marchie et ibi per vicinos et amicos communes qui sunt quasi justiciarii debent hujusmodi querele

feature of marcher law, however, was the right of waging private war, without the intervention or direction of the Crown. It was this privilege which clearly differentiated them from the other members of the nobility, even the great earls palatine.[103] The Statute of Wales, issued in 1284, did not interfere with the existing structure of marcher law, and indeed in 1280 Edward I had expressly agreed that disputes in the march should be settled " according to the custom of those parts." [104] But the king clearly did not have in mind sanctioning the resort to arms. Private war was, in his view, an anachronistic relic of a past age, and incompatible with the principle of the supremacy of legal process enunciated by Edward in his great series of statutes and judicial inquiries. He was not prepared to tolerate its continued usage. It was this position which led to the most spectacular incident of the first half of his reign, and which resulted in the trial and disgrace of two of the greatest magnates of the realm, Humphrey de Bohun, earl of Hereford and lord of Brecknock, and Gilbert de Clare, earl of Gloucester and lord of Glamorgan.[105]

Trouble had been brewing between the two men for some time. In 1265, Gilbert had been granted custody of Brecknock along with the right of Humphrey's marriage. When Humphrey came of age in 1270, the lordship was restored to him. At the same time he purchased his marriage from the earl for £1,000, which Gilbert claimed had not yet been paid in full by 1290. Moreover, Humphrey resented the fact that Gilbert had been put in charge of operations in Brecknock in the campaign of 1287.[106] But the

---

proponi et per consensum marchie emendantur. . . ." PRO, Coram Rege Roll Easter 19 Edward I, KB 27/127 m. 26d.

[103] This point is clearly brought out in Edwards, " The Normans and the Welsh March," p. 173.

[104] *The Welsh Assize Roll*, p. 309. Cf. the similar position taken by Henry III and Richard of Cornwall in the dispute between Gilbert and Llywelyn in 1270 (note 24, above).

[105] The entire case involving the earls was recorded in a parliament held at Westminster at Michaelmas term 19–20 Edward I, and is printed in *Rot. Parl.*, I, 70–77. Another copy is preserved in PRO, Welsh Roll 20 Edward I, C 77/5 mm. 3–5, and is calendared in *Cal. Welsh Rolls*, pp. 334–49. The best secondary account is that of Morris, *Welsh Wars*, pp. 224–37.

[106] *Cal. Pat. Rolls 1258–66*, p. 495; *Close Rolls 1268–72*, pp. 205–6; PRO, Coram Rege Rolls, Mich. 2–3 Edward I, KB 27/11 m. 11d.; Easter 18 Edward I, KB 27/123 m. 54; Trinity 18 Edward I, KB 27/124 m. 49; Morris, *Welsh Wars*, p. 223.

chief source of contention was a castle Gilbert was building at
Morlais on a tributary of the Taff in the ill-defined border area
between Brecknock and Uwch–Caiach in Senghenydd. The earl
undoubtedly intended Morlais to secure his power in the region
between Brecknock and Caerphilly, but Bohun claimed the disputed region was within his own boundaries, and protested to
the king. The castle is never mentioned by name in the judicial
records, but there can be no doubt that its construction was a
potential source of armed conflict between the two. On June 26,
1289, Edmund of Cornwall, acting in his capacity as regent, wrote
Earl Gilbert to suspend " until the king's arrival in England the
construction of a castle in the land of Brecknock (*Breghenowe*),"
for the king had learned from Humphrey that Gilbert, " having
collected an immense number of armed men, has begun to erect
a castle in the aforesaid land to Humphrey's disinheritance, and
that he keeps such armed men there." [107] The earl seems to have
disregarded the order. Prior efforts by Queen Eleanor [108] and
John Peckham, archbishop of Canterbury,[109] to resolve the dispute
peaceably had met with no success. The matter was up to the
king.

Edward I returned from Gascony in August, 1289, determined
to brook no truculence from Gilbert. On January 20, 1290, Bohun
formally appealed the earl for trespasses committed on the march,
but Gilbert failed to answer the summons to appear before the
court of King's Bench.[110] Five days later the king issued a proclamation forbidding private warfare in the march. Gilbert's response
was immediate and defiant. On February 3 some of his men,
displaying his banner, entered Brecknock, killed some of Bohun's
men and carried off livestock and other chattels, presumably back
to the new castle. Earl Gilbert was distinctly cognizant both before
and after the fact, and indeed he received a third part of the

---

[107] *Foedera*, I, 710, from the Close Roll (*Cal. Close Rolls 1288–96*, p. 47). Cf.
Dunstable, p. 370: hostilities had erupted " ratione cujusdam castri, quod comes
Gloverniae vi et armis fecerat in Marchia ad alterius comitis nocumentum."
[108] In February, 1289, Gilbert, at the request of the queen, appeared before the
king's council to confirm a deed stating that he had not broken the truce with
Humphrey, PRO, Parliamentary and Council Proceedings (Chancery), C 49/2/13.
But in fact he had.
[109] *Reg. Epist. Peckham*, III, 960–61 (June 4, 1289).
[110] PRO, Coram Rege Roll Hilary 18 Edward I, KB 27/122 m. 1.

booty, " according to the law and custom of the march." [111] This custom was an integral part of the right of waging private war, and had been taken over by the marchers from the Welsh princes they had displaced. The fact that the Red Earl received a third of the spoils is clear evidence that he had initiated and condoned the raid.[112]

A second incident occurred in early June, shortly after Gilbert had married the king's daughter, Joan of Acre, and a third in November, after a dispute over the earl's rights in the bishopric of Llandaff had been resolved in favor of the Crown. Morris has established that each raid was a premeditated act of defiance of the king.[113]

The marriage between Gilbert and Joan had long been planned and long delayed. Joan was Edward's second surviving daughter, born when her father was still on crusade in 1272. In 1276 Rudolf of Hapsburg, the German Emperor, had proposed a marriage between the girl and his son Hartmann. Negotiations were conducted in 1277 and 1278, but the whole project had to be abandoned when Hartmann was accidentally killed in December, 1281. In May, 1283, the king agreed to a marriage between his daughter and Earl Gilbert. The earl had been separated from Alice de Lusignan since 1271, but a formal annulment was now required, and the marriage was finally dissolved in May, 1285. The king and the earl still had to wait for a papal dispensation for the new marriage, and it was only forthcoming in November, 1289.[114] When the final arrangements were made, the king imposed conditions that must have caused Earl Gilbert considerable displeasure. By this time he had control of the entire inheritance, aside from the manors held by Alice de Lusignan and his brothers Bogo and Thomas. His mother, the dowager Countess Maud, had died the previous year, and on March 10, 1289, Gilbert received seisin of the third of the estates she had held in dower.[115] On April 17, 1290, he surrendered all his lands in England, Wales, and Ireland into the king's hands. The marriage was celebrated

---

[111] " Prout decet dominum tempore guerre habere, secundum usum et consuetudinem Marchie." *Rot. Parl.*, I, 71–72.
[112] See Edwards, " The Normans and the Welsh March," pp. 170–74.
[113] Morris, *Welsh Wars*, pp. 225–26.
[114] *Foedera*, I, 628–29, 654, 721.
[115] *Cal. Close Rolls 1288–96*, p. 6.

at the beginning of May, and on May 27 the estates were restored jointly to Gilbert and Joan for life. The inheritance was to pass to their heirs or, failing such heirs, to Joan's children by any subsequent marriage.[116] Although Gilbert had married into the royal family, he resented the restrictions placed on the descent of the estates by the new enfeoffment. In effect, he had only a life interest in his properties. If Joan were to die without issue, the king, not the earl, could dispose of the inheritance, since Gilbert's children by Alice de Lusignan were excluded. If the earl were to die without issue, and Joan were to have children by a second marriage, the estates would pass to them. In short, it was conceivable that Gilbert would have no control whatsoever over the descent of the inheritance. His fears were unfounded, as he and Joan were to have a son and heir and three daughters. But the earl could not have foreseen that. At the time of the marriage he was nearly fifty, and there was no guarantee that he would have children by his new wife. There can be no doubt that he did not envisage such restrictions when the marriage was first proposed in 1283. In certain important respects, therefore, the marriage was less an increase in his prestige than a reduction of it.[117] It seems likely that the earl's sense of independence was aroused, and he showed his displeasure by staging a second raid in Brecknock, this one on June 5. Again the earl received a third share of the booty and was clearly guilty after the fact.[118]

The third raid occurred in November. Gilbert was involved in a suit with the king over the right of custody of temporalities in the bishopric of Llandaff and the collation to dignities and prebends *sede vacante.* Such powers had long been enjoyed by the lords of Glamorgan, but the king was determined to eliminate them. On October 23 the earl was forced to renounce his claims, and although these rights were restored to him for life " of the king's special grace " on November 3, he had in fact lost one

[116] *Cal. Fine Rolls 1272–1307*, pp. 274–75; *Cal. Pat. Rolls 1281–92*, pp. 350–52, 359–60; *Littere Wallie*, p. 177.

[117] Cf. *G. E. C.*, V, 707, 709; Powicke, *King Henry III*, II, 678, and for Gilbert's oath regarding the succession to the throne (printed in *Foedera*, I, 742), *ibid.*, II, 705, 732–33, 788. This account of the marriage needs to be amplified in light of the remarks of K. B. McFarlane, " Had Edward I a ' policy ' towards the earls?," *History*, L (1965), 153–54 and *passim*. This article unfortunately appeared too late for me to utilize in my own discussion.

[118] *Rot. Parl.*, I, 71, 72.

of the major privileges of his marcher standing. The third raid was a " prompt answer of defiance " following Gilbert's surrender of his claims.[119]

In the meantime Earl Humphrey, whose original plea was continuously postponed from session to session because Gilbert failed to appear, had entered a fresh protest to the king about Gilbert's raids.[120] Marcher sympathies lay with the lord of Glamorgan, for he was defending marcher privileges, and there is some evidence that by the beginning of 1291 Humphrey was prepared to withdraw his complaint for the sake of the marcher position. But Edward was determined to continue the case, to demonstrate the supremacy of the monarchy and reduce marcher independence. On January 18, 1291, he commissioned William de Valence, William de Louth, bishop of Ely, and two royal judges to summon the parties to appear at Ystradfellte in Brecknock on March 12, " even should the earls or one of them withdraw from the prosecution or defense." At the same time the marcher lords of southern Wales were summoned, as were knights from the adjoining counties, to give evidence. Gilbert and some of the marchers failed to appear, and an adjournment was ordered to Llanthew near Brecon for March 14.[121] Again the Red Earl did not appear. The commissioners attempted to empanel a jury of marchers in accordance with a royal mandate. The marchers unanimously refused: they would only acknowledge a writ ordering the matter to be settled according to marcher custom.[122] The judges' reply was a clear statement of the efficacy of the royal prerogative: marcher liberties could not exclude the lord king " qui, pro com-

---

[119] *Ibid.*; Morris, *Welsh Wars*, p. 226. For the dispute over Llandaff, see *Rot. Parl.*, I, 42–43; *Littere Wallie*, p. 178; *Cal. Pat. Rolls 1281–92*, p. 393; *Cal. Chart. Rolls 1257–1300*, p. 372. The entire question will be discussed in detail below, pp. 273–75.

[120] *Cal. Close Rolls 1288–96*, p. 126 (February 12, 1290). For the plea, see PRO, Coram Rege Rolls, Easter 18 Edward I, KB 27/123 m. 1; Trinity 18 Edward I, KB 27/124 m. 12d.; Mich. 18–19 Edward I, KB 27/125 m. 2; Hilary 19 Edward I, KB 27/126 m. 2. Indeed, Gilbert brought his own suit, claiming the money still owed him by Humphrey since 1270 and an additional 1,000 marks in damages: KB 27/123 m. 54; KB 27/124 m. 49. Bohun's original plea ran concurrently with the later inquest. See below, notes 126, 132.

[121] *Rot. Parl.*, I, 70–71; *Cal. Pat. Rolls 1281–92*, pp. 452, 454; Morris, *Welsh Wars*, pp. 227–29.

[122] They argued " quod nuncquam consimile mandatum regium venit in partibus istis, nisi tantum quod res tangentes marchiam istam deducte fuissent secundum usus et consuetudines partium istarum." *Rot. Parl.*, I, 71.

muni utilitate, per prerogativam suam in multis casibus est supra leges et consuetudines in regno suo usitatas. . . . ." [123] Still the marchers refused,[124] and a jury of twenty-four was finally assembled from the men produced by the king's brother, Edmund of Lancaster, Robert Tibetot, justiciar of West Wales, and the sheriffs of Gloucestershire and Herefordshire.[125] Their testimony produced the facts about the raids committed by Gilbert's men in 1290, as outlined above. The earl was clearly guilty *ex post facto*, and failure to appear at the inquest had added to his contempt. The judges reiterated the royal prohibition against the resort to arms, and reported their findings to the king. Edward ordered a new jury summoned and the parties arraigned before him at Abergavenny in October. He was prepared to act swiftly and severely to crush the most distinctive and troublesome feature of the custom of the march. The affair may have originated as a private dispute, but in his view it had become a matter of public welfare, and local custom could not be permitted to deal with it. As Edward put it, the case involved the person of the king and the dignity of the Crown.[126]

At Abergavenny Edward struck hard. Bohun had clearly been the aggrieved party in 1290, but his actions since the preliminary hearing had brought him under grave suspicion. He was tried and found guilty of having staged retaliatory raids in Glamorgan after the commission had retired from Llanthew. He had taken the law into his own hands. It was a foolish blunder. Humphrey was committed to jail and his lordship seized into the king's

---

[123] *Ibid.* The implications of this position are discussed in L. Ehrlich, *Proceedings against the Crown, 1216–1377* (Oxford, 1921), p. 59. It is significant that one of the judges, William de Valence, was himself lord of the palatine county of Pembroke—and the king's uncle.

[124] They answered " quod nichil inde facerent sine consideratione parium suorum." *Rot. Parl.*, I, 71.

[125] *Ibid.*

[126] *Ibid.*, I, 72: " res ista specialiter tangit dominum Regem, et coronam et dignitatem suam." Shortly after the hearing, Gilbert finally went to Westminster to answer Humphrey's original plea. He protested that the court could not have cognizance of such a dispute until it had first been discussed at a " day of the march " (note 102 above). The court postponed a ruling on this point until Michaelmas term, when it was decided that Gilbert's objection would not be allowed. PRO, Coram Rege Roll Mich. 19–20 Edward I, KB 27/129 m. 36d. Undoubtedly, the king had instructed his judges to dismiss Gilbert's claim. See also note 132.

hands.[127] Edward turned to Gilbert, who had not dared to absent himself this time. The earl must have known what was coming; he dropped his show of defiance and attempted to evade his responsibility by raising technical objections. The court summarily dismissed them.[128] His contumacious behavior since 1290 was clear beyond a doubt. He and his men had acted in contempt of the king, "believing that they could escape by their liberty of the march the penalty and peril they would deservedly have incurred if they had committed such excesses elsewhere in the realm outside the march." The earl and his sheriff were committed to prison, and the lordship of Glamorgan confiscated.[129] Both Gilbert and Humphrey were soon released on the surety of their friends and ordered to appear in parliament in January 1292 for final sentencing.[130]

At Westminster both men put themselves at the king's mercy. Edward was determined fully to vindicate his authority. Glamorgan and Brecknock were declared forfeit for life, and the earls returned to jail at the king's pleasure. On February 19 Roger Burghull, sheriff of Herefordshire, was appointed guardian of the lordships.[131] The sentences, however, were not meant to be enforced literally. The king knew when to stop. The earls were soon allowed to redeem their bodies, Gilbert for a fine of 10,000 marks, Humphrey, whose offense was deemed less serious, for 1,000 marks. On May 7 Glamorgan was restored to Gilbert, although Humphrey did not recover Brecknock until July 15.[132]

[127] Rot. Parl., I, 73–74.

[128] Ibid., I, 72–73, 74–75, summarized by Morris, Welsh Wars, pp. 233–35.

[129] Rot. Parl., I, 75: "quia hec omnia audacius et praesumptuosius per ipsum comitem et homines suos de Morgannou fiebant, credentes quod per libertatem suam de marchie possent evadere a pena et periculo que merito incurrisse debuissent, si extra marcham alibi in regno talem excessum perpetrassent . . . , (et) propter contemptum et inobedientam domino Regi factam contra inhibitionem predictam, consideratum est, quod idem comes, et similiter predictus Johannes de Crepping qui presens est, committantur gaole . . . et etiam libertas predicti comitis de Glamorgan cum pertinentibus capiatur in manum domini Regis." The like wording, mutatis mutandis, was used with Bohun.

[130] Ibid., I, 75–76.

[131] Ibid., I, 76–77; Cal. Pat. Rolls 1281–92, pp. 477–78. He was replaced by Walter Hackelute in April. See note 145 below.

[132] Rot. Parl., I, 77; Cal. Pat. Rolls 1281–92, pp. 489, 501. The bailiffs of the two earls were also fined small amounts, except for Crepping, who was fined 500 marks. Rot. Parl., I, 77; PRO, Coram Rege Roll Hilary 20 Edward I, KB 27/130 m. 20. Gilbert did not pay the fine before his death. Cal. Close Rolls 1288–96, p. 469.

The drama was completed. The dignity of the Crown had been fully asserted at the expense of the mightiest lords of the march. The king did not interfere in the internal organization of the lordships, nor did he seize the earls' other estates; but he had successfully appealed to concepts of public welfare and the supremacy of royal prerogative to eliminate the best known feature of marcher custom. Miss Otway-Ruthven has pointed out that Edward's actions marked the beginning of a " consistent pattern of bringing pressure to bear on the greatest franchises throughout the British Isles," and this pattern can be discerned in his relations with the other marcher lords, the great Anglo–Irish magnates of Meath and Leinster, and the bishop of Durham.[133] In the march, Edward had already asserted his supremacy in the bishopric of Llandaff and humbled the lords of Glamorgan and Brecknock. In 1291–92 he exacted a tax of a fifteenth on movables from the marchers, although promising not to use the grant as a precedent to the prejudice of their liberties.[134] In cases in 1291 and 1299 he reduced the independent privileges of two more marchers, Theobald Verdun, lord of Ewyas Lacy, and William de Braose, lord of Gower.[135] In these instances, as in the Clare–Bohun trial, Edward successfully but heavy-handedly employed all the techniques of political and personal pressure and the sometimes tortuous avenues of legal process he could muster. There can be little doubt that, however much Edward felt his actions to be justified by the prerogatives of monarchy, they could not but create a feeling of deep resentment among the magnates; and this resentment was to culminate in a major baronial revolt in the last years of the king's reign and to contribute in large measure to the troubled reign of his son. In the end, Edwardian kingship and its legacy proved to be politically unworkable.

Earl Gilbert's problems were not over. In 1293 the Irish in

Humphrey's original plea against Gilbert for trespasses committed before 1290 was still pending in 1293–94. PRO, Coram Rege Rolls, Trinity 21 Edward I, KB 27/137 m. 12; Hilary 22 Edward I, KB 27/139 m. 40d. No further mention of it is found on subsequent rolls.

[133] Otway-Ruthven, "The Great Lordships of South Wales," p. 15. For the case of Bishop Anthony Bek, see C. M. Fraser, "Edward I and the Regalian Franchise of Durham," *Speculum*, XXXI (1956), 329–42.

[134] *Cal. Pat. Rolls 1281–92*, pp. 419, 499–500, 502–3, 510–11, and for Gilbert, *Littere Wallie*, p. 181.

[135] See Otway-Ruthven, "Great Lordships," pp. 18–19, and Morris, *Welsh Wars*, pp. 238–39.

Kilkenny revolted, and Gilbert was forced to sail with a large body of knights to pacify the region.[136] He seems to have arrived in Ireland in October of that year, and to have remained there at least until the beginning of April, 1294.[137] Shortly after his return to England, a fresh revolt erupted in Wales.[138] It spread to Glamorgan, where it was led by Morgan ap Maredudd, the son of the Welsh chieftain whom Gilbert had expelled in 1270.[139] Morgan, who had unsuccessfully brought suit against Gilbert in 1278 for Machen, Edelegan, and Llefnydd,[140] seems to have been associated with Dafydd ap Gruffydd in 1283; but nothing more is known about him until this time.[141] The revolt apparently commanded the support of all the Welsh in the lordship: the tradition of resistance to their Norman overlord was not entirely forgotten. The rebellion erupted in October and was at first completely successful. The rebels captured a number of castles, apparently including Morlais, and expelled the earl from the land. According to the account of the Dunstable chronicler, Gilbert "barely escaped alive."[142]

In April 1295 the Red Earl counterattacked. He was formally summoned for military service in November, 1294, but his activities were confined to Glamorgan, presumably with King Edward's approval. His force consisted mainly of his own knights, but included such barons as John Wake and John Lovel, who had led independent cavalry units in the campaign in Cardigan in the fall

[136] Wykes, p. 336; *Annals of Ireland 1162–1370*, in *Chartularies of St. Mary's, Dublin*, ed. J. T. Gilbert (Rolls Series LXXX, 1884–86), II, 322. Cf. the letters of protection, *Cal. Pat. Rolls 1292–1301*, pp. 9–13 *passim*, 19–20, 22–23, 27–28, 30, 39, 60. Among those who went with him were John de Hastings, lord of Abergavenny, Peter fitz Reginald, a younger brother of the lord of Blaenllyfni, and John Bigod, brother of the Earl Marshal.

[137] *Ann. Ireland*, II, 322, 323. On April 1, 1294, Earl Gilbert sat with Richard de Burgh, earl of Ulster, John de Hastings, and others, on the king's Irish council in the preliminary stages of a case involving William de Vescy, lord of Kildare. PRO, Coram Rege Roll Trinity 22 Edward I, KB 27/141 m. 36.

[138] Full details of the war are given in Morris, *Welsh Wars*, pp. 240–70.

[139] His identity is established in *Cal. Anc. Corr., Wales*, p. 208. According to the *Annales Wigornia*, p. 526, the leader was named Rhys ap Morgan.

[140] *The Welsh Assize Roll*, pp. 268, 276.

[141] *Littere Wallie*, pp. 75, 133.

[142] *Ann. Wigornia*, p. 526; Dunstable, p. 387; Rishanger, *Chronica*, p. 144; cf. *Brut Peniarth*, p. 122. The fate of Morlais is unknown. It is not mentioned in the inquisitions *post mortem* of the Clares or their descendants, and it may have been destroyed by Morgan and never rebuilt. Morris, *Welsh Wars*, p. 237, thinks King Edward had confiscated it in 1292.

of 1294. By the middle of May, Gilbert was once again in control of Cardiff, but was unable to inflict a decisive defeat on Morgan ap Maredudd and his supporters.[143] By the beginning of June, the general revolt elsewhere in southern Wales subsided. Morgan had claimed only to be fighting against the earl, and now professed his loyalty to Edward. By June 7, 1295, he had been received into the king's peace "against the earl's wishes," and the other rebels quickly followed suit.[144] Shortly thereafter, Edward took Glamorgan into his own hands and exacted a promise from Earl Gilbert to be attendant to Walter Hackelute whom the king appointed as custodian of the lordship.[145] The reasons for Edward's action are not entirely clear. He was involved in another dispute with Gilbert, who had delayed surrendering custody of the temporalities of the bishopric of Llandaff even after the election of John de Monmouth to the see. It is possible that Edward wanted to remind Gilbert forcibly that he did not intend to tolerate such behavior. Since the earl was not in control of the lordship for most of this time, however, and probably could not have complied fully with the order, a more likely explanation for Edward's action is that he feared a recurrence of fighting in Glamorgan if Earl Gilbert were to resume control of it immediately after Morgan's capitulation.[146] At any rate, the king kept Glamorgan for over four months, restoring it to the earl only on October 20.[147]

Six weeks later Earl Gilbert was dead. On December 7 he died at Edmund of Lancaster's castle of Monmouth, and was buried two weeks later at Tewkesbury Abbey.[148] Most of the

[143] Cf. Dunstable, p. 387, and Cal. Pat. Rolls 1292–1301, p. 140. The summons is in Parl. Writs, I, 265. For the contingent, see Morris, Welsh Wars, p. 261, and Calendar of Chancery Warrants 1244–1326 (H.M. Stationery Office, 1927), pp. 54, 61, 63.

[144] Ann. Wigornia, p. 526, and for the date, Cal. Anc. Corr., Wales, p. 208. See also Morris, Welsh Wars, p. 265. For Morgan's activities after 1295, see below, Chapter VIII, notes 7, 126.

[145] PRO, Ancient Correspondence, SC 1/16/40 (not given in the Cal. Anc. Corr., Wales). It is however possible that this letter, which is undated, refers to the forfeiture of 1292, for Hackelute was custos of Glamorgan from April 12 to May 7 in that year. Cal. Fine Rolls 1272–1307, p. 309; Cal. Pat. Rolls 1281–92, p. 489.

[146] See also below, p. 275. The texts relating to Llandaff are printed from the Parliament and Chancery rolls in Cartae de Glamorgan, III, 905–9.

[147] Cal. Pat. Rolls 1292–1301, p. 154.

[148] Monasticon, II, 61; Ann. Wigorn., p. 524. Gilbert may have stopped at

chroniclers merely noted his death without further comment, although an interpolation in the chronicle of Walter of Guisborough refers, in rather conventional fashion, to the earl's military prowess and staunch defense of his rights.[149] The Red Earl's last years were spent under the shadow of Edward I's domination, and his stormy career ended in dispirited humiliation. Perhaps the soundest judgment is that contained in the otherwise undistinguished Osney chronicle. In referring to the earl's marriage to Joan of Acre in 1290, the chronicler calls Gilbert the greatest of the magnates of the realm in nobility and eminence, and incomparably the most powerful man in the kingdom—next to the king.[150] Later events proved that the chronicler's qualification was more significant than he could have realized at the time.

Monmouth on his way from Glamorgan to Westminster, to which he had been summoned to attend parliament. *Parl. Writs.*, I, 33.

[149] " Vir prudens in consiliis, strenuus in armis et audacissimus in defensione sui juris." *Chronicle of Walter of Guisborough*, ed. Harry Rothwell (Camden Society, 3rd ser., vol. LXXXIX, 1957), p. 259, note j.

[150] *Annales Monasterii de Oseneia*, ed. H. R. Luard (*Annales Monastici*, vol. IV, Rolls Series XXXVI, 1869), p. 323: " summae et singularis inter regni magnates nobilitatis et praeminentiae et incomparibilis post regem potentiae."

CHAPTER V

THE LAST EARL

Bannockburn

On December 14, 1295, Edward I ordered the estates of Gilbert de Clare taken into custody. The Red Earl had left as his heir a son Gilbert, born in 1291. But the king was deprived of the opportunity to enjoy the revenues from the estates during the minority of the heir. By the terms of the marriage settlement of 1290, the Countess Joan had been jointly enfeoffed of the lands, and the king could not abrogate her rights to their control. On January 20, 1296, Edward, having taken her homage, formally restored the inheritance.[1]

Edward had plans for his daughter. A young widow with a great landed endowment was a valuable commodity, and the king began to cast about for a suitable marriage alliance. But Joan had become attracted to Ralph de Monthermer, a young knight of modest circumstances who had served in Earl Gilbert's *familia*, and planned to marry him. Edward learned of the scheme, and in January, 1297, seized the estates in an attempt to remind her that she had no say in such matters. On March 16 the king formally announced the betrothal of his daughter to his cousin and ally, Amadeus V, count of Savoy. But Joan had been persistent. She and Monthermer were already married.[2] Edward was furious and summarily imprisoned Ralph in Bristol castle. He eventually relented, however, and Ralph, together with his wife, did fealty

[1] *Cal. Fine Rolls 1272–1307*, p. 368; *G. E. C.*, V, 712; *Cal. Close Rolls 1288–96*, p. 470.
[2] *Cal. Close Rolls 1296–1302*, p. 12; *Cal. Fine Rolls 1272–1307*, p. 383; *Chronicle of Walter of Guisborough*, p. 259. The contract with Amadeus is printed in *Foedera*, I, 861. For his relations with Edward I, see Powicke, *Thirteenth Century*, pp. 653, 665, who does not however mention this betrothal.

157

to the king on August 2. Edward restored the estates, with the exception of the honor of Tonbridge and the Isle of Portland, which he kept in custody until 1301.[3]

In the decade following his marriage to Joan of Acre, Ralph de Monthermer controlled the Clare inheritance. His position has often been commented on by modern peerage writers. By virtue of his marriage, he was styled earl of Gloucester and Hertford *vita uxoris*, although the earliest mention of him as earl does not occur until November 12, 1297, over three months after he had performed homage and fealty. He had no legal claim to the title apart from his marriage and did not receive the formal grant of the third penny of the pleas of the shire. Had Joan of Acre lived beyond 1307, Ralph would have remained earl of Gloucester only until the majority of her son and heir, Gilbert, and no longer. As it was, his interest in the Clare lordships and the comital title lapsed at her death in April, 1307. He immediately reverted to his original status and was thenceforth regarded as an ordinary baron.[4]

Ralph de Monthermer acted with circumspection in the great struggle between king and baronage which marked the last years of Edward's reign.[5] He certainly did not wish to incur a repetition of the king's disfavor, and he must have realized that the great hereditary earls regarded him as an upstart and intruder. In addition to administering the Clare estates with Joan of Acre, he spent much of his public career serving in the wars with Scotland. He raised a paid contingent of 100 men for the campaign of 1298, leading in addition a force of 46 unpaid soldiers. He also served with pay in the campaigns of 1299, 1300, 1301–2, 1304 and 1306.[6]

[3] Rishanger, *Chronica*, p. 173; *Parl. Writs.*, I, 296; *Cal. Fine Rolls 1272–1307*, p. 389.

[4] *G. E. C.*, V, 709 and note (b), 712 and note (f); *Cal. Close Rolls 1296–1302*, p. 527; *ibid. 1302–07*, p. 495; *Rotuli Scotiae*, ed. D. Macpherson *et al.* (Record Commission, 1814–19), I, 48; *Parl. Writs*, indexes to vols. I–II (Edward I–II).

[5] The conflict was intimately connected with the outbreak of warfare in Scotland and the war against Philip the Fair in Gascony and Flanders. This aspect has been treated at length in Morris, *Welsh Wars*, pp. 271–305. For a recent interpretation of the constitutional issues involved, see Harry Rothwell, "Edward I and the Struggle for the Charters, 1297–1305," in *Studies in Medieval History Presented to Frederick Maurice Powicke* (Oxford, 1948), pp. 319–32.

[6] *Rot. Scot.*, I, 48; *Cal. Docs. Scotland*, II, nos. 1044, 1896; Morris, *Welsh Wars*, pp. 285, 290, 301; *Parl. Writs*, I, 297, 323, 327, 336–37, 348, 360. Various sums allowed to Ralph for his expenses in the campaigns of 1301–2 and 1304 are recorded in PRO, Exchequer, KR Accts. Var. (Army and Navy), E 101/10/4.

Edward recognized his loyalty and abilities. In November, 1301, the king restored Tonbridge and Portland " in consideration of [Ralph's] good service in Scotland," and in the fall of 1306 granted him the forfeited Scottish earldom of Athol.[7]

Joan of Acre died on April 23, 1307, and the Clare estates reverted to the Crown during the minority of the young Gilbert de Clare, then a youth of sixteen. On June 24 Ralph agreed to surrender the earldom of Athol to David de Strathbogie, son of the earl who had forfeited. In return, David was to pay him 5,000 marks and Edward granted him custody of the Clare estates in Wales in lieu of a like amount. Ralph's renewed control of Glamorgan and the other lordships, however, was brief. On July 7 Edward II succeeded to the throne, and shortly thereafter granted seisin of the estates to the young Earl Gilbert. Ralph was forced to relinquish custody of the Welsh lands in exchange for the sum promised by Edward I, and his last connection with the family was severed. In 1306 he had been earl of Gloucester and a peer of Scotland; less than a year later he was once more the relatively obscure knight he had been before 1297.[8]

Edward II was not a forceful man, and he was beset with problems which threatened to overwhelm him. He was unable to cope with the grave military and financial burdens which the last years of his father's reign had imposed upon the realm. Although he maintained a precarious truce with France, he could not contain the Scots under Robert Bruce, and the English defeat at Bannockburn in 1314 was to secure Scottish independence for almost four centuries to come. In addition, Edward found himself engaged in a bitter struggle for power with a majority of the baronage, occasioned by the generosity he showed to his favorite, Peter Gaveston. Personal animosities to Gaveston culminated in the reform Ordinances of 1310–11, which attempted to place the

---

[7] Cal. Close Rolls 1296–1302, p. 473; Cal. Chart. Rolls 1300–26, p. 72.

[8] Cal. Pat. Rolls 1301–07, p. 534; ibid. 1307–13, p. 5. The 5,000 marks owed by Earl David were still unpaid in 1311. Cal. Chanc. War., p. 350. Ralph fought in the Scottish campaigns of 1309, 1311, and 1314. Cal. Docs. Scot., III, no. 393; Cal. Close Rolls 1307–13, p. 485; Tout, Chapters, II, 295. He also had a career in the royal service. From 1315 to 1320 he was keeper of the forest south of Trent, and served in various other judicial and administrative capacities as well. He died in 1325. Cal. Pat. Rolls 1313–17, p. 55; Cal. Fine Rolls 1307–19, pp. 230, 314; ibid. 1319–27, p. 23; G. E. C., IX, 140–42. For his children by Joan of Acre, see G. E. C., V, 534, IX, 143–45.

royal household and central administration firmly under baronial control. But Edward's first seven years were not a complete series of disasters for the monarchy. He might be foolish, as his stubborn adherence to Gaveston showed; but he was not wholly incompetent, and he enjoyed the support of a number of influential men, including Henry de Lacy, earl of Lincoln, and the young Gilbert de Clare. Only after the crushing defeat at Bannockburn was the king placed at the mercy of the leader of the baronial opposition, Thomas of Lancaster; and Lancaster's regime was even more unhappy than Edward's had been.[9]

Gilbert de Clare was on good terms with Edward II. His friendship did not, as has sometimes been assumed, stem from the fact that he was a boyhood playmate of the prince before 1307. Miss Johnstone has shown that the " Gilbert de Clare " referred to as Edward's *familiaris* was actually the last Earl Gilbert's cousin, the son of Thomas de Clare and himself lord of Thomond in Ireland from 1299. Earl Gilbert was brought up by his mother Countess Joan and his stepfather Ralph de Monthermer until 1301, when he was transferred to the household of Queen Margaret.[10] In any event, the new king cultivated the young heir's favor. Almost immediately after Edward succeeded to the throne, he allowed Gilbert to obtain seisin of his estates for a fine of 1,000 marks, a sum which was itself soon remitted, and by March, 1308, Gilbert was already styled earl of Gloucester, despite the fact that he was not quite seventeen years of age.[11]

Earl Gilbert served the king better than most of the other great magnates of the realm. He quickly distinguished himself in the Scottish campaigns. From October, 1308, to March, 1309, he was warden of Scotland and in December, 1308, led an expedition to relieve the castle of Rutherglen in Lanarkshire (near Glascow).[12]

---

[9] There are many good books dealing with the reign. The most recent account of the political troubles in the period 1307–14 is that of May McKisack, *The Fourteenth Century* (Oxford, 1959), pp. 1–32. The Ordinances are analyzed from the administrative point of view by J. Conway Davies, *Baronial Opposition to Edward II* (Cambridge, 1918), pp. 357–94, and T. F. Tout, *The Place of the Reign of Edward II in English History* (Manchester, 1914; 2nd ed. by Hilda Johnstone, 1936), Chapter III. For Edward's career prior to 1307 and his early relations with Gaveston, see Hilda Johnstone, *Edward of Carnarvon* (Manchester, 1946).

[10] Johnstone, *Edward of Carnarvon*, p. 75; *Cal. Pat. Rolls 1292–1301*, pp. 592, 606; below, Chapter VI, note 123.

[11] *Cal. Pat. Rolls 1307–13*, pp. 1, 21, 50; *Cal. Close Rolls 1307–13*, p. 10.

[12] *Rot. Scot.*, I, 58, 62; *Foedera*, II, 64.

In September, 1309, he was again captain in Scotland and the northern marches, and served in operations in the area in 1310 and 1311 as well. In July, 1311, the king recognized his aid by granting him 5,000 marks or its equivalent in custodies and marriages " in consideration of the earl's great expenses in the king's service in Scotland and elsewhere," and he made numerous additional grants of lands and money in subsequent years. There is no reason to believe that Edward was trying to buy his support; Gilbert saw already one of the wealthiest magnates in the kingdom, and the gifts seem to be expressions of the king's gratitude for his genuine friendship and loyalty.[13] But individual efforts displayed by such men as Gilbert or Aymer de Valence, the new earl of Pembroke, were not an adequate substitute for a concerted series of campaigns against the Scots utilizing the full resources of the realm. Between 1307 and 1313, Robert Bruce was able to subdue Inverness, Dundee, and Perth, thus securing the entire region north of the Tay River, and to begin attacking the center of English power in Lothian; and Edward, faced with financial crisis and growing political dissension at home, was unable to contain him.

Earl Gilbert maintained a middle ground in the struggle between king and baronage. He remained neutral in the early manifestations of hostility to Peter Gaveston which resulted in the favorite's banishment to Ireland in April, 1308. Gilbert's position was a difficult one. He did not oppose the sentence of exile, probably because he hoped it would help satisfy baronial grievances and lead to a reconciliation between Edward and his opponents. At the same time he did not actively support it, partly because of friendship with the king, and partly because of personal ties to Gaveston, who married the earl's full sister Margaret in October 1307.[14] After Gaveston's recall in 1309, however, Gilbert tended to oppose him. Edward's continued loyalty to his favorite was creating a dangerous political situation which threatened the internal security of the realm and prospects for a common effort against the Scots. The increased power which Gaveston enjoyed after his recall, combined with his overweening arrogance,

---

[13] *Rot. Scot.*, I, 74; *Foedera*, II, 91; *Cal. Pat. Rolls 1307–13*, pp. 376, 381; *ibid. 1313–17*, p. 89; *Cal. Chart. Rolls 1300–26*, p. 130; *Cal. Chanc. War.*, p. 305.
[14] *Vita Edwardi Secundi*, pp. 2, 4.

had the effect of bringing baronial opposition to a head. In March, 1310, Edward was forced to agree to the appointment of a committee of ordainers to draft proposals for the reform of the realm. After numerous delays, the Ordinances were published in October, 1311.[15]

Gilbert served on the committee of ordainers. Although he opposed Gaveston and in principle favored some reforms, he sought a moderate settlement for he did not wish an oligarchic regime imposed on an unwilling monarch. Edward recognized his antipathy to the extreme measures proposed by the Lancastrian faction. On March 4, 1311, he appointed the earl as his regent in England while he himself was in Scotland.[16] While Gilbert was mainly involved with routine administrative affairs such as the hearing and redressing of grievances brought to his attention under writs issued by the king, he also acted on matters of more general importance concerning the progress made by the ordainers. It was a critical period, for Lancaster and his chief supporters, including the earls of Hereford and Warwick, were in London, having refused to serve with the king in the Scottish campaign. There were doubts as to their intentions, and the king relied on Gilbert's loyalty and personal standing to avoid possible trouble.[17]

Gilbert's mediating influence, however, had little effect on the program of reform. The Ordinances of 1311 were seemingly a complete triumph for Edward's opponents. Gaveston was forced into a second exile. The exercise of executive power and control of the central administration were placed under baronial direction, and the king was compelled to follow the counsel of his barons in the affairs of state.[18] The Ordinances bear a resemblance to the old Provisions of Oxford, except that the normal royal council was not replaced by a baronial one. An even more profound difference lay in the quality of leadership: Thomas of Lancaster,

[15] Davies, *Baronial Opposition*, pp. 358–67.

[16] *Foedera*, II, 129. He succeeded Henry de Lacy, the royalist earl of Lincoln, who had died the previous month.

[17] For Gilbert's activities as *custos,* see Davies, *Baronial Opposition*, pp. 259, 365, 427, and Appendix, no. 107; *Cal. Chanc. War.*, pp. 347, 351, 357, 362–63, 369, 377; PRO, Ancient Correspondence, SC 1/45/152, 155, 157, 159–63.

[18] The Ordinances are best analyzed in Davies, *Baronial Opposition*, pp. 368–88, and B. Wilkinson, *Studies in the Constitutional History of the 13th and 14th Century* (Manchester, 1937), pp. 228–43.

as later events were to prove, had neither the ability nor the vision of a Simon de Montfort.

The promulgation of the Ordinances, far from producing a period of internal harmony, marked the beginning of increased political strife. Gaveston had no sooner left England when Edward began intriguing for his return. By the spring of 1312 the two had joined forces in the north. Baronial hatred of the favorite was implacable, and even Earl Gilbert, who had only reluctantly agreed to the second exile, now gave his tacit support to a sworn confederation of four earls, which resulted in Gaveston's capture and murder.[19] But the resort to violence shocked moderate opinion. Pembroke and other important magnates such as the Earl Warenne now threw their support behind the king. Open hostilities, however, were prevented by the timely intervention of Earl Gilbert who, after much hard effort, finally managed to effect at least a superficial reconciliation.[20] In this period Edward came to rely even more heavily on Gilbert's counsel and support. During the course of the lengthy negotiations the king made a brief trip to France, again leaving the earl as guardian of the realm and his deputy for the session of parliament, which formally opened on July 1, 1313. In addition, the earl went to France as the king's envoy in February, 1314, to conduct negotiations about Gascony.[21] Gilbert's activities reveal both Edward's increased reliance on him in the affairs of state, and his ability— as evidenced by his success in averting a potential civil war following the murder of Gaveston, through his influence and moderate position.

The greatest problem facing the king after his reconciliation with Lancaster was the steady advance of Robert Bruce who by March, 1314, had secured the strategic castle of Roxburgh and Edinburgh and even attacked Berwick itself.[22] His main objective was Stirling, the last remaining English stronghold north of the Tweed, but Edward was determined to retain it at all costs. Accordingly, the king raised a large army of foot and cavalry

---

[19] *Vita*, pp. 20–21, 22–23, 25–26. The parties to the murder were Lancaster, Hereford, Warwick, and Arundel.

[20] *Ibid.*, pp. 32–38, 42–43; *Cal. Pat. Rolls 1307–13*, p. 546. He acted in conjunction with John de Brittany, earl of Richmond, and some French envoys.

[21] *Vita*, p. 39; *Cal. Pat. Rolls 1307–13*, p. 514; *Foedera*, II, 244.

[22] *Vita*, p. 48.

and set north, coming within three miles of the castle on June 23. The front line of the army was commanded by the earls of Gloucester and Hereford. Gilbert engaged in a brief skirmish with the Scots on the 23rd, but although unhorsed, escaped without injury. The next day he advised Edward to order a day's rest for the army. The king foolishly spurned his advice as deceitful and treacherous. Gilbert retorted sharply and impetuously plunged into battle.[23] He led a gallant charge against the Scots line commanded by Robert's brother Edward, but failed to receive adequate support from his own troops or the English bowmen. His horse was cut down, and Gilbert, deserted by his followers, was slain. His body was later recovered from Robert Bruce and brought back to Tewkesbury Abbey for burial at the right hand of his father. Earl Gilbert's death marked the beginning of a complete rout of the English forces. Scottish independence was assured.[24]

Gilbert de Clare, the last member of the senior branch of the family in the male line, was also one of its most attractive. In spite of his youth he displayed qualities of leadership and military ability which held great promise. Had he not been killed, he might have continued to exercise a salutary effect on the relations between the king and the barons led by Thomas of Lancaster, which would have mitigated the worst excesses of the period immediately following Bannockburn.[25] As it was, his consistent efforts to effect a moderate solution in the struggle between the two factions did much to prevent the outbreak of civil war before his death. He had served the king valiantly to the last.

[23] *Vita*, p. 52: Gilbert " consuluit regi ne ipso die in bellum prodiret, sed propter festum [the birth of John the Baptist] potius vacaret, et exercitum suum valde recrearet. Sed rex consilium comitis sprevit, et proditionem et prevaricationem sibi imponens in ipsum vehementer excandit. ' Hodie,' inquit comes, ' erit liquidum quod nec proditor nec prevaricator sum,' et statim paravit se ad pugnandum."

[24] *G. E. C.*, V, 714; *Monasticon*, II, 61; *Vita*, pp. 52-54. The best and most recent account of the entire campaign is in G. W. S. Barrow, *Robert Bruce* (Berkeley, 1965), pp. 290–332.

[25] For the period of Lancaster's supremacy after 1314, see McKisack, *Fourteenth Century*, pp. 45–51, and Davies, *Baronial Opposition*, pp. 394–425.

The Partition

For Edward II, the ultimate results of the extinction of the senior line of the Clare family were tragic. The death of Earl Gilbert meant not only the loss of a gallant ally and close friend; it further involved the partition of his great inheritance among three men, hitherto of little prominence, whose rivalries were to shatter the political equilibrium established after Lancaster's brief period of supremacy, and whose actions were to prove an important factor in the eventual downfall of the king himself.

After the loss at Bannockburn, Edward II and the disorganized remnants of his army fell back to Berwick-on-Tweed. On July 10, two weeks after the battle, he ordered the escheators to seize the lands late of Gilbert de Clare, earl of Gloucester. Three days later he appointed keepers for the earl's estates.[26] The death of a great baron always involved numerous inquisitions and difficulties. The escheators and other royal officials had to determine the identities and ages of the rightful heirs. Valuations of the manors, castles, and other properties had to be made, and the services by which they were held certified to the exchequer and chancery. Dower had to be assigned to the widow, and the claims of all parties adjusted. Even under more routine circumstances, the business was long and complicated; but the death of one of the greatest magnates of England without issue was to provide complexities and have political and territorial repercussions that could not be foreseen at the time.

The situation was immediately made difficult by the terms of the marriage settlement of 1290, which had entailed the inheritance on the issue of Earl Gilbert the Red by Joan of Acre. Since the last earl died without any surviving heirs of his own,[27] this meant that unless his widow Maud de Burgh were pregnant, the nearest heirs would be the young Gilbert's three full sisters, Eleanor, wife of Hugh Despenser the younger, Margaret, widow of Peter Gaveston, and Elizabeth, widow of John de Burgh, Countess Maud's brother. His two half sisters Isabella and Joan,

---

[26] *Cal. Fine Rolls 1307–19*, pp. 201–2, 204. On October 10, Tonbridge was released to the archbishop of Canterbury. *Ibid.*, p. 214.

[27] See above, p. 40.

the daughters of Earl Gilbert the Red by his first marriage to Alice de Lusignan, were excluded from the inheritance.[28]

Uncertainty as to whether the countess was indeed pregnant, confusion as to the proper identities of the sisters, and efforts by King Edward to delay or avert the partition and thus keep the inheritance intact, all contributed to the fact that over three years elapsed between the last earl's death and the actual division of the estates. The inquisitions *post mortem* ordered by the king in the fall of 1314 produced considerable diversity of opinion as to the rightful heirs. Countess Maud was generally believed to be pregnant. The majority of the returns named Eleanor, Margaret, and Elizabeth as the heiresses if the countess were not pregnant, although the returns for a number of counties named an Isabella as the third sister.[29] In December, 1314, and February, 1315, the king assigned one-third of the estates to the countess in dower, including the lordship of Usk with Caerleon, confident that she would produce the expected heir.[30] At this point the eagerness of Eleanor's husband, Hugh Despenser, enticed by the prospect of obtaining a third of the great Clare inheritance, brought him into conflict with the king. In May, 1315, he seized Tonbridge castle from its keeper, the archbishop of Canterbury, and refused to surrender it.[31] Hugh's action was probably intended to bring the entire matter to a head; he never believed the story of the countess' pregnancy and was impatient at the delays caused by the confusion surrounding the names of the sisters. In June he released Tonbridge to King Edward, who restored it to the archbishop,[32] and then appeared at the chancery and later before the council to demand that the partition be effected. He asserted that there was no sister named Isabella who could be considered as an heiress, and stated that he was prepared to do homage and fealty for his wife's share of the estates.[33]

The king, however, attempted to delay Hugh's demands as long

---

[28] Above, p. 149.

[29] *Cal. Inq. Post Mortem*, V, no. 538 (pp. 326–31); *Rot. Parl.*, I, 353.

[30] *Cal. Close Rolls 1313–18*, pp. 131–39. At the same time the king reassigned the remaining estates to various keepers, many of whom had been members of Earl Gilbert's household. *Cal. Fine Rolls 1307–19*, pp. 224–30.

[31] *Cal. Inq. Post Mortem*, V, no. 538 (pp. 351–52).

[32] *Cal. Pat. Rolls 1313–17*, pp. 306–7.

[33] *Rot. Parl.*, I, 353.

as possible. An heir to the inheritance would prevent its division and would provide him with considerable revenue during the subsequent period of wardship, which under normal circumstances would thus last twenty-one years. The integrity of the inheritance was of obvious political and financial advantage to him, and he was determined to give the countess, who was still young and attractive,[34] every opportunity to vindicate her claims. Edward was obliged, however, to clear up the uncertainty as to the identities of the last earl's sisters, in the event the partition would eventually have to be made. In the summer of 1315 he ordered a further investigation as to the names of the sisters. Edward's action may have been necessary to exclude any claims the half sister Isabella might make. The confusion was clearly over the name of Gilbert's youngest full sister, Elizabeth de Burgh, for the original returns had all stated that the heiress "Isabella" was twenty years of age or younger. The proper half sister was over fifty and still unmarried in 1314, but Hugh Despenser's insistence on this point indicates he feared she might be tempted to claim part of the inheritance for herself.[35]

The new inquisitions, held in August, 1315, showed that the first set of returns had erred as to Elizabeth's correct name.[36] Satisfied on this point, Hugh continued to press his own claims. By now he was throughly convinced that the countess' alleged pregnancy was only a convenient personal or political fiction. In October, 1315, he again petitioned the council, arguing with impeccable logic and complete justification that more than the normal period of gestation had elapsed; if Maud were still to have a child, he urged, it could not be considered Gilbert's.[37] Learned contemporary opinion supported his position. The author of the *Vita Edwardi Secundi* wrote that if a posthumous child were born more than eleven months after its alleged father's death, it could

---

[34] In 1308, the last Earl Gilbert sent envoys to select one of Earl Richard de Burgh's three daughters for his wife. They chose Maud "as being the fairest." John de Birmingham, to whom she had originally been betrothed, was forced to settle for her presumably less attractive sister Avelina. *G. E. C.*, V, 714 note (c); *Cal. Papal Letters*, II, 209.

[35] *Rot. Parl.*, I, 353.

[36] *Cal. Inq. Post Mortem*, V, no. 538 (pp. 352–53).

[37] *Rot. Parl.*, I, 353–54: "tantum tempus est efluxum quod si dicta Comitissa esset pregnans, secundum communem cursum pariendi quod non posset dici a prefato Comite impregnata."

not be claimed as legitimate.[38] King Edward, however, was not easily swayed by such arguments; he still hoped to preserve the inheritance intact. In reply to Hugh Despenser, it was answered for the king that the pregnancy was common knowledge, and that owing to the difficulty and novelty of the case, the matter was to be adjourned and heard in parliament. At the parliament of Lincoln, held in January, 1316, Hugh once more urged the partition. Edward again temporized, and on a technicality ordered Hugh to appear at Easter term before the council.[39] Further delays ensued until in December, 1316, the king finally appointed new custodians of the estates in his name pending the final settlement of the issue by a parliament or an afforced meeting of the king's council.[40]

By this time it was obvious to even the most optimistic and lenient observers that the countess' hopes for an heir were illusory. It is impossible to determine what her motives had been. She may well have been pregnant in 1314 and miscarried; perhaps she had a personal antipathy to Hugh Despenser and hoped to postpone the division indefinitely. The king certainly exerted every effort to counter his claims and provide her the time to substantiate her own. But more than two years had now elapsed since Earl Gilbert's death; the partition could not be postponed much longer.

The fate of the younger heiresses was now a question of paramount importance. The king arranged for their marriage to knights already high in his favor. The second sister, Margaret, had been married to Peter Gaveston in 1307. After his execution the king granted her dower, and additional gifts, including lands which had been held in dower by her aunt, another Margaret, widow of Edmund of Cornwall.[41] On April 28, 1317, she was married to Hugh D'Audley, a member of the lesser nobility, and a knight of the royal household.[42] The youngest daughter, Elizabeth, had been married in 1308 to John de Burgh, son of the

[38] *Vita*, p. 62.
[39] *Rot. Parl.*, I, 354. Hugh had refused to assent to a medical examination of the countess to be made " per milites et matronas discretas."
[40] *Ibid.; Cal. Fine Rolls 1307–19*, pp. 313–14, 318.
[41] Davies, *Baronial Opposition*, pp. 82, 85; PRO, Chanc. Misc., C 47/9/52 no. 2; PRO, Exchequer, KR Mem. Roll 11 Edward II, E 159/91 m. 48.
[42] *G. E. C.*, V, 715; Davies, *Baronial Opposition*, pp. 173 note 5, 182 note 4, 221, 432–33.

earl of Ulster. After his death in 1313, she seems to have resided in Ireland with their son William (d. 1333). Edward recalled her and placed her under his custody at Bristol castle in February, 1316, pending a marriage settlement. Theobald Verdun, lord of Ewyas Lacy and a former justiciar of Ireland, abducted and married her without the king's license and presumably without the lady's acquiescence, although he later claimed they had been betrothed in Ireland. Theobald had discovered a simple and pleasant way to gain a share of the Clare estates, and obviously felt he would eventually regain Edward's favor; but his plans were frustrated by his death in July, 1316.[43] In May, 1317, Edward married Elizabeth to Roger Damory, a favorite household knight and one of the leading members of the "Middle Party" being built up under the leadership of the earls of Pembroke and Hereford in opposition to the antiroyal faction headed by Lancaster.[44] Shortly thereafter, the council reviewed the entire situation. The countess had not given birth; the claims of the heiresses and their husbands had to be accepted. The partition was ordered and the homage and fealty of Despenser, D'Audley and Damory were received.[45] The lands were to remain in the king's hands until the partition was effected and on May 22, 1317, Edward ordered new valuations made for the purpose of arriving at an equitable division of the estates.[46] The process was a long and difficult one, producing further delays, and the partition was not handed in to chancery until the fall. Finally, on November 15, 1317, Edward ordered delivery of the portions of the inheritance to the three coparceners.[47]

A complete and nearly contemporary copy of the partition has been preserved.[48] It records the share of each heir on a separate roll, and includes the values of the manors and courts each received, along with the knights' fees and advowsons arranged by

[43] *Rot. Parl.*, I, 352–53; *Cal. Inq. Post Mortem*, VI, no. 54.

[44] Davies, *Baronial Opposition*, pp. 431–32; *G. E. C.*, IV, 43–44. For the personnel and activities of the Middle Party, see Davies, *Baronial Opposition*, pp. 425–72.

[45] *Rot. Parl.*, I, 355.

[46] *Cal. Pat. Rolls 1313–18*, pp. 660–61, 666. On May 12 he had written the chancellor, John Sandall, bishop of Winchester, to see that the partition would be made "reasonably, and in good and courteous manner and without riot." *Cal. Chanc. War.*, p. 470.

[47] *Cal. Fine Rolls 1307–19*, pp. 350–51.

[48] PRO, Chancery Miscellanea, C 47/9/23–25.

county. In addition, the share each was to receive of Maud de Burgh's dower lands is entered at the foot of the roll containing his original portion. It is possible that an agreement was reached in advance as to the subsequent partition of her dower and that the documents may be dated to 1317, but it seems more likely that the surviving rolls are revised and expanded copies of the originals and should be dated sometime after 1320, when the countess died.[49]

The long wait had been well worth while. Hugh Despenser and Eleanor received the lordship of Glamorgan, the most important of all the Clare holdings, along with Rotherfield in Sussex and scattered manors in Devon and Somerset.[50] Hugh D'Audley and Margaret obtained the honor of Tonbridge and manors in Surrey, various estates appurtenant to the honors of Gloucester and Clare in Northampton, Huntingdon, Wiltshire, Norfolk, and Southampton, and the manor and town of Thornbury in Gloucestershire. D'Audley also received the lordship of Gwynllwg, hitherto dependent on Glamorgan, which was now organized as a fully separate county.[51] Roger Damory and Elizabeth took the bulk of the honor of Clare in East Anglia, including the castle and manor of Clare and the pleas of the honor court, as well as Cranbourne and the other Dorset manors and boroughs. His only property in Wales was two-thirds of the manor of Llangwm in Usk, as the lordship was held in dower.[52] In addition, each heir acquired two-ninths of the liberty of Kilkenny in Ireland, although there is no evidence that any of them ever visited it.

The death of the countess in the summer of 1320 completed the division of the estates among the heirs. Maud probably died

[49] Each roll records, in addition to the original share, the subsequent partition " de terris et tenementis que Matilda qua fuit uxor prefati comitis tenet in dotem et alias ad terminum vite sue."

[50] PRO, Chanc. Misc., C 47/9/24. A full list of the manors acquired by all three heirs is given below, Appendix II.

[51] PRO, C 47/9/23; Appendix II. It was stipulated that henceforth Gwynllwg was to be totally independent of Glamorgan: " Memorandum quod juxta istas particiones, comitatus de Wenthlok isti parti assignatur, ita quod de cetero comitatus ille seu homines terre aut tenementa infra eundem comitatum existencia sint omnino separata a comitatu de Glamorgan, et quod eidem comitatui de Glamorgan in nullo subjaceant seu intendant, sed solomodo corone Angliae imperpetuum." This proviso was necessary, as Gwynllwg had under the Clares been treated for administrative purposes as dependent on Glamorgan. See below, Chapter VIII.

[52] PRO, C 47/9/25; cf. Cal. Inq. Post Mortem, VI, no. 129.

on July 2, and the properties she held in dower must have been partitioned shortly thereafter.[53] Each received an equal portion of her third of Kilkenny. More importantly, Despenser obtained a substantial share of the honor of Gloucester, including the manor and town of Tewkesbury, the manor of Bushley and the castle and manor of Hanley in Worcester, and other demesne lands in Berkshire, Oxford, and Buckingham. D'Audley received properties in Wiltshire which had originally formed part of the Marshal estates, along with manors and boroughs of the honor of Clare in Suffolk, Norfolk, Surrey and Kent. Damory's share was the now unified lordship of Usk–Caerleon, with Edelegan and Llefnydd.[54]

The partition of the Clare estates has been described as " the most important territorial upheaval of the reign." [55] The titles of earl of Gloucester and earl of Hertford lapsed, and although the former was revived for Hugh D'Audley and others by Edward III and subsequent kings, they were not bestowed on any of the heirs by Edward II himself.[56] Moreover, the honors of Gloucester and Clare and the liberty of Kilkenny were permanently divided and were never restored to the size and composition they had assumed under the Clares. Modern statements that the lordships and honors remained unified and passed to a single lord are erroneous. Roger Damory and Elizabeth de Burgh received not the entire honor of Clare but only the East Anglian portion of it, and the bulk of the honor of Gloucester was fairly evenly divided between Hugh Despenser and Hugh D'Audley.[57] Each heir, however, was legally regarded as having inherited a third of each

[53] *Monasticon*, II, 61, where the year is wrongly given as 1315. The executors of her will are mentioned on August 11, 1320 (*Cal. Close Rolls 1318–23*, p. 323), and their mention on the Close Roll might indicate that they were arranging the partition of her dower with the heirs at that time.

[54] PRO, C 47/9/23–25; Appendix II.

[55] Denholm-Young, *Vita Edwardi Secundi*, Introduction, pp. xii–xiii.

[56] *G. E. C.*, V, 715 note (d) errs in claiming that Margaret de Clare was styled countess of Gloucester and Hertford in 1316. The document cited (*Feudal Aids* [H. M. Stationery Office, 1899–1921], II, 270) clearly confuses her with the dowager Countess Maud (Matilda), who held Tewkesbury in dower in 1316, and does not refer to Margaret, who moreover did not marry Hugh D'Audley until 1317.

[57] *G. E. C.*, V, 715 note (d) wrongly states that in 1317 Despenser acquired Glamorgan and Gloucester, D'Audley received Tonbridge, Usk, Gwynllwg and Kilkenny, and Damory obtained the honor of Clare. Sanders, *English Baronies*, pp. 6, 35, repeats some but by no means all of these errors.

honor: in 1350, D'Audley's heir Ralph Stafford was charged 50 marks relief " pro tercia parte comitatus Glovernie." [58]

The partition was of the greatest political as well as territorial importance. It directly conditioned the last decade of Edward II's reign, for it brought to prominence Hugh Despenser the younger, and the rivalries his ambition engendered led the country to civil war. A brief summary of Hugh's activities subsequent to the partition forms a fitting epilogue to the history of the senior branch of the Clare family.

The three great marcher lordships of Glamorgan, Gwynllwg, and Usk–Caerleon provided the focus for Hugh's ambitions: once again, marcher affairs became the dominant aspects of the politics of the kingdom at large. Hugh was already lord of Glamorgan from 1317, but immediately after the partition he began to intrigue against his brothers-in-law. Some chronicles give the impression that he wished to usurp all the properties of Hugh D'Audley and Roger Damory and reunite the entire inheritance in his own hands.[59] There is no evidence, however, that he desired the English estates. His activities centered on the march, and his real aim was to make himself the natural successor to the Clares as the greatest of the marcher lords. He cultivated the king's favor and by a thinly disguised combination of force and fraud succeeded in obtaining Gwynllwg from D'Audley in May, 1320.[60] His actions aroused suspicions among the other marchers, and his subsequent efforts to obtain Cantref Bychan in Carmarthen, Gower, and the Damory lordship of Usk served to drive them into a confederation with the earl of Lancaster. As a direct result of Hugh's aggressive actions, the Middle Party disintegrated and warfare erupted briefly in Glamorgan. In August, 1321, the triumphant baronage, headed by Lancaster, forced King Edward to submit to the exile of Despenser and his father.[61]

[58] *Feudal Aids*, II, 293.

[59] E. g., the *Chronicon Laudunense* states that Hugh desired "omnes porciones trium sororum sibi usurpare et sic comes Glovernie vocari. . . ." Brit. Mus., Cotton MS Nero A IV, fol. 53v., printed in *Cartae de Glamorgan*, III, 1089.

[60] J. Conway Davies, "The Despenser War in Glamorgan," *Transactions of the Royal Historical Society*, 3rd ser., IX (1915), 28–30; PRO, Parliamentary and Council Proceedings (Chancery), C 49/4/22; *Cal. Pat. Rolls 1317–21*, pp. 103, 120–21, 208, 257, 415, 456.

[61] These events have been fully described in Davies, "Despenser War," pp. 33–62 *passim*; Davies, *Baronial Opposition*, pp. 472–82; McKisack, *Fourteenth Century*, pp. 59–64.

Less than a year later, the Despensers themselves returned in triumph. The king managed to win over to his side many of Lancaster's allies, and fighting again broke out, culminating in the royalist victory at Boroughbridge on March 22, 1322. Lancaster and his chief supporters, including Roger Damory and Bartholomew de Badlesmere, were executed, while D'Audley and the Mortimers were imprisoned. King Edward was at the height of his power. He lavished gifts of lands forfeited by the rebels on his followers, many of them to the Despensers, and had the Ordinances of 1311 annulled by the famous Statute of York. Edward allowed himself to fall completely under the domination of the Despensers. For the next four years, they were the real rulers of England.[62]

The ambitions of Hugh Despenser the younger were still unfulfilled, and he refused to heed the warning of the earlier warfare and exile. After recovering Glamorgan and Gwynllwg, his first step was to acquire Usk. In July, 1322, he was granted the forfeited lordship of Gower, and forced Damory's widow, Elizabeth de Burgh, to exchange Usk for it.[63] He had thus reunited the Clare dominions in the march in his own hands, but they proved to be only the starting point of his territorial designs. In 1324, he arranged with the former lord of Gower, William de Braose, to recover the lordship from Elizabeth by a fraudulent assize of *novel disseisin*. When Braose was successful, he promptly granted Gower to the elder Despenser, who then gave it to his son.[64] Hugh skillfully exploited his position as power behind the throne, and by 1325 had also acquired in one form or another the lordships of Isgenen, Striguil, Abergavenny, Cilgerran, and Pembroke.[65] With these additions to the former Clare lordships and Gower,

[62] McKisack, *Fourteenth Century*, pp. 64–79, provides a convenient general account of Lancaster's fall and the subsequent period of the Despensers' supremacy.

[63] *Cartae de Glamorgan*, III, 1100–1; *Cal. Chart. Rolls 1300–26*, pp. 448–49; G. A. Holmes, " A Protest against the Despensers, 1326," *Speculum*, XXX (1955), 208.

[64] *Cartae de Glamorgan*, III, 1127, 1128–30; PRO, Coram Rege Roll Hilary 18 Edward II, KB 27/259 m. 115; Holmes, " Protest against the Despensers," p. 209.

[65] *Cal. Chart. Rolls 1300–26*, p. 450; *Cal. Pat. Rolls 1321–24*, pp. 341–42; *Cal. Close Rolls 1323–27*, pp. 288–89; *Cat. Ancient Deeds*, III, 115–17. In addition, Hugh's chief minister and sheriff of Glamorgan, John Inge, had custody of the Mortimer lordships of Wigmore and Ludlow in October, 1324. *Cal. Fine Rolls 1319–27*, p. 306.

Hugh was the master of South Wales from the Wye to the Teifi. His aim had been the systematic acquisition of the whole of the southern march, and the reintegration of the Clare lordships had served both as the starting point and the nucleus of this policy.[66]

Hugh Despenser achieved his aims, but his very success soon spelled not only his own downfall, but that of King Edward as well. His acquisitions were cloaked in the outward forms of correct legal procedure, but in every case they betrayed misuse of royal authority and engendered implacable hostility. His control of the king and the royal administration left no other course for the expression of opposition than open rebellion, and the tragic sequel to Hugh's spectacular career quickly ensued. In September, 1326, Queen Isabella and her paramour Roger Mortimer, who had escaped from the Tower in 1323 and gone to France, landed in England. Their return touched off full-scale civil war. Edward and Hugh fled to Glamorgan, but they were unable to rally support. In mid-November they were captured in Neath Abbey. Shortly thereafter, Hugh was hanged and King Edward deposed and imprisoned.[67] In 1327–28, the regents for the young Edward III nullified the exchanges and acquisitions which Hugh had exacted, and restored all the estates and lordships to the sisters of the last Earl Gilbert in accordance with the original partition of 1317–20. Thenceforth the estates remained in the possession of the heiresses and their descendants until they became vested in the Crown in the later fifteenth and early sixteenth centuries.[68] Of more immediate consequence, however, was the fact that Hugh Despenser had learned no lesson from the Glamorgan war of 1321. In a sense, it is befitting that his capture and downfall occurred in the very lordship whose acquisition had originally given rise to his ambitions and successes. The partition of the Clare inheritance not only brought him to power, but also led directly to the civil wars which convulsed first the march and later the entire kingdom, and which eventually doomed not only Hugh, but the king himself.

[66] Cf. the remarks of Holmes, "Protest against the Despensers," pp. 209–10, who points out the similar designs of the elder Despenser in northern Wales and England.

[67] See, in general, McKisack, *Fourteenth Century*, pp. 79–96.

[68] *Cal. Pat. Rolls 1327–30*, pp. 30, 32; *Cal. Close Rolls 1327–30*, pp. 27, 76, 275–76, 283. For the descendants, see above, pp. 40–41.

CHAPTER VI

YOUNGER BROTHERS

The first chapter of this study attempted to demonstrate the ways in which the entire family served as a basis of action and cohesion in medieval English society. Primogeniture and the full heritability of land had only evolved slowly in the period since the Conquest, but by the thirteenth century they were firmly established in the common law of the kingdom.[1] This meant that the eldest son followed his father in the inheritance as a matter of course, and from youth was trained for his later career. But a baron usually had other children, daughters and younger sons, who under normal circumstances had no hope of succeeding to the estates, and he had a responsibility for their welfare as well. To great magnates such as the earls of Gloucester, these matters were of considerable importance, and the various provisions made for their children well illustrate this concern.

The careers of Bogo and Thomas de Clare, the brothers of Earl Gilbert the Red, deserve detailed and separate consideration. They offer perhaps the best examples in thirteenth century English history of the opportunities available to younger members of baronial families. Both men possessed considerable abilities, but in many ways, they stood in sharp contrast to each other. One embarked upon an ecclesiastical career, amassing great wealth and influence which he used to promote his own interests and those of his relatives. The other served in the royal administration, and through this service developed a substantial landed endowment of his own in western Ireland, an area hitherto relatively free of Norman penetration and authority. There were important

[1] S. E. Thorne, "English Feudalism and Estates in Land," *Cambridge Law Journal* (1959), pp. 193–209. There were of course important differences in the legal positions of tenants-in-chief and the holders of mesne fiefs. See also Pollock and Maitland, *Hist. English Law*, II, 266–74, 292–94.

175

differences in their personalities and character as well. Thomas had a sense of responsibility and public-mindedness wholly lacking in his brother. Both acted from motives of private interest and ambition, but while Bogo exploited the Church and squandered his wealth, Thomas achieved his aims by serving as one of King Edward I's most capable and trusted agents. Viewed together, their careers provide a vivid picture of the choice of action open to such men in the contemporary social structure and of the advantages each took of his opportunities and talents.

Bogo de Clare: "Nec Rector sed Incubator"

A lifetime spent in the service of the Church provided a great attraction for many men, regardless of their social station. It offered security and perhaps some measure of temporal importance and influence, and it was the surest path to eternal salvation. It certainly proved popular with many members of the nobility, for it afforded a ready means of providing for their younger sons. Many of the men who entered the Church in this way, however, had no intention of pursuing their calling seriously. They entered under the force of circumstance and, attracted by the opportunity for amassing wealth and position, lived in indolence and luxury. The ranks of the English clergy in the thirteenth century contained numerous examples of this kind, but none more famous or conspicuous than Earl Richard's youngest son Bogo.[2]

Bogo de Clare was born on July 21, 1248.[3] The name is an unusual one. In the Tewkesbury chronicle he is called Beves, while in an early sixteenth century register of the abbey his name is given as Benedict.[4] In the government records and his own household accounts edited by Giuseppi, however, the name regu-

---

[2] In general, however, the higher ranks of the ecclesiastical hierarchy in the thirteenth century were comprised of men of less exalted social station and background than Bogo. None of the bishops under Edward I, for example, came from families of comital rank. See J. H. Moorman, *Church Life in England in the 13th Century* (Cambridge, 1945), pp. 20–26, and for a detailed consideration of this point for the early fourteenth century, Kathleen Edwards, "The Social Origins and Provenance of the English Bishops during the Reign of Edward II," *Transactions of the Royal Historical Society*, 5th ser., IX (1959), 51–79.

[3] Tewkesbury, p. 136.

[4] Brit. Mus., Add. MS 36985, fol. 18v.

larly appears as "Bogo," and this form is followed here.[5] From
his childhood, his father intended him for a clerical career. As
early as 1255, Earl Richard secured for his son a papal dispensation
to hold two benefices with care of souls in England, along with
the church of Callan in Kilkenny, despite the fact that he was
underage. In addition, he was named a papal chaplain.[6] Bogo was
at Oxford along with his brother Thomas from 1257–59. It is
impossible to determine precisely what sort of training and study
the brothers were engaged in, for the documents merely note gifts
from Henry III to Bogo and Thomas, "scholaribus Oxonie." In
1259 the two left, Bogo probably feeling at the age of eleven or
twelve sufficiently prepared to embark on the ecclesiastical career
awaiting him.[7]

He rapidly began to acquire further benefices. In May, 1258,
he was presented by his father to Rotherfield (Sussex), but failed
to obtain admittance until 1280 due to litigation over his title,
occasioned by the opposition of the bishop of Rochester, who also
claimed the right of presentation. The king then presented him
to the two livings in England provided in the dispensation, St.
Peter's-in-the-East, Oxford, on August 25, 1259, and the deanery
of the royal free chapel of St. Mary's, Stafford, on September 10
following.[8] Thenceforth he amassed benefices with extraordinary
rapidity and success. By 1261, armed with another papal dispensation, he had acquired three more rectorships. Between 1261 and
1280 he accumulated thirteen more rectorships and three canonries,
and by the time of his death in 1294 he had to his credit the out-
standing total of almost thirty rectorships and some dozen canonries and other dignities, including the offices of treasurer of York
and chancellor of Llandaff, which made him the greatest pluralist
in the English Church.[9] His income has been placed by Giuseppi
at about £1,000 per year on the assumption that the sums recorded
in the wardrobe accounts represent all the major sources of

[5] "Wardrobe and Household Accounts of Bogo de Clare, 1284–86," ed. Giuseppi,
pp. 19–56 passim. Cited hereafter as Giuseppi.
[6] Cal. Papal Letters, I, 317.
[7] Close Rolls 1256–59, pp. 73, 270; ibid. 1259–61, p. 9. On the subject of
student patronage, see Frank Pegues, "Royal Support of Students in the Thirteenth
Century," Speculum, XXXI (1956), 454–62.
[8] Registrum Roffense, ed. J. Thorpe (London, 1769), pp. 591–92, 595; Cal. Pat.
Rolls 1258–66, pp. 40, 42.
[9] See Appendix III for a full list and details.

revenue.[10] These figures, however, do not include the income from the treasurership of York, which was valued at 600 marks a year.[11] He also acquired some other lucrative positions after 1286. At the time of his death, then, Bogo's income probably approached the figure of some £1,500 annually. Archbishop Romeyn thought his income from the province of York alone amounted to almost £1,300. While this figure seems to be an exaggeration,[12] it is at any rate indicative of the immense wealth concentrated in Bogo's hands and attests to the grasping reputation he had acquired while amassing his fortune. Moreover, he consistently squandered his wealth. In the period March, 1285, to June, 1286, according to the wardrobe accounts printed by Giuseppi, expenditures exceeded recorded income by £375.[13]

Bogo only achieved his position in the face of stiff competition. Pluralism flourished throughout the thirteenth century despite the constitution *De Multa* issued by the Fourth Lateran Council. In the middle of the century John Mansel, Henry III's most influential clerk and adviser, had at least fifteen churches with an estimated annual income of 4,000 marks.[14] In 1280 Adam de Stratton, the notorious Christian usurer, had twenty-three benefices, Geoffrey de Haspal fifteen and William de Brunton ten. Bogo was credited with holding thirteen, but the list is incomplete in his case.[15] Pluralism was only effectively checked in the early fourteenth century by John XXII's bull *Execrabilis*. In the middle of the century, the greatest pluralist in England was William de Wykeham, keeper of the king's privy seal, who had only five prebends and the archdeanery of Lincoln, with an annual income

[10] Giuseppi, p. 12. The accounts run from June, 1284, to June, 1286, with a three-month gap from September–December, 1285. Total recorded income in the 21-month period is over £1,800. Moorman, *Church Life in England*, p. 27, estimates annual income at £2,200, but his discussion of Bogo's finances seems to be based on a misreading of the figures in the wardrobe accounts.

[11] *Register of John le Romeyn, Lord Archbishop of York, 1286–96*, ed. William Brown (Surtees Society, vols. CXXIII, CXXVIII, 1913–16), I, 396.

[12] *Reg. Romeyn*, I, 396–97; A. Hamilton Thompson, "Pluralism in the Medieval Church," *Associated Architectural Societies' Reports and Papers*, XXXIII (1915), 55. Romeyn lists the value of Simonburn at 500 marks. This is probably a slip for 50 marks.

[13] Giuseppi, pp. 27, 35–36, 41–42, 55–56.

[14] Thompson, "Pluralism in the Medieval Church," pp. 50–52.

[15] The lists are printed in a survey of 1280 contained in the register of Robert Winchelsey, archbishop of Canterbury from 1294 to 1313. *Reg. Winchelsey*, II, 1146–50. For Stratton's connections with Thomas de Clare, see note 95, below.

of £843 6s. 8d.—a far cry from the great days of the "indiscriminate pluralism" of the preceding century.[16]

Bogo de Clare had a passion for collecting benefices and other ecclesiastical positions in much the same way as a lay baron amassed lands and fees. There is no trace of religious interest, much less dedication, in any of his activities; he regarded the Church as existing solely for his private benefit, and exploited its institutional structure while totally failing to acknowledge any reciprocal responsibilities or duties for the wealth and power gathered into his hands. He whiled away his time in a sumptuous London establishment, where he organized his household, and exerted himself only to take possession of newly acquired benefices, to engage in litigation concerning them, or to attend to purely secular matters, often in conjunction with his brother, Earl Gilbert.[17]

Bogo's interests were almost entirely identical with those of the English baronage. He moved freely among its ranks, finding his most congenial ties with such men as his brother-in-law, Roger de Mowbray, Edmund Mortimer of Wigmore, John de Beauchamp, brother of the earl of Warwick, and John de Hastings, lord of Abergavenny. He lavished gifts of furs and plate on these men, most of whom were also close associates of Earl Gilbert.[18] In addition, he established particularly close ties with the other members of his family. His activities on behalf of his mother, the dowager Countess Maud, and his sisters Rohese and Margaret, wives of Roger de Mowbray and Edmund of Cornwall, have already been discussed. In return, he was rewarded with a

[16] A. Hamilton Thompson, *The English Clergy and their Organization in the Later Middle Ages* (Oxford, 1947), p. 12 and note 1; Kathleen Edwards, *The English Secular Cathedrals in the Middle Ages* (Manchester, 1949), p. 88. Cf. also W. A. Pantin, *The English Church in the XIVth Century* (Cambridge, 1955), pp. 35–41, and the annotated notes on pluralities in the diocese of Lincoln in 1366, published by Thompson as an appendix to his paper on pluralism: *Associated Architectural Societies' Reports and Papers*, XXXIV (1917), 1–26; XXXV (1919–20), 87–108, 199–242; XXXVI (1921), 1–41.

[17] Good indications of Bogo's activities and the organization and magnificence of his London house are to be found in the wardrobe and household accounts printed by Giuseppi, pp. 19–56, and his commentary on them, pp. 1–18.

[18] Giuseppi, pp. 37, 39. Edmund Mortimer was Bogo's predecessor as treasurer of York and renounced his ecclesiastical career when he succeeded his brother Roger (d. 1282) in the marcher lordship of Wigmore. *York Minster Fasti*, ed Sir Charles Travis Clay (Yorkshire Archaeological Society, Record Series, vols CXXIII–CXXIV, 1958–59), I, 26.

number of benefices over which they had advowsonary rights.[19] His brother Earl Gilbert also presented him to some benefices, and probably used his authority and influence to have him named chancellor of Llandaff in 1287, a position he immediately used to assist the earl.[20] Bogo held the manors of Tregrug and Llangwm and tenements in Llantrissent, all in the lordship of Usk, of his brother, and often went to Wales to visit them.[21] He also employed men in his own household who had close connections with the earl. Raymond de Sully, who administered his Usk estates, came from a prominent Glamorgan family.[22] David le Graunt, who was Bogo's household seneschal in 1282, was a canon of Llandaff in 1290 and *camerarius* of the royal exchequer, and he held lands of Earl Gilbert in Rhymny in the lordship of Gwynllwg.[23]

Bogo held the great prelates of his day in contempt, for his ambitions and interests were entirely at odds with theirs. John Peckham, archbishop of Canterbury, who bitterly denounced him for opposing his plan to curb pluralities, called Bogo a ravisher (*raptor*), not a rector, of his churches.[24] The leading figures in the York archdiocese maintained a steady but fruitless effort to make him attend to his duties. Archbishop Wickwane in 1283 ordered him to be ordained a priest within a year, a charge he blithely ignored.[25] Archbishop John Romeyn, Wickwane's successor, was reputed to have threatened him with excommunication in 1287,[26] and when Peckham in 1291 asked Romeyn's opinion of Bogo's character, the prelate was forced to admit that he could say little, for Bogo rarely bothered to venture north.[27]

[19] See above, pp. 36, 48–49; also below, pp. 183–84, and Appendix III.
[20] Above, pp. 49–50. Appendix III.
[21] *Cal. Inq. Post Mortem*, IV, no. 435; *Cal. Pat. Rolls 1272–81*, pp. 268, 329, 437.
[22] Giuseppi, pp. 22, 27; *Cartae de Glamorgan*, II, 650.
[23] PRO, Min. Accts., SC 6/925/5, 1028/7; PRO, Exchequer of Pleas, Plea Roll 19 Edward I, E 13/17 m. 15; *Cal. Papal Letters*, I, 519.
[24] *Reg. Epist. Peckham*, I, 370–72. Cf. Powicke, *Thirteenth Century*, p. 475.
[25] *Register of William Wickwane, Lord Archbishop of York, 1279–1285*, ed. William Brown (Surtees Society, vol. CXIV, 1907), pp. 114–15.
[26] PRO, Parliamentary and Council Proceedings (Chancery), C 49/44/8–9. Romeyn was acting in conjunction with the bishop of Lincoln. The exact cause of the alleged action is not stated. There doubtless were many they could have chosen from.
[27] ". . . super moribus, autem, de quibus vestra missiva meminit, nichil certum scribimus, quia idem dominus Bogo ad partes nostras rarum habet accessum modicumque in ipsis dicitur conversari." *Reg. Romeyn*, I, 397.

Bogo's officials shared the utter disdain with which he viewed his position. When a clerk of Archbishop Peckham came to London to serve a writ on him, some of the household staff beat and imprisoned the messenger and forced him to eat the letters and seals.[28] Bogo was able to escape punishment by pleading that he had neither known of nor consented to the deed, but it may be supposed that he heartily approved of it.[29] A letter of 1290 addressed to him in his capacity as treasurer of York, preserved in Wickwane's register, provides an amusing example of the way his deputies attended to their responsibilities. The dean and chapter of York, writing out of " extrema necessitas," complained, among other things, that his men left vestments and books in a state of disrepair, failed to replace such items as wax, candles, and bell-cord, left the grass uncut and the hay unmowed, and refused to contribute to even ordinary church expenses and burdens. In addition they were wont to go out of the church in the evening, leaving the keys lying around where anyone could find them, and to engage in boisterous quarrels late into the night. They also connived with thieves. What was more, they used church ornaments and palls for such strangely unspiritual purposes as gifts to brides and women in labor. Besides, the sub-treasury was somehow depleted.[30]

Bogo exerted much energy and ingenuity in devising sharp practices designed to increase his income and power and incidentally to reward his friends. Peckham accused him of usurping tithes from other rectors,[31] and of attempting, apparently unsuccessfully, to exchange some manors he held with another noted pluralist, Tedisius de Camilla, in return for the rectorship of Wingham.[32] On the manors he held by virtue of his rectorships,

---

[28] *Rot. Parl.*, I, 24–25. Peckham was trying to secure Bogo's approval of the nomination of William de Hothum as bishop of Llandaff. Hothum's was the second unsuccessful candidacy, the first being that of Philip de Staunton. He later became archbishop of Dublin. See Greenway, " The Election of John de Monmouth," pp. 10–11.

[29] Sayles, *Select Cases*, II, no. 10; PRO, Coram Rege Roll Hilary 21 Edward I, KB 27/135 m. 8.

[30] *Reg. Wickwane*, I, 286–87.

[31] *Reg. Epist. Peckham*, III, 1062.

[32] *Ibid.*, II, 558–60. Camilla, Henry III's household clerk, was made archdeacon of York in 1266 and subsequently dean of Wolverhampton. See *Cal. Pat. Rolls 1258–66*, p. 573; *ibid. 1266–72*, pp. 306, 310, 523, 532, 607, 681–82, 711.

he usurped jurisdictions and franchises. He would summon people who were " extra feodum " to his courts, and when they failed to appear, amerce them.[33] He lavished cash gifts on various persons, such as royal justices and clerks, who might be of service or importance to him.[34] Occasionally he worked these connections to rather spectacular advantage. Edmund, earl of Cornwall, who was recently separated from Bogo's sister Margaret, was on his way to a meeting of the council at Westminster in 1290, when Bogo, acting on behalf of Archbishop Peckham, served an illegal writ on him, which threatened Edmund with excommunication if he refused to rejoin his wife.[35] The earl ignored the writ, and when Bogo, apparently on his own initiative, tried to imprison the earl, he was himself promptly dispatched to the Tower of London for a time and fined 2,000 marks.[36] He found a champion in Queen Eleanor, however. She had the fine reduced first to 1,500 and later to 1,000 marks. Bogo even borrowed the money from her to pay it.[37] His association with Eleanor stemmed from the fact that in his capacity as treasurer of York he was patron of the church of Nether Wallop, and in 1286 had presented her minister, Robert de Bures, to it.[38] Bures had become notorious for his extortions while steward of her properties in Wales, and was jailed after a royal investigation; his entrance into the Church should probably be regarded as an act of prudence rather than a sign of repentance.[39] Bogo used his position to secure the advancement of other clerical friends as well. Most notable among these was Walter Langton, also an energetic pluralist. Under Bogo's guidance he advanced rapidly. After Bures' death in 1289, he collated Langton to Nether Wallop, and in the following year used his authority as chancellor of Llandaff to have Langton

[33] PRO, Coram Rege Roll Trinity 9 Edward I, KB 27/62 m. 4 (Berkshire); for usurpations on his lands in Oxford and elsewhere, see *Rotuli Hundredorum* (Record Commission, 1812–18), II, 35, 800, 802, 805; *Plac. Quo War.*, p. 810.
[34] See Giuseppi, p. 13.
[35] *Rot. Parl.*, I, 17; *Reg. Epist. Peckham*, III, 969. The writ was invalid because the Roman Curia had jurisdiction over the matter. *Reg. Sutton*, III, 33–36.
[36] *Rot. Parl.*, I, 17.
[37] *Cal. Fine Rolls 1272–1307*, p. 288; *Cal. Close Rolls 1288–96*, p. 158; Sayles, *Select Cases*, II, no. 13; PRO, Coram Rege Roll Hilary 19 Edward I, KB 27/126 m. 14d.
[38] *Reg. Pontissara*, I, 22.
[39] PRO, Assize Rolls, JI 1/1149.

nominated as treasurer of that diocese.[40] Langton later went on to become keeper of the royal wardrobe, treasurer of England in 1295, and bishop of Coventry and Lichfield in 1296.[41]

When not engaged in such activities, Bogo spent enormous amounts of time and money in litigation to add to his collection of churches. He participated in complicated legal proceedings with Roger de Mowbray and the royal justices to obtain Melton Mowbray in 1284. When he saw that his title rested on shaky foundations, he leased or sold it to the priory of Lewes for an annual rent of £80.[42] He spent a quarter of a century in protracted litigation in an ultimately vain attempt to secure the church of Adlingfleet in the archdiocese of York. The story of his efforts to obtain title reveal both the complications the system of lay patronage could produce and the dogged determination with which Bogo pursued affairs he deemed to be to his interest and profit.

The right of presentation originally belonged to John d'Eyville. While he was a minor, the guardian of his lands, Roger de Mowbray, presented John le Frounceys to the church. When d'Eyville was of age in 1256, he sold lands in Adlingfleet, along with the advowson of the church, to Richard de Clare for £400 and a yearly rent of 1d.[43] By the terms of the deed, right of presentation was to be reserved to Richard and his heirs, but after the earl's death Henry III granted it in dower to his widow Maud.[44] When Frounceys died in December, 1267, great confusion ensued as to who had the right of presentation. D'Eyville felt that assigning it in dower invalidated his original sale, and on December 29 he presented Godfrey Giffard, archdeacon of York and brother of Archbishop Walter Giffard. On January 2, 1268, Countess

---

[40] *Reg. Pontissara*, I, 37–38; *Cal. Papal Letters*, I, 519; *Cal. Pat. Rolls 1281–92*, p. 387. He was soon forced to resign both positions, however.

[41] The most recent account of Langton's career is in Alice Beardwood, " The Trial of Walter Langton, Bishop of Lichfield, 1307–1312," *Transactions of the American Philosophical Society*, new ser., LIV (1964), pt. 3.

[42] Giuseppi, pp. 13–16, and PRO, Exchequer, KR Memoranda Roll 25–26 Edward I, E 159/71 mm. 12d., 55, which mentions the rent as a source of income Bogo's executors used to help pay off his debts. Bogo must have resigned the rectorship shortly after he acquired it, probably by 1286: see Giuseppi, p. 16 note 1.

[43] *Feet of Fines for the County of York, 1246–72*, ed. John Parker (Yorkshire Archaeological Society, Record Series, vol. LXXII, 1932), p. 104.

[44] *Close Rolls 1261–64*, p. 288.

Maud presented her son Bogo.[45] Earl Gilbert, feeling that by the terms of the sale he was entitled to the advowsonary rights, presented his clerk Richard Jocelin in the following September. In the meantime, Godfrey Giffard had been collated to the bishopric of Worcester, and d'Eyville in October presented Hervey de Borham, formerly a seneschal of the honor of Clare and one of Earl Gilbert's closest advisers.[46] Early in 1269 Maud appealed to Henry III, who reaffirmed that the right of presentation lay with her.[47] The situation was further complicated when Archbishop Giffard rejected all candidates and himself collated Robert de Scarborough on March 25, 1269.[48] Bogo immediately instituted an action which carried on unabated against the archbishop and his successor Wickwane;[49] and Maud brought suit for the right of presentation against d'Eyville and Earl Gilbert before the itinerant justices in York.[50] Only under Archbishop Romeyn were the issues resolved. In 1286, after nearly two decades of litigation and delay, Maud finally resigned her claims and withdrew entirely from the matter.[51] Bogo was not so easily deterred, however. He carried his case to the Roman Curia,[52] but apparently without success, for in 1287 he finally released his claims as well.[53] In 1286 Romeyn had purged Scarborough, who since 1279 had also been dean of York, on various grounds, including Scarborough's refusal to indemnify the archbishop against Bogo.[54] In 1289 he appointed Master Nicholas de Lovetot to the church on the presentation of his father John de Lovetot, who had in the meantime acquired full legal title to the advowson by purchase from d'Eyville.[55] Bogo achieved some sort of partial satisfaction when his friend Walter Langton was collated to Adlingfleet in 1292.[56]

[45] Register of Walter Giffard, Archbishop of York 1266–1279, ed. William Brown (Surtees Society, vol. CIX, 1904), p. 20 (nos. 48–49).
[46] Ibid., pp. 27–28 (nos. 85–86).
[47] Close Rolls 1268–72, p. 103.
[48] Reg. Giffard, p. 30.
[49] Ibid., pp. 268–69; Reg. Wickwane, pp. 240–41, 267–68. The case went to Rome in 1282. Cal. Papal Letters, I, 466.
[50] PRO, Assize Rolls, JI 1/1050 m. 91.
[51] Reg. Romeyn, I, 47: " advertentes nos jus presentandi ad eandem (ecclesiam) non habere, quam de facto ad eandem fecimus."
[52] Ibid., I, 62–63, 74. Cf. Giuseppi, p. 35, where various sums are allowed members of Bogo's household staff " pro expensis suis versus Curiam Romanam."
[53] Reg. Romeyn, I, 74.
[54] Ibid., I, 62–63; II, Introduction, pp. xx–xxi.
[55] Ibid., I, 91–93; Cal. Papal Letters, I, 525; Cal. Inq. Post Mortem, III, no. 207.
[56] Reg. Romeyn, I, 117.

When Bogo did obtain title to a benefice, he immediately farmed it out, often for sums far in excess of its official valuation. Swanscombe and Rotherfield, which were valued at 20 and 30 marks, were farmed for £31 18s. 6d. and 80 marks respectively.[57] In the wardrobe accounts printed by Giuseppi, income from farms constitute the major source of revenue. No individual sums are recorded for the churches in the northern diocese, however; Bogo probably used the Mozzi and other Italian societies, who were also widely used by the papacy to collect its revenues,[58] as agents for his more remote benefices.[59] There is some evidence, however, that he at least supplied the churches with men of ecclesiastical training. William de Bocking was both chaplain and farmer of Rotherfield, while Holywell was farmed in 1284 by a Master Stephen de Balliol.[60]

Bogo watched over his farmers closely, sending his officials out of the household on a regular basis to supervise them. He employed his most important ministers, such as Thomas le Fox and Walter de Regny, both of whom served as wardrobers, for his affairs in the northern provinces.[61] He held his farmers to strict accountability, on one occasion going before the Barons of the Exchequer to collect £65 8s. owed in arrears of the farm of Kilkhampton by a certain William de Penland.[62] While Bogo engaged extensively in farming, the practice as a whole was not as prevalent in the thirteenth century as it was to become in the fourteenth, when even baronial patrons farmed out their advowsonary rights.[63]

[57] *Reg. Sutton*, II, 3; Giuseppi, p. 27; PRO, Min. Accts., SC 6/1028/7.
[58] On this subject see W. E. Lunt, *Financial Relations of the Papacy with England to 1327* (Cambridge, Mass., 1939), *passim.*
[59] See Giuseppi, pp. 12, 27, for evidence and commentary.
[60] PRO, Min. Accts., SC 6/1028/7; *Cartulary of the Hospital of St. John the Baptist,* ed. H. E. Salter (Oxford Historical Series, vols. LXVI, LXVIII–LXIX, 1914–16), II, 347.
[61] Giuseppi, p. 33, where payments are allowed " in expensis dominorum Thome le Fox (et) Walteri de Reygny de London usque Ebor', Dunholm', Ceterinton' et Donecastr' a festo sancti Petri in Augusto . . . per Lj dies."
[62] PRO, Exchequer, KR Memoranda Roll 13–14 Edward I, E 159/59 mm. 12, 12d.
[63] A list of the values of farms of advowsons in the possession of the Bohun family, dating from the last third of the fourteenth century, is contained in PRO, Rentals and Surveys, Portfolio Series, SC 12/18/32. For instances in which farming was employed in the thirteenth century, see Lunt, *Financial Relations,* pp. 315–16, 323, 491.

Bogo's relationships with his farmers and regular officials varied considerably, according to the degree to which they served their master faithfully. Walter de Chausey was farmer of Holywell from at least 1273 to 1281, and seems to have left office peacefully.[64] William de Bocking, chaplain and farmer of Rotherfield, did not fare as well. His account was audited and he was charged with owing some £40 which he had claimed as legitimate expenses. Some of Bogo's men formed a sort of posse, came down, expelled him, destroyed his writs and tallies, and had him thrown into jail in Fleet Street until he paid up.[65] Occasionally the tables could be turned on Bogo, as when he charged his wardrober Walter de Regny with arrears on his accounts during his term of office. The case went to the Exchequer of Pleas, and after lengthy proceedings, Regny was acquitted.[66] On the whole, however, Bogo's staff seems to have acted diligently in his behalf, and he rewarded them well with lavish banquets and amusements and costly liveries of furs and other items.[67]

Bogo de Clare was obviously uninterested in an ecclesiastical career devoted to piety and good works; but just as obviously, he was well at home in the institutional structure of the Church. He was stirred to action only when he had an opportunity to add to his wealth or position. Apart from aiding the other members of his family, he never intended to use his energies or abilities, which were considerable, for any other purpose than his own amusement and gain. He developed a reputation that has long outlived him. When he died in October, 1294, the event was noted with scorn by the authors of the Dunstable chronicle and the *Flores Historiarum*, while the Lanercost chronicler, with more

[64] *Cart. Hosp. St. John the Baptist*, II, 346–47, 350–51, 365–66, 369 (deeds to which Walter is witness within these dates).

[65] PRO, Min. Accts., SC 6/1028/7. See Giuseppi, p. 27, where a sum of 7 marks in part payment of the debt is received " de fideiussoribus domini W. de Boking'." By destroying his records of course, Bogo's men eliminated any evidence he could have used to clear himself.

[66] The case is printed in *Select Cases in the Exchequer of Pleas*, eds. Hilary Jenkinson and Beryl Fermoy (Selden Society, vol. XLVIII, 1931), no. 170, and is summarized in Denholm-Young, *Seignorial Administration*, pp. 156–58. On the forms of procedure involved, see Plucknett, *Legislation of Edward I*, p. 153 and note 2. The accounts printed by Giuseppi owed their survival to the fact that they were produced during the proceedings and were preserved in the exchequer archives.

[67] Cf. the remarks of Giuseppi, pp. 8–11, 17–18.

zeal than style, painted a sardonic picture of him.[68] In the present day, he has been described as a man to whom the collecting of benefices and livings was " an occupation and a passion." [69] He was, in short, simply the most successful and notorious example of a certain breed of worldly and greedy churchmen of his day, who earned the denunciation of more spiritual men, and whose actions, in Giuseppi's words, " were to bring their whole order into discredit, and to excite in the succeeding century the bitter invective of a Langland and the good-humoured sarcasm of a Chaucer." [70]

Thomas de Clare and Ireland

The career of Bogo's elder brother Thomas exemplifies the other major course open to younger sons in great baronial and comital families. Many members of the lesser nobility were attracted to a public career. Barons such as Geoffrey de Genevill and Robert de Tibetot served King Edward in the affairs of state; and the younger brothers of the earls of Hereford and Warwick occasionally were employed in the royal administration. But aside from Hugh Bigod, brother of the earl of Norfolk, whose activities as justiciar in the period of the baronial reform movement took place under exceptional circumstances, Thomas de Clare represents the best example of a landless member of a comital family engaged in service to the Crown in the later thirteenth century.[71]

The date of Thomas' birth is unknown, but it probably falls sometime between that of Gilbert in 1243 and Bogo in 1248.[72] It is possible that his father intended a clerical or administrative career for him, since he attended Oxford with Bogo from 1257

[68] Dunstable, p. 400: "dives multum in beneficiis ecclesiasticis, sed moribus pauper." *Flores Hist.*, III, 93: " multarum rector ecclesiarum-vel potius, incubator." *Chronicon de Lanercost*, ed. J. Stevenson (Bannatyne Club, 1839), I, 158: " In dicto festo (*sc.* All Saints) recessit a seculo solemni nomine, sed non conversatione, Bovo (*sic*) de Clare, non satis, ut dicitur, claro fine et merito, quippe qui innumeras occupaverat ecclesias, et male gubernaverat eas quas Christus suo commercio adquisierat, nam curales exercens ordines non curavit, curam animarum exsufflavit, proventus ecclesiarum dilapidavit. . . ."

[69] Thompson, " Pluralism," p. 53.

[70] Giuseppi, p. 18.

[71] Cf. the remarks of Powicke, *King Henry III*, II, 698–701.

[72] Tewkesbury, pp. 130, 136.

to 1259.[73] While sedentary and scholarly pursuits appealed no more to him than they did to his brother, he found different outlets in which to develop his capabilities. He became involved in political affairs, and soon assumed an active role in the rising conflict between the king and the reform movement led by Simon de Montfort and Earl Gilbert the Red. At first, undoubtedly under the influence of Gilbert, he sided with Earl Simon, and was knighted by him before the battle of Lewes.[74] After Simon's victory, he became an important aide. In August, 1264, he assisted the earl in arranging the exchange of hostages to ensure the co-operation of the marchers, and in April, 1265, Simon appointed him to the strategic position of constable of St. Briavel's castle in Gloucestershire.[75]

About this time, Thomas began to form what was to grow into a lasting friendship with the Lord Edward. He seems quickly to have become one of Edward's most intimate advisors, for Wykes describes him as the " familiaris et cubicularius " of Henry III's heir as early as 1265.[76] When the break between Edward and Gilbert on the one hand and Simon on the other erupted in the spring of that year, Thomas helped Edward escape to join forces with his brother.[77] He fought with Gilbert at Evesham, both gaining the king's pardon for their previous allegiance to Montfort.[78] Like the earl, Thomas engaged in wholesale seizures of rebel lands after the battle, often acting in close conjunction with his brother.[79] He seemed to have a marked preference for the estates of Henry de Hastings, whom he had personally captured and jailed.[80] In addition, the king rewarded him with various escheats and forfeitures,[81] including a grant of all the lands of Peter de Montfort, whose son later redeemed them for £1,000.[82]

---

[73] See the references cited in note 7, above.

[74] *Ann. Wigorn.*, p. 451.

[75] *Cal. Pat. Rolls 1258–66*, pp. 344, 419. He retained St. Briavel's until 1284. *Cal. Close Rolls 1279–88*, p. 276.

[76] Wykes, pp. 162–63.

[77] Powicke, *King Henry III*, II, 497–98.

[78] *Cal. Pat. Rolls 1258–66*, p. 460.

[79] *Rotuli Selecti*, pp. 141, 225; *Cal. Inq. Misc.*, I, nos. 610, 656, 673, 809, 846, 895.

[80] *Cal. Inq. Misc.*, no. 613. Hastings managed to escape and took refuge in Kenilworth.

[81] *Cal. Pat. Rolls 1266–72*, pp. 57, 63, 187.

[82] *Close Rolls 1264–68*, pp. 378–79, 540–41.

Thomas' association with the Lord Edward became increasingly more intimate. Unlike Earl Gilbert, he participated in the crusade, taking the cross at St. Paul's, London, in 1267, at the instigation of the legate Ottobuono.[83] In August, 1269, he accompanied Edward to Paris to make final arrangements with Louis IX, and set out with some eighty other knights in the summer of 1270.[84] In the Holy Land he found ample opportunity to exercise his knightly prowess, and is said to have returned with four Saracen captives.[85]

Thomas was back in England by February, 1272,[86] but left again in April for Gascony as the envoy and secretary of King Henry and Edward, to deal with administrative matters and to do homage on their behalf for the Agenais, which was owed the king of France by the terms of the Treaty of Paris of 1259. This commission occupied Thomas for the remainder of the year, and he did not return to England until January, 1273.[87]

From the first, Edward encouraged his father to make use of Thomas' talents in the public administration of the kingdom, and continued this policy after he himself succeeded to the throne. Positions of importance and prestige in England rapidly accrued to the Red Earl's brother in this period. He was entrusted with control of a number of major castles in addition to St. Briavel's. He became constable of Colchester in October, 1266, a position which he retained until April, 1268, and held custody of Rockingham from April, 1272, until September, 1275.[88] In addition, he was keeper of Porchester castle from February, 1272, to August, 1273, when it was assigned in dower to Henry III's widow Eleanor.[89] Thomas also held the stewardship of a number of royal

[83] *Flores Hist.*, III, 14.

[84] Powicke, *King Henry III*, II, 576; *Cal. Pat. Rolls 1266–72*, pp. 440, 461, 479.

[85] *Flores Hist.*, III, 24.

[86] *Cal. Pat. Rolls 1266–72*, pp. 625–26. The Waverly and Worcester chronicles erroneously state that he returned with Edward in August 1274. *Ann. Waverly*, p. 376; *Ann. Wigorn.*, p. 459.

[87] *Cal. Pat. Rolls 1266–72*, pp. 643, 646, 649, 651–52, 661–62; Powicke, *King Henry III*, II, 587–88. The question of the Agenais was not fully settled, however, until 1279. Powicke, *Thirteenth Century*, pp. 289, 291–93; Thomas N. Bisson, "An Early Provincial Assembly: the General Court of Agenais in the Thirteenth Century," *Speculum*, XXXVI (1961), 271–72.

[88] *Cal. Pat. Rolls 1258–66*, pp. 642, 645, 649; *Cal. Pat. Rolls 1266–72*, p. 218; *Cal. Fine Rolls 1272–1307*, p. 57.

[89] *Cal. Pat. Rolls 1266–72*, p. 626; *ibid.* *1272–81*, p. 27.

forests. He was appointed steward of the forest of Essex in October, 1266, and although he surrendered it in 1275 his descendants claimed hereditary title to the office.[90] He was also steward of the forest between Oxford and Stamford from April, 1272, a post which did become hereditary in his family.[91] He seems to have held the stewardship of the forest of Dean in 1284 as well.[92] These offices indicate the favor Thomas enjoyed from the monarchy. The positions were quite lucrative, and largely honorary; they entailed no arduous duties, the performance of which would in any case be deputized.[93] Edward employed him in a number of other capacities as well. After his return from Gascony, Thomas occasionally acted as justice of oyer and terminer for Norfolk and Suffolk, and as late as November, 1275, when he had become absorbed in Irish affairs, he returned to England to act as mediator for the king in a dispute between the bishop and citizens of Norwich. He was also chief assessor and collector for Oxford and Berkshire of the fifteenth on movables granted in that year.[94]

Thomas' connections with Ireland were also the direct result of his friendship with Edward. In April, 1269, Edward, as overlord of Ireland, granted him the custody of the lands and the marriage of the heir of Maurice fitz Gerald, third baron of Offaly, who had died in 1268.[95] As he was about to depart with Edward on crusade, Thomas sold the wardship to William de Valence, lord of Pembroke, for 3,500 marks in March, 1270.[96] The experience,

---

[90] *Ibid.* 1266–72, p. 680; *Cal. Close Rolls 1272–79*, p. 520; *Rot. Parl.*, I, 205 (1307).

[91] *Cal. Pat. Rolls 1266–72*, p. 642; *Cal. Fine Rolls 1307–19*, p. 14.

[92] *Cal. Close Rolls 1279–88*, p. 276.

[93] E.g., the forest in Oxford was almost immediately deputized: *Close Rolls 1268–72*, p. 489. Forest administration is discussed by G. J. Turner, *Select Pleas of the Forest* (Selden Society, vol. XIII, 1899), Introduction.

[94] *Cal. Pat. Rolls 1272–81*, pp. 4–5, 121; *Cal. Close Rolls 1272–79*, pp. 12, 65, 217, 251.

[95] *Close Rolls 1268–72*, p. 111. Thomas appointed Adam de Stratton, an unsavory churchman, as his representative in England while he was in Ireland attending to the matter. Stratton also appears as a witness to one of Thomas' charters in 1275. *Ibid.*; *Cartulary of St. Mary Clerkenwell*, ed. W. O. Hassall (Camden Society, 3rd ser., vol. LXXI, 1949), pp. 265–66. For Stratton's career, see Powicke, *Thirteenth Century*, pp. 364–65; Denholm-Young, *Seignorial Administration*, pp. 77–85.

[96] *Close Rolls 1268–72*, pp. 268–70, and cf. *Royal Letters*, II, 345–46 (February, 1270). Later, both the grant to Thomas and the subsequent sale were successfully

however, must have impressed Thomas, opening to him the possibilities of independent action and position in Ireland. Powicke has suggested that he may have wished to free himself from the dominating influence of Earl Gilbert, and that Edward, realizing this fact and recognizing Thomas' abilities, felt he would be a valuable asset in consolidating royal authority there.[97]

The subject must have been discussed between them when Edward returned to England in August, 1274, because Thomas sailed to Ireland in the fall of 1274 and quickly established himself as one of Edward's most able lieutenants for Irish affairs. He was employed in judicial activities with Edward's chief officials, and developed a close friendship with the justiciar, Geoffrey de Genevill, who appointed him sheriff of Limerick, a post he held until June, 1276. Thomas also became chancellor of Ireland in 1275 and acted on various commissions for the king.[98] Early in 1275 he firmly established himself in Ireland by marrying Juliana, daughter and eventual heir of Maurice fitz Maurice (d. 1286), a former justiciar and an important landowner in Connaught and elsewhere.[99]

Edward also made use of Thomas' military abilities in his efforts to extend royal authority in the country. Thomond, a dependent territory in Limerick held by the Irish for a tributary rent, was being ravaged by an uprising of the local chieftains, the O'Briens. On January 26, 1276, Thomas was granted the

---

challenged by Roger Mortimer, who claimed that control fell to him in right of his share of the Marshal inheritance. *Cal. Docs. Ireland 1252–84*, no. 1039. See also *Cal. Pat. Rolls 1272–81*, pp. 12–13; Sayles, *Select Cases*, II, no. 35.

[97] Powicke, *King Henry III*, II, 700.

[98] Thomas came to Ireland sometime after October, 1274, when letters of protection were issued to him. *Cal. Close Rolls 1272–79*, p. 131. For his commissions and the chancellorship, see *Cal. Pat. Rolls 1272–81*, pp. 96, 117; Orpen, *Ireland under the Normans*, IV, 65; *Cal. Docs. Ireland 1252–84*, no. 1163. Thomas surrendered the office of sheriff when Genevill was replaced as justiciar by Robert de Offord. He was probably granted the office shortly after his arrival, for Genevill had been given power to appoint sheriffs in September, 1274. *Cal. Pat. Rolls 1272–81*, pp. 57, 149. See also *Irish Pipe Roll 5 Edward I* (36th Report of the Deputy Keeper of the Public Records, Ireland [Dublin: H.M. Stationery Office, 1904]), p. 39 (hereafter cited as D.K. Report).

[99] Orpen, IV, 66; *Cal. Docs. Ireland 1285–92*, no. 1142. Maurice was a younger son of the Maurice fitz Gerald who died in 1268. As a marriage portion, Juliana brought the manor of Corkmoyth, Limerick, to Thomas. Thomas was also lord of Youghal, Cork, in June 1275, although it is not known how he acquired it. *Cal. Pat. Rolls 1272–81*, p. 98.

whole of the territory to be held as a fief for the services of ten knights' fees—and the responsibility for pacifying it.[100] He rapidly began to fill out his possessions in his new lordship. He was granted custody of Castle–Connel, and was allowed to make an exchange of land with Robert de Muscegros (lord of the castle and liberty of Bunratty with other lands), who had surrendered them into the king's hands for safekeeping during the uprising.[101] Edward gave Thomas license to acquire these properties in exchange for various manors he held in Oxford and Berkshire, and the transaction was completed by March 4, when the justiciar was ordered to surrender the lands to him.[102] In addition, in 1278, he obtained the manor of Knockainy in Limerick from Edmund de Bassingbourne in exchange for the manor of Blyborough, Lincoln.[103] Both Thomas and Edward stood to profit by these transactions. Thomas clearly intended to secure a well-defined and substantial endowment in Thomond for himself and his heirs, while the king had made the grant to him as a reward for his previous services and in return for his ability to pacify the territory.

At the same time an expedition, led by Thomas, his father-in-law Maurice fitz Maurice, and Geoffrey de Genevill, was sent against the MacMurroughs of Glenmalure. A second expedition, led by Thomas and the new justiciar, Robert de Offord, was required before the MacMurroughs were captured and the territory subdued in the fall of 1277.[104] Thomas had a personal interest in the success of the campaign, for Edward had promised in return to supply him with knights to help him conquer Thomond.[105] Fighting raged intermittently while Thomas awaited the promised

[100] *Cal. Chart. Rolls 1257–1300*, p. 198; *Cal. Pat. Rolls 1272–81*, p. 135. He was allowed to hold the liberty for five fees in his lifetime, his heirs to do the service of ten fees. *Cal. Pat. Rolls 1272–81*, p. 134. On the rising of the O'Briens, see Orpen, *Ireland under the Normans*, IV, 61–65. Most of Thomond is now comprised in modern county Clare, but despite the coincidence the name does not derive from the family: see Orpen, *Ireland under the Normans*, IV, 65 note.
[101] *Cal. Pat. Rolls 1272–81*, pp. 107, 134; *Cal. Chart. Rolls 1226–57*, pp. 377–78. Muscegros also held the cantred of Tradery and the theod of Ocormok.
[102] *Cal. Fine Rolls 1272–1307*, p. 66; *Cal. Pat. Rolls 1272–81*, p. 136. The text of the exchange with Muscegros is preserved in PRO, Exchequer, KR Memoranda Roll 13–14 Edward I, E 159/59 m. 20.
[103] *Cal. Chart. Rolls 1257–1300*, p. 210.
[104] See Orpen, *Ireland under the Normans*, IV, 17–19.
[105] *Cal. Close Rolls 1272–79*, p. 471.

reinforcements. In 1277 he captured and killed Brian O'Brien, allegedly breaking a compact between them, but the following year Brian's son, Duncan, defeated Thomas in a pitched battle, destroying most of his force. Thomas' response was to build the great castle of Quin to safeguard his frontiers.[106] He petitioned the king's council at Westminster for aid in 1278,[107] but it was not until 1281 that a force led by Robert de Offord and Theobald Butler finally enabled Thomas to put down the resistance and complete the building of his castle.[108]

The ensuing period of peace allowed Thomas to engage in other activities in the royal service. He sat on the king's Irish council in 1280 [109] and in 1282 served as Edward's agent in raising loans in Ireland to help meet the expenses of the Welsh wars.[110] He came to England in November, 1283, and frequently appears as a witness to charters issued by the king at Carmarthen and elsewhere in England and Wales at this time. He remained in England for nearly a year, until a fresh outbreak in Thomond caused him to return to the lordship in the fall of 1284. The disturbance was quickly put down, and Thomas resumed his activities on behalf of the Crown in 1285–86. He died on August 29, 1287, at about the age of forty, of unknown but apparently natural causes. The story which appears in some local chronicles that he was killed by the Irish has been discredited.[111]

By the time of his death, Thomas de Clare had built up a great landed endowment for his descendants. He held numerous properties in England, including the manor of Tarrant Rushton and the hundred of Coombsditch, Dorset, and lands in Standon, Hertford, all by enfeoffment of his brother, Earl Gilbert the Red. In

[106] *Annals of Loch Cé*, ed. and trans. W. M. Hennessy (Rolls Series LIV, 1871), I, 481, 483; *Annals of Inisfallen*, ed. and trans. Sean Mac Airt (Dublin, 1951), pp. 373, 375.

[107] PRO, Council and Parliamentary Proceedings (Chancery), C 49/1/9.

[108] *Cal. Docs. Ireland 1252–84*, nos. 1835, 1860, 1892; Orpen, *Ireland under the Normans*, IV, 105–6. The war is described in detail by Orpen, IV, 67–72.

[109] *Cal. Close Rolls 1279–88*, p. 55. On the council, see H. G. Richardson and G. O. Sayles, *The Irish Parliament in the Middle Ages* (Philadelphia, 1952), pp. 20–38.

[110] *Foedera*, I, 617; *Parl. Writs*, I, 225; *Cal. Welsh Rolls*, pp. 239–40.

[111] *Cal. Pat. Rolls 1281–92*, pp. 16, 134, 188; *Reg. Pontissara*, II, 419, from the charter rolls; *Cal. Docs. Ireland 1252–84*, no. 206; Robert Brentano, *York Metropolitan Jurisdiction and Papal Judges Delegate 1279–1296* (Berkeley, 1959), p. 137; Orpen, *Ireland under the Normans*, IV, 74, and for his death *ibid.*, IV, 99–104.

addition he had purchased or been granted lands and tenements in Cambridge, Suffolk, Oxford, and Middlesex.[112] The bulk of his estates, however, were in Ireland. Besides the liberty of Thomond granted by Edward, and Bunratty, Knockainy, Youghal and Corkmoyth, all obtained through marriage or purchase, he had scattered manors in various counties, including Mahoonagh in Limerick, Inchiquin in Cork, and Ballydugall in Kerry. After 1286 he also held half the lands of his father-in-law, Maurice fitz Maurice, who died in that year. Interestingly enough, Thomas held no manors in his brother's liberty of Kilkenny.[113]

It is difficult to describe the organization of his Irish lands in detail. Thomond seems to have been organized as a shire along much the same lines as the liberty of Kilkenny held by the senior branch of the Clares, with Bunratty forming the *caput* of the lordship.[114] The royal government, however, seems still to have regarded it as a division of Limerick, and both military service and the rents and farms due for various lands within it were entered on the exchequer records under that county.[115] Thomond itself does not appear as a separate shire on the Irish Pipe Rolls except in times of escheat.[116] In his original grant, Edward stipulated that Thomas was to hold Thomond " as fully as the Marshals or others " had held their liberties. This meant that the king reserved to himself control over episcopal lands and appointments within the lordship, as well as the four major pleas of the Crown and the right of appeal to the court of the justiciar.[117] While the former property of the O'Briens was held by knight service, other lands within the lordship were held at fee farm. Tradery was

[112] Cal. Inq. Post Mortem, IV, no. 435 (pp. 314–15); Pedes Finium or Fines Relating to County Cambridge, 7 Richard I–Richard III, ed. Walter Rye (Cambridge Antiquarian Society, 1891), p. 48; Calendar of Feet of Fines for Suffolk, ed. Walter Rye (Suffolk Institute of Archaeology and Natural History, 1900), p. 65; Rot. Hund., II, 186–87; Cat. Ancient Deeds, I, 493, II, 163.
[113] Cal. Docs. Ireland 1285–92, no. 459; PRO, Chanc. Misc., C 47/10/17 no. 12.
[114] Cal. Docs. Ireland 1285–92, no. 459 (p. 208), mentions under Bunratty the perquisites of the county court. See also Cal. Inq. Post Mortem, III, no. 507.
[115] E. g., Cal. Docs. Ireland 1252–84, no. 2329.
[116] Irish Pipe Roll 26 Edward I (38th D.K. Report, 1906), p. 39; Irish Pipe Roll 12 Edward II (42nd D.K. Report, 1911), p. 20.
[117] Cal. Chart. Rolls 1257–1300, p. 198; Cal. Pat. Rolls 1272–81, p. 135. For similar restrictions placed on his brother's liberty of Kilkenny, see below, Chapter IX. For Thomas' relations with the bishopric of Limerick, see The Black Book of Limerick, ed. Rev. J. MacCaffrey (Dublin, 1907), pp. 31, 102, 105–6.

held for an annual rent of 6s. 8d., Ogashin for 200 marks, Castle Connel for £6 8s. and the cantred of Clare for 41 marks.[118] A great deal of the revenues of the lordship derived from tributary rents of the O'Briens. Bunratty was worth £170, of which £120, about two-thirds, came from such rents.[119] Thomas probably commanded an annual income of some £950 from his Irish properties in Thomond and elsewhere, and a total of over £1,000 including his English estates and perquisites of the administrative and judicial offices he held. By means of diligent service to the royal government and private resourcefulness, Thomas de Clare had risen from a landless member of a comital house to the head of a great Anglo–Irish family.[120]

The inheritance, however, did not long outlast him. Thomas left two sons who succeeded to the estates, two daughters, the eventual coheiresses, and an illegitimate son, Master Richard.[121] The eldest son, Gilbert, was born in 1281. In 1299, although still underage, he was granted seisin of his father's lands, and the following year, when his mother Juliana died, he recovered the lands she had held in dower as well.[122] Gilbert, however, spent little time in Ireland and seems to have largely neglected his estates. In 1300, he was admitted to the household of the prince of Wales, the future Edward II. He served as a valet of the prince and became one of his closest friends and companions. He has sometimes been confused with his cousin and namesake, the last Earl Gilbert, who was also friendly with Edward, but the earl at this time was a member of the household of Queen Margaret.[123] Gilbert remained in Prince Edward's household until

---

[118] *Cal. Docs. Ireland 1252–84*, no. 2329; PRO, Chanc. Misc., C 47/10/17 no. 12.

[119] *Cal. Docs. Ireland 1252–84*, no. 2329. The O'Briens had held the land of the king for 120 marks before their uprising. Thomas was originally charged with their debts, but was absolved in 1280. *Ibid.*, nos 1675, 2329.

[120] The figure for the Irish estates is derived from the escheator's accounts entered on *Irish Pipe Roll 16 Edward I* and *18 Edward I* (37th D.K. Report, 1905), pp. 35–36, 42. It receives further verification from the fact that the widow of Thomas' son Richard held one-third of the lands in dower in 1318 with a stated value of some £300. *Irish Pipe Roll 12 Edward II*, p. 20.

[121] For the latter, see below, pp. 239–40.

[122] *Cal. Close Rolls 1296–1302*, pp. 272, 366. Juliana had married Adam de Creting in 1292. He died in 1296 without issue. *Cal. Docs. Ireland 1285–92*, no. 1142.

[123] *Cal. Docs. Scot.*, II, no. 1352, from PRO, Chanc. Misc., C 47/22/4 no. 34. The editor, Bain, confuses him with the earl (see Index, p. 595), and the incorrect

1307. He served in the Scottish campaigns of 1303–4, although for some reason he failed to serve in the campaign of 1306, and his English estates were confiscated for a time.[124]

Gilbert died without issue in 1308 and was succeeded as lord of Thomond by his younger brother, Richard. Like Gilbert, Richard's identity has also been confused. He has been identified with his bastard half brother, Master Richard, but the legitimate Richard was never a clerk.[125] Unlike Gilbert, Richard was continuously engaged in Irish affairs. He was sheriff of Cork in 1309 and again from 1312 to 1316.[126] He also fought for the king during the invasion of Ireland by Edward Bruce,[127] and in May, 1316, was granted custody of the liberty of Kilkenny, in the king's hands following the death of the last Earl Gilbert.[128] Richard's major task, however, was fighting uprisings in his own lordship of Thomond. He was faced with a number of rebellions, probably inspired by his brother's largely absentee overlordship and Bruce's invasion, in the period after 1308, and although generally successful, he was finally slain by the Irish in 1318.[129]

Richard's death in effect marked the end of the Norman lordship of Thomond. He did leave a son Thomas, but the young heir died in 1321 at the age of three. His death brought the male line of the cadet branch of the Clares to an end. The estates were divided between Richard's sisters, Maud, wife of Robert de Welle, and Margaret, wife of Bartholomew de Badlesmere.[130] Neither husband, whose interests lay in England, seems to have

---

identification has misled a number of scholars. Johnstone, *Edward of Carnarvon*, p. 75.

[124] *Cal. Fine Rolls 1272–1307*, pp. 543–44; *Cal. Close Rolls 1302–07*, pp. 481–82, 530–31; PRO, Exchequer, KR Accts. Var., E 101/91/9–10, 357/28, 360/17; *Cal. Chanc. War.*, pp. 169, 187, 225; *Parl. Writs*, I, 378, 379.

[125] *G. E. C.*, V, 701.

[126] *Cal. Fine Rolls 1307–19*, p. 48; *Irish Pipe Roll 16 Edward II* (42nd D.K. Report, 1911), p. 49.

[127] The fullest account of Bruce's invasion is in Orpen, *Ireland Under the Normans*, IV, 169–205. See also J. F. Lydon, "The Bruce Invasion of Ireland," *Historical Studies*, IV (1963), 111–25.

[128] *Cal. Pat. Rolls 1313–17*, p. 459.

[129] Orpen, *Ireland under the Normans*, IV, 94–95. His wife died in 1322.

[130] *Cal. Chanc. War.*, p. 526; PRO, Exchequer, LTR Originalia Roll 15 Edward II, E 371/81 m. 14. Maud had first married Robert de Clifford of Westmoreland in 1295. He died at Bannockburn in 1314. Margaret was married in 1289 to Gilbert de Umphraville, son of the earl of Angus. Gilbert died before 1307, and she married Badlesmere in 1312.

concerned himself with Thomond and the other estates in Ireland. Badlesmere was executed in 1322, and Robert de Welle seems to have died about the same time. The estates escheated to the Crown, and although the sisters petitioned for their return in 1327,[181] neither they nor the king could have exercised effective overlordship by that date. Following the death of Richard de Clare in 1318, the native Irish had quickly resumed full control, and English rule in Thomond thus came to an end until the Tudor reconquest in 1543.[182] For the second time in the history of the Clare family, the failure of the male line prevented a cadet branch from assuming a position of lasting power and importance among the great Anglo–Irish families. The association of the Clares with Ireland, which had begun so auspiciously with Strong-bow's conquest of Leinster, ended in disorder and neglect a century and a half later.

---

[181] *Cal. Fine Rolls 1327–37*, pp. 30–31.
[182] Orpen, *Ireland under the Normans*, IV, 95–96.

PART II: THE ESTATES

CHAPTER VII

EARL OF GLOUCESTER

In the thirteenth and early fourteenth centuries, the head of the house of Clare was one of the greatest landholders in the British Isles. At once powerful English earls, the greatest of the marcher lords of Wales, and important Anglo–Irish landlords, the Clares had the standing and the material resources to play a vigorous and sometimes decisive role in the political life of the kingdom. Like the Marshals, Bigods, Mortimers, and the other great baronial families, the Clares were more interested in the business of war and politics, in hunting and in tournaments, than in the system of estate management or the diversification of crops. But they by no means neglected these affairs. They strove constantly to increase the profitability of the inheritance and to make its administration and control more effective; and they associated with themselves a host of estate and household officials and other *familiares* to serve their interests. The inheritance, an interdependent complex of manors, courts, and fees, was the basis of their power. A study of the organization of its three major components, in England, Wales, and Ireland, forms a natural complement to the discussion of the political activities of its lords.

Introductory. The Wealth of the Earls

The over-all economic structure of the inheritance is unfortunately obscured in a number of important places by a relative scarcity of information. Very few central financial records of the family have survived, and it is necessary to rely mainly on government accounts and valuations made during periods of royal control to estimate the gross annual income of the earls or to consider their wealth on a comparative basis with other great baronial houses in the period of this study. The results are far from satisfactory, and all that can be said with full certainty is that income tended to rise steadily throughout the entire thirteenth and early fourteenth centuries, and that the Clares were easily among the two or three richest families in England in this period.

Very little evidence remains for the early thirteenth century. The fullest information derives from the Pipe Roll accounts for the period of Richard de Clare's wardship from 1230 to 1243, but these accounts, while helpful, are incomplete. The lordship of Glamorgan, the honor of Tonbridge and numerous other manors in England were held in custody at various times by Richard of Cornwall, Gilbert Marshal, Hubert de Burgh, the archbishops of Canterbury and other prominent men, and it is impossible to make any precise calculation of the value of the entire inheritance at any given time. The accounts rendered by the keeper, Richard de la Lade, for 1237–42 indicate a gross annual income of about £500 from some scattered estates in Dorset, Gloucestershire, and Oxford appurtenant to the honor of Gloucester and in royal custody during those years. A somewhat fuller but still incomplete account for the honor of Clare, including Clare and other manors in Essex, Hertford, Kent, Norfolk, Northampton, Suffolk, and Sussex, reveal a gross income of almost £750 in 1237–38 and about £600 per annum for the period 1238–42. Since these figures do not include all the demesne manors of the honors of Gloucester and Clare, there is no way of knowing their total value in the early decades of the thirteenth century.[1] Under Henry II and John, to judge from the Pipe Roll accounts dating from their reigns, the honor of Gloucester seems to have been worth between £450 and £600 a year, with Bristol supplying some 20–25 per cent of the total; and the lordship of Glamorgan brought in about £225 in 1184–85, when it came into Henry II's hands following the death of William, earl of Gloucester.[2] No estimate is possible for the honor of Clare in this period. No estate accounts have survived, and as Richard, earl of Hertford and the first Earl Gilbert were of full age when they succeeded to the honor, the

---

[1] PRO, Pipe Rolls 21 and 25 Henry III, E 372/81 r. 14, E 372/85 r. 4.
[2] Sidney Painter, *Studies in the History of the English Feudal Barony* (Baltimore, 1943), pp. 70 and note 159, 166; *Cartae de Glamorgan*, I, 170–73.

Pipe Rolls are also silent. The twelfth-century earls of Hertford were well off, but it seems reasonable to surmise that the addition of the honor of Gloucester and the lordship of Glamorgan to the Clare inheritance in 1217 more than doubled annual income, despite the loss of Bristol.

The fullest statements of the family income are those contained in the government valuations of 1266–67, when dower was reassigned to Earl Richard's widow Maud, and 1317–20, when the estates were partitioned among the sisters of the last Earl Gilbert.[3] The figures, if at all reliable, indicate that total income rose by more than 50 per cent between the two dates. In 1266–67, the honor of Clare was officially valued at £1,200, and the Gloucester and Giffard lands at £950. The Welsh lordships of Glamorgan and Usk (the latter acquired in 1246) were said to be worth £850, thus bringing the total to £3,000. This set of figures, however, is not complete, for the Dorset manors and the estates appurtenant to the honor of Tonbridge and to the lordship of Kilkenny are not included in the survey. Kilkenny was worth about £350 at this time,[4] and the Dorset and Tonbridge lands, to judge by some later evidence, in all likelihood brought in at least a similar amount, although there are no adequate figures for the mid-thirteenth century. Total gross income at the time of Earl Richard's death, therefore, was probably around £3,700 or perhaps somewhat higher.

In 1317 the inheritance seems to have been worth close to £6,000. The English estates, including those held in dower by the last earl's widow, were valued at some £3,000, the Welsh lordships at almost £2,500, and Kilkenny at about £500. Some of the valuations of individual properties, especially the marcher lordships, may be too high.[5] Holmes, however, regards the £6,000 figure for the entire inheritance as substantially accurate,[6] and the general reliability of the figures, at least for the English estates, is borne out by some earlier and more precise evidence. A surviving

---

[3] PRO, Rentals and Surveys, General Series, SC 11/610 mm. 1–7 (an expanded and corrected version of the 1262 valuations entered on *Close Rolls 1261–64*, pp. 284–93); PRO, Chanc. Misc., C 47/9/23–25.

[4] Below, Chapter IX.

[5] On this point, see below, pp. 257–58.

[6] G. A. Holmes, *Estates of the Higher Nobility in Fourteenth Century England* (Cambridge, 1957), p. 36 and note 1.

receiver's account for the East Anglian manors of the honor of
Clare for 1307–8 reveals a gross income that year of just under
£1,000 excluding arrears, while the honor of Tonbridge and
appurtenant estates in southeastern England yielded almost £700
in 1299–1300, when they were in royal custody following their
seizure by Edward I after he learned of Joan of Acre's marriage
to Ralph de Monthermer.[7] It is likely that the lands comprising
the honor of Gloucester and the other family properties in western
England were worth at least £1,300 in the late thirteenth and
early fourteenth centuries. The value of the honor of Gloucester
had undoubtedly increased over the £950 figure given in the
valuation of 1266–67, if only because of the Dorset manors, which
were not included in that survey. The Marshal estates acquired
in 1275 at the death of Eleanor de Montfort, dowager countess
of Pembroke and Leicester, were themselves valued at £200. If
these sums are added to the precise figures available for Tonbridge
and Clare in 1299–1300 and 1307–8, the total value of the inheritance in England would thus amount to about £3,000, approximately the same figure as that derived from the valuations given
in the partition.[8]

Unfortunately, few adequate figures exist for the inheritance
under Earl Gilbert the Red. Denholm-Young estimates the annual
income of Earl Gilbert and his father at between £3,000 and
£4,000, but it is not clear whether he has taken into account the
fact that one-third of the estates were held in dower by Richard's
widow for most of the Red Earl's career. In the inquisition *post
mortem* of 1295, the English lands were valued at somewhat over
£2,200. The Welsh lordships were said to be worth only about
£800, but in view of the other valuations and the fact of the
widespread devastation caused by Morgan ap Maredudd's uprising in 1294–95, this figure seems much too low.[9] It is impossible

---

[7] PRO, Min. Accts., SC 6/1109/12; PRO, Exchequer, KR Escheators' Accts.,
E 136/1/19a. The overlapping in the calendar years in explained by the fact that
estate accounts, whether private or royal, used Michaelmas (September 29) as the
termini of the fiscal year.

[8] PRO, Chanc. Misc., C 47/9/20. In 1317 the properties in Dorset and elsewhere not mentioned in the 1266–67 survey were included, as were the Marshal
manors and other estates acquired since that time.

[9] Denholm-Young, *Seignorial Administration*, p. 22; PRO, Chanc., Inq. Post
Mortem (Edward I), C 133/77/3, bundle 1, mm. 1–25, bundle 2, mm. 1–22,
bundle 3, mm. 1–20.

to estimate with any precision the degree to which his mother's long widowhood adversely affected his income, but between 1290 and 1295, when all the estates were once again in his hands, gross annual income was in all likelihood in the neighborhood of £4,500–5,000, while his son, the last Earl Gilbert, to judge from the 1317 figures, commanded some £6,000 per annum at the time of his death.

The discussion of baronial income is obviously a treacherous business, but some comparisons with other great comital families might usefully be made. In the middle years of the thirteenth century Earl Richard, with about £3,700, was probably the third richest magnate in the kingdom, surpassed only by the Lord Edward, who before 1272 was worth some £8,000–10,000, and Richard of Cornwall, Henry III's brother, whose annual income has been estimated between £5,000 and £6,000.[10] In 1245 the last of William Marshal's sons had a gross income of £3,500, while somewhat later the Bigods, earls of Norfolk, probably approached that figure as well.[11] No other earl seems to have come near these levels. The estates of William de Ferrers, earl of Derby, John de Brittany, earl of Richmond, and Robert de Quincy, earl of Winchester, were officially valued at 2,000 marks, £1,200 and £400 in 1254, 1261, and 1264 respectively.[12]

A similar picture emerges for the reigns of Edward I and Edward II. Edmund of Cornwall (d. 1300) enjoyed an income roughly comparable to that of his father, while Thomas, earl of Lancaster had an income of about £8,000 in 1313–14.[13] If Earl Gilbert the Red commanded between £4,500 and £5,000 in 1295, and his son some £6,000, they would rank next. Roger Bigod, earl of Norfolk, had about £4,000 at the time of his death in

---

[10] Denholm-Young, *Seignorial Administration*, pp. 9, 22; *idem, Richard of Cornwall*, p. 163.

[11] PRO, Chanc. Misc., C 47/9/20, collated with the other versions of the partition (above, Chapter II, note 84); Painter, *Studies*, p. 174; Denholm-Young, *Seignorial Administration*, p. 22.

[12] Painter, *Studies*, p. 174; Denholm-Young, *Seignorial Administration*, p. 22; *Cal. Pat. Rolls 1247–58*, p. 285; *ibid. 1258–66*, p. 160; *Close Rolls 1261–64*, pp. 407–8.

[13] For Edmund, see *Ministers' Accounts of the Earldom of Cornwall 1296–1297*, ed. Margaret Midgley (Camden Society, 3rd ser., vols. LXVI, LXVII, 1942–45). Painter, *Studies*, p. 174, gives a somewhat lower figure, based on other sources. For Thomas, see PRO, Duchy of Lancaster, Min. Accts., DL 29/1/3, and Tout, *Chapters*, II, 185.

1306, while Isabella de Fortibus, dowager countess of Devon and Aumale (d. 1293) had an income of over £2,500 per annum.[14] The Warennes, earls of Surrey and the Lacies, earls of Lincoln in all probability had over £2,000, but more precise figures are lacking. Other great comital families, such as the Beauchamps, earls of Warwick, the Bohuns, earls of Hereford and Essex, and the Valences, earls of Pembroke, must have had comparable annual incomes, but no estimates are available.[15] While all the figures given here are very approximate and tentative, they at least clearly indicate the dominant position enjoyed by the Clares in the ranks of the higher nobility. It is quite likely that William Marshal (d. 1219) and his sons, as earls of Pembroke and lords of Netherwent and Leinster, commanded an income greater than that of the first Earl Gilbert, but after the extinction of the Marshal family in 1245, Earl Richard and his descendants were surpassed only by the earls of Cornwall and Lancaster, the brothers and cousins of Henry III and his successors. In the second half of the thirteenth and the early fourteenth centuries, the Clares were the wealthiest and most powerful magnates in the British Isles outside the immediate royal circle itself.

The Structure of Landed Property

The great aggregate of lands and fees controlled by the Clares in England extended to almost every county in the southern half of the kingdom. Most of the estates were held as members of the three great family honors of Gloucester, Clare, and Tonbridge. In addition, the earls had half of the old Giffard honor of Buckingham and the barony of St. Hilary, both acquired by Richard, earl of Hertford in the late twelfth century. In two separate transactions in the mid-thirteenth century, Earl Richard purchased two-thirds of the Huntingdon barony of Southoe, while in 1275 a number of properties which originally formed part of the Marshal inheritance came into the possession of his son, Earl Gilbert the Red. Some other estates were held individually of

[14] For Bigod, see *Cal. Pat. Rolls 1301–07*, p. 460, and for Isabella de Fortibus, Denholm-Young, *Seignorial Administration*, pp. 22–23.
[15] Painter, *Studies*, p. 177.

religious houses, of the Crown, or as fiefs of other tenants-in-chief. The composition of the demesne often changed through subinfeudation, exchange or other means of alienation, but it is possible to enumerate those properties which remained more or less constantly in the earls' hands throughout the period.[16]

The bulk of the lands which comprised the honor of Gloucester lay in western and southwestern England.[17] It included the following properties: Stanford (Berkshire); Little Brickhill (Bucks); Chittlehampton and Langtree (Devon);[18] the manors and hundreds of Cranbourne and Pimperne, the manors of Steeple and Tarrant Gunville, the borough of Wareham and the hundreds of Hasilor, Rowbarrow, and Rushmore (Dorset); the manors, towns, and hundreds of Tewkesbury and Thornbury, the manors of Fairford and Sodbury and lands in Rendcombe and Campden (Gloucestershire); the borough of Petersfield and lands in Mapledurham and Clatford (Hants);[19] Burford, Skipton, and the hundred of Chadlington (Oxford); Easton (Somerset); Titsey and lands in Camberwell (Surrey); and the manor of Bushley and the manor and castle of Hanley (Worcs). The honor of Clare, centered in East Anglia but including lands in outlying counties as well, was almost as large. It included Bardfield, Claret, Thaxted, and lands in Hersham (Essex);[20] lands in Popeshall and Standon (Hertford); Yalding (Kent); Bircham, Crimplesham, Great and Little Walsingham, Warham, Wells, and Wiveton (Norfolk); the manor and hundred of Rothwell with its members (North-

---

[16] The following information is largely based on the inquisitions *post mortem* of 1262 (Earl Richard), 1295 (Earl Gilbert the Red), 1307 (Joan of Acre), and 1314 (the last Earl Gilbert). *Cal. Inq. Post Mortem*, I, no. 530, III, no. 371, IV, no. 435, V, no. 538. Widely scattered rents, tenements, and other small holdings are not listed in detail, nor are lands held at any particular time by reason of wardship or escheat.

[17] Some manors had been absorbed in the twelfth century from the honors of Chester, Dover, and Leicester, and are not differentiated here.

[18] Chittlehampton was obtained in 1285 from Matthew fitz John for some other estates in Devon, Wiltshire, and Southampton, but was returned in the 1295 inquisition as held of the honor. *Devon Feet of Fines*, eds. O. J. Reichel, F. B. Prideaux, and H. Tapley-Soper (Devon and Cornwall Record Society, 1912–39), II, 101.

[19] Petersfield and Mapledurham were added to the honor when Amaury of Evreux (created earl in 1200) married the daughter of Hugh de Gournay. Powicke, *Loss of Normandy*, p. 341.

[20] Claret was technically held as of the honor of Boulogne at fee farm, but was normally regarded as a member of Clare.

ants);[21] the castle, manor, and borough of Clare, the manor and borough of Sudbury, the manors of Disning, Haverhill, and Hundon (Suffolk); the manor and borough of Bletchingley, the manors of Chipstead, Ockham, Tillingdon, and Waldingham (Surrey); and the manor and hundred of Rotherfield and the manor of Eridge (Sussex). The honor of Tonbridge was held as a serjeanty of the archbishops of Canterbury, and consisted of the castle and borough of Tonbridge and the manors of Brasted, Edinbridge, Hadlow, Hetherede, and Hildenborough (Dacherst), all in Kent. For the honor the Clares owed suit at the archiepiscopal court of Otford twice yearly. They also served as the steward and butler of the archbishop at the feast celebrating his enthronization, but they often deputized these ceremonial functions. In return, the Clares received gifts of robes, horses, wine, and grain on these occasions.[22]

The remaining properties were held in various other ways. The Giffard lands remaining in demesne were Great Marlowe and Stewkley in Buckingham and Bottisham in Cambridge. The Marshal lands acquired in 1275 at the death of King John's daughter Eleanor, the widow of William Marshal the younger and Simon de Montfort, included Spenhamland (Berkshire), Caversham (Oxon), and the borough of Great Bedwyn, the manor of Wexcombe, and the hundred of Kinwardstone (Wilts).[23] Southoe was the *caput* of the barony of that name in Huntingdon, which Earl Richard acquired in 1259. Corhampton in Hampshire was held of the St. Johns for one fee, while Westpeckham in Kent was held of John Aguillon for a money-rent. The manor of Lackenheath and the village of Southwold in Suffolk were held of the priors of Ely and the abbots of Bury St. Edmunds respectively. Finally, the Dorset manors of Portland and Wyke and

[21] Rothwell may originally have been a St. Hilary manor; see Sanders, *English Baronies*, p. 44 and note 5. It was royal demesne in 1086.

[22] A copy of the agreement between Earl Richard and Boniface of Savoy in May 1258 setting forth these terms is in Brit. Mus., Cotton MS Vitellius A VIII, fols. 103v–109v. A shorter version is in Brit. Mus., Add. MS 6159 (Register of Christ Church, Canterbury), fols. 155v–156r. The original deed is in the archives of the Dean and Chapter of Canterbury, Chartae Antiquae, A 28. The agreement was renewed in 1273 by Earl Gilbert the Red and Boniface's successor, Robert Kilwardby, and is in PRO, Chanc. Misc., C 47/9/59. Gilbert's oath of fealty to Archbishop Peckham in 1279 is printed in *Reg. Epist. Peckham*, III, 997.

[23] Caversham was technically a Giffard manor which had passed to the elder William Marshal in 1189. Painter, *William Marshal*, p. 78.

the borough of Weymouth, all obtained in 1258 from the priory of St. Swithun's for some lands in Mapledurham, remained in demesne despite strenuous efforts by the Crown on behalf of the priory and the bishopric of Winchester to dislodge them.[24]

Not all of these estates were necessarily in the earls' possession at any given time. A number of manors were alienated for varying lengths of time and for various social purposes. Examples have been cited in an earlier chapter of the grants made by the earls to their brothers, to their daughters and sisters as marriage portions, and in the case of Earl Gilbert the Red, to his first wife Alice de Lusignan following the annulment of their marriage in 1285.[25] In addition to formal enfeoffment, grants of demesne lands to political associates among the lesser baronage were often made for brief periods of time, for example to John Giffard, lord of the Gloucestershire barony of Brimpsfield and Isgenen in Cantref Bychan, who held the town of Burford under Earl Gilbert the Red.[26] After the statute *Quia Emptores* in effect put an end to subinfeudation in 1290, life grants of demesne estates became a frequent means of attracting or strengthening political and tenurial ties. Bartholomew de Burghersh, nephew of Bartholomew de Badlesmere, the husband of the last Earl Gilbert's cousin Margaret and one of his closest associates, held the manor of Stewkley in this fashion. Roger Damory, who later was to marry Gilbert's youngest full sister Elizabeth, held Easton, also by the earl's grant.[27] The dower assigned to Earl Richard's widow Maud is the only example of a pronounced reduction of the demesne, however. From 1263 to 1289, almost the entire time her son was earl of Gloucester, the countess held one-third of the inheritance, including such important manors as Great Marlowe (Bucks), the Oxford estates of the honor of Gloucester, and the manor of Clare itself.[28] It is possible, however, that Earl Gilbert the Red

[24] PRO, Parliamentary and Council Proceedings (Chancery), C 49/2/5 (11 Edward I), and the references cited above in Chapter IV, notes 19–20.

[25] Above, pp. 50–51.

[26] *Cal. Inq. Post Mortem*, III, no. 544. Giffard also held the Gloucestershire manor of Badgworth (part of the Marshal inheritance) of the earl. *Cat. Ancient Deeds*, I, 107.

[27] PRO, Chanc. Misc., C 47/9/23, 25. For the estates held by Badlesmere and his wife, see *Cal. Pat. Rolls 1313–17*, p. 131.

[28] *Close Rolls 1261–64*, pp. 286–88; PRO, Rentals and Surveys, General Series, SC 11/610 mm. 1, 3, 7.

had at least *de facto* control of Clare castle by 1266, and the borough of Clare was always in his hands.[29]

These examples illustrate both the shifting composition of the demesne and the various political and social reasons for the alienation of property. With the important exception of Maud's long widowhood and the consequent diminution of her son's holdings, however, such transfers did not seriously affect the economic picture. Most of these manors were of more social than economic interest to the earls, and their loss could be partially offset by increased demesne productivity or the acquisition of other manors by purchase, exchange, or as in the case of the Marshal estates in 1275, by marriage connections. The inheritance, in short, was expected to support more than just its lords; but while the earls cared for the interests of sisters and daughters, friends and discarded wives, they did not neglect their own.

The rise in the official valuations of the Clare estates, as reflected in the governmental surveys of 1266–67 and 1317–20 discussed above, provides a general indication of the over-all tendency to an increased profitability of the inheritance in the period of this study. The lump sums, however, afford no clue as to the internal organization of the estates, the kinds of income or their relative importance. Unfortunately, the manorial accounts which have survived date mainly from the first decade of the fourteenth century, and the information they contain refers for the most part to the family properties in eastern England. Additional information, however, survives in the Pipe Roll accounts and other government sources, which combined with the private estate accounts and deeds of purchase, affords enough evidence to provide at least a general picture of the economic organization of the English estates and some detailed information on a number of important points.

It seems reasonably clear that the period witnessed a steady increase in manorial activity and demesne expansion. The best indication of this is afforded by the growth in the amount of land

---

[29] Maud let him use the castle to store goods seized after Evesham. There is no evidence that Gilbert sued for recovery of the manor and castle when he brought suit successfully for Usk and Trellech castles in 1266–67; it therefore seems likely that he reached a private agreement with his mother whereby he regained control of Clare castle, perhaps around this time. *Rotuli Selecti*, p. 134; PRO, Curia Regis Roll Mich. 50–51 Henry III, KB 26/177 mm. 3, 13–13d. For the borough, cf. *Parl. Writs*, I, 388.

brought under direct cultivation, as reflected in the numerous deeds of purchase of small parcels from freeholders and other tenants. From at least the mid-thirteenth century there was a marked tendency to acquire not only entire manors through exchange or purchase, but also to add smaller properties to the manors already in demesne. Many of the deeds recording such transactions are no longer extant, but are known from late fourteenth-century transcripts in the cartularies of the Mortimer family, into whose hands passed a number of estates in 1368–69, including the Dorset lands and the East Anglian manors of the honor of Clare.[30] The cartularies record a host of additions to the Norfolk, Suffolk, Essex, and Hertford manors, dating mainly from the reign of Edward I.[31] The most noticeable effort to increase demesne acreage, discussed briefly by Holmes, concerns the Hertford manor of Standon. In a remarkable series of transactions dating from the period 1277–87, Earl Gilbert the Red purchased the holdings of Geoffrey de Leukenor, Richard de Aston, and William de Kanmille or Canvill, among others. The first two men, at least, had long-standing connections with the family. Geoffrey de Leukenor, who served as a royal commissioner and itinerant justice in the 1260's and 1270's, was a bailiff in Essex under Earl Gilbert in 1265, acting on the earl's behalf in the seizure of rebel lands following Evesham. He may have been related to Nicholas de Leukenor, the keeper of the royal wardrobe from 1265–68, who held two and a quarter fees in Kent under Earl Richard and was one of the earl's executors, and whose son Roger served as a knight in the retinue of Thomas de Clare in 1272.[32] Richard de Aston was one of the Disinherited. He was a member of Earl Gilbert's *familia* in 1267 and like Roger de Leukenor was in Thomas de Clare's retinue in 1272. He seems

---

[30] See Holmes, *Estates of the Higher Nobility*, pp. 11 note 3, 17, 38.

[31] The deeds are recorded in Brit. Mus., Add. MS 6041, fols. 61–63v (Clare), 64v–66 (Bardfield), 67 (Sudbury), 69v–70 (Walsingham), 71–72 (Hundon), 72v (Bircham), 73–77 (Stanton), 82 (Claret), 83 (Lackenheath). Additional purchases in Thaxted, and fuller details of some of the transactions relating to Lackenheath and Standon are given in the other cartulary, Brit. Mus., Harleian MS 1240, fols. 79–87.

[32] *Cal. Pat. Rolls 1258–66*, pp. 75, 490; *ibid. 1266–72*, pp. 9, 643; *ibid. 1272–81*, pp. 70, 131, 412; *Cal. Inq. Post Mortem*, I, nos. 530, 678; *Cal. Inq. Misc.*, I, nos. 285, 666; PRO, Fine Roll 46 Henry III, C 60/59 m. 7, 50 Henry III, C 60/63 m. 3; Brit. Mus., Add. Ch. 20039.

to have entered royal service thereafter, and in 1292 was sheriff of Southants and constable of Winchester castle.[33] Unfortunately the available records shed little light on the third individual. He may be identical with a certain William de "Kamvile" who witnessed a fine in the court of the earl of Pembroke in 1301, or with the William de Ca(u)nvill who served as a royal commissioner in the principality of Wales in the last decade of Edward I's reign. Aside from the deeds in the Mortimer cartularies, there is no direct evidence of his relations with the Clares, and there is no way of knowing if his lands in Standon were held of Earl Gilbert by knight service or some other form of tenure before their purchase.[34] At any rate, the numerous deeds of purchase in Standon indicate the earls' interest in direct demesne enterprise, and the manor appears in the surviving Ministers' Accounts for the period 1304–14 as one of the most valuable family properties in eastern England.[35]

The tendency noted for Standon and the neighboring East Anglian estates is confirmed by similar transactions involving demesne manors in other parts of the kingdom. Purchases of lands in Cranbourne and the other estates in Dorset, in Easton, Tonbridge, Brasted, and Hadlow in Kent, almost all dating before 1314, are also listed in the Mortimer cartularies.[36] Moreover, some of the original deeds by which Earl Richard and his descendants acquired lands, rents, and villein services on such manors as Clare, Tonbridge, Hadlow, Popeshall, Southwold, Rotherfield, Little Brickill, and Stewkley have survived.[37] The over-all impression given by this evidence is that of a gradual but deliberate

---

[33] *Cal. Pat. Rolls 1266–72*, pp. 146, 643; *Cal. Inq. Misc.*, I, no. 936; *Cal. Close Rolls 1288–96*, p. 226.

[34] *Cat. Ancient Deeds*, III, 546; *Cal. Pat. Rolls 1292–1301*, p. 317. The deeds relating to Kanmille are in Brit. Mus., Add MS 6041, fols. 74v–77, Harleian MS 1240, fols. 81–84.

[35] Cf. Holmes, *Estates*, p. 88, and PRO, Min. Accts., SC 6/868/17–18.

[36] Brit. Mus., Add. MS 6041, fols. 80v–81, 84, 85, 87–89, 90–91.

[37] *Cat. Ancient Deeds*, II, 181, 492, IV, 400, V, 509–510, VI, 5–6, 7, 10, 15, 27, 33, 118, 228, 276, 277; *Feet of Fines relating to County Sussex* [1249–1307], ed. L. F. Salzmann (Sussex Record Society, vol. VII, 1908), p. 112; *Calendar of Feet of Fines for Bedfordshire*, ed. G. Herbert Fowler (Bedford Historical Record Society, vol. XII, 1928), pt. III (Edward I), p. 20; *Calendar of Feet of Fines for Buckingham* [1195–1260], ed. M. W. Hughes (Buckinghamshire Record Society [Buckinghamshire Archaeological Society, Records Branch], vol. IV, 1940), p. 93.

buildup of demesne acreage and rent-paying tenements, both contributing to and reflecting a high level of domanial enterprise; as
Holmes has remarked, these deeds are the " best indication that
this is the final stage of a period of great manorial activity." There
were few significant additions to the East Anglian estates after
1314, and the process of demesne leasing began in the mid-fourteenth century, when the estates passed to Lionel, duke of Clarence,
and then to the Mortimers, earls of March, following the death
of the last Earl Gilbert's youngest sister and heiress, Lady Elizabeth de Burgh.[38] Earl Gilbert the Red seems to have been somewhat more active than either his father or his son in the acquisition
of rents and acreage, probably reflecting his desire, also noticeable
in the numerous usurpations of franchisal privileges recorded in
the *quo warranto* inquests, to minimize by every available method
the adverse effects of his mother's dower holdings on his own
economic position.[39]

A comparison of the Clares with other great landholders yields
some interesting results. The pattern of piecemeal addition to
the demesne was also followed by a number of comital families,
notably the Bohuns, earls of Hereford, and the Beauchamps, earls
of Warwick, and by some ecclesiastical houses, such as the abbey
of Bec on its Wiltshire properties. The process, however, was not
universal. The estates of the bishopric of Ely, for example, under-
went some decline in total demesne acreage at the turn of the
fourteenth century. On most of the estates of Edmund, earl of
Cornwall in 1296–97, there was little or no direct agricultural
activity, the revenues being derived largely from rents and farms.
The demesne manors in the Percy barony of Alnwick in Northumberland were entirely leased to the tenants by 1314, and the
Fortibus estates of the honor of Cockermouth in Cumberland were
similarly farmed as early as 1266–67. For the Clares, however,
the increase in demesne acreage as reflected in the deeds of purchase makes it clear that at least for the second half of the thirteenth and the early fourteenth centuries, the inheritance was characterized not by stabilization or contraction, but rather by expansion in direct manorial exploitation and enterprise.[40]

[38] Holmes, *Estates*, pp. 88–89, 92.
[39] *Plac. Quo War.*, pp. 183–85, 337–41, 348–50, 703–4, 774–76; PRO, Exchequer,
KR Miscellanea, E 163/2/30; Painter, *Studies*, pp. 87–88, 109, 114–15; Sutherland, *Quo Warranto Proceedings, Edward I*, pp. 22, 146–47.
[40] The early fourteenth-century evidence relating to the Bohun and Beauchamp

The sources directly relating to the internal organization of the estates reveal no radical departures from the well-known features of the economy. Manorial resources, especially rents and the sale of agrarian produce, formed by far the most important items of revenue, although income from boroughs, non-manorial courts and various feudal incidents were by no means insignificant. The fullest information for the early thirteenth century derives from the Pipe Roll account of February 2, 1242–Michaelmas, 1243, just prior to Richard de Clare's seisin, when almost all the lands were back in royal control.[41] The surviving Ministers' Accounts refer mainly to some half dozen East Anglian manors of the honor of Clare, and almost all of the accounts date between 1300 and 1314.[42] Some other evidence, notably court rolls, also comes mainly from this period. Unfortunately there is almost nothing for the properties in western England. Although the evidence is too limited to discern any short-term but significant fluctuations in the pattern of income, it would seem that the general characteristics of the economic structure remained relatively stable throughout the period of this study.

On the manors, the sale of grain formed the major item of income, and in 1242–43 brought in over £800, about 45 per cent of all revenues. Wheat, oats, and barley were the usual crops, although rye and occasionally some other cereals were also cultivated. What was not consumed directly by the lord's household was sold, mainly in local markets but sometimes in large cities

---

families is discussed in Holmes, pp. 113–14. For Bec, see Morgan, *English Lands of the Abbey of Bec*, p. 84, and for Ely, Edward Miller, *The Abbey and Bishopric of Ely* (Cambridge, 1951), pp. 99–105. The Cornwall accounts (cited above, note 13) are discussed in Holmes, *Estates*, p. 112. The Cockermouth and Alnwick accounts, PRO, Min. Accts., SC 6/824/6–7, are briefly discussed in J. M. W. Bean, *The Estates of the Percy Family 1416–1537* (Oxford, 1958), p. 12. Cf. also the general remarks of Edward Miller, "The English Economy in the Thirteenth Century," *Past and Present*, no. 28 (July, 1964), pp. 25–26, 31–33.

[41] All references in the following paragraphs to 1242–43 figures and percentages derive from PRO, Pipe Roll 27 Henry III, E 372/87 r. 3d. Total income for the properties represented in the account was £1,870, of which the honor of Gloucester yielded £920 and the honor of Clare £950. The account is not complete. Other estates in Essex, Hertford, and Kent only appear on r. 4–5. They show no significant differences in the kinds of income, and have not been included in the figures.

[42] Some statistics from these accounts have been tabulated by Holmes, *Estates*, pp. 150–54, and I have verified my figures with his. The most important accounts are for Clare, Standon, Bircham, Claret, Lackenheath, and the Dorset manor of Wyke.

such as London as well. Considerable profit could be realized in this way. Clare, with 500 acres, had the largest demesne of any of the East Anglian manors, and grain production in the early fourteenth century approached 1,000 quarters per annum (8,000 bushels), about half of which went to the household and the other half for cash. A Minister's Account for 1308–9 shows that over two-thirds of the total manorial income for that year came from the sale of grain.[43] On the much smaller Norfolk manor of Bircham, which had less than 70 acres in demesne, sale of grain in 1311–12 yielded well over half the income, while on the Dorset manor of Wyke in 1294–95, the sale of grain accounted for over one third of the total.[44] There were other kinds of agrarian produce as well, but they were of less importance. The sale of livestock and dairy products such as butter, cheese and milk brought in comparatively small sums, averaging about 5–10 per cent for each of these three manors.[45] There is little evidence of other commodities. The earls regularly imported large quantities of wine from the Continent, but some was also made at Tewkesbury, presumably for direct consumption by the earl and his household, although some of it may have been sold locally, perhaps to the nearby abbey.[46] Sheep farming does not seem to have been engaged in extensively. There are references to shepherds and the sale of wool and of the animals themselves at Cranbourne, Sudbury, and some other places, but both flocks and income were small. There is little mention of sheep at Clare or the other Suffolk or Norfolk manors before about 1320, and as Holmes points out, wool production only became an important part of the economy of these estates after 1330, with the introduction of sheep farming on such manors as Claret, Woodhall, and Standon.[47]

[43] PRO, Min. Accts., SC 6/992/8. Total income, excluding arrears and money received from the reeve of Claret, was £288. For the sale of wheat in London in 1266, see *Cal. Pat. Rolls 1258–66*, p. 590.

[44] PRO, Min. Accts., SC 6/930/2, 834/22.

[45] In 1242–43 they brought in only £80 out of a total of £1870, just over 4 per cent.

[46] In 1235 there were wine growers on the demesne staff at Tewkesbury (PRO, Min. Accts., SC 6/1109/6 m. 2), and the sale of wine regularly produced small amounts in the Pipe Roll accounts at this time. For the importation of wine via London, see *Close Rolls 1251–53*, p. 90; *ibid. 1254–56*, p. 23; *ibid. 1256–59*, p. 214; and *passim*.

[47] See Holmes, *Estates*, pp. 89–90. The thirteenth-century references are PRO, Min. Accts., SC 6/1109/6 m. 2 (Cranbourne, 1235); SC 6/1117/13 (Rothwell

Freehold and customary rents (mainly in cash, but including some in kind) formed the next largest item of income. Their importance varied greatly, and they were less susceptible to the hazards of weather and other variable factors which could disrupt normal demesne exploitation. It is clear, however, that nowhere did they form the predominant source of revenue characteristic of the later middle ages. In 1242–43 rents came to £600, about a third of the stated income. By 1300 the over-all percentage seems roughly to have been the same. At Claret rents brought in somewhat less than half the total income in 1307–8, while at Lackenheath in 1290–91 and Bircham in 1310–11 they accounted for about 40 per cent of the total. At Standon in 1304–5 and 1311–12, rents provided well over a quarter of the total revenues.[48] On some other properties, however, rents were much less prominent. At Crimplesham in 1304–5, the sale of grain and stock accounted for two-thirds of the income, while only one eighth derived from rents. At Wyke in 1294–95 rents yielded only about 15 per cent of the total, while on Clare manor itself in 1308–9 they were insignificant, yielding only some 3 per cent of the total income of nearly £300 for that year.[49] Only after the first quarter of the fourteenth century did rents become the predominant item of revenue. Holmes has calculated that they provided about half the income at Standon and Bircham, about 35 per cent at Claret and comparable percentages at other East Anglian manors, while at Clare they increased to approximately 10 per cent of the total.[50] For most of the fourteenth century, income from rents provided the single largest item of revenue, and arable farming tended to decline in importance. Although the examples cited for the period before 1314 are isolated, their relatively late date and the tendency to continual demesne expansion discussed above afford ample evidence that the Clares themselves exhibited no proclivity to become *rentier* landlords at the turn of the fourteenth century. While rents were clearly an important source of manorial revenue for the lords,

---

and Burford, 1234–36); Pipe Roll 1 Edward I, E 372/117 r. 7 (Sudbury, account for 1262–63).

[48] PRO, Min. Accts., SC 6/838/9, 1001/5, 930/1, 868/17–18.

[49] PRO, SC 6/933/18, 834/22, 992/8.

[50] Holmes, *Estates*, pp. 89, 145–47, 150–56. The increased percentage at Clare is due not to a rise in the amount of rent collected, but to a decline in the over-all net income on the manor.

direct agrarian production remained the backbone of the economy throughout this entire period.

There were many other sources of revenue connected with the manor which supplemented the sale of agricultural produce and rents. These included the sale or lease of pasture and meadow rights, the sale of wood, forest fines, issues or farms of mills and fisheries, income from manorial courts, and the sale of villein services. These items ranged widely in profitability, depending on the size and geographical composition of the manor and on local conditions in any given year. The sale of pasture rights and miscellaneous fees for their use in other respects accounted for about a quarter of the total income at Claret in 1307–8, about 15 per cent at Standon and 8 per cent at Clare, but only about 2–4 per cent at Bircham in 1310–11 and 1311–12.[51] Income from mills was probably more important than the extant accounts would indicate. At Tonbridge in 1299–1300 they brought in 40 marks, and although the estate was in royal custody at the time, the figure probably reflects normal annual income from this source.[52] Otherwise, however, the recorded sums were small. At Wyke, mills yielded some 7 per cent of the total, at Clare income was almost completely balanced by expenses for upkeep and repair, and on some other manors they are not mentioned at all.[53] Domanial courts, on the other hand, were a permanent feature on every manor, and they brought in a small but steady profit. In 1242–43 pleas and perquisites amounted to almost 5 per cent of all manorial income, and this percentage seems to be valid for the entire period. The surviving Ministers' Accounts for the late thirteenth and early fourteenth centuries reveal comparable percentages for small manors such as Bircham, Claret, Crimplesham, Lackenheath, and Wyke, and for the larger manors of Standon and Clare as well. A similar picture emerges for the manors of Rotherfield, Yalding, and Hadlow in 1299–1300, when they were in royal custody.[54]

---

[51] PRO, Min. Accts., SC 6/838/9, 868/18, 992/8, 930/1–2.

[52] PRO, Exchequer, KR Escheators' Accounts, E 136/1/19 a m. 1.

[53] PRO, Min. Accts., SC 6/834/22, 992/8. The portion of the account for Wyke recording expenses is mutilated, and it cannot be determined how much of the actual income was clear profit.

[54] PRO, Min. Accts., SC 6/930/1–2, 838/9, 993/18, 1001/5, 834/22, 868/17–18, 992/8; PRO, KR Escheators' Accounts, E 136/1/19a m. 1.

Other kinds of supplementary sources of income could be more valuable. Forests in particular were quite profitable. The sale of wood, supplemented by the collection of forest fines such as pannage, brought in over £100 from Rotherfield chase and the forests of Northfrith and Southfrith adjoining the Kent manors of Hadlow and Hetherede in 1299–1300. These sums may not be entirely reliable, as the Crown would naturally tend to waste these resources for immediate profit.[55] In 1307–8, however, the sale of wood from forest lands at Clare and Popeshall yielded almost £50.[56] Most of the timber was probably sold locally, but some was also brought to London for sale as firewood.[57]

The sale of villein works was a regular source of manorial income, and its development reflects a number of important features of the economy. Although the Clares used villein services extensively, they converted a large number of them into cash, which could be used to hire part-time laborers for a variety of purposes, the most important of which would be spring planting and autumn harvesting. These workers received both wages and liveries of food, and supplemented the permanent wage-earning demesne *familia*. There is no way of knowing whether hired laborers were recruited from the villeins themselves, but the regular demesne staff were probably drawn from excess population among the villeinage or possibly from men whose holdings were purchased by the family in the course of the century. The size of the staffs would vary according to the relative importance of continued villein services at each manor, but in general they included ploughmen, carters, mowers, reapers, harrowers, and dairy-maids (*daye*). There were also a vintner and eight *vindemiatores* at Tewkesbury, shepherds and smiths at some other places, and an *ancilla* at Clare whose job was to make pottage for the others. Most villein services were still exacted in the early fourteenth century, but enough had been converted into cash payments before then to bring in over £20 at Clare, about 7 per cent of the total income in 1307–8. Relatively substantial sums on the smaller manors were realized in the same way, and in 1242–43 the sale of works brought in over £200, or about 12 per cent of total

---

[55] PRO, E 136/1/19a m. 2; cf. Painter, *Studies*, pp. 165–66.
[56] PRO, SC 6/1109/12.
[57] E.g., *Cal. Pat. Rolls 1258–66*, p. 590 (May, 1266).

income. The use of full and part-time hired labor was undoubtedly more efficient than the reliance on traditional villein obligations, and although it was not the dominant feature of the work force, its development reflects an increased concern with manorial organization and enterprise as the main source of family income.[58]

Important sums were also derived from boroughs and especially feudal and franchisal resources. The Clares were lords of a number of prominent boroughs, including Clare, Tonbridge, Tewkesbury, Thornbury, and Cranbourne, and realized a steady income from them. Revenues consisted mainly of burgage rents, seigneurial dues (such as prise of ale, tolls, or farms of markets), and borough courts. Most of the income was clear profit, as the boroughs required little in the way of heavy expenditures normally needed for the upkeep of manors. The only major expenses were wages to the borough officials themselves. Clare borough was small and was valued chiefly as an administrative center. An account for 1311–12 shows a total income (excluding arrears) of £16 10s., of which about 23 per cent derived from rents, just under a third from the farm of the market, and the remainder from court fees and fines. These percentages remained fairly constant throughout the thirteenth and fourteenth centuries, and only in the fifteenth century did income increase as Clare became an important center of the cloth industry.[59] Detailed figures for other boroughs are lacking, but Tonbridge brought in £10 8s. and Bletchingley £8 10s. in 1299–1300,[60] and Tewkesbury was said to be worth £19 in 1295.[61]

Of greater importance were the revenues derived from feudal resources, franchises, and honorial courts. The Clares had extensive jurisdictional rights throughout their holdings which, combined with the incidents of feudal lordship, could be of considerable financial value. The central court of the honor of Clare, which for reasons to be discussed below drew suitors from only

[58] In addition to the Ministers' Accounts already cited, see also PRO, SC 6/1109/ 6–7, extracted from the Pipe Roll accounts of 1234–40. Again the 1242–43 figures may not be entirely reliable, but they are indicative of this tendency.

[59] PRO, Min. Accts., SC 6/992/9; Holmes, *Estates*, pp. 92–93, 157.

[60] PRO, Escheators' Accts., E 136/1/19a mm. 1, 4.

[61] PRO, Chanc. Inq. Post Mortem (Edward I), C 133/77/3 bundle 1 m. 13. The figures for Tewkesbury and Thornbury given by Painter, *Studies*, p. 167, are misleading, for the sources used do not differentiate between borough and manor. In each case over 90 per cent of the total actually derived from the manor.

the East Anglian counties, dealt with a wide range of business. Civil actions between military tenants were comparatively infrequent, and the bulk of the revenues derived from petty criminal actions, fines for respite of suit and nonattendance, payments connected with homage, fealty and relief, and entry fines.[62] The earliest surviving Clare court roll, dating from 1308–9, shows an income of £57 10s.[63] In 1309–10 the court brought in £59 7s. and in 1312–13 £40 15s.[64] The sums were actually collected by bailiffs of fees (*ballivi feodorum*) for the individual counties, and they also accounted for the local honorial courts as well as for a number of scattered rent-paying tenements and some franchisal revenues. Over £200 was realized in 1307–8 from these sources.[65] The account of the bailiff of fees for Essex for 1309–10 reveals the varied nature of the income, but also its profitability. Of a total income of £67, about a fifth came from sums assessed by the central court at Clare, 40 per cent from local franchisal and honorial courts, while £22 10s.—almost exactly a third of the total—came from a relief assessed at £5 on the knight's fee, and the rest from isolated rents and views.[66] Some of the smaller courts were quite profitable in themselves. The Sudbury leet court was worth £12 6s. in 1314,[67] while income from leets and local courts of the honor of Gloucester appurtenant to the Cambridge manor of Bottisham brought in over £31 in 1308–9.[68]

Large sums could be collected from purely feudal sources. By

---

[62] Cf. Brit. Mus., Add. Ch. 1263–64, portions of rolls recording entry fines in Standon, Haverhill, Hundon, Clare and some other manors, *ca.* 1307–14. The large number of fines testify to the lively traffic in land among the Clare tenants. The sums average about 6d.–1s., but there is also a reference to Hugh D'Audley who owed 8s. "pro tenementis quedam Alicie la Blunde" in Haverhill. For the importance of entry fines in the *rentier* economy of the fifteenth and early sixteenth centuries, see Bean, *Estates of the Percy Family*, pp. 51–67.

[63] The roll is printed in *Court Rolls of the Abbey of Ramsey and the Honor of Clare*, ed. Warren O. Ault (New Haven, 1928), pp. 75–110. A roll for 1307–8 exists but cannot be used.

[64] PRO, Court Rolls, SC 2/213/34, 35. The latter figure does not include £5 12s. from some local court leets also entered on the roll (mm. 4–5).

[65] PRO, Min. Accts., SC 6/1109/12.

[66] PRO, Min. Accts., SC 6/1109/13. One other account survives, that of the Suffolk bailiff for 1310–11 (SC 6/1109/14). Income was only £7 14s., and was derived entirely from sums assessed by the central court and some rents. The other revenues were accounted for separately.

[67] PRO, Court Rolls, SC 2/213/112 m. 3.

[68] PRO, Court Rolls, SC 2/214/2 m. 1d.

the later thirteenth century, military tenure was regarded almost entirely in monetary terms. Adam de Creting, who married the widow of Thomas de Clare in 1292, held lands in Suffolk of Earl Gilbert the Red. The number of fees owed, however, is not recorded; Adam merely rendered half a mark for scutage " when it shall happen." A somewhat earlier example indicates clearly the complexities involved in fractional knight service and the degree to which the actual holder of the fee was separated from the ultimate lord. Elena de Besford held a small amount of land in Gloucestershire:

of the gift of John de Solariis, and this John of Walter de Solariis, and this Walter of Constancia de Leye, and she (holds it) of Sir William de la Mare, and this William of the earl of Gloucester, for the service of one tenth part of a knight's fee; and the earl (holds it) of the king.[69]

Under such circumstances, the only possible value of this fee to the Clares was the scutage that might be collected for it. At the end of the thirteenth century, the Clares were assessed for 495 fees, a total far greater than that of any other magnate, but they in fact held about 520 in England. When granted, the net profit to the earls from scutage, if collected at the rate of 40 shillings per fee, would thus amount to some £50.[70] Reliefs, which were assessed at £5 per fee, also appear from time to time in the accounts.[71] Other feudal incidents were still lucrative as well. In 1308 Robert Baynard paid £40 for the custody and marriage of a certain Roger atte Ash.[72] In 1251 Earl Richard exacted an

[69] Cal. Inq. Post Mortem, II, no. 492; Feudal Aids, II, 242.
[70] The 520 total is derived from the figures given in the 1317 partition (PRO, Chanc. Misc., C 47/9/23–25). The KR Memoranda Roll for 24–25 Edward I (PRO, E 159/70 mm. 14–14d.) is the fullest list of those fees liable to Crown service or scutage. King Edward demanded scutage for all the fees despite the fact that Earl Gilbert the Red had performed service with some of them in the Welsh wars. A total of 494 9/10 is made up as follows: Gloucester 261 ½, Clare and St. Hilary 141 ⅔, Giffard (acquired in 1189) 43, Giffard (acquired in 1272) 9 ¼, Marshal estates (acquired in 1275) 27, honor of Gloucester in Kent 9, Southoe (one-third of barony) 3 ½.
[71] In addition to the account of the Essex bailiff of fees mentioned above (PRO, Min. Accts., SC 6/1109/13), reliefs from Clare mesne tenants are also recorded in some of the Pipe Roll accounts, e.g., 20 Henry III, E 372/80 r. 1; 27 Henry III, E 372/87 r. 3d.; 51 Henry III, E 372/111 r. 28d.; 1 Edward I, E 372/117 r. 7. An example from 1338 is given in Holmes, Estates, p. 93 note 3.
[72] PRO, Min. Accts., SC 6/1109/12. I have been unable to trace Roger's holdings.

aid of two marks per fee for the marriage of his eldest daughter Isabel, even though there was no prospective husband in sight at that time,[73] and as late as 1327 Lady Elizabeth de Burgh, Demory's widow, collected a " reasonable aid " for the knighting of her son William.[74] In short, if by the thirteenth century feudal relationships were almost entirely financial, still they were valued and tenaciously preserved, precisely for that purpose, and they formed not an insignificant aspect of the total income of the earls of Gloucester.

Estate Administration

For administrative purposes, the estates were divided into a number of bailiwicks, clusters of geographically convenient manors, courts, and fees, whose only unity lay in the fact that they were under the general supervision of the same receiver and the same seneschal, the major financial and judicial officials. By the thirteenth century, for the great magnates at least, the honor was no longer the characteristic unit of territorial organization it had been in the Norman and Angevin period, and its theoretical indivisibility had ceased to have much practical significance.[75] The estates of Edmund, earl of Cornwall were divided into bailiwicks which had no relation to the original feudal boundaries of his properties,[76] and the organization of the Clare inheritance affords other evidence of this point. Although the exact details are obscure, it is clear that the Marshal and Giffard lands did not maintain their separate identities when absorbed by the family. They were administered as parts of larger bailiwicks, and were treated as units only by the Crown for the purpose of assessing scutage. While the executors of Earl Gilbert the Red were charged with scutage and 50 marks relief for one-third of the Southoe barony in 1297, the manors and fees appurtenant to it were other-

[73] Tewkesbury, p. 146, and cf. *Close Rolls 1254–56*, pp. 192–93. Isabel married the marquis de Montferrat in 1258, but there is no evidence that Earl Richard tried to collect a second aid at this time.

[74] This is known from a fifteenth century transcript in PRO, Duchy of Lancaster, Returns of Knights' Fees, DL 40/1/4.

[75] Cf. the remarks of Denholm-Young, *Seignorial Administration*, pp. 40–41, 93. For the honor in the twelfth century, see Stenton, *The First Century of English Feudalism*, pp. 54–66.

[76] *Ministers' Accounts of the Earldom of Cornwall, passim.*

wise thoroughly absorbed into the administrative organization of the honor of Clare.[77]

Nor did the honors of Clare and Gloucester remain unified. At some point in the early or mid-thirteenth century the properties of these honors in Kent, Surrey, and Sussex were transferred to the administrative and judicial control of the honor of Tonbridge. The earliest definite evidence for this dates from 1269, when Earl Gilbert ordered his seneschal of Tonbridge to hand over to Merton College some mesne manors in Surrey appurtenant to Bletchingley which Walter de Merton had previously acquired. Although Bletchingley was a member of the honor of Clare, all administrative and judicial matters came under the ultimate control of the central officers of Tonbridge.[78] It is reasonable to suppose that the change took place in 1263, when Clare itself came into the hands of Countess Maud; but it is also possible that it had already been effected before that date for the sake of administrative convenience, perhaps under the first Earl Gilbert after 1217 or under Earl Richard after 1243. At any rate, the situation was not changed by the recovery of the entire inheritance at Maud's death in 1289. The bailiwick of Tonbridge as it existed at the end of the thirteenth century included all the family manors, courts, and fees in Kent, Surrey, and Sussex, regardless of the original honors to which the properties had pertained.[79] For the purposes of estate management, the "honor" of Clare was thus transformed into a bailiwick comprising the demesne manors of Norfolk, Suffolk, Essex, and Hertford, along with Southoe in Huntingdon and the fees and courts in those counties and Cambridge.[80] The central honor court drew suitors only from Norfolk, Suffolk, and Essex, and on rare occasion Cambridge;[81] and the bailiff of fees for

[77] PRO, Exchequer, KR Mem. Roll 24–25 Edward I, E 159/70 mm. 14–14d; PRO, Min. Accts., SC 6/1109/12. For some reason, the other third of Southoe controlled by the earl was not assessed.

[78] *Rot. Parl.*, I, 12, and *Surrey Manorial Accounts*, ed. Helen Briggs (Surrey Record Society, vol. XV, 1935), pp. 10, 21, 27, 38, 40; Introduction, pp. xxvii–xxviii, xli–xliv.

[79] The manor of Yalding in Kent was technically a member of the honor of Clare, but the reeve accounted to the receiver of Tonbridge. PRO, Min. Accts., SC 6/1247/11 (2 Edward II). The escheator's account of 1299–1300 lumps all the lands in the three counties under the rubric "honor of Tonbridge." PRO, E 136/1/19a.

[80] PRO, Min. Accts., SC 6/1109/12.

[81] PRO, Court Rolls, SC 2/213/34 mm. 7, 8; 213/35 m. 8. No suitors from Cambridge appear in the roll edited by Ault (note 63 above).

Essex accounted to the receiver of Clare not only for the fees and courts of the honor in his county but also for the fees and courts originally pertaining to the honors of Gloucester and Giffard and the Marshal inheritance.[82]

The division of the honor of Gloucester itself is impossible to describe with much confidence in view of the almost total lack of surviving information. Beyond the fact that the properties in eastern England were administered as parts of the Clare and Tonbridge bailiwicks, little is known. After the loss of Bristol, no attempt was made to establish a single new *caput*. The honor was probably divided into two or three bailiwicks for financial and judicial purposes. One centered on Cranbourne, which had its own receiver in 1295 and which drew suitors to its court from Dorset and Wiltshire. In view of their geographical proximity, the estates in Devon and Southampton may have accounted to Cranbourne as well, but there is no direct evidence of this. Tewkesbury most likely formed the center of another bailiwick. It drew suitors to its "honor court" from Gloucester, Worcester, and probably Somerset, and it was the most valuable property the family possessed in western England.[83] Simply no evidence survives for the organization of the estates in the central parts of the kingdom. The important Northamptonshire manor of Rothwell, technically a member of the honor of Clare, does not appear in the receiver's account for the bailiwick of that honor in 1307–8. Since Rothwell was not alienated, it may well have served as the center of a third bailiwick, comprising the estates and fees of the honor of Gloucester in Northants, Oxford, Buckingham, Berkshire and Bedford; but the lack of contemporary family accounts for the properties in these shires makes it impossible to verify this conjecture.

Although the number of bailiwicks comprising the honor of Gloucester is obscure, it seems reasonably clear that there was only one seneschal for the entire complex. In 1218–19 and 1290, for example, Robert de Bermondsey and Robert Bardolf are each described as "seneschallus honoris Gloucestriae."[84] Other evi-

[82] PRO, Min. Accts., SC 6/1109/13.
[83] PRO, Min. Accts., SC 6/834/22; PRO, Rentals and Surveys, General Series, SC 11/610 m. 5; *Cal. Inq. Post Mortem*, II, nos. 154, 770, 806, III, no. 404; *Close Rolls 1227–31*, p. 445.
[84] PRO, Exchequer, LTR Memoranda Rolls 2–3 Henry III, 18–19 Edward I, E 368/1 m. 2, E 368/62 m. 31.

dence is even more conclusive. A number of documents involving some lands in Dorset held of Earl Gilbert the Red by the abbey of St. Peter's, Gloucester, contain references to the earl's seneschal, and the context provides strong grounds for presuming that he was the only seneschal for the entire honor. The documents, which date from the late 1260's, consistently refer to a Geoffrey de Mores as " seneschallus honoris Gloucestriae " or " seneschallus Gloucestriae." Contemporary writs from Earl Gilbert to his seneschals of Tonbridge and Clare always state the bailiwick precisely, and it is difficult to imagine the earl using the term " seneschal of the honor of Gloucester " loosely, if he actually meant the seneschal " of Cranbourne " or " of Tewkesbury." [85] On the other hand, an entry in the Hundred Rolls dating from around 1275, and an account in the Tewkesbury chronicle of a dispute between the abbey and Earl Richard in 1249–50, mention a " seneschal of Rothwell " and a " seneschal of Cranbourne " respectively. In each instance, however, the term is applied by someone other than the earls themselves, and is ambiguous; it may be used loosely to describe what actually was the local hundredal bailiff, or possibly to describe the seneschal of the honor holding his court at Rothwell and Cranbourne, either on tourn or perhaps as the chief manors of the local bailiwicks. There is no other mention of the existence of a separate seneschal for these two estates, nor does there seem to be any reference in the sources to a seneschal whose activities were confined to Tewkesbury and its appurtenant estates. On balance, the wording of the sources in the cartulary of St. Peter's, Gloucester, which implies the existence of a single seneschal for the whole honor, outweighs these other references. Indeed, the chief value of the latter lies in providing some circumstantial evidence for supposing the existence of bailiwicks centered on Cranbourne and Rothwell as part of the reorganization of the honor of Gloucester following its acquisition by the Clares without Bristol as the *caput*.[86]

To manage both their household and their vast estates, the Clares employed a host of professional salaried officials, men well

---

[85] *Historia et Cartularium Monasterii Sancti Petri Gloucestriae*, ed. W. H. Hart (Rolls Series XXXIII, 1863–67), II, 23–24, 25, 26, 70. For Gilbert's letter to the seneschal of Tonbridge (1269), see *Rot. Parl.*, I, 12.

[86] *Rot. Hund.*, II, 12; Tewkesbury, p. 513 (Appendix). In the Tewkesbury case, Earl Richard himself uses the term " baillivus."

versed in the techniques of efficient administration. In this respect the earls of Gloucester were by no means unique. The complex economic and judicial structure of a great inheritance required a well-organized and co-ordinated administrative system staffed by trained laymen and clerks, and the general features of the administration closely resemble those found on other great estates in this period.[87] The seneschal, who at Clare was paid 40 marks a year, was the major executive officer within the bailiwick in all matters of administration and justice. He presided over the central honor court, hearing pleas, levying fines, and issuing writs to the appropriate bailiff of fees to take the necessary actions. Although he had general authority over the activities of the court, his actions could be superseded at times by orders from the household auditors, to whom he accounted, or by the earl himself. There is also evidence that the seneschal made a tourn of the local manorial courts at fixed times of the year, presumably to handle business involving freeholders and tenants by knight service who did not owe suit to the central court.[88] He also figured prominently in more general administrative matters. When a mesne tenant alienated his holdings to another, the seneschal would deliver seisin.[89] He often witnessed the earls' deeds[90] and occasionally kept their seal, issuing charters in their name.[91] Robert de Bermondsey, seneschal of Gloucester under the first Earl Gilbert, also acted as his attorney in negotiations involving the payment of scutage to the Crown. When Earl Gilbert the Red was about to go overseas in 1279, probably to Ireland, he appointed a seneschal, Richard Heydon, as his attorney in England. In 1308, Robert

[87] See, in general, Denholm-Young, *Seignorial Administration*, which deals most fully with the Fortibus and Bigod estates. For an ecclesiastical estate, see Miller, *Bishopric of Ely*, pp. 252–75. The administrative system in the Norman and Angevin period is discussed in Stenton, *First Century*, pp. 66–83.

[88] *Court Roll of Honor of Clare*, pp. 80, 97 and *passim*; PRO, Court Rolls, SC 2/214/1 m. 4 (Crimplesham and Wiveton, Norfolk, 2 Edward II); PRO, Min. Accts., SC 6/1247/11 (Yalding, Kent, 2 Edward II).

[89] *Surrey Manorial Accounts*, pp. 10–11, 21; *Rot. Parl.*, I, 12.

[90] *Cat. Ancient Deeds*, II, 158, 492; VI, 5–6, 277.

[91] E.g., a charter in favor of Oseney Abbey in 1268 was issued " per manum domini Hamoni Hauteyn tunc senescalli nostri." *Cartulary of Oseney Abbey*, V, ed. H. E. Salter (Oxford Historical Series, vol. XCVIII, 1935), 252–53. There was no separate chancery for the English lands. The earl usually kept the seal although a scribe would draft the charters and writs. The archives, which have not survived, were probably deposited in the central household.

de Bures, seneschal of Clare, represented the last Earl Gilbert in parliament.[92]

Many of the Clare seneschals put their experience to good use in later service to the Crown, and indeed some may have been royal commissioners while still members of the Clare *familia*, although there is no direct evidence of this in the period. John de Cornherd, seneschal of Richard, earl of Hertford, in 1199, held a number of important positions under King John and Henry III, including that of keeper of the archiepiscopate of Canterbury *sede vacante*.[93] Richard Heydon, seneschal in 1279, became a royal justice in 1283, while Roger de Scaccario, who was seneschal of both Tonbridge and Clare at various times between 1247 and 1258, was also active in judicial capacities for the Crown by 1259–60.[94]

On the other hand, a number of seneschals had already had royal careers before entering the service of the family. Robert de Bures was custodian of the royal forest of Cannock in Stafford from 1295 to 1306 and was a royal justice as late as April, 1307. He served as seneschal of the honor of Clare from Michaelmas, 1307, to 1309, and was once again a royal justice of oyer and terminer in Norfolk by April, 1314, and a member of Edward II's household by at least 1322.[95] Similarly, one of Earl Gilbert the Red's closest advisers, Hervey de Borham, passed easily between royal and private service and managed an ecclesiastical career in the last years of his life as well. He was seneschal of Clare under Earl Richard in 1259 and a royal commissioner by 1261. He served in the Montfortian government in 1264–65, and was appointed keeper of the peace for Essex and Hertford by Henry III in 1266.

---

[92] PRO, Exchequer, LTR Memoranda Roll 2–3 Henry III, E 368/1 m. 2; KR Memoranda Roll 3 Henry III, E 159/2 m. 8; *Cal. Pat. Rolls 1272–81*, p. 306; PRO, Min. Accts., SC 6/1109/12. Heydon's bailiwick is unknown.

[93] *Memoranda Roll 1 John*, pp. 22, 55, 79–81; *Memoranda Roll 10 John*, ed. R. Allen Brown (Pipe Roll Society, vol. LXIX, new ser. XXXI, 1957), pp. 33, 54, 57; PRO, Exchequer, KR Memoranda Roll 2 Henry III, E 159/1 m. 2d.; LTR Memoranda Roll 2–3 Henry III, E 368/1 m. 4.

[94] For Heydon, see *Cal. Pat. Rolls 1281–92*, p. 102, and for Scaccario, *ibid. 1258–66*, pp. 49, 53, 101. He was seneschal of Tonbridge in 1247 and of Clare *ca.* 1258. *Cartulary of the Priory of St. Gregory, Canterbury*, ed. Audrey M. Woodcock (Camden Society, 3rd ser., vol. LXXXVIII, 1956), p. 161; *Select Cases of Procedure without Writ, Henry III*, eds. H. G. Richardson and G. O. Sayles (Selden Society, vol. LX, 1941), pp. 96–97.

[95] PRO, Min. Accts., SC 6/1109/12, 992/8; *Cal. Pat. Rolls 1301–07*, p. 543; *ibid. 1313–17*, p. 146; *Cal. Close Rolls 1313–18*, p. 541; Brit. Mus., Stowe MS 553, fol. 42.

His ability to serve very different masters is further evidenced by
the fact that in the spring of 1267 he was back with the Clares,
acting on behalf of Earl Gilbert in the negotiations concerning the
Disinherited. In 1268, he represented the earl in the dispute with
Llywelyn ap Gruffydd over Senghenydd. In the same year, John
d'Eyville attempted unsuccessfully to present him to the church
of Adlingfleet coveted by Bogo de Clare, but by the 1270's he was
rector of a number of churches and in 1276 was dean of St. Paul's,
London. At the same time he was once again in royal service,
acting as an itinerant justice for Essex in 1276.[96] Finally, Hamo
Hautein, a seneschal under the Red Earl in 1268, had been sheriff
of Lincoln in 1259–60, a royal escheator in 1261 and sheriff of
Lincoln again in 1262. He was an official in the king's wardrobe
in 1263, and somewhat later was sheriff of Norfolk and Suffolk
as well. The length of his tenure with the Clares is unknown, but
he served in a variety of positions for Edward I from at least 1273
to 1286.[97]

These examples provide detailed illustrations of the reliance of
both the Crown and the great comital families on men of proven
administrative ability and experience. For the most part, the Clare
seneschals were not prominent landholders under the earls. In
the twelfth century the baronial seneschal may have been a mesne
tenant of considerable local importance in terms of his military and
territorial position; [98] but in the thirteenth century he was a professional bureaucrat, with a sound knowledge of contemporary
legal practice and with an ability to perform a variety of administrative functions. As the careers of Robert de Bures, Hervey
de Borham, and Hamo Hautein demonstrate, a significant number
of seneschals did not view baronial service as the prerequisite to

[96] *Select Cases of Procedure without Writ, Henry III*, p. 97; *Cal. Pat. Rolls
1258–66*, pp. 146, 668; *ibid. 1266–72*, pp. 143, 716; *Close Rolls 1261–64*, p. 348;
ibid. 1264–68, pp. 11, 79; PRO, Coram Rege Roll Easter 4 Edward I, KB 27/21
m. 34; *Littere Wallie*, p. 102; *Rotuli Ricardi Gravesend, diocesis Lincolniensis*, ed.
F. N. Davis (Lincoln Record Society, vol. XX, 1925), pp. 113, 116, 133, 182,
183; *The Great Chartulary of Glastonbury*, ed. Dom Aelred Watkin (Somerset
Record Society, vols. LIX, LXIII–LXIV, 1944–49/50), I, p. (xiv). For Adlingfleet,
see above, p. 184.

[97] *Oseney Cartulary*, V, 252–53; *Close Rolls 1259–61*, p. 470; *ibid. 1268–72*,
p. 323; PRO, Pipe Roll 48 Henry III, E 372/108 r. 4; *Cal. Pat. Rolls 1272–81*,
p. 32; *ibid. 1281–92*, pp. 211, 259; *Cal. Close Rolls 1272–79*, pp. 167, 251.

[98] For a general discussion of this question and some specific examples from
the twelfth century Clares, see Stenton, *First Century*, pp. 75–79.

appointment in the royal administration, but rather were attracted to private positions for varying lengths of time after employment by the Crown. The responsibilities of the seneschal were heavy, but he seems to have discharged them well. The frequency with which he entered the royal administration indicates that the Crown recognized both his prior experience and his abilities; conversely, his use by the earls following service for the king indicates the impact of the royal example on great baronial families such as the Clares in the recruitment and employment of professional administrative personnel.

Subordinate to the seneschal were the estate bailiffs who managed the demesne economy and, before 1300 at least, were responsible for local judicial and franchisal administration, and the bailiffs of fees. The functions of the latter officials have already been indicated. The system of feodaries for each county of the bailiwick can only be established definitely for Clare, but it may have existed for the Tonbridge and Gloucester bailiwicks as well, at least by the early fourteenth century. For the Clare bailiwick in 1308, there were five such bailiffs, one each for Norfolk, Suffolk, and Essex, one for Cambridge and Huntingdon, and a separate one for the " March," which probably represents the local courts and fees of the Gloucester, Clare, Marshal, and Giffard lands centered on Stambourne Marsh in Essex.[99] This grouping was not always rigidly observed, however. The Essex bailiff in 1309–10 accounted for the Stambourne court receipts. Thomas Merveylus, who was arrested for irregularities in his account in 1291, was bailiff of fees for both Norfolk and Suffolk in that year.[100] The development of the system of feodaries probably reflects an attempt to remove some of the burdens of administration from the estate bailiffs, but there is no way of knowing when it was introduced. The earliest indication of the system for Clare bailiwick is the reference to Merveylus in 1291, but such officials existed on the Fortibus estates by 1275.[101] Much of the routine work involved in executing the orders of the honor court, holding

---

[99] PRO, Min. Accts., SC 6/1109/12; cf. PRO, Chanc. Misc., C 47/9/25 and *Cal. Inq. Post Mortem*, VI, no. 129.

[100] PRO, Min. Accts., SC 6/1109/13. For Merveylus, see PRO, Exchequer of Pleas, Plea Roll 19 Edward I, E 13/17 m. 34d., and cf. Denholm-Young, *Seignorial Administration*, p. 159.

[101] Denholm-Young, *ibid.*, pp. 34, 159–60.

views and collecting feudal incidents was actually done by an under bailiff, who accounted to the chief bailiff at Clare castle. He in turn delivered the bulk of the cash income to the receiver, although his own account seems to have gone directly to the household for final audit by the central financial officers after a preliminary view by the seneschal.[102] Little is known of the men who served as feodaries. In 1291 Thomas Merveylus combined the office with that of estate bailiff on some Norfolk manors, and in 1307–8 John Beneyt was both sub-bailiff of Norfolk and bailiff of the borough of Clare. Both men were undoubtedly mesne tenants of the Clares, but neither seems to have been an important landholder. The office in Suffolk was a paid serjeanty: certain tenants held their lands in returning for providing a bailiff of fees for the county from among their ranks. The bailiff of Essex received 26s. 8d. per annum in wages, and the Suffolk bailiff 33s. 4d.; the amounts paid the others in this period do not survive.[103]

The duties of the estate bailiffs, who were generally paid between 5 and 10 marks a year, were numerous. In most instances there was a separate one for each manor, although Thomas Merveylus was bailiff of Wells, Warham, and Walsingham in 1291 and John de Toucestre, who was constable and bailiff of Clare in both 1307–8 and 1308–9, also appears as bailiff of Hundon, Sudbury, Haverhill, Disning, and Bardfield in the receiver's account for 1307–8.[104] The bailiff, with his assistant the beadle or serjeant (*serviens*), supervised the entire operation of the demesne economy, although the reeve or in some cases the *serviens* accounted for manorial income and expenditure to the receiver.[105] It is in his judicial capacities that the estate bailiff figures most prominently. By the beginning of the fourteenth century many of his functions had been assumed by the bailiff of fees, but the evidence clearly shows the varied tasks which the estate bailiff was expected

---

[102] PRO, Exchequer of Pleas, E 13/17 m. 34d.; PRO, Min. Accts., SC 6/1109/13–14; *Court Roll of Honor of Clare*, p. 77, and cf. *ibid.*, pp. 93, 99.

[103] PRO, Min. Accts., SC 6/1109/12–14; *Court Roll of Honor of Clare*, pp. 77, 79, 82–83. In the early 1320's, the bailiff of Cambridge and Huntingdon received 50s. per annum and the bailiff of Norfolk 26s. 8d. PRO, Min. Accts., SC 6/1109/17–18.

[104] PRO, Exchequer of Pleas, E 13/17 m. 34d.; PRO, Min. Accts., SC 6/992/8, 1109/12.

[105] SC 6/1109/12. Little can be said of the reeve beyond the fact that he was unpaid, probably overworked, and a villein.

to perform in the earlier period. He was the seneschal's deputy in judicial and franchisal administration, presiding at most of the sessions of the manorial and hundredal courts and in the Oxford hundred of Chadlington holding the view of frankpledge. He also collected scutage from the mesne tenants and made distraints and attachments at the precept of the seneschal, at times however acting illegally outside the area of his lord's fee; and on some occasions he can be found representing the earl in cases pending before the royal justices in eyre.[106] In certain ways, moreover, the bailiff assumed functions normally reserved to the officials of the Crown. The Clare tenants in the banlieu of Tonbridge were exempt from common summons before the justices in eyre for Kent. The royal justices had to hold a special session within the banlieu, and before 1279 the earls had the right to appoint one of their own men as coroner to make presentments.[107] In addition, the Clares enjoyed or usurped the privilege of return of writs in many of their holdings, including the honor of Tonbridge and the Suffolk lands within the liberty of Bury St. Edmunds, and they claimed it for all their lands and fees in Somerset and numerous other places as well.[108] All royal writs which affected the Clare tenants in these lands had to be executed by the bailiffs in place of the sheriff. Most of the time they complied with the royal directives, but instances in which they defaulted in their responsibilities are occasionally recorded as well.[109]

Financial administration in the bailiwick was under the control of the receiver. The fullest information concerning his activities

[106] *Curia Regis Rolls 1230–32*, pp. 126–27, 360–61; *Select Cases of Procedure without Writ, Henry III*, p. 97; *Rot. Hund.*, I, 168, II, 12, 746; *Surrey Manorial Accounts*, pp. 38, 40; Introduction, p. xliii; *Somerset Pleas*, III (1–7 Edward I), ed. Lionel Landon (Somerset Record Society, vol. XLI, 1926), p. 151.

[107] *Patent Rolls 1225–32*, p. 297; *Cal. Pat. Rolls 1247–58*, p. 617; *ibid. 1258–66*, pp. 49–50. In 1279 Edward I recovered the exercise of the office of coroner. *Plac. Quo War.*, p. 340, and cf. Sutherland, *Quo Warranto Proceedings, Edward I*, p. 147 note 1. The earls kept all the revenues for themselves. *Close Rolls 1256–59*, p. 196.

[108] *Plac. Quo War.*, pp. 253, 343; *Rot. Hund.*, II, 172; PRO, Coram Rege Roll Mich. 13–14 Edward I, KB 27/94 m. 28d.

[109] E.g., *Calendar of Plea Rolls of the Exchequer of the Jews*, eds. J. M. Rigg and H. Jenkinson (Jewish Historical Society, 1905–29), I, 190–91, II, 82. A good example involving the bailiffs of Countess Maud in 1269 is contained in *Somerset Pleas*, II (41–57 Henry III), ed. Lionel Landon (Somerset Record Society, vol. XXXVI, 1923), pp. 66, 77, 91.

is contained in the account of Robert de Abethrop for the bailiwick of the honor of Clare in 1307–8.[110] He collected over £960, excluding arrears, from the reeves or other officials of the demesne manors in Suffolk, Norfolk, Essex, Hertford and Huntingdon, from the bailiffs of the boroughs of Clare, Sudbury and Southwold, from the bailiffs of fees for the various counties, and from a fine assessed for the wardship of a mesne tenant. He paid the salaries of the seneschal, the constable of Clare, the estate bailiffs and park-keepers, some of the household officials and himself. He also paid the expenses of various household officials engaged in a variety of legal and financial affairs for Earl Gilbert, and reimbursed some of the household knights for horses killed in a tournament at Dunstable. The remaining cash, about £800, was delivered to the earl's wardrobe, and the entire series of financial transactions was carefully controlled by an elaborate system of writs, tallies, and letters of acquittance. Abethrop's own account was subject to audit by the wardrobe clerks, although the methods employed and the time and place of the view are not apparent.

The Household

The central household imposed a unity of administration on all the Clare estates in England, Wales, and Ireland. Unfortunately no household rolls have survived, and what is known of its organization derives mainly from indirect references in the receivers' accounts. All the evidence, however, points to a highly centralized and elaborate body, at least by the late thirteenth century. The financial side in particular was carefully managed. Only the main features of its organization can be discerned, but these reveal many similarities to the system employed by the king, and it is probable that they were developed on that model. In the twelfth century and under the first Earl Gilbert, the chamber was the central financial office, but at some point after the mid-thirteenth century it was superseded by the wardrobe. The last men-

[110] PRO, Min. Accts., SC 6/1109/12. The document is summarized in Denholm–Young, *Seignorial Administration*, pp. 41–42, but is misdated 1–2 Edward I. Abethrop remained as receiver until at least 1312. PRO, SC 6/992/8, 1109/13–14, 930/2.

tion of a Clare chamberlain occurs in 1252, when Earl Richard imprisoned a certain Milo at Usk, possibly for theft.[111] It seems reasonable to suppose that the earl reorganized the financial system at that time, but the earliest definite mention of a wardrobe only dates from 1292, when Earl Gilbert the Red requested a respite on a plea at Westminster to consult the officials of the wardrobe, who were in Wales at the time.[112] The receivers of the English bailiwicks delivered their cash receipts directly to the wardrobe, but the Clares had receiverships at Cardiff and Usk, where the profits from the Welsh and perhaps the Irish estates would go. The wardrobe may have been in Wales to take control of the cash, or possibly to audit the accounts of the receivers.[113] The wardrober was essentially a receiver-general. He supervised all financial transactions, paid the fees of the household staff and was responsible for the major purchases of food, clothing, and luxury items for the earl, his family and his retinue. Smaller sums required for food and supplies as the earl and countess traveled from manor to manor were handled by household clerks under his direction.[114] The auditors examined the accounts of all local officials and the central financial ministers. Apart from some corrections of figures or dating on a number of accounts, which may however have been made by the local officials themselves, no details survive to indicate the procedure the auditors employed. With the wardrober, they also served more generally as the earl's most important advisers on all matters of administration. By the turn of the century there was also a dependent wardrober, who

[111] *Curia Regis Rolls 1219–20*, p. 62; Tewkesbury, p. 149.

[112] *Rot. Parl.*, I, 83. The Red Earl's brother Bogo had a wardrobe system by 1284, and the accounts printed by Giuseppi indicate that it was not new at that date.

[113] In most of the Usk receivers' accounts, the bulk of the money went to the wardrobe, but sums were also delivered to Cardiff. No accounts survive for Kilkenny or Cardiff itself. By 1296–97, the Cardiff receiver was replaced by a treasurer. See below, Chapter VIII, ("The Administration of the Lordships"), and for Kilkenny, below, Chapter IX, note 40.

[114] Cf. PRO, Chanc. Misc., C 47/3/32 no. 28, a damaged roll entitled "billa de debitis apud Clare pro hospicio domini et domine tempore . . . pro W. de Wallingford et Stephano de Muchdene clericis officiorum," which records small sums allotted to various estate officials at Clare, Hundon, and Sudbury for the purchase of household supplies. Since the last Earl Gilbert was not married until Michaelmas, 1308, the document probably dates *ca.* 1309–14. It may however refer to Joan of Acre and either Earl Gilbert the Red or Ralph de Monthermer, or perhaps to Roger Damory and Lady Elizabeth de Burgh.

managed the household finances of Joan of Acre's children by Earl Gilbert the Red and Ralph de Monthermer. In the surviving receivers' accounts for the lordship of Usk, certain sums were paid at this time to men described as the " wardrobers of the countess' children." Richard de St. Fagans, the chief wardrober from 1300 to 1306, held this position in 1296–97, and a certain Roger Capellus held it from 1302 to 1305.[115] Finally, Richard de Loughteborough is described in Abethrop's account as the " forensic wardrober " in 1307–8. The meaning of this term is uncertain. Earl Gilbert had houses in London, and the account mentions expenses connected with bringing £125 to the city, possibly for deposit or for payment to various merchants. Loughteborough may have had charge of these and similar sums. It is more likely, however, that he was the dependent wardrober of the last earl's youngest full sister Elizabeth and perhaps his half sister Isabella. Both were still unmarried in 1307–8, and presumably resided in the household.[116]

By the late thirteenth century the major administrative body supervising the activities of all the local and central officials was the permanent salaried council. In this period every great lord must have had a council of some sort, but in most cases, almost nothing is known either of its composition or its activities.[117] The surviving references to the Clare council are few, but explicit enough to reveal something of its scope. It is likely that it only came into existence under Earl Gilbert the Red, despite some evidence which on first sight suggests that it was already functioning by the mid-thirteenth century. In the judicial proceedings involving Earl Richard and Richard Siward, lord of Llanbleddian, in 1245, the latter is described as " de familia et . . . de consilio comitis." [118] In a dispute between Earl Richard and the abbot of Tewkesbury in 1249, the earl was dissuaded from allowing the abbot's claim " per consiliarios suos contrarios." A decade later Matthew Paris described Walter de Scoteny, Richard's seneschal (and alleged

---

[115] PRO, Min. Accts., SC 6/927/2, 5, 6, 8. The young Gilbert was transferred to the household of Queen Margaret in 1301, but his sisters remained with their mother and stepfather.

[116] PRO, Min. Accts., SC 6/1109/12. Elsewhere in the account he is described as the former "(chief) wardrober," indicating that he had held this latter position in the previous year, 1306–7.

[117] See Denholm-Young, *Seignorial Administration*, pp. 25–30.

[118] *Cartae de Glamorgan*, II, 550, 551.

poisoner) as his "principal counselor."[119] In these instances, it seems clear that the earl was relying on the informal counsel of his leading household knights and estate officials, who did not in themselves constitute a permanent, official advisory body. In this latter sense, the earliest indication of an institutionalized council probably dates from March, 1284, when Archbishop Peckham wrote Earl Gilbert the Red suggesting that disputes between them might best be settled if the earl and his council (*conseyl*) met with the archbishop and his council in or near London.[120] In 1314, a dispute between the last Earl Gilbert and the newly consecrated archbishop of Canterbury, Walter Reynolds, was similarly settled by the councils of the two men.[121] The other references to the Clare council suggest that it dealt with difficult or unusual situations, and that it exercised a general supervisory control over all affairs throughout the family estates and lordships, at least in England and Wales. In 1299 it sat with the sheriff of Glamorgan at the Cardiff county court to try a case.[122] In 1308 Robert Baynard paid £40 for a wardship "pro fine facto coram concilio comitis apud Clerkenwelle," and in 1309 Adam de Llantrissent, receiver of Usk from August to Michaelmas, 1307, while it was in royal custody, was pardoned a debt of £5 "per concilium domini comitis." It is known from Robert Abethrop's account that the members of the council were paid, receiving at least £31 in 1307–8.[123]

The identities of the putative councilors of 1284 is unknown, but there seem to have been eleven of them in 1299. Seven were prominent household knights, including Robert Bardolf, a former

---

[119] Brit. Mus., Cotton MS Cleopatra A VII, fol. 96; Tewkesbury, p. 512; Matthew Paris, *Chronica Majora*, V, 737–38.

[120] *Reg. Epist. Peckham*, II, 689. The archiepiscopal council is known to have existed by 1282.

[121] " Acorde est et aconeunu entre le consayl del honorable Pere en Dieu Sire Wauter . . . d'une part (et) le consayl de haut homme et noble Monsieur Gilbert de Clare." Irene J. Churchill, *Canterbury Administration* (2 vols.; London, 1933), I, 13 and note 4, from the unpublished register of Archbishop Reynolds, fol. 4. This dispute related to the services owed by the earl at Reynold's enthronization, services eventually rendered by Bartholomew de Badlesmere as Gilbert's representative. The dispute between the Red Earl and Peckham may have concerned usurpations of franchises in Tonbridge, a practice in which the earl was quite proficient. Cf. Painter, *Studies*, p. 115.

[122] *Cartae de Glamorgan*, III, 911. See also below, p. 264.

[123] PRO, Min. Accts., SC 6/1109/12, 1247/29.

seneschal of Gloucester, Robert de Grendon, sheriff of Glamorgan in 1307 and 1313–14, and John de St. John, eldest son of the John de St. John who was lord of the Hampshire barony of Basing and a member of the Red Earl's *comitiva* in the Welsh war of 1282. There were also four clerics: Master Thomas de Pulesdene, Master Henry de Llancarfan, who served as treasurer of Cardiff from 1304 to 1308, Robert de Chenington, who was also a councilor in 1313 and one of the last earl's executors, and John de Bruges, the wardrober under Joan of Acre and Ralph de Monthermer in 1297 and again under the last Earl Gilbert in 1307–8.[124] Unfortunately, Abethrop's account recording the payment of £31 to the councilors does not indicate their number or identities, and there is no way of knowing if the composition of the council of 1299 was at all exceptional. It is likely, however, that the wardrober at least was a permanent member of the council, perhaps its presiding officer. In 1313 Richard de Estdene was a councilor; he appears as wardrober from 1308 to 1311, and again for the widow of the last earl in 1315, and he was her executor as well. It would seem safe to say that the permanent members of the council included the wardrober, probably the auditors, and a number of household knights, while the other members would vary according to the particular nature of the council's activities and its location at any given time.[125]

In addition to the financial officers and their clerks, the household contained a vast number of knights, attorneys, and assorted esquires, grooms, pages, ladies-in-waiting, and domestics. The magnitude of the *familia* may be judged from the fact that when Earl Gilbert the Red and Countess Joan visited her brother Prince Edward in February, 1293, they brought along over two hundred knights, esquires and maids of honor.[126] Nothing can be said about the great majority of these followers beyond the fact that they wore their master's robes and attended to the details of his domestic affairs. The knights and bachelors who formed the retinue in war and tournaments were for the most part minor

---

[124] *Cartae de Glamorgan*, III, 911, 1017; PRO, Min. Accts., SC 6/920/16, 922/28, 927/2, 1109/12, 1247/17, 1247/29; *Cal. Papal Letters*, II, 113; *Cal. Pat. Rolls 1313–17*, p. 202.

[125] *Cal. Papal Letters*, II, 113; PRO, Min. Accts., SC 6/920/18, 927/15, 1247/29; *Cal. Close Rolls 1318–23*, p. 323; *Cal. Inq. Misc.*, II (1307–49), nos. 497–98.

[126] PRO, Exchequer, KR Accts. Var., E 101/353/18 m. 3d.

landholders in their own right and were often employed at various times in administrative positions. A list of knights in the retinue of the last Earl Gilbert, contained in a document relating to a tournament at Dunstable in 1309, may be taken as representative. The contingent included Roger Tyrel, who served under Ralph de Monthermer and the last earl in the Scottish campaigns of 1303, 1311, and 1314; Nicholas Poinz and Fulk Payforer, who came from small landholding families that had long-standing personal and tenurial ties with the Clares; Henry de Penbridge and William Fleming, mesne tenants in Glamorgan who were prominent in the local administration of that lordship, Penbridge having served as sheriff of Glamorgan *ca.* 1300; and the earl's cousin Richard, the son of Thomas de Clare and by 1308 lord of Thomond.[127] A list of the *familia* with Earl Gilbert the Red in London in 1267 reveals a similar pattern of social composition and territorial and administrative connections with the family.[128] There is evidence to suggest that by the early fourteenth century at the latest, some of the knights were permanent salaried retainers, receiving an annual wage in place of enfeoffment on the English or Welsh estates or some other form of reimbursement for their services. In 1305–6 Robert de Grendon was paid a retaining fee in installments by the receiver of Usk. The account of Robert de Abethrop for the bailiwick of Clare in 1307–8 reveals a partial payment of £10 " pro feodo suo " to Giles de Argentine, a prominent member of the last Earl Gilbert's retinue who fought and died with the earl at Bannockburn.[129] No other evidence, however, survives to indicate the use of the indenture system coming into prominence at this time. There is an early indenture, dating from 1297, which involves two Clare military tenants in Usk, but the contract does not relate directly to service in the lord's *comitiva*.[130]

---

[127] These and other examples are cited in A. Tomkinson, "Retinues at the Tournament of Dunstable, 1309," *English Historical Review*, LXXIV (1959), 72–73. The document is partially reproduced in *Collectanea Topographica et Genealogica*, vol. IV (London, 1837), 61–72.

[128] *Cal. Pat. Rolls 1266–72*, pp. 145–47. See Jacob, *Studies*, pp. 128–33, and above, pp. 113–14.

[129] PRO, Min. Accts., SC 6/927/9, 1109/12. Grendon was paid £19 for some horses apparently killed in the Scottish campaign that year " simul cum feodo predicti domini Roberti de termino Sancti Michaelis." For Argentine, see *Vita Edwardi Secundi*, p. 53; Johnstone, *Edward of Carnarvon*, pp. 116–17.

[130] Brit. Mus., Add. Ch. 1531, discussed below, pp. 279–80.

The only other class of household officials about whom there is some information is the attorneys. Many of them were professional lawyers who can be found representing other barons besides the Clares.[131] Some, however, were permanent members of the household and held a variety of positions for the earls; they either served as attorneys on the basis of their prior administrative and legal experience, or else advanced to higher positions after employment in this capacity. When Earl Gilbert the Red went to Ireland in 1293, he named Simon de Hengham, who had been receiver of Clare bailiwick in 1290–91, and Robert Bardolf, seneschal of Gloucester in 1290, as his attorneys in England.[132] John de Chelmersford, attorney de banco in 1307–8, became wardrober in 1312 and later entered royal service.[133] A number of attorneys also had clerical careers. Chelmersford was presented to the rectorship of Stanford in the Vale, Berkshire, by the last Earl Gilbert in 1311, and he eventually rose to the position of deacon in the diocese of Salisbury. Richard de la Lade, custos of the honors of Gloucester and Clare during Earl Richard's minority from 1234 to 1243, was an attorney under the first Earl Gilbert, who presented him to the church of Northill in Bedford in 1224.[134] The attorneys acted as the earls' representatives in legal matters concerning both their relations with the Crown and the internal organization of the inheritance. There is no evidence that the Clare council ever visited Kilkenny, but attorneys were sent out of the household on a regular basis to supervise the affairs of the liberty and audit the accounts of the local treasurer and

[131] E.g., Geoffrey Costentin, Cal. Close Rolls 1272–79, pp. 54, 119.

[132] PRO, Min. Accts., SC 6/1001/5; Cal. Pat. Rolls 1292–1301, p. 19. Hengham was also an attorney for Gilbert's son-in-law, Duncan, earl of Fife, in 1287. He later served as one of the Red Earl's executors. Cal. Pat. Rolls 1281–92, p. 262; ibid. 1292–1301, p. 292.

[133] PRO, Min. Accts., SC 6/1109/12; Calendar of Letter Books of the City of London, Letter Book B, ed. Reginald Sharpe (London, 1900), p. 46; Cal. Chanc. War., pp. 409, 587; Cal. Fine Rolls 1307–19, p. 201 (keeper of the honor of Clare after Bannockburn); Cal. Pat. Rolls 1317–21, p. 175. He was an attorney for Bartholomew de Badlesmere in 1320–21. Ibid., pp. 426, 535, 553.

[134] Registrum Simonis de Gandavo, diocesis Saresbiriensis, 1297–1315, eds. C. T. Flower and M. C. B. Dawes (Canterbury and York Society, vols. XL–XLI, 1934), II, 760, 902, 904; Close Rolls 1227–31, p. 229; Curia Regis Rolls 1227–30, p. 175; Cal. Pat. Rolls 1232–47, p. 54; Close Rolls 1242–47, p. 44; Rotuli Hugonis de Welles, episcopi Lincolniensis, 1209–1235, ed. W. Phillimore et al. (Lincoln Record Society, vols. III, VI, IX, 1912–14), III, 10.

seneschal. This procedure presumably originated under Earl Richard, and it was continued by his successors despite the formation of the permanent council.[135]

The career of Master Richard de Clare may well serve as a final example of the administrative personnel of the earls of Gloucester. Richard was a bastard son of the Red Earl's brother Thomas, and was born around 1286.[136] He has sometimes been confused with his legitimate half brother Richard, who was lord of Thomond from 1308 to 1318.[137] By 1306, Master Richard was rector of Bunratty and Youghal in Thomond and Maltby in York, and in 1305 served as the attorney for Ralph de Monthermer in a suit against Thomas' eldest son Gilbert (d. 1308) for tenements in Plashes-juxta-Standon in Hertford.[138] The suit was unsuccessful, and sometime between 1308 and 1318 the legitimate Richard, now lord of Thomond, gave the lands to his "clerk and kinsman," Master Richard.[139] After the last Gilbert became earl in 1307, Master Richard entered his service. He was Gilbert's chancellor of Cardiff in 1313, and along with John de Chelmersford was appointed the earl's attorney in March, 1314.[140] After Gilbert's death he was one of the keepers of the honor of Gloucester, and served with Robert de Chenington and Bartholomew de Badlesmere as Gilbert's executor.[141] In addition, Richard was the executor of the earl's aunt, Margaret, dowager countess of Cornwall, sister of Earl Gilbert the Red, who died in 1312.[142]

After the last Earl Gilbert's death, Master Richard entered royal service. From 1315 to 1318 he was *custos* of Ramsey Abbey during vacancy, and he served as escheator south of Trent from 1318

---

[135] Below, p. 290.

[136] His paternity is proved in *Cal. Papal Letters*, II, 12.

[137] E.g., *G. E. C.*, V, 701. Both Richards appears as witnesses to a charter of Bartholomew de Badlesmere in 1309, along with some other important Clare officials and associates. *Cal. Close Rolls 1307–13*, p. 246.

[138] *Cal. Papal Letters*, II, 12; *Cal. Chanc. War.*, p. 245.

[139] PRO, Duchy of Lancaster, Cartae Miscellaneae, DL 36/1/243. In 1320–21, Master Richard gave these lands to his half sister Margaret and her husband, Badlesmere. PRO, Duchy of Lancaster, Ancient Deeds, Series L, DL 25/2021.

[140] *Cal. Papal Letters*, II, 113; *Cal. Pat. Rolls 1313–17*, p. 86.

[141] *Cal. Pat. Rolls 1313–17*, p. 202; *Cal. Fine Rolls 1307–19*, p. 201. His account for the honor is in PRO, Pipe Roll 10 Edward II, E 372/162 r. 42–43.

[142] *Cal. Pat. Rolls 1313–17*, p. 459. It was at her request that a papal dispensation was granted to Master Richard in 1306 to hold benefices in addition to Bunratty, Youghal, and Maltby. *Cal. Papal Letters*, II, 12.

to 1320.[143] All during this time, he continued to amass ecclesiastical positions as well, the most important of which was the office of dean of Wimborne Minster, Dorset, which he acquired in 1317 and held until his death in 1338.[144] Master Richard's career is a prime example of the ways in which various members of the Clare family provided services to each other; of equal significance, it affords still another example of the ease with which a professional administrator could combine the duties of cleric, baronial official, and royal servant in the Middle Ages.

[143] PRO, Exchequer, KR Memoranda Roll 11 Edward II, E 159/91 m. 64d.; PRO, Exchequer, KR Escheators' Accounts, E 136/1/29, 238/23.

[144] Cal. Papal Letters, II, 84, 145, 326; Cal. Inq. Misc., II, no. 1614; Registrum Henrici Woodlock, diocesis Wintoniensis, 1305–16, ed. A. W. Goodman (Canterbury and York Society, vols. XLIII–XLIV, 1940–41), I, 616; Registers of Roger Martival, Bishop of Salisbury, 1315–1330, eds. Kathleen Edwards and C. R. Erlington (Canterbury and York Society, vols. LV, LVII, 1959–63), I, 87–88; Cal. Fine Rolls 1337–47, p. 74.

CHAPTER VIII

LORD OF THE MARCH

For almost exactly a century, from 1217 to the death of the last Earl Gilbert at Bannockburn, the Clares were among the most powerful lords of the Welsh march. Their great dominions in southern Wales, extending from the Wye to the Tawe, comprised a large part of modern Monmouthshire and the whole of modern Glamorganshire with the exception of the Gower peninsula. The largest and most important of these territories, the great palatine county of Glamorgan with the dependent lordship of Gwynllwg, came to the family in 1217 along with the earldom and honor of Gloucester. The other lands were acquired as a result of the partition of the Marshal inheritance. In 1246 Earl Richard obtained the lordship of Usk with its members, and in 1268–69 his son purchased Caerleon, like Usk a former portion of the Marshal lordship of Netherwent.[1] Within these areas the Clares exercised an authority almost completely free of royal control. They interpreted and applied a system of law independent of the English common law and the king's writ. They owed no military service for their lordships, but the system of fiefs created in these lands provided them with a body of knights who formed the mainstay of their military strength; and until the end of the thirteenth century they in effect treated the bishop of Llandaff as their own tenant and the landed property of the bishopric as mesne fiefs. The Clares jealously guarded their liberties, and more than once came into conflict with the Crown over them. Edward I displayed the strength of the monarchy and the royal prerogative by crushing the most distinctive feature of marcher law, the right of waging private war, compelling Earl Gilbert the Red to surrender his

---

[1] In 1246 the Clares also obtained the barony of Castle Walwyn in Pembroke, but did not add it to their demesne holdings. See above, Chapter II, note 85.

regalian rights over Llandaff, and in other ways limiting the privileges of both the Clares and the other marchers as well. Nevertheless, the Clares, as lords of the march, still enjoyed independent political and judicial powers they could never possess as English earls.

Englishry and Welshry

The most striking feature of the economic and social structure of the Clare lordships in southern Wales is the division between those areas in which Norman (English) institutions predominated and those characterized by the persistence of the ancient Welsh tribal organization. In general, this division was much more pronounced in Glamorgan than in the lands east of the Ebbw River. The original conquest of Glamorgan and Gwynllwg by Robert fitz Hamon and his followers had only resulted in the Norman settlement of the more prosperous lowlands, leaving the structure of the outlying regions largely undisturbed. The latter were marked by a pastoral economy, and Celtic social and legal institutions retained their vitality. The lowlands, on the other hand, were subject to the growth of manorialism and a system of mesne fiefs. This dichotomy continued under fitz Hamon's successors to the early thirteenth century. Although the Clares conquered the areas under the control of the local chieftains, and in most cases dispossessed them, no attempt was made to interfere with the existing social structure. The local unit of tribal organization, the commote, styled in Latin *patria*, still retained its identity, and the Clares were largely content to exact the established tributary rents and dues. In Glamorgan and Gwynllwg, the separation into a manorialized south and a tribute-paying, pastoral north predominated. In the lordships of Caerleon and Usk, on the other hand, these distinctions, although present, were not as marked. These areas were located on the eastern edge of the march, where they were more subject to English influence, and they lacked a sharp division between mountainous uplands and more fertile lowlands. Such differences as naturally existed in the early stages of Norman penetration had largely disappeared by the thirteenth century. Manors and boroughs were not concentrated in a limited geographical area, and the commote, usually termed a bedelry in these lordships, was more a unit of administrative organization than an area which marked the territorial boundaries of the dominance of Welsh institutions.[2]

The division into Englishry and Welshry in Glamorgan is clearly reflected in the territorial distribution of the demesne estates. For each commote or *patria*, there tended to be a castle and a small group of manors and boroughs in the lowlands to serve as the center of local administration and overlordship. The castle and borough of Cardiff formed the *caput* of the entire lordship. Associated with Cardiff were the manors of Roath and Leckwith and the *patria* of Cibwr, the southernmost of the three commotes which comprised the ancient Welsh cantred of Senghenydd. After 1267 Earl Gilbert the Red also controlled directly the remaining commotes, Uwch–Caiach and Is–Caiach, taken from the native dynasty represented before that time by Gruffydd ap Rhys.[3] The great castle of Caerphilly with the borough and the appurtenant manors of Merthyr Tydfil and Whitchurch, along with some smaller properties, henceforth formed the nucleus of the family control of these commotes. West of the river Taf were the castle and borough of Llantrisant with the manors of Cloun, Pentyrch, and Radyr and the *patriae* of Meisgyn and Glynrhondda. Until the mid-thirteenth century these commotes were held by local chieftains, descendants of Iestyn ap Gwrgant, the last king of Glamorgan before fitz Hamon's invasion. In 1228 Hywel ap Maredudd, lord of Meisgyn, seized Glynrhondda from his cousin Morgan ap Cadwallon, holding both commotes until he in turn was dispossessed by Earl Richard in 1246. Under Richard, half of Glynrhondda was held by Morgan ap Cadwallon's sons, but Earl Gilbert the Red seems to have been in control of the entire area.[4] Further west and south were the great castle and manor of Llantwit with the *patria* of Llanharry; the castles and manors of Talyfan and Llanbleddian with Talyfan and Rhuthun *patriae*, confiscated from Richard Siward in 1245;[5] the castles and boroughs of Kenfig

[2] See, in general, Rees, *South Wales,* pp. 26–31, and the map showing the distribution of manors throughout the entire region, *ibid.*, p. 129. For Caerleon and Usk in particular, cf. the remarks of Holmes, *Estates,* p. 103, and the detailed map, *ibid.*, p. 102.

[3] Above, pp. 123–26.

[4] *Cartae de Glamorgan,* II, 651; *Cal. Inq. Post Mortem,* III, no. 371; above, pp. 59, 69–71, 73–74.

[5] Above, pp. 70–74.

and Cowbridge and the castle of Llangynwyd with the *patria* of
Llangynwyd or Tiriarll ("The Earl's Land"); and the castle,
manor and borough of Neath with Neath *patria*, the manor of
Britton (acquired in 1289 from the abbey) and some other holdings between the Nedd and Tawe Rivers.[6]

A similar pattern of distribution of the demesne estates can be
discerned in the much smaller lordship of Gwynllwg, which
originally was a cantred within the ancient Welsh kingdom of
Morgannwg. Gwynllwg was divided into two commotes. The
northern commote of Machen, situated between the Rhymny and
the Ebbw, was held by a local Welsh dynasty until Earl Gilbert
the Red seized it from Maredudd ap Gruffydd in 1270.[7] The
southern commote, on the other hand, which stretched across the
Ebbw to the confluence of the Usk and the Bristol Channel, was
from the beginning subject to heavy Norman colonization and
settlement, and indeed its original name is lost. The Clares had
a few scattered properties in Machen, notably the manor of
Dyffryn Ebbw, but the bulk of the demesne lands were in the
south, and consisted of the castle and borough of Newport, the
caput of the lordship, and the manors of Stowe, Dowlais, and
Rhymny.[8]

A number of fees in these lordships were still held by Welsh
tenants, and descended according to Welsh rules of tenure, but
the only large area remaining under the autonomous control of a
native chieftain by the beginning of the fourteenth century was
the commote of Afan in Glamorgan, between the Nedd and Afan
Rivers. It was held as a serjeanty by the descendants of the eldest
son of Maredudd ap Caradog ap Iestyn, who in the late thirteenth
century adopted the Normanized surname of de Avene. Otherwise

[6] In return for Britton and the other properties, the Clares paid an annual rent
of £100. The charter is printed from a later *inspeximus* in *Cartae de Glamorgan*,
IV, 1203–5. The money was still being paid by the lords of Glamorgan as late
as 1492 and presumably until the dissolution of Neath Abbey in 1539. PRO,
Duchy of Lancaster, Min. Accts., DL 29/665/10334 m. 15d.

[7] Above, p. 129. His son Morgan ap Maredudd led the revolt in Glamorgan
in 1294–95 (above, pp. 154–55). When Morgan came into the king's peace in
June, 1295, he probably expected Edward I to restore the territories held by his
father, but this was not done. Under Ralph de Monthermer he held a life interest
in Edelegan to the value of £15 per annum, but the last Earl Gilbert replaced
this with a grant of somewhat lesser value. *Cal. Close Rolls 1313–18*, p. 263.

[8] Rhymny was held in dower by Countess Maud from 1267 to 1289. PRO,
Rentals and Surveys, General Series, SC 11/610 m. 1.

the broad plains between the Ogwr and the Rhymny were divided into a number of Anglo–Norman fiefs, the most important of which were the lordship of Coety, held by the Turberville family as a serjeanty; Dinas Powys, held by the de Somerys, who also held the Worcestershire barony of Dudley in chief of the Crown; Penmark, held for four fees by the Umphravilles; and Ogmore, which passed with the marcher lordship of Kidwelly in modern Cardiganshire from the de Londres to Patrick de Chaworth, lord of the Gloucestershire barony of Kempsforth, and later to Henry, second son of Edmund of Lancaster and successor to his elder brother Thomas (d. 1322) as earl of Lancaster.[9]

Caerleon and Usk present a somewhat different picture. Demesne manors and boroughs were scattered throughout the lordships, and both the number and size of subordinate fiefs were smaller. Caerleon, which until 1314 was administered as a member of Glamorgan, consisted of the castle, manor, and borough of Caerleon, the manors of Liswerry or Llefnydd, Little Tintern and Undy, and the commotes or bedelries of Caerleon, Edelegan and Llefnydd, the latter two taken in 1270 from Maredudd ap Gruffydd.[10] Usk was administered as a separate lordship, but most of it was in the earls' possession only from 1247 to 1262 and from 1289 to 1314. It included the castle, manor, and borough of Usk with the appurtenant manor of New Grange, the castle, manor, and borough of Trellech, the castles and manors of Llantrissent and Tregrug, the manors of Troy, Cwmcarvan, and Llangwm, and the bedelries of Usk and Trellech. From 1267 to 1289, Countess Maud held Troy, Cwmcarvan, Trellech, and the manor and borough of Usk, along with the manor of Rhymny in Gwynllwg, in dower, and Bogo de Clare held Tregrug, Llangwm and some other properties in Llantrissent until his death in 1294. Only the castles of Usk and Llantrissent and some scattered holdings re-

[9] For the lords of Afan, see above, pp. 57–59, 69, 134. A list of fees, compiled when dower was reassigned to Earl Richard's widow in 1266–67, is printed from PRO, Exchequer, KR Ancient Extents, E 142/88 m. 9 in *Cartae de Glamorgan*, II, 650–51. A similar list of fees acquired by Hugh Despenser in 1317 was copied from the original (PRO, Chanc. Misc., C 47/9/24) by Sir Robert Cotton, and is printed in the *Cartae*, III, 1052–55, from Brit. Mus., Cotton MS Julius B XII, fol. 169.

[10] Although Little Tintern was within the boundaries of the Usk lordship, it was treated as a member of Caerleon (cf. *Cal. Inq. Post Mortem*, IV, no. 435), and does not appear in the Usk accounts before 1314.

mained with Earl Gilbert the Red. In December, 1314, Edward II assigned both Caerleon and Usk in dower to the last Earl Gilbert's widow, and henceforth they were organized as a single lordship.[11]

The economic structure of the lordships reproduces most of the features found on the English estates, but with some significant differences in emphasis, especially in Glamorgan. Income from boroughs, mills, seigneurial dues, and natural resources such as forests seem to have been more important in these areas than in the family properties in England, and substantial sums were also collected from the Welsh population in the form of tributary rents, dues, and perquisites of courts. On the manors themselves, freehold and customary rents were a major source of revenue, although the production of grain was still the main activity. The sale of grain, however, was not always the most important item of profit on every manor. The endemic warfare against the Welsh, particularly in Glamorgan, frequently disrupted normal manorial enterprise, and a considerable amount of the annual yield went directly to the earl and his household, who were often in residence on the Welsh estates. Moreover, a major purpose of direct demesne exploitation was to provide food supplies for the castle garrisons, although there is no way of calculating exactly how much of the total was consumed in this way. The account of Humphrey de Bohun, earl of Hereford and *custos* of the lordships in 1262–63, reveals the large staffs required even in peacetime, and there was a castle attached to almost every manor and borough in the lordships.[12] A similar problem would not arise in the English lands, where the only castles were located at Clare, Tonbridge, and Hanley in Worcestershire. Undoubtedly a large proportion of the grain was sold in local markets, but the income realized did not necessarily form the largest item of revenue in every instance.

Unfortunately, little evidence has survived for Glamorgan and

[11] PRO, Rentals and Surveys, General Series, SC 11/610 m. 1; *Cal. Inq. Post Mortem*, IV, no. 435; *Cal. Close Rolls 1313–18*, p. 132; PRO, Chanc. Misc., C 47/9/25. Tregrug was located in Edelegan bedelry in Caerleon, but appears in the Usk receivers' accounts after Bogo's death.

[12] PRO, Min. Accts., SC 6/1202/1. There were 52 people housed in Neath castle, including the constable, 12 foot soldiers, a chaplain, the cook, a laundress and other domestics, and a number of grooms. There were 28 people at Llangynwyd, 42 at Llantrisant, and 20 at Cardiff.

Gwynllwg. The fullest information is contained in the accounts of Bartholomew de Badlesmere and John Giffard of Brimpsfield, keepers of the lordship after the death of the last Earl Gilbert in 1314. Their accounts, however, reflect the unsettled conditions attendant upon the earl's death, in particular the widespread disorder caused by the abortive uprising led by Llywelyn Bren,[13] rather than the normal pattern of economic activity and income.[14] Combined with some earlier evidence, dating mainly from periods of royal control, the accounts at least indicate the importance of tributary rents and dues, and a reliance on the profits of boroughs, mills, and courts to supplement income from the sale of demesne produce and manorial rents.

The largest items of manorial income recorded in Badlesmere's account derive from the sale of grain and livestock, but almost all the revenues were released to Payn de Turberville, his successor as keeper of the lordship, for the expenses of munitioning the castles and paying the fees of the other royal officials. For example, Roath manor yielded small sums, £5 or less, from rents, the lease of pasture rights, and court profits, but over £56 from the sale of grain and almost £29 from the sale of stock. On the larger manor of Llantwit, which probably had about 700 acres in demesne,[15] sums ranging from £20 to £33 were collected from rents, the farm of mills, and the sale of wood and demesne works (both lumped under the heading "exitus manerii"), while the sale of grain and stock together came to over £146.[16] Most of the figures presumably represent normal or near normal income, but the sums realized from the sale of grain and stock in all likelihood do not. Faced with extraordinary expenses and the difficulties of safeguarding the area, the Crown seems to have ex-

[13] For the rising, see *Vita Edwardi Secundi*, pp. 66–68, and Davies, *Baronial Opposition to Edward II*, pp. 31–32.

[14] Badlesmere's account, which runs from Michaelmas, 1314, to Michaelmas, 1315, is in PRO, Min. Accts., SC 6/1202/7. An earlier account, from June 24–Michaelmas, 1314 (SC 6/1202/6), is of little use. John Giffard's account runs from April 20 to Michaelmas, 1316, and is partially printed from SC 6/1202/9 in *Cartae de Glamorgan*, III, 813–48. An account for the period Michaelmas, 1315–April 20, 1316, rendered by Payn de Turberville, lord of Coety and keeper of Glamorgan between Badlesmere and Giffard, is in SC 6/1202/8, but is incomplete and partly illegible.

[15] In the 1260's it had 565 acres of arable and over 125 acres of pasture. *Cartae de Glamorgan*, II, 663.

[16] PRO, Min. Accts., SC 6/1202/7 mm. 1–2, 10.

ploited these resources for immediate profit, and there is evidence that it took little care to keep up an adequate supply of seed and farm animals in the succeeding years. In Turberville's account the sale of grain and livestock is recorded for only a few manors, and only at Stowe and Llantwit, where it brought in about £50 on each manor, was it a major item of revenue. In Giffard's account there is little mention of agricultural enterprise; indeed, there was a concerted effort to lease both pasture and arable, but in a number of cases it was unsuccessful " pro defectu emptorum causa guerre." [17] Only two original Ministers' Accounts have survived, one for the large manor of Rhymny in Gwynllwg for 1300–1, and the other for Dowlais in the same lordship for 1307–8. At Dowlais rents and farms provided half the total income. The issues of mills and the sale of grain brought in about 20 per cent each, and insignificant sums were realized from profits of courts and assorted seigneurial dues. At Rhymny, on the other hand, the sale of grain and stock accounted for a third of the gross income. The other items of profit were freehold and customary rents, which brought in about 30 per cent, issues of mills and dues, which yielded 20 per cent, and court profits, which amounted to about 8 per cent of the total. The remainder derived from various items such as the sale of wood and the lease of pasture rights.[18]

Despite the evidence afforded by these manors and the accounts of Badlesmere and Giffard, the extant sources are too limited to permit a more precise calculation of the overall importance of demesne production in the economy of the lordship. It is clear, however, that other kinds of income, less prominent or non-existent on the English estates, were quite profitable in these areas. A small but steady income was realized from a varied assortment of Welsh tributary rents and dues such as cylch and commorth, which represented marcher adaptations of pre-conquest rents paid by the native tribesmen to the court of their king or chieftain, or a general tributary payment replacing a host of ancient food renders and labor services.[19] Another example of a source

[17] PRO, SC 6/1202/8 and Cartae de Glamorgan, III, 815 (Roath), 821 (Leckwith), 824 (Llanbleddian), 835 (Kenfig), 843 (Cloun).
[18] PRO, Min. Accts., SC 6/925/5, 1202/4. An account for the manor of Merthyr Tydfil, SC 6/1202/2, is illegible.
[19] E.g., Giffard accounted for £3 6s. 8d. " receptis de auxilio Walensi de Talevan quo dicitur Commorth hoc anno." Cartae de Glamorgan, III, 825. For the origin and nature of these rents, see Rees, South Wales, pp. 10–12, 227–33.

of revenue peculiar to the marcher lordships was mining operations. According to the Tewkesbury chronicle, the first Earl Gilbert found silver, lead, and iron mines in Glamorgan in 1228. Unfortunately the extant accounts do not mention any exploitation of these mines by the Clares, or even their exact location, but in 1319 Hugh Despenser, as lord of Glamorgan, hired some royal iron and lead miners to work for him. Hugh may have been working these mines for the first time, but it is also possible that they had been exploited or perhaps farmed out under the Clares.[20] Of greater importance, the farm of mills, occasionally supplemented by the farm of fisheries and forest rights, was an item of profit on almost every manor, and in some instances the income could be of considerable importance. In Badlesmere's account, income from mills was almost as large as freehold and customary rents, and in one case was much more valuable. At Cloun, income from the farm of mills in the dependent commotes of Meisgyn and Glynrhondda was only slightly less than the amount collected in rents. On larger manors such as Llantwit and on the small manor of Pentyrch, a similar pattern emerges, with rents and the farm of mills yielding roughly equivalent amounts in each case. At Stowe in Gwynllwg, however, mills seem to have been very profitable, bringing in about three times as much as rents. Finally, the sale of wood and charcoal usually brought in small amounts, but in Machen forest it was a considerable source of revenue, yielding £40 in 1314–15.[21]

Income from boroughs was also more prominent in Glamorgan than in the English bailiwicks, although the sources of revenue were generally the same. An extent of Cardiff borough made in 1266 shows a total value of almost £100, of which about half derived from issues of mills and about 20 per cent from burgage rents. The remainder consisted principally of revenues of prise of ale, valued at some 15 per cent of the total, fisheries and market

[20] Tewkesbury, p. 70; *Cal. Close Rolls 1318–23*, p. 127. In Giffard's account for Is–Caiach commote in Senghenydd, there is mention of a farm of a coal mine which brought in nothing "pro defectu operariorum causa guerre." *Cartae de Glamorgan*, III, 847.

[21] PRO, SC 6/1202/7 mm. 4, 6, 8, 10 and *passim*. Cf. also *Cartae de Glamorgan*, III, 825 (Llanbleddian), 830 (Llantwit), 839 (Neath fisheries). By 1316, however, some mills had been destroyed in Llywelyn Bren's uprising, e. g., *ibid.*, III, 822 (Whitland), 843 (Cloun and Glynrhondda *patria*).

tolls, worth 10 and 5 per cent respectively. In 1314–15, Cardiff brought in £113, and in most cases the amounts and percentages from these sources had remained remarkably stable over the intervening half century. Only income from prise of ale and fisheries had risen significantly, bringing in twice as much as in 1266.[22] Bartholomew de Badlesmere's account for Kenfig, Neath, and Newport in 1314–15 presents a similar picture. The largest items of income were burgage rents and the farm of mills and fisheries, while smaller amounts were realized from market tolls, prise of ale, perquisites of the borough courts, and in Kenfig, from a fine of 5 marks from 12 tenants for commutation of castle-guard duty. An independently surviving account for Neath in 1311–12 reveals some differences in the actual sums collected, but no significant changes in the over-all nature of income. Such items as market tolls, fisheries, and prise of ale would naturally tend to vary from year to year, but they invariably figured as sources of revenue. Unfortunately, no evidence has survived to indicate any policy the Clares might have undertaken to encourage the formation of new borough settlements or the growth of existing ones within their lordships.[23]

Finally, large sums were also realized from feudal and commotal courts. The *curia comitatus* at Cardiff brought in £50 in 1262–63 and £33 14s. 7d. in 1314–15. Under Turberville and Giffard, it yielded £25 3s. 3d. in 1315–16. These sums are representative, since all pleas, held in these years by the Crown by reason of wardship, would normally be held by the officials of the Clares themselves. An additional £15 5s. was received annually for commutation of castle-guard, a service nominally owed at Cardiff by every military tenant in the lordship.[24] The court at Newport brought in over £20 under Badlesmere, and over £30 was also collected from the dependent *patria* of Machen. Pleas and perquisites in the Glamorgan Welshries were also lucrative, with sums varying from £36 to £50 recorded for Meisgyn and Glynrhondda, the two northern commotes of Senghenydd, and Neath.[25] The totals probably include incidental tributary dues

[22] *Cartae de Glamorgan*, II, 657–58; PRO, Min. Accts., SC 6/1202/7 m. 1. In 1262–63, the entire borough was farmed for 100 marks. PRO, SC 6/1202/1.
[23] PRO, SC 6/1202/5, 1202/7 mm. 5, 11, 11–12.
[24] PRO, SC 6/1202/1, 1202/7 m. 3, 1202/8; *Cartae de Glamorgan*, III, 823. Cf. also Rees, *South Wales*, p. 65.
[25] PRO, SC 6/1202/7 mm. 4, 5, 6, 11, 14.

and fees collected through the courts in addition to regular judicial profits, and there is no indication as to the amounts derived solely from pleas involving Welsh tenants. However, it is clear that control over the commotes was both politically and financially of great value to the Clares.

The economic structure of Caerleon and Usk presents a similar picture, but with some important variations in the over-all pattern of income. Although Caerleon was administratively a member of Glamorgan until 1314, its economy more closely resembles that of Usk, and the two may be considered together. A large number of original Ministers' Accounts have survived for the late thirteenth and early fourteenth centuries which provide a clearer picture of economic conditions in these lordships than can be discerned for Glamorgan and Gwynllwg. The Welsh bedelries were quite lucrative, and large sums were collected through the local courts. There seems, however, to have been less emphasis on tributary rents and dues and more on direct manorial enterprise as sources of income, reflecting the fact that the division into Englishry and Welshry was not as pronounced in these areas as in Glamorgan. On the manors, the sale of grain was usually the most important item of revenue, followed by rents, assorted dues connected with the lease of pasture and forest rights, farms of mills and fisheries, and court perquisites, although not always in that order. There were sheep on some of the manors, but they did not form an important aspect of the economy in this period.[26] The boroughs again were more important in these lordships than in the English honors, but the sources of income were similar to those in Glamorgan. Finally, the sale of wood and charcoal brought in more cash in these areas than in any of the other family holdings in England or Wales.[27]

The surviving manorial accounts clearly indicate a flourishing and well-rounded economy at the turn of the fourteenth century. The manor of Usk, with appurtenant demesnes at New Grange, is well represented by a good series of accounts, the earliest of

[26] See Rees, *South Wales*, p. 196, for references.

[27] A number of items in the surviving accounts for Usk and Troy manors and the boroughs of Usk, Caerleon, and Trellech have been tabulated in Holmes, *Estates*, pp. 161–63. His discussion of the economy of these estates (*ibid.*, pp. 103–7) is more detailed for the period after 1315, when they were joined into a single lordship, than for the early years of the century.

which dates from 1292–93. In that year the sale of wheat and stock brought in about one-third of the total, the farm of a mill one-fifth, issues from other mills, the sale of dairy produce, seigneurial dues, and the lease of pasture rights 30 per cent, while court profits and rents accounted for the bulk of the remainder. In 1304–5, most of these profits were roughly the same, except that two mills were demised at farm in this year, doubling the income from that source. In 1305–6 gross income rose sharply, with a marked increase in the amount of grain sold accounting for the bulk of it. In all three years income from the sale of demesne works was insignificant, indicating a heavy reliance on villein labor, although the reeves' accounts mention sums paid to part-time autumnal workers and annual wages to the usual assort-ment of demesne workers, including a reaper (*messor*), a park-keeper, a gardener, and a milkmaid (*daya*). The small amount of rent is explained by the fact that for some reason the bulk of the cash was actually collected by the receiver himself and only appears in his own accounts. The receiver also accounted directly for most of the rents from the borough and from scattered outlying properties held by Welsh customary tenants, and he regularly collected about £40 per annum from these sources. Since all the income was lumped together and entered under the heading " ville de Usk," there is no way of knowing how important freehold and customary rents were on the demesnes of Usk and New Grange themselves.[28] Some other accounts for Usk for the period 1303–23 present a very similar pattern of revenue, although the income from rents accounted for directly by the reeve tended to rise after 1307.[29] At Caerleon in 1292–93, rents were insignificant, and there was also less emphasis on grain production than at Usk. The bulk of the revenues at Caerleon derived from the farm of mills and the " exitus manerii," comprised mainly of the sale or lease of farm animals and the sale of pasture rights. In the 1320's this somewhat exceptional pattern was still unchanged.[30]

On some other manors rents were a more prominent source of income, but they were still less important than other kinds of

[28] PRO, Min. Accts., SC 6/1247/25, 26; 927/10. For the outlying properties attached to the manor, see Rees, *South Wales*, p. 143 note 2.

[29] See Holmes, *Estates*, pp. 103–4, 161.

[30] PRO, Min. Accts., SC 6/920/13; Holmes, *Estates*, p. 105.

manorial activity. At Llantrissent in 1307–8, about a quarter of the total was collected "de redditu liberorum, villanorum et Walensum," while the sale of grain and stock brought in a like amount, court profits and the sale of villein services somewhat smaller sums, and seigneurial dues and the sale of pasture the remainder. In 1308–9, however, total income rose sharply to almost £90, triple the amount for the preceding year, but it is not clear from the accounts which was more indicative of normal annual income. Rents remained stable, but all other sources rose noticeably, especially the sale of grain, which more than quadrupled its value as compared to the 1307–8 figure.[31] Three separate accounts for Troy manor, dating from 1292–93, 1307–8 and 1310–11, reveal a marked continuity in economic organization. In each instance, gross annual income was about £50, with rents accounting for just under 30 per cent of the total. The amounts realized from the sale of grain varied between 30 and 50 per cent of the whole, with the remainder deriving principally from pasture and related dues, and from the courts. The over-all characteristic of Troy manor, at least for the late thirteenth and early fourteenth centuries, is thus one of stability in rents and the continued importance of direct demesne exploitation as the major source of income.[32] Finally, on at least one manor, Liswerry, rents provided the dominant source of revenue in 1307–8, although this may have been due to a bad harvest that year which ruined the cereals, or to other factors not apparent from this isolated account. In any event, rents brought in 55 per cent of the total, while the sale of grain and livestock accounted for only about 10 per cent. Small sums were realized from the usual farms, court perquisites, seigneurial dues and fees, and the sale of villein works. No other accounts for Liswerry have survived, and there is no way of knowing whether the seeming reliance on rents in 1307–8 was exceptional; in any case, this manor is the only significant exception to the fact that in the lordships of Usk and Caerleon, as in the English bailiwicks, direct demesne enterprise, rather than rents, was the major feature of the economy.[33]

[31] PRO, SC 6/923/25, 1247/19. For the demesne cultivation on this manor between 1323 and 1326, see the table in Rees, *South Wales*, pp. 192–93.

[32] PRO, SC 6/926/11, 16, 17. After 1315 there was a noticeable tendency for rents to rise. Holmes *Estates*, pp. 105–6, 161.

[33] PRO, SC 6/923/10.

Few borough accounts have survived for this period, but it is clear that profits derived from the usual sources. The earliest account for Usk covers only the fifteen-week period from Michaelmas, 1293, to Hilary, 1294, and is of little use for comparative purposes. The first extant account covering a full year dates from Michaelmas, 1296, to Michaelmas, 1297. Most of the burgage rents were collected by the receiver and entered under Usk *ville*, but the bailiff accounted directly for £8 12s. Borough issues brought in about twice as much, the bulk of which derived from the prise of ale, with most of the remainder deriving from profits of courts. Other evidence, however, indicates that the 1296–97 figures are not representative of normal income. In 1308–9 rents came to £14 18s., a figure which remained fairly constant for the remainder of the fourteenth century. The income from dues and markets, and from courts, increased sharply to about triple their value in 1296–97, indicating a marked upturn in commercial activity. The net income from the borough as recorded in the receivers' accounts seems to have fluctuated sharply. In 1292–93 it produced £44 in clear profits, but in 1296–97 yielded only £24 12s. In 1302–3 and 1303–4, income was £64, with rents and dues providing almost half, and the farms of fisheries and prise of ale bringing in the rest. In 1304–5, however, net income was only £43, but in 1305–6 it rose to £79. The precise reasons for these fluctuations are hidden.[34]

Less information is available for the other boroughs. Gross income at Caerleon in 1310–11 was about £47, with about half coming from prise of ale, fisheries, and market tolls, 30 per cent from rents, and the rest from farms of mills and the courts. Trellech, on the other hand, was not well situated for trading purposes, and the bulk of the revenues derived from rents and judicial profits. The earliest account dates from 1289, when Earl Gilbert the Red recovered the borough after his mother's death. Rents provided about half the income, while the " exitus burgi," undifferentiated in the account but presumably including prise of ale, market tolls and other dues, brought in only about 15 per cent. An additional 25 per cent derived from court profits, including a fine of £6 13s. 4d. paid to the earl " de recognicione

[34] PRO, SC 6/926/31, 927/2, 3, 5, 6, 8, 14. For the period after 1315, see Holmes, *Estates*, pp. 107, 162.

burgensum . . . post mortem Matildae comitissae." In 1315–16, the percentages were about the same, except that there is no mention of a similar fine levied by the last Earl Gilbert's widow, and small sums were recorded for *cylch*, items usually accounted for by the officials of Trellech forest and bedelry.[35]

Extant information about the forests and bedelries is scant, but it is clear that both were valuable. The net receipts from the sale of wood and charcoal in Trellech forest were £22 in 1296–97, £51 10s. in 1308–9 and £41 in 1314–15, and by the late 1320's they had risen to nearly £200 per annum.[36] Smaller but still substantial amounts, averaging between £10 and £30, are also found regularly in the Usk receivers' accounts from the forests of Gwehelog, Pillgwenlly and Coedcwnwr. The sums, which were collected by the beadles, included perquisites of the forest courts and customary payments such as *cylch* in addition to profits derived from the sale of charcoal and wood. By the reign of Edward III charcoal-burning and iron-making developed into local industries of considerable importance in these areas and in Machen commote in Gwynllwg, but nothing can be said in detail about these developments before 1314.[37]

Finally, considerable sums were collected from the bedelries. The profits, which usually came through the courts, consisted of judicial fines and amercements, along with miscellaneous dues and tributary rents. These were sometimes supplemented by the sale of animals (presumably heriots or escheated chattels, which were then sold to other tribesmen), and more importantly, by the collection of rents from the holders of scattered customary tenements. Usk and Trellech bedelries were usually accounted for by a single beadle. In 1307–8, total income excluding arrears was £67 9s., of which 7s. came from the sale of animals and all the rest from perquisites of the local Welsh courts. There were ten court sessions in each bedelry that year. The profits of each session

[35] PRO, SC 6/920/18, 1247/21, 925/30.

[36] PRO, SC 6/927/2, 1247/29, 927/15; Holmes, *Estates*, p. 107 and note 6.

[37] For the entire question of the importance of forests in the marches, see Rees, *South Wales*, pp. 109–28. In 1292–93 Gwehelog forest brought in £22 6s. 8d. and Coedcwnwr £7 5s. In 1305–6, Gwehelog, Pillgwenlly, and Coedcwnwr yielded £14 13s., £4 4s., and £1 6s. respectively, and there was an additional £2 10s. from Adam ap Knayche (?), called " collector kylch de Weloc." PRO, SC 6/926/31, 927/9. In other years the sums were smaller. The original beadles' accounts for 1305–6 still survive (SC 6/922/26, 925/3).

averaged between £2 and £3, although in one instance an Usk court brought in £7 17s. and the Trellech court £6. Presumably the main business of the court was given over to hearing pleas between the customary tenants, but the large sums may represent the payment of *cylch* or some other tributary rent.[38] In the receivers' accounts, net income from these bedelries varied considerably. In 1305–6 they brought in £66 13s. 4d., but went as low as £20 in 1296–97 and as high as £89 in 1308–9. Otherwise they seem to have averaged between £40 and £50. Surviving original accounts for the 1320's indicate that gross income averaged about £70 to £80.[39] The surviving accounts for the small bedelry of Caerleon also indicate a great fluctuation in profitability, varying between £47 in 1292–93 and £12 in 1304–5. It would seem that the latter figure was more representative, for when the bedelry appears in the Usk receivers' accounts after 1314, it regularly yielded between £7 and £18 per annum. It is possible that the 1292–93 figure reflects an extraordinary fine imposed by Earl Gilbert the Red, but the reasons for any such action are not apparent. Income from the larger bedelry of Edelegan was also erratic. In 1284–85, Edelegan brought in £58, three-quarters of which came from court fines and the remainder from rents. In 1292–93, however, the court was worth only £10 16s., although rents remained fairly constant. After 1315, annual income averaged £25–£30, again indicating that the large court profits in 1284–85 were due mainly to a heavy but unexplained fine.[40] The only usable figures for Llefnydd date from 1307–8 and 1311–12, when it accounted jointly with Edelegan. It cannot be determined what proportion of the income derived solely from Llefnydd, but in each instance the courts provided the majority of the income, with rents contributing only a relatively small portion of the total.[41] These accounts reveal the financial profitability of the bedelries to the Clares, although there was little consistency in income. Even though the division between Welshry and Englishry was less important in the old Marshal lordships than in Glamorgan and Gwynllwg, the distinction nevertheless was there, and could be used to good financial advantage.

[38] PRO, SC 6/927/13.
[39] PRO, SC 6/927/2, 9; 1247/29; Holmes, *Estates*, p. 107 note 5.
[40] PRO, SC 6/920/14, 16; 927/17, 21, 24.
[41] PRO, SC 6/922/13, 28; 1247/18.

Reasonably reliable estimates can be made of the gross value of all the Clare lordships in Wales in the early fourteenth century. In Badlesmere's account for 1314–15, total income for the Glamorgan estates was about £1,140 and for Gwynllwg almost £350. In 1315–16, as far as can be made out, Glamorgan yielded about £1,000 and Gwynllwg £300. These figures cannot be used with complete confidence, since the tendency to deplete the supply of grain and stock brought abnormally high profits from these sources in 1314–15, a fact confirmed by the correspondingly lower sums in the keepers' accounts for the following year. On the other hand, there was a tendency to farm out mills, pasture, and even the entire manors of Radyr and Whitchurch in 1314–15, at figures presumably below their normal yield. Of greater importance, heavy losses were sustained " per guerram," especially during Llywelyn Bren's uprising of 1316. Unfortunately the surviving original estate accounts are too few in number to provide an adequate check against the amounts recorded in the keepers' accounts, but it seems safe to surmise that under normal conditions annual income from the lordships would amount to some £1,300–£1,500 with Glamorgan supplying about £1,000–£1,150 and Gwynllwg £300–£350. When the estates were partitioned in 1317, Glamorgan was officially valued at £1,275 and Gwynllwg at £460, but in view of the earlier figures, these valuations seem somewhat exaggerated.[42]

For the lordships of Usk and Caerleon, estimates can be made with more confidence. In 1317 these lordships were valued at some £750, and this figure seems to be accurate, at least more so than the figures for Glamorgan and Gwynllwg given above. Since Usk and Caerleon were in private hands from 1315, the royal commissioners charged with making the partition had in all likelihood more reliable data to work with, and to judge from the surviving receivers' accounts for the period 1315–20, their estimate seems substantially correct. In 1315–16 net income, excluding arrears, was £550, in 1316–17 £600, and in 1318–19 £540, and it is reasonable to suppose that before expenses and wages, gross income averaged about £700 to £750 in those years.[43] The entire

[42] PRO, Min. Accts., SC 6/1202/7–9; Chanc. Misc., C 47/9/23–24.
[43] PRO, Chanc. Misc., C 47/9/25; Min. Accts., SC 6/927/17, 21, 24.

Clare inheritance in South Wales, then, was in all likelihood worth at least £2,000 and possibly as much as £2,250 gross in the early years of the fourteenth century.

The Administration of the Lordships

For the purposes of administration, the Clare estates in the march were divided into two distinct units: the relatively small lordship of Usk, which had its own seneschal and receiver, and the great palatine county of Glamorgan, including the dependent lordships of Gwynllwg and (after 1269) Caerleon, in which the administrative organization was much more elaborate, with a sheriff, treasurer, chancellor, and coroner. Both lordships, however, shared that remarkable legal and constitutional independence of royal authority characteristic of all the marcher territories, which lasted, in greater or lesser degree, throughout the entire Middle Ages.

The lordship of Usk was administered in much the same way as a normal English bailiwick, although it applied marcher and Welsh law, not English common law, in its courts. The seneschal performed the usual functions associated with his counterpart in the bailiwick of Clare. He was the central officer in charge of judicial administration and was accountable for his actions not to the Glamorgan officials but directly to the earl and his household. He held the central court of the lordship at Usk and controlled the seal, and he was assisted by a staff of bailiffs for the manors and boroughs and beadles for the Welsh lands.[44] Unfortunately no court rolls have survived, and nothing can be said in any detail about the kinds of pleas heard in the courts. The seneschal presumably presided at the manorial courts at fixed times of the year and held most of the sessions of the commote and forest courts, but the reeve or beadle accounted for the profits to the receiver.[45] The seneschal also served as constable of Usk castle and with the estate bailiffs and the other constables had responsibility for the military organization of the lordship, although the duty of raising

[44] PRO, SC 6/927/17, mentions expenses incurred by the seneschal in holding the court. The seal of the lordship is mentioned in *Close Rolls 1264–68*, p. 264.
[45] Cf. the manorial accounts cited above, and for Usk bedelry PRO, SC 6/926/32.

foot soldiers levied by Edward I and Edward II for their campaigns in Wales and Scotland and on the Continent was undertaken by special commissioners appointed by the king.[46] Under the Clares, the seneschal was the highest paid officer in the lordship, receiving a yearly wage of 20 marks and an additional 10 marks " de dono comitis," which probably represents his fee as constable. Of the lesser officials, the constable of Tregrug received 8 marks in 1314, while the beadle of Usk was paid 5 marks and the estate bailiffs between 5 and 10 marks.[47]

More information is available about the financial organization. Nothing is known about the period of Earl Richard's control, but under his widow, who held the bulk of the lordship in dower for over a quarter of a century from 1263 to 1289, some evidence on this point has survived. It is clear that the receivership centered not at Usk, probably because after 1266 the castle was in the hands of the countess' son, but at Trellech. An account for Trellech manor in 1285 reveals that the bulk of the net profit was released to a Henry Gretton or Gretham, " receptor de Trillech." [48] When the entire lordship reverted to Earl Gilbert the Red after Maud's death, a local receivership at Trellech remained, although the central office was henceforth located at Usk, where it presumably had been under Earl Richard before 1262. In 1289 the officials of the manors of Trellech, Troy, and Cwmcarvan accounted to the local receiver at Trellech. The total receipt was £59, of which £50 was then released to the receiver at Cardiff and only £6 to the receiver at Usk, indicating that Earl Gilbert had not yet fully established an organized central receivership for his newly acquired lordship.[49] The local receipt still existed as late as 1292–93, but it was confined to the issues from Trellech manor, borough, and forest. Of a total receipt of £145, £32 went to Cardiff and £106 to Usk.[50] By 1296–97, the office at Trellech had disappeared, and in the surviving fourteenth century accounts all revenues were delivered to Usk and the receiver collected directly from the bailiffs and beadles themselves.

[46] E.g., *Parl. Writs*, I, 295–96 (1297).
[47] PRO, Min. Accts., SC 6/926/32, 927/2, 5, 8, 9; *Cal. Close Rolls 1313–18*, p. 408.
[48] PRO, SC 6/923/20.
[49] PRO, SC 6/925/21, and cf. the Usk account, SC 6/926/30. The bailiff of Trellech borough in 1289 delivered his entire net profit to Cardiff. SC 6/1247/21.
[50] PRO, SC 6/925/22, 926/31.

The duties of the receiver of Usk closely corresponded to those noted for Robert de Abethrop, receiver of Clare bailiwick from 1307 to 1312, except that the Usk receiver collected the bulk of the money rents from the manor and borough in place of the reeve and bailiff. The lack of a fully organized receivership before 1294, already noticed in the survival of a similar office at Trellech, is also apparent from the extant accounts. In 1289 only a few properties accounted to Usk, and income amounted to only £49, of which £40 was released to Cardiff.[51] The first full account dates from 1292–93, when only Tregrug, still held by Bogo de Clare, is missing from the roll. Receipts totaled £355, including arrears, but the bulk of the cash, £275, was released to the receiver of Cardiff, and not directly to the wardrobe as was common thereafter. The other *liberationes* included £10 10s. to two prominent household officials, Henry de Llancarfan, who later was treasurer of Cardiff, and Robert de St. Fagans, later the wardrober, for the arrears of previous receivers; and £10 allocated to the bailiff of Usk manor for repairs at New Grange. The remainder of the cash was expended on salaries and various incidental allowances, including £10 for the expenses of the *familia* of the Red Earl's young son, making a "short visit" at Usk castle.[52] In the later accounts, most of the cash was allocated to the central wardrobe, with smaller amounts going to the dependent wardrobers of Joan of Acre's children and the remainder for wages, repairs, purchases of supplies, and other incidental expenses. Only one account survives for the period of the last Earl Gilbert. In 1308–9, total income was £572, including almost £125 in arrears. Of this sum, £420 was delivered to Richard de Estdene, the earl's wardrober, in four installments. Most of the remainder was used to pay the wages of the seneschal, the receiver himself, the constables of some of the castles, and a few lesser officials such as the foresters. Over £40 was also expended on upkeep and repairs at the castle and on purchases of food and supplies. The money still unaccounted for, about £9 11s., was undoubtedly carried over and entered as arrears on the account for 1309–10, which has not survived. The accounts were audited by the clerks of the central

[51] PRO, SC 6/926/30.
[52] PRO, SC 6/926/31. Llancarfan and St. Fagans may have been serving as auditors at this time.

household, but again, nothing is known of the procedure involved. The receivership was held by a number of men two or three times, but not in successive years, and the receivers do not seem to have been prominent in other administrative positions. The office itself was a serjeanty. Both it and some small tenements were held in return for an annual rent of £5 4s., but the sum was regularly respited by the Clares. Otherwise the receiver was paid 13s. 4d. per annum and had a robe of equal value.[53]

The administrative organization of the lordship of Usk closely parallels the system found in most of the other marcher lordships. In Glamorgan, however, as in the other great lordships of southern Wales such as Pembroke and Brecknock, a much more complex system was developed. But this structure only slowly evolved over the course of the thirteenth century. The Clares had subjected Glamorgan to a process of territorial and political integration no less important or remarkable in its way than the original penetration into southern Wales by the first generation of Norman adventurers in the late eleventh and early twelfth centuries. In the wake of this consolidation, there was an increased efficiency and centralization of the administrative organization designed to supplement or in some instances to replace the loosely knit structure which had obtained under fitz Hamon and his twelfth century successors. The main components of this system resemble the pattern found in the English palatinates and the great Anglo–Irish franchises, and even to some degree the royal government itself.[54]

The lordship of Glamorgan seems to have been organized as a shire from the very moment of the Norman conquest in the late eleventh and early twelfth centuries. A certain William, " vicecomes de Kard(iff)," [55] witnessed a charter dated *ca.* 1102, although the first mention of a *comitatus* of Glamorgan only

---

[53] PRO, SC 6/1247/21, and for the surviving accounts from 1296–97 to 1306, SC 6/927/2, 5, 6, 8, 9. Holmes, *Estates*, p. 162, dates SC 6/927/9 to 1309–10 (i. e., 3–4 Edward II), but the document itself is dated 33–34 Edward [I], and the names of the receivers given in the manorial accounts for 1305–6 and 1309–10 confirm this date.

[54] Cf. Smith, " The Lordship of Glamorgan," pp. 10, 16–17, 30–31, 37, and Otway-Ruthven, " The Great Lordships of South Wales," *passim.*

[55] " Cardiff " is often found in the documents as synonymous with Glamorgan, and the two terms were used interchangeably throughout the Middle Ages, both by the Crown and by the lords themselves.

dates from the end of the first quarter of the century.[56] The sheriff was from the beginning the head of the central administration, assuming the functions normally associated with the seneschal or *dapifer*, who never appears as a separate officer in the lordship.[57] Under the Clares, the sheriff, who was paid 100 marks a year,[58] had a wide range of duties and responsibilities. His best-known function was to preside at the monthly meetings of the *curia comitatus*, sometimes called a *parliamentum*,[59] to hear pleas involving the tenants of the lordship and to conduct other business within the cognizance of the court, such as the enrolling of private charters and deeds. He regularly acted in conjunction with a body of suitors drawn from the tenants in chief of the lordship, although on at least one occasion in 1299 he sat with the central council of Joan of Acre and Ralph de Monthermer.[60] The sheriff also held the fixed sessions of the courts at Newport and Caerleon, the *capita* of the dependent lordships of Gwynllwg and Caerleon. In 1313 the last Earl Gilbert addressed a writ to Robert de Grendon, sheriff of Glamorgan, ordering him to conduct an inquiry with the aid of jurors from his bailiwick (*baillie*) of Newport and Caerleon. This document affords ample evidence that although Gwynllwg and Caerleon were technically independent lordships, administrative and judicial matters came under the authority of the sheriff of Glamorgan.[61] The same document, along with some other evidence, shows that the sheriff also made a regular tourn of the local manorial and possibly the commotal courts as well, both in Glamorgan and in the other lordships. His assistants, the local bailiffs and beadles, who were responsible for executing the writs and collecting fees and fines, accounted for the revenues directly

---

[56] *Cartae de Glamorgan*, I, 38, 57; *Hist. et Cart. Mon. Gloucestriae*, I, 347.

[57] In one or two twelfth century charters, the term *senescallus* or *dapifer* seems to have been used as an equivalent for *vicecomes* (*Cartae de Glamorgan*, I, 75, 117), but in other instances these designations clearly refer to the seneschal of the honor of Gloucester (e. g., *ibid.*, 106, 108, 116).

[58] *Cal. Close Rolls 1313–18*, p. 407.

[59] The term is found in documents dating from *ca.* 1218 and 1247. *Cartae de Glamorgan*, II, 360, 547.

[60] *Ibid.*, II, 543, 565, III, 911, 1017–19.

[61] *Hist. et Cart. Mon. Glouc.*, III, 275. Earl Humphrey de Bohun's account for 1262–63 mentions under Newport expenses of the sheriff " in holding the county court " (PRO, Min. Accts., SC 6/1202/1 m. 2), but there is no evidence to indicate that this refers to a separate sheriff of Gwynllwg. When the lordships escheated to the Crown in 1314, Edward II continued to use a single sheriff for both. Cf. *Cal. Pat. Rolls 1313–17*, p. 540.

to the central financial officers at Cardiff. There is no evidence that the sheriff himself performed this latter function, unlike his counterpart in the English shires.[62] The sheriff also figured more generally in the over-all administration. He regularly witnessed the charters and deeds both of the earls and of their tenants, occasionally acting as surety to fulfill the terms of the transactions.[63] He often served as his lord's representative in other matters. William de St. Elena was a seneschal of the honor of Gloucester under Earl Richard before 1250, and served as sheriff of Glamorgan in the following decade. Geoffrey de Fanencourt, sheriff in 1249, was also Earl Richard's attorney in all pleas concerning the partition of the Marshal inheritance, and in 1262 he was one of the earl's executors.[64] Robert le Veel, who was sheriff on at least two separate occasions under Earl Gilbert the Red, and John de Crepping, who held the office in 1289, 1292, and 1293, also acted as attorneys.[65] Most of the known sheriffs seem, like Robert de Grendon, to have been knights in the earls' *comitiva*, and many came from long-standing Glamorgan families. Bartholomew de la More, sheriff in 1266, was one of the Red Earl's *familiares* pardoned by Henry III following the settlement of the Disinherited crisis in 1267. In 1262 the sheriff was Walter de Sully, presumably appointed by Richard de Clare shortly before his death. Walter, who held two fees in Sully and two fees in Wenvoe in the southwestern part of the lordship, may have been descended from one of Robert fitz Hamon's original companions. Other men who held the office in the early fourteenth century, such as Henry de Penbridge and Simon de Raleye, similarly came from established and prominent local families.[66] Finally, a number of sheriffs also entered the

---

[62] *Hist. et Cart. Mon. Glouc.*, III, 275; *Cartae de Glamorgan*, III, 839 (Neath manor and possibly *patria*, 1316), 847 (Uwch– and Is–Caiach, Senghenydd).

[63] *Cat. Ancient Deeds*, III, 433; *Cartae de Glamorgan*, II, 535; III, 917, 977, 978

[64] *Cartae de Glamorgan*, II, 273–75, 565; *Cartulary of St. Mark's Hospital, Bristol*, ed. C. D. Ross (Bristol Record Society Publications, vol. XXI, 1959), p. 200; *Close Rolls 1247–51*, p. 114; PRO, Fine Roll 46 Henry III, C 60/59 m. 7.

[65] *Cartae de Glamorgan*, III, 714, 895–96, IV, 1205; "Chronicle of the Thirteenth Century," p. 282; *Littere Wallie*, p. 181; *The Welsh Assize Roll*, pp. 276, 277, 283; *Cal. Pat. Rolls 1281–92*, pp. 262, 290; *ibid. 1292–1301*, p. 19. Crepping, who was tried and imprisoned with Earl Gilbert the Red in 1291–92, was the earl's attorney in Ireland in 1287–88.

[66] *Cartae de Glamorgan*, II, 650, 685, III, 911, 965, 976–78, 979; *Royal Letters*, II, 218; *Cat. Ancient Deeds*, III, 433.

service of the Crown, although this phenomenon seems to have been more common among the seneschals of the family honors in England. John de Crepping was a commissioner of array in York at the end of the thirteenth century. Robert de Grendon was sheriff of Shropshire and Staffordshire and constable of Shrewsbury in 1318, and later appears as one of Edward II's household knights in the Scottish campaign of 1322. Little can be said about the other Glamorgan sheriffs in this regard, and most of them presumably spent their entire careers in association with the Clares.[67]

The lordship also had its own coroner, who held both the major and minor Crown pleas in the name of the earl and made presentments and indictments before the sheriff at the central courts and in eyre. The earliest direct reference to a coroner, however, dates from 1299, and it is possible that the office was a relatively late development. In a case heard at Cardiff in that year before the sheriff and the central council of Countess Joan and Ralph de Monthermer, the beadle of Tiriarll was convicted of usurping the office of coroner, properly held by the *famulus comitatus*, and was imprisoned.[68] The meaning of the term *famulus* in this connection is uncertain, but it was probably used as an equivalent for the *ballivus comitatus*, a term found elsewhere to denote the sheriff's deputy at the Cardiff sessions. The only other mention of a *famulus*, a word otherwise applied elsewhere to permanent demesne laborers, dates from the early or mid-thirteenth century, when a certain Thomas Baudewine witnessed a charter by that title.[69] It seems likely that the formal office of coroner was only established in the later thirteenth century, as part of the administrative reorganization attendant upon the political consolidation of the lordship effected by Earl Richard and Earl Gilbert the Red. At any rate, the coroner was a relatively minor functionary under the Clares, but under Richard Nevill, earl of Warwick and lord of Glamorgan in the mid-fifteenth century, he seems to have assumed most of the sheriff's duties,[70] and under Jasper Tudor,

---

[67] *Cal. Pat. Rolls 1292–1301*, pp. 438, 512; *Cal. Fine Rolls 1307–19*, p. 381; Brit. Mus., Stowe MS 553, fols. 60, 65.

[68] *Cartae de Glamorgan*, III, 911.

[69] *Ibid.*, II, 275, and for the term *ballivus comitatus, ibid.*, III, 823, 912.

[70] E.g. *ibid.*, IV, 1618, a writ from the earl, dated March 24, 1450, was addressed to the sheriff, but in October, 1452 (*ibid.*, p. 1631) another writ was addressed

earl of Pembroke, to whom Henry VII granted the lordship, the coroner accounted to the exchequer at Cardiff for the court revenues in much the same fashion as the sheriff of a normal English shire accounted to the royal exchequer.[71]

For the purposes of financial administration, Glamorgan, Gwynllwg, and Caerleon were organized as a single receivership centered at Cardiff until the death of Earl Gilbert the Red. No original accounts of the receivers have survived, but it can safely be assumed that the nature of their duties was no different from that of their counterparts for Usk or the English bailiwicks. In the extant accounts for the Caerleon estates prior to 1295, the local officials of the manors, boroughs and bedelries accounted directly to the receiver, and undoubtedly he handled the cash from the Glamorgan and Gwynllwg properties as well.[72] Moreover, after Earl Gilbert recovered Usk lordship in 1289, the Cardiff receiver seems to have assumed partial responsibility for its finances, at least until 1293. In the Usk receiver's account for 1289, income was recorded only from Usk bedelry, Coedcwnwr forest, and the local receipt at Trellech, which comprised Trellech, Troy, and Cwmcarvan manors. It is known that the bailiff of Trellech borough accounted directly to Cardiff, and presumably the other estate and forest officials in the lordship did the same. Moreover, the Usk receiver delivered the bulk of his cash receipts to Cardiff, and it is possible that his account was viewed by the Cardiff receiver before a final audit by the clerks of the central wardrobe.[73] In 1292–93 the Usk estates accounted directly to the receiver of that lordship, but he still delivered the revenues to Cardiff, and some of the local officials, including the Usk beadle, also delivered small sums to Cardiff themselves.[74] No Usk re-

---

to the coroner, and no mention of a sheriff was made. Cf. also Otway-Ruthven, " Great Lordships of South Wales," p. 6.

[71] PRO, Duchy of Lancaster, Min. Accts., DL 29/665/10334 m. 1. After the complete separation of Glamorgan and Gwynllwg in the fourteenth century, the latter lordship had its own sheriff and coroner. *The Marcher Lordships of South Wales 1415–1536: Select Documents*, ed. T. B. Pugh (Board of Celtic Studies, History and Law Series, no. XX, Cardiff, 1963), pp. 211–14.

[72] E.g. PRO, Min. Accts., SC 6/922/13 (Edelegan bedelry, 1284–85); 920/14 (Caerleon bedelry, 1292–93); 920/13 (Caerleon manor, 1292–93).

[73] PRO, SC 6/926/30, 1247/21.

[74] The receiver's account is in PRO, SC 6/926/31. The beadle of Usk released £10 to the Usk receiver and £10 to the Cardiff receiver (SC 6/926/32), and the " local receiver " at Trellech released £106 to Usk and £32 to Cardiff (SC 6/925/22).

ceiver's account survives for 1293–94 or for 1294–95, but an incomplete roll for Usk manor, borough, and bedelry dated Michaelmas, 1294–Hilary, 1295, contains no reference to the Cardiff receiver. All *liberationes* went directly to Usk, and it is probable that the two receiverships were independent by this time.[75]

By the end of the thirteenth century, the Cardiff receivership was replaced by an exchequer under the control of a treasurer, indicating an improvement in the machinery of financial administration, probably inspired by the methods introduced by the Crown into the principality of Wales. There is no evidence of a treasurer under Earl Gilbert the Red, and it seems likely that the office was established by Countess Joan after his death, perhaps when she married Monthermer. Although the first mention of an exchequer dates only from 1318,[76] the earliest indication of the change is contained in the Usk receiver's account for 1296–97, which records a payment to a certain Roger de Walcote, "thesaurarius de Kaerdif." [77] In the surviving Ministers' Accounts for the early fourteenth century, the estate officials in Glamorgan, Gwynllwg, and Caerleon accounted directly to the treasurer, and no mention is made of a receiver.[78] In 1303–4 Caerleon manor served as a local office of receipt for the revenues of the manors, boroughs and bedelries in that lordship, but there is no other mention of this arrangement in the period.[79] The treasurer assumed all the functions of a receiver but presumably kept a more elaborate series of rolls to record financial transactions. No documents have survived, however, and nothing can be said about the detailed organization of the exchequer. Little is known of most of the men who served as treasurers, but Master Henry de Llancarfan, who held office in the first decade of the fourteenth century, was an important household official and a member of the council in 1299, and after the death of Countess Joan was appointed both chancellor and " receiver " (treasurer?) of the lordship by Edward I. Llancarfan

[75] PRO, SC 6/927/1.
[76] *Cat. Ancient Deeds*, III, 116.
[77] PRO, Min. Accts., SC 6/927/2.
[78] E.g., PRO, SC 6/1202/5 (Neath borough, 1311–12); 925/5 (Rhymny manor, 1300–1301); 1202/4 (Dowlais manor, 1307–8); 920/16 (Caerleon bedelry, 1304–5); 922/18 (Llefnydd bedelry, 1307–8); 920/18 (Caerleon borough, 1309–10); 922/14 (Edelegan bedelry, 1312–13).
[79] PRO, SC 6/1247/17.

came from a family long prominent in the affairs of the bishopric of Llandaff, and in Pope Nicholas' taxation of 1291, he was stated to hold a small prebend in the see, worth 5s. 10d. per annum.[80] Little can be said about the chancery. The term is not found as such in any of the extant sources, and the only evidence for its existence comes from a few widely scattered and unsatisfactory references to a chancellor. In 1247 a certain Master Robert de Evreux (*de Ebrioic'*) witnessed one of Earl Richard's charters as *cancellarius*, but nothing further is known of him.[81] In 1307 Edward I appointed Master Henry de Llancarfan chancellor of Glamorgan, and in 1313 Master Richard de Clare obtained a papal dispensation to acquire two benefices at the request of the last Earl Gilbert, "whose chancellor he is." [82] The other great lordships of the southern march, Pembroke, Brecknock, and Gower, also had chanceries, about which something is known, and presumably the Glamorgan chancery was organized along the same lines.[83] The chancellor kept the seal of the county, issuing writs in the lord's name respecting pleas heard in the *curia comitatus*. Evidence for this point is afforded by an order issued by Edward I when he seized the lordship following the imprisonment of Earl Gilbert the Red in 1292. The king appointed Roger de Burghull, sheriff of Hereford, as keeper, with the provision that " all those of the said lands who ought to plead there by writ come to the (royal) chancery and obtain writs on their actions, and plead them before the said Roger in like manner as they formerly did before the bailiffs (i. e., the sheriff and his subordinates) of the earl." [84] The chancellor seems also to have assumed the functions of a controller, keeping duplicate rolls of the charters and other business enacted in the courts. The sheriff kept rolls of the pleas and

---

[80] PRO, SC 6/920/16, 922/28, 1247/17; *Cal. Fine Rolls 1272–1307*, p. 556; *Cartae de Glamorgan*, III, 911, 952. The history of the Llancarfan family is discussed in *Episcopal Acts relating to Welsh Dioceses 1066–1272*, ed. J. Conway Davies (Historical Society of the Church in Wales, nos. I, III, 1946–48), Introduction, II, 506–37.

[81] *Cart. Priory St. Gregory, Canterbury*, p. 61. The editor styles him Master Robert " of York " in the index.

[82] *Cal. Fine Rolls 1272–1307*, p. 556; *Cal. Papal Letters*, II, 113.

[83] See Otway-Ruthven, " Great Lordships of South Wales," pp. 7–8. The chancery of the Bohun lordship of Brecknock is mentioned in 1256. *Cal. Anc. Corr., Wales*, p. 211.

[84] *Cal. Pat. Rolls 1281–92*, pp. 477–78. This order similarly applied to the lordship of Brecknock.

property transactions in the course of his judicial activities, and duplicate rolls were probably deposited in chancery.[85] The archives, which were located at Cardiff castle, have not survived, being destroyed in the Despenser war in Glamorgan in 1321. Only after 1327, when Glamorgan and Gwynllwg were permanently separated, does the chancery come into clearer focus, and by this time a distinct chancery for Gwynllwg was also instituted. The Cardiff chancery is first mentioned by name in 1329, when the then lord of Glamorgan, William la Zouche, second husband of the last Earl Gilbert's eldest sister, Eleanor Despenser, issued a charter to Margam Abbey using the seal " de cancellaria nostra de Kaerdif." After Zouche's death the lordship reverted to Hugh Despenser's heirs, and they regularly used the chancery seal on charters and writs.[86] On at least one occasion the chancellor doubled as treasurer under the Despensers,[87] and it is possible that Henry de Llancarfan also held both offices simultaneously under the Clares, although he is merely styled treasurer in the documents. In 1313 at least, however, the two offices were distinct, for the document in which Master Richard de Clare is styled chancellor is dated May 28, when William de Everton was treasurer.[88]

The Law of the March

As lords of Glamorgan, the Clares enjoyed an almost complete independence of the Crown in the normal exercise of administration and justice. Neither the king's writ nor the king's law ran in the march, and only by virtue of his position as feudal overlord and under exceptional circumstances did the king assert or establish the right to intervene in the internal affairs of the lordship. Enough evidence remains to indicate both the nature and scope of

[85] For the term " controller," see *Cal. Close Rolls 1313–18*, p. 407, and cf. Rees, *South Wales*, pp. 87 note 3, 89. For the sheriff's rolls " des pledz et de porchaz," see *Hist. et Cart. Mon. Glouc.*, III, 275.

[86] For Zouche, see *Cartae de Glamorgan*, III, 1158, and for the Despensers, *ibid.*, IV, 1217, 1224, 1244, 1261, 1266, 1298, 1411. The Gwynllwg chancery at Newport under Hugh D'Audley's heirs, the Staffords, dukes of Buckingham, is mentioned in *Marcher Lordships 1415–1536: Select Documents*, p. 214.

[87] *Cartae de Glamorgan*, IV, 1266: one of the witnesses to a Despenser charter *ca.* 1345 was " domino Johanne de Coventre tunc thesaurario et cancellario. . . ."

[88] *Cal. Papal Letters*, II, 113; *Cartae de Glamorgan*, III, 1017–19.

marcher jurisdiction and the limitations imposed by the Crown, notably under Edward I.

In their central courts at Cardiff, Newport and Caerleon, the Clares conducted most of the business which in England was normally reserved to the royal courts. They held both the major and minor Crown pleas, and entertained pleas commenced under writs, but these writs were issued in their own name and applied to their own system of marcher law. The earliest known instance in which the Clares adopted the possessory assizes developed by Henry II dates from the beginning of the second quarter of the thirteenth century, when John Norreis brought suit in the Cardiff county court for the recovery of land in Bonvileston under a writ issued by the first Earl Gilbert.[89] Explicit references to cases begun under writ later in the century are rare. A plea of land heard at Cardiff in 1247 between Margam Abbey and Lleision ap Morgan, lord of Afan, was held under an assize of *novel disseisin* issued by Earl Richard. In 1290 Earl Gilbert the Red, involved in a dispute with the prior of Goldclive over the advowsonary rights to Undy church, impleaded the prior in his court at Caerleon on a writ of *quare impedit*.[90] In addition to hearing pleas by writ, the courts served as courts of record, at which charters and deeds were enrolled and final concords recorded, and there is evidence that in at least some instances fines were drawn up in triplicate, with the third copy probably deposited in the chancery in much the same manner as that of the royal government.[91] The courts also handled more routine matters, such as proofs of age (in conjunction with the bishops of Llandaff) and titles to franchises. The local manorial and commote courts presumably dealt with petty actions involving freehold and customary tenants, both English and Welsh, but no records have survived.[92]

Separate courts for Englishry and Welshry existed not only in the lands controlled directly by the family, but in some of the larger mesne fiefs as well. John Giffard's account for 1315–16

---

[89] *Cartae de Glamorgan*, II, 427–28.

[90] *Ibid.*, II, 543; PRO, Coram Rege Roll Trinity 18 Edward I, KB 27/124 m. 33d. For *quare impedit*, see Pollock and Maitland, *History of English Law*, II, 139.

[91] *Cartae de Glamorgan*, II, 565, records a fine in 1249 between the sons of Morgan ap Cadwallon, then lords of Glynrhondda, and Margam Abbey, with the endorsement " comes habet tertiam partem istius cyrographi."

[92] *Ibid.*, II, 432–33; III, 1017–19; VI, 2328–29.

mentions revenues of courts " Anglicanorum et Wallensium de Laniltwyt (Llantwit) et Ruthyn." There was a Welsh " hundred " court at Margam in the late twelfth century, and by the mid-fourteenth century, and probably much earlier, there was a *curia anglicana* in the Turberville lordship of Coety and presumably a Welsh court for the dependent *patria* of Glyn Ogwr.[93] Little can be said about the application of Welsh law in these commotal areas, but a number of knights' fees were held according to native rules of tenure and descent. The fees were partible among all heirs and descended in both the male and female lines, and in most cases, the Clares could claim only a limited number of the normal feudal aids and incidents. Those chieftains still holding commotes at the time of Earl Richard's death in 1262 held " per Walescarium et non (faciunt) aliquid servicium nisi heriettum videlicet equum et arma cum moriantur." In the inquisitions *post mortem* of 1295 and 1314, certain Welsh tenants were stated to hold fees which were only liable to a relief of 50s. per fee, and the Clares had no right of wardship or marriage of the heirs.[94]

Of wider significance, the Clares consistently maintained their claim to full cognizance of all civil and criminal jurisdiction, without interference from the Crown. Under Henry III they upheld this position successfully, as the appeal *coram rege* by Richard Siward in 1247, already discussed, indicates.[95] Earl Gilbert the Red made similar claims under Edward I, but he was only partially successful; Edward did not hesitate to impose his own authority if he had the opportunity. The Statute of Westminster I, issued in 1275, laid down the principle that appeals could be made to the royal courts even by those tenants whose lands were in areas " where the king's writ does not run." [96] In general, the marchers seem to have accepted this principle, although vigorously insisting on the prior right to try cases in their own courts, and claiming, in the event of a dispute between two marcher lords themselves, the right of a *dies marchie*.[97] In cases involving his

[93] *Ibid.*, I, 122, III, 831, IV, 1301, VI, 2277.
[94] *Ibid.*, II, 651, VI, 2310–11; *Cal. Inq. Post Mortem*, III, no. 371 (p. 247), V, no. 538 (p. 337). See also Rees, *South Wales*, pp. 145–47.
[95] PRO, Curia Regis Roll 31–42 Henry III, KB 26/159 mm. 2, 10–11; above, pp. 70–73.
[96] Stat. Westm. I, c. 17, in *Statutes of the Realm*, I, 31.
[97] Cf. above, Chapter IV, note 102.

own tenants, Earl Gilbert's claims were generally accepted. In 1278, the king established a commission to try all pleas in Wales and the marches " according to the laws and customs of those parts," and juries were assembled from the Crown lands and the marcher lordships (except Glamorgan and Brecknock) to give evidence in all disputes.[98] Pleas were heard under this commission until 1284, and Earl Gilbert was party to a number of cases. Richard de St. Brigida brought suit against him for burgage tenements in Caerleon. Gilbert claimed the prior cognizance of his court, arguing that he ought not to answer before the justices " unless his court had failed in right to anyone complaining there." Despite the plaintiff's objection that he did not hold of the earl in chief, Gilbert's claim was allowed.[99] Similarly, William Corbet, lord of St. Nicholas in Glamorgan, sued the earl for the wardship and marriage of Adam de Somery, claiming Adam as his own tenant. The justices allowed Gilbert's claim for his own court, but with the provision that Corbet could appeal if " full and speedy justice " were not done.[100]

Of greater importance were Earl Gilbert's attempts to maintain this position in cases involving other great tenants-in-chief of the Crown. As early as 1281, at the very time Edward I was subjecting the English franchises to the rigors of the *quo warranto* campaign, he came into conflict with the king on this score. Gilbert was summoned *coram rege* to answer William de Braose, lord of Gower, on a plea of assault allegedly committed by Robert le Veel, the earl's bailiff (sheriff), while William was traveling along a " royal highway " near Newport on his way to Gower.[101] The mention of the " royal highway " and the later circumstances of the action suggest that Edward was deliberately contriving a test case; in any event, the case foreshadows later and more spectacular conflicts between the earl and the king. Gilbert claimed the regality (*regale*) of his lordship, arguing that he ought not to plead *coram rege* unless Braose could show default of justice in the earl's own court. When Braose pointed out that he held

[98] *Cal. Welsh Rolls*, p. 163.
[99] *The Welsh Assize Roll*, p. 292.
[100] *Ibid.*, pp. 283, 304.
[101] PRO, Coram Rege Roll Mich. 9–10 Edward I, KB 27/64 m. 35, printed in *Cartae de Glamorgan*, III, 810–11. Cf. the commentary of Sayles, *Select Cases*, I, Introduction, pp. lvii–lviii.

Gower in chief of the Crown, not of the earl, and that the trespass had been committed in contempt of the king, Edward's council dismissed the claim. Gilbert then replied that he did not have to answer the plea until the accusation against his bailiff, the principal defendant, had first been proved in his own court (*quousque principale in curia ista convincatur*). He also argued more generally that he held his marcher lordships *per conquestum*, not by delegated right, and hence need not reply without the deliberation of his peers, those magnates who held similar liberties in the march. The case unfortunately ends at this point, and although it was still pending in later terms, with the king himself a party to William de Braose's writ, it was never formally resolved at law.[102] Gilbert may have been forced to pay part or all of the damages claimed by Braose, but there is no evidence on any of the subsequent Coram Rege rolls that Veel was tried for trespass, and the loss of the Cardiff court records makes it impossible to determine if indeed he was ever tried at all.[103]

Despite its inconclusive nature, the case involving Earl Gilbert and William de Braose is significant in marking the beginning of the conflict between the king and the lord of Glamorgan over the nature and scope of marcher jurisdiction and autonomy. When Earl Humphrey de Bohun, lord of Brecknock, brought suit in the *curia regis* for the alleged raids into his dominions in 1290, Earl Gilbert pleaded forcefully but unsuccessfully for the prior right to hold a *dies marchie* to settle the matter.[104] On the other hand, a less spectacular but similar case involving the Red Earl and Roger Bigod, earl of Norfolk and lord of Striguil, seems to have been settled by marcher custom at this very time. In 1290, Roger complained to the king that Gilbert's men had entered his lordship " vi et armis," carrying chattels off to Caerleon. He further charged that the lord of Glamorgan illegally withdrew suit owed by certain tenants in Usk and Trellech to the central court of his lordship at Striguil (Chepstow). In May, 1292, however, Roger

---

[102] PRO, Coram Rege Roll Hilary 10 Edward I, KB 27/65 mm. 15, 17; Trinity 10 Edward I, KB 27/67 m. 1d. No further mention of the suit is found on subsequent rolls.

[103] In 1281 Braose claimed £500 damages, and in 1290 Gilbert was said to owe him 200 marks. PRO, Exchequer of Pleas, Plea Roll 19 Edward I, E 13/17 m. 47.

[104] PRO, Coram Rege Roll Easter 19 Edward I, KB 27/127 m. 26d., partially printed above, Chapter IV, note 102.

withdrew his plea, and King Edward accepted the statement of both parties that the disputes " amicabiliter sunt sedati," probably by private agreement but possibly at a full *dies marchie.* There can be little doubt that Roger withdrew the suit when he saw the fate that had befallen Gilbert and Humphrey in the meantime; but it is also noteworthy that Edward, having just established the efficacy of the Crown in matters of this sort, was content to allow the case to be settled outside the sphere of royal jurisdiction.[105]

In another highly important respect, however, Edward I definitely limited Earl Gilbert's independent position. The issue involved the earl's claims to custody of the temporalities of the bishopric of Llandaff within the lordship, along with the collation of prebends and dignities, *sede vacante.* Such powers were reserved to the Crown in all the other bishoprics of England, Wales, and Ireland,[106] but they were seemingly enjoyed by the lords of Glamorgan over Llandaff from the early twelfth century. These privileges were first questioned during a vacancy in 1240, when Henry III summoned Gilbert Marshal, *custos* of Glamorgan during Richard de Clare's minority, to show by what right he claimed the temporalities.[107] Henry later took the custody of the temporalities and the right of presentation to vacant prebends into his own hands. Even after Earl Richard attained his majority in 1243, the king overrode his attempt to present his own nominee as archdeacon, ordering the earl to appear *coram rege* to defend his claims.[108] The king did not press this point further, however, and although Bishop William de Burgh stated in 1250 that he held

---

[105] The initial plaint is in PRO, Coram Rege Roll Easter 18 Edward I, KB 27/123 m. 1, and full details of the raids, committed in January, 1290, are contained in PRO, KB 27/125 m. 6 (Mich. 18–19 Edward I). Edward's acceptance of the withdrawal of the suit, dated May 6, 1292, is in PRO, Coram Rege Roll Easter 20 Edward I, KB 27/131 m. 22. On May 7, Gilbert recovered the lordship of Glamorgan.

[106] Margaret Howell, *Regalian Right in Medieval England* (London, 1962).

[107] See Otway-Ruthven, " Great Lordships of South Wales," pp. 17–18. The case is in PRO, Curia Regis Roll Mich. 25 Henry III, KB 26/121 m. 17d. Cf. above, p. 68.

[108] Tewkesbury, p. 131; PRO, Curia Regis Roll Hilary 28 Henry III, KB 26/131 m. 3d. He also ordered the other marchers who claimed the temporalities of the see within their lordships to appear before him. PRO, KB 26/131 m. 16. For Henry's control of the vacant see in the early 1240's, cf. *Cal. Pat. Rolls 1281–92,* p. 393.

directly of the Crown and not of any marcher lords, the Clares and
their neighbors seem to have had full possession of the temporalities during the vacancies of 1256 and 1266.[109]

Under Edward I, the power of the lords of Glamorgan over the
bishopric of Llandaff was broken. After the death of Bishop
William de Braose in 1287, the king ordered the temporalities
seized in his own name. The escheator attempted to execute the
king's writ in the march, but found Roger Bigod, lord of Striguil,
Humphrey de Bohun, lord of Brecknock, William de Braose, lord
of Gower and the bishop's uncle, and Edmund of Lancaster, lord
of Monmouth, already in possession of the properties of the see
within their lordships, and Earl Gilbert the Red in possession of
the Glamorgan estates along with the archdeaconry and other
vacant prebends. When pressed by the king, all the marchers
except Gilbert surrendered their claims. The Red Earl, however,
was not prepared to abandon easily such notable signs of his
power and status. The affair came before a parliament. Gilbert
contended that the bishopric's lands within his lordship were
subject to the same exclusive rights of control he enjoyed over
any of his mesne fiefs during wardship or escheat. He argued
that King Henry's possession of the temporalities and prebends
was due solely to Earl Richard's minority, and pointed out that
both he and his father had enjoyed their accustomed rights during
the two subsequent vacancies. Edward I, on the other hand, cited
Henry's custody of the temporalities, his appointment of an archdeacon and some other officials in 1243, and especially the acknowledgment of Bishop Burgh in 1250 that he held in chief of
the Crown, as evidence that Llandaff was in the same position
as all the other bishoprics of the kingdom, and that Gilbert's
possession of the temporalities and prebends in 1287 was in fact
a usurpation of the rights of the Crown. On October 23, 1290,

---

[109] For Bishop de Burgh, see PRO, Curia Regis Roll 31–42 Henry III, KB
26/159 m. 6 (Mich. 34–35 Henry III), printed from a later copy in *Cartae de
Glamorgan*, II, 576. For Earl Richard's control of the temporalities in 1256, see
Close Rolls 1254–56, pp. 361–62. Since Glamorgan was in royal custody after
April, 1266, Earl Gilbert the Red could have maintained control for only a short
time following the death of Bishop William de Radnor in January of that year.
Radnor's successor, William de Braose, was elected in April, 1266, and consecrated
the following month. Cf. *Cal. Pat. Rolls 1258–66*, pp. 542, 581. For the first
Earl Gilbert's control of the temporalities during the vacancy of 1229–30, see
Patent Rolls 1225–32, pp. 326–27, *Close Rolls 1227–31*, pp. 375, 432–33.

Gilbert finally surrendered his claims, and although ten days later Edward, " de gratia sua speciali," restored the rights to the earl and Joan of Acre for life, he had in fact successfully asserted all the powers of the monarchy to bring Llandaff into line with the other bishoprics of the realm.[110] When John de Monmouth was finally named bishop to succeed Braose in the spring of 1295, Gilbert was accused of delay in restoring the temporalities. This was the period of Morgan ap Maredudd's rebellion, however, and undoubtedly the earl did not have effective control of the lordship. At any rate, when the rebellion had subsided, the king again brought pressure to bear by seizing Glamorgan and keeping it in his own hands for over four months. Edward was largely prompted by military considerations, but part of his actions may be due to the fact that he had effectively deprived Earl Gilbert of one of the greatest privileges his marcher standing bestowed, and that he wished to remind the earl forcibly of that fact.[111] In 1318, Edward II granted the right of custody *sede vacante* to the chapter of Llandaff, and it retained this right in the following decades.[112]

The dispute over Llandaff is the only major instance in which the Crown intervened in the relations between the Clares and the ecclesiastical bodies within the lordship. The family retained both rights of protection and secular jurisdiction over the great Cistercian abbeys of Neath and Margam, and there is no indication that the king attempted to abrogate their position. Moreover, the Clares often placed men of their own choosing in high positions in the bishopric itself. The Red Earl's brother Bogo was chancellor of the diocese from 1287 to at least 1290, and Robert de St. Fagans, the wardrober under Countess Joan and Ralph de Monthermer from 1300 to 1306, was also treasurer of Llandaff in 1301. Even when custody of the bishopric was in royal hands, the Clares sometimes managed to have their friends collated to vacant dignities. Before restoring the temporalities to Gilbert

---

[110] PRO, Parliamentary and Council Proceedings (Exchequer, KR), E 175/1/8; *Rot. Parl.*, I, 42–43; *Littere Wallie*, pp. 178–79; *Cal. Pat. Rolls 1281–92*, p. 393.

[111] Above, pp. 154–55. The problems of finding a successor to Bishop Braose are discussed fully in Greenway, " The Election of John de Monmouth," pp. 3–22. It is more than coincidental that Monmouth was only approved in 1295—the year after the death of Bogo de Clare.

[112] *Cartae de Glamorgan*, III, 1010–13 (misdated 1311; cf. *Cal. Fine Rolls 1307–19*, pp. 355–56); Glanmor Williams, *The Welsh Church*, pp. 47–48, 54–55, 68–69, 143.

and Joan of Acre in 1290, Edward presented Walter Langton, Bogo de Clare's protégé, to the office of treasurer.[113]

In one other relatively minor but characteristic instance, however, Edward I did manage to extend his authority over ecclesiastical matters at Earl Gilbert's expense. As lord of Caerleon, Gilbert was patron of the priory of Goldcliff, founded in 1122 by Roger de Chandos as a cell of the abbey of Bec. In 1290, the prior claimed advowsonary rights over the church of Undy against the earl. When Gilbert countered by impleading him at Caerleon under a writ of *quare impedit*, the prior immediately appealed to the king, claiming he held in frankalmoign tenure and was answerable only to writs issued by the king himself. Edward I became a party to the suit with the prior, and the vigor with which he defended the cognizance of the royal court indicates that he was anxious to extend his power of entertaining all pleas relating to advowsons in the march, a right already recognized by most of the marchers,[114] into the Clare lordships as well. The plea came *coram rege* in June, 1290, and appears on almost every roll for the next few years. Earl Gilbert—who was having more serious problems with King Edward at the time—was usually content to have his attorney claim the cognizance of his own court, and the earl appeared in person in only a few instances. For his defaults, the royal court ruled against him, and he was ordered to respond to subsequent complaints entered by the prior in regard to trespasses and distraints made while the original plea was still pending. These cases dragged on without settlement until the earl's death, and some were even revived in 1298 and 1304 against his widow. Once again the Crown was successful: by the early fourteenth century not only did the prior have the advowson of Undy, but the king was patron of the priory itself.[115]

---

[113] *Cartae de Glamorgan*, II, 413–14, 426, 464, 543, 565, 699; III, 911, 1017–19; Williams, *Welsh Church*, p. 68; Browne Willis, *Survey of the Cathedral Church of Llandaff* (London, 1719), pp. 84, 120–24; *Reg. Winchelsey*, I, 411; *Cal. Pat. Rolls 1281–92*, p. 387.

[114] Otway-Ruthven, " Great Lordships of South Wales," pp. 10–11.

[115] The original plea is in PRO, Coram Rege Roll Trinity 18 Edward I, KB 27/124 m. 33d. It or the subsequent pleas are found on almost every roll from Easter 19—Mich. 23–24 Edward I (KB 27/ rolls 127–146), and some pleas were revived in 1298 (Mich. 26–27 Edward I, KB 27/156 m. 43d.) and 1304 (*Cal. Chanc. War.*, p. 212). See also *Cal. Close Rolls 1288–96*, p. 197; *Rot. Parl.*, I, 82–83; Morgan, *English Lands of the Abbey of Bec*, pp. 29–30. On July 1, 1290,

Finally, mention should be made of the other areas in which the powers of the Crown extended to the march. The king, as feudal overlord, had the right to try all cases in which the title to lordships was in question, and also to hear all disputes arising out of the partition of any of these lands. The Marshal partition in particular resulted in innumerable suits, some of which were not fully settled even by the end of the thirteenth century. The cases involving the Clares were relatively minor, consisting mainly of pleas relating to scattered tenements and rents contested by Earl Gilbert, Countess Maud (as part of her dower portion) and some other Marshal heirs such as the Mortimers.[116] The Crown also had the right to summon juries from the neighboring lordships in disputes resulting from the king's attempts to extend his jurisdictional powers into areas bordering on Cardigan and Carmarthenshire, and on a number of occasions the sheriff of Glamorgan was ordered to raise a jury in such cases.[117] Moreover, the Crown seems to have maintained its normal right of custody of the goods of deceased Jews, at least in Caerleon; [118] and in 1245 Henry III ordered the sheriff of Glamorgan to assist the bishop of Llandaff in executing orders of excommunication as if he were the sheriff of a normal English county.[119]

Edward I imposed other limitations on marcher independence. The methods by which he eliminated, at least for the duration of his reign, the marcher privilege of private war have been discussed at length in a previous chapter.[120] In 1291–92, he subjected the marcher lordships, including Glamorgan, to a tax on movables, although promising the marchers that he would not use the grant as a precedent to the detriment of their liberties.[121] Edward also

---

the prior, having just brought the case *coram rege*, was thoughtful enough to have all his charters confirmed by Edward I. *Cal. Chart Rolls 1257–1300*, pp. 358–61.

[116] E.g. PRO, Coram Rege Roll Trinity 4 Edward I, KB 27/24 m. 6; Mich. 6–7 Edward I, KB 27/41 mm. 12d., 33; Mich. 8–9 Edward I, KB 27/57 m. 22d.

[117] *Cal. Welsh Rolls*, p. 298; *Cal. Pat. Rolls 1292–1301*, p. 478. Cf. also *Welsh Assize Roll*, p. 327; PRO, Coram Rege Roll Michaelmas 27–28 Edward I, KB 27/160 m. 37d.

[118] *Cal. Fine Rolls 1272–1307*, p. 93.

[119] *Episcopal Acts relating to Welsh Dioceses*, II, 733–34. For other examples involving felons and outlaws who had fled to Wales, see *Close Rolls 1253–54*, p. 80; *ibid. 1254–56*, p. 201.

[120] Above, Chapter IV, ("Trouble on the March").

[121] Above, p. 153. For the normal immunity of the march lands and other areas within the kingdom, see James F. Willard, *Parliamentary Taxes on Personal Property 1290–1334* (Cambridge, Mass., 1934), pp. 26–32.

established the right of the Crown to raise levies of foot soldiers from the march during the Welsh wars, and he continued this policy in his Scottish wars and even the Flemish campaign of 1297. In 1277 he ordered Robert le Veel to raise a squadron of paid troops in Glamorgan and put it under the command of Pain de Chaworth, lord of Kidwelly and Ogmore and captain of the royal army in western Wales.[122] In 1287, Earl Gilbert himself led forces of 5,000 and 3,500 foot soldiers, but they served under royal wages.[123] In later years the Crown assumed direct control of the forces raised in this way. About 900 footmen were raised for service in Flanders in 1297,[124] and in the Scottish campaigns of 1298–99 and 1307 contingents of 500 and 975 men were recruited from the lordship.[125] In addition, Edward II regularly raised troops from the marcher estates for the campaigns against Robert Bruce. The numbers recruited from Glamorgan for the campaigns of 1310 and 1314 are unknown, but 1,000 were raised in the summer of 1317, and 500 served in 1318 and 600 in 1322, when Hugh Despenser held the lordship.[126]

Despite these instances of royal intervention, the Clares maintained full control over their own tenants-in-chiefs within the lordships and governed them in accordance with their own body of marcher custom and law. They owed no military service for the marcher estates, and the normal Crown right of prerogative wardship did not apply to the fiefs within them. When Roger de Somery died in 1273, the Crown seized the estates appurtenant to his Worcestershire barony of Dudley, but his manor of Dinas Powys in Glamorgan was controlled by Earl Richard's widow, the dowager Countess Maud, as one of the fees assigned as part of her dower portion.[127] Another example of the survival in

---

[122] Cal. Anc. Corr., Wales, p. 65. Cf. also Morris, Welsh Wars, pp. 131–32.

[123] Morris, Welsh Wars, pp. 211, 213.

[124] Cal. Pat. Rolls 1292–1301, p. 294; Cal. Anc. Corr., Wales, p. 208; N. B. Lewis, "The English Forces in Flanders, August–November 1297," in Studies . . . Powicke, p. 317.

[125] PRO, Exchequer, KR Accts. Var. (Army and Navy), E 101/12/17 m. 2, E 101/13/23.

[126] Parl. Writs, I, (pt. II), 396–97, 424; Cal. Close Rolls 1313–18, p. 563; PRO, Exchequer, KR Accts. Var., E 101/15/27; Brit. Mus., Stowe MS 553, fol. 80v. The 1317 contingent was raised by Morgan ap Maredudd, son of Maredudd ap Gruffydd of Machen, Edelegan and Llefnydd, whom Earl Gilbert the Red had dispossessed in 1270. Morgan was in royal service until at least 1322. Cal. Anc. Corr., Wales, p. 101.

[127] Cal. Inq. Post Mortem, II, no. 16; Cartae de Glamorgan, III, 770–71.

marcher custom of an old feature of Anglo–Norman customary law was the lord's right to the goods of a tenant who died intestate. This right had been eliminated in common law, but in 1305 Edward I refused to heed a petition by the bishop of Llandaff to extend common law usage to the march: " rex intendit quod talis est consuetudo patrie quam in praejudicium hominum patrie illius annullare non debet."[128] Moreover, the records of the Cardiff court sessions produced in Richard Siward's unsuccessful appeal to Henry III in 1247 provide ample evidence that the Clares had full power to deal with rebellious vassals themselves, including the use of a *dies marchie*, without the intervention of the Crown. The fact that Earl Richard's officials arranged the truce in 1242 among Hywel ap Maredudd of Meisgyn, Rhys ap Gruffydd of Senghenydd and Gilbert de Turberville of Coety is another indication that as long as their warfare was confined to Glamorgan, the Crown could not interfere.[129]

Finally, there is evidence that a number of the earls' knights were paid retainers, at least by 1300. Robert de Grendon, a member of Monthermer's council in 1299 and later sheriff of Glamorgan under the last Earl Gilbert, was paid a retaining fee in 1305–6 by the receiver of Usk, and Giles de Argentine was paid a similar fee by the receiver of Clare bailiwick in 1307–8.[130] There is also some evidence to indicate that at least part of the earls' forces in the Scottish campaigns of Edward I and Edward II were recruited by means of the indenture system. In 1297 a permanent indenture was arranged between John Bluet, who held two fees in Llangstone and Whitson in the lordship of Caerleon, and William Martel, who held a partial fee at Redcastle in the same lordship. In return for an annual wage and other perquisites, Martel agreed to serve " ben e lealment " as John's knight in the Flemish campaign and in all subsequent wars in England or Wales.[131] Bluet, who was from a long-standing marcher family, appears in Ralph de Monthermer's *comitiva* in Scotland in the campaign of 1303, and

---

[128] *Memoranda de Parliamento*, ed. F. W. Maitland (Rolls Series XCVIII, 1893), pp. 73–74. Cf. Otway-Ruthven, " Great Lordships of South Wales," p. 13, who cites other evidence on this point from the mid-fourteenth century.

[129] *Cartae de Glamorgan*, II, 547–55; Tewkesbury, pp. 124–25.

[130] Above, p. 237.

[131] Brit. Mus., Add. Ch. 1531. For their holdings, see *Cal. Inq. Post Mortem*, V, no. 538 (p. 336).

later served under the last Earl Gilbert in the 1314 campaign which culminated in the great Scots victory at Bannockburn. There seems to be no mention of Martel in either campaign, but he probably served as one of the knights Bluet owed for his estates.[132] No other indentures involving Clare military tenants survive for this period, and it cannot be determined to what degree the system was used directly by the Red Earl and his descendants to supply knights for the king's army or their own household.

As lords of the march, the Clares enjoyed a position of virtual independence of royal control. The emphasis given in preceding paragraphs to the powers of the Crown in the march is in a sense largely a matter of the availability of sources. Relatively little has survived, for example, to provide a comprehensive analysis of the judicial structure of the courts or the routine processes of administration. Much more information, on the other hand, is available in the royal records to denote those areas in which the Crown extended its jurisdiction and authority at the expense not only of the Clares, but of other marcher lords as well. Under all normal circumstances, the king's powers of intervention or control were severely limited, and in the thirteenth and early fourteenth centuries, the Clares, like the other lords of the march, held what amounted to a series of small, virtually independent principalities. This position was argued by Earl Richard, and in effect accepted by Henry III, as the case involving Richard Siward in 1245–47 reveals; but Edward I would not tolerate some of the claims of Earl Gilbert the Red, in particular the right of waging private war and the control over the bishopric of Llandaff. He made little effort, however, to modify or destroy most of the other distinctive features of marcher custom, and his successors were for the most part either less capable or less interested in maintaining many of the precedents he had set. It was not until 1536 that another and greater monarch, Henry VIII, united England and Wales, shired the march lands, and eliminated the system of marcher lordships and marcher law.[133]

---

[132] Cal. Docs. Scot., IV, no. 1796; Cal. Pat. Rolls 1313–17, p. 86.

[133] The Act of Union, 27 Henry VIII c. 26, is printed in Statutes of the Realm, III, 563–69. By this Act, Glamorgan and Gower were joined as a single county, and Gwynllwg, Caerleon and Usk became parts of the new county of Monmouth. The other shires created at this time were Pembroke, Brecon (Brecknock), Radnor, Montgomery and Denbigh.

CHAPTER IX

LORD OF KILKENNY

The liberty of Kilkenny in southeastern Ireland was a portion of the great palatine lordship of Leinster which had been conquered in 1170 by Richard fitz Gilbert de Clare, earl of Pembroke ("Strongbow"). After Strongbow's death Leinster passed by marriage to the Marshals and after the extinction of the male line, was divided in 1247 into the five lordships of Carlow, Kilkenny, Kildare, Dunamase, and Wexford. These divisions were regarded as having the same privileges and structure as the original lordship and were organized as shrievalties. Leinster and its components failed, however, to develop the same independence and authority as the great lordships of the marches of Wales, due mainly to the early introduction of the English common law, and the effective control exercised by the English kings.

In 1166 Dermot McMurrough, king of Leinster, sought aid from Henry II and the marchers to help him regain the lands from which his rivals had expelled him. In 1169 the vanguard of the expedition arrived, and the following year Strongbow, its captain, reached Ireland and quickly restored Dermot to his territories. Strongbow was nominally acting as Henry II's agent, but his real aim was to establish an independent position for himself. He married Dermot's daughter, Eva, on the understanding that the kingdom would descend to him on Dermot's death. This agreement naturally found no support among the native chieftains and was contrary to local law, but when the king died in the spring of 1171, Strongbow assumed royal jurisdiction and subdued local disturbances.[1] Henry II became alarmed at Earl Richard's show of independence and hastened over to Ireland in October,

[1] On the Norman conquest of Ireland in general, see Orpen, *Ireland under the Normans*, I, *passim*.

281

1171. His effective intervention at this point proved decisive. He compelled the earl to surrender the kingdom, and regranted it to him as a fief to be held for the service of 100 knights. In addition Henry reserved to the Crown the cities of Dublin and Waterford, but in all other respects Strongbow was confirmed in his full control over administration and justice.[2] It is interesting to note, however, that the lordship was never styled an earldom, probably because Strongbow already held the title by virtue of his Pembroke estates.[3] The earl died in 1176, leaving as his heir a son Gilbert, who was about five years old. King Henry took Leinster into custody, and in 1185 entrusted it to his son John, lord of Ireland. The young Gilbert died shortly thereafter, and John held Leinster until 1189, when William Marshal, who had married Strongbow's daughter Isabel, inherited her father's territories.[4]

The early organization of Leinster is difficult to describe in much detail. The Marshals completed the subinfeudation of the lordship begun by Strongbow, founded a number of religious houses, and encouraged the development of towns and markets.[5] Strongbow had entrusted the duties of administration, which consisted mainly in putting down local rebellions, to the constables of his chief castles. In his earliest charters of enfeoffment, the constable appears at the head of the list of witnesses, and is the only administrative officer named.[6] By 1200, however, William Marshal established a seneschal for the lordship, and by 1225 there was also a separate sheriff for each of the four major subdivisions. There was a county court at Wexford by 1204, a sheriff of Kilkenny by 1202–14, and a sheriff of Kildare by 1224. The other shrievalty within the lordship, Carlow, must also date from this time.[7] The seneschal held the county courts twice a

---

[2] See Painter, *William Marshal*, pp. 150–51.

[3] This situation is analogous to that of Glamorgan, which was never formally raised to the dignity of an earldom, probably because its holders already had the title in right of their other properties. See T. F. Tout, "The Earldoms under Edward I," *Transactions of the Royal Historical Society*, new ser., VIII (1894), 149.

[4] *G. E. C.*, X, 357–58; Painter, *William Marshal*, pp. 66, 77, 151.

[5] Painter, *ibid.*, pp. 152–53, 167–68, for details.

[6] *Calendar of Ormond Deeds*, ed. Edmund Curtis (Irish MSS Commission, 1933–43), I (1172–1350), nos. 1–2.

[7] *Register of the Abbey of St. Thomas, Dublin*, ed. John T. Gilbert (Rolls Series XCIV, 1889), nos. 144–46; J. Otway-Ruthven, "The Medieval County of Kildare," *Irish Historical Studies*, XI (1959), 185–88. Dunamase was only organized as a shire in 1247 to facilitate the partition of the lordship.

year for major jurisdiction, leaving the lesser courts to the sheriff.[8] In addition, the Marshals organized a chancery for the lordship, and they began to make use of royal assizes and forms of action, initiating them under writs issued by the chancery in their own name.[9] Finally, they also improved the financial organization, establishing a permanent exchequer at Kilkenny, which replaced the chamber system used by Strongbow.[10]

While the Marshals vastly increased the efficiency of their control, their judicial powers and autonomy were not as extensive as those originally enjoyed by Strongbow. William Marshal quarreled with King John in 1207–8, and as part of the truce effected in the spring of 1208, a new charter was issued for Leinster which effectively limited its palatine nature. The four major pleas of the Crown (arson, rape, treasure-trove, and fore-stall or ambush), and more importantly, control over episcopal appointments and the custody of church lands (*cruciae*) during vacancy, rights previously enjoyed by the lords of Leinster, were reserved to the king acting through the justiciar and the sheriff of Dublin. Writ of error was also adjudged to run in the lordship, so that judgments could be appealed to the royal courts. In addi-tion, in the event of the death of a military tenant-in-chief, the lord had control of only those fees that lay in Leinster; all others, along with custody and marriage of the heir, were reserved to the king, although in the mid-thirteenth century Henry III seems to have relaxed this last provision.[11] The liberty was also subject to taxation, the earliest instance dating from 1212.[12] The fact that

[8] *Cal. Docs. Ireland 1252–84*, no. 1647, from an inquisition of 1279.

[9] The first appearance of such writs can be dated to about 1225: Otway-Ruthven, " Medieval Kildare," p. 190. Two charters, one of Gilbert Marshal (d. 1241) and the other of his brother Walter (d. 1245), include a chancellor among the witnesses. Eric St. J. Brooks, " Irish Possessions of St. Thomas of Acre," *Pro-ceedings of the Royal Irish Academy*, LVIII (1956–57), Section C, nos. 10, 12 (pp. 32–33).

[10] *Cal. Docs. Ireland 1252–84*, no. 861 mentions the Marshal exchequer. The Strongbow chamber, which naturally peregrinated with the lord and served as central financial office for all his estates, is mentioned in a charter of 1174: *Calendar of Christ Church* (Dublin) *Deeds* (20th D. K. Report, 1888), no. 3, p. 36.

[11] *Rotuli Chartarum 1199–1216*, ed. T. D. Hardy (Record Commission, 1837), p. 176. Similar restrictions were placed on the Lacy lordship of Meath. *Ibid.*, p. 178. For the quarrel, see Painter, *William Marshal*, pp. 153–58, and for Henry III, *Close Rolls 1247–51*, p. 178.

[12] *Irish Pipe Roll 14 John*, eds. Oliver Davies and David B. Quinn, *Ulster Journal of Archaeology*, IV (1941), Supplement, 16–21.

the later subdivisions of Leinster were always represented in Irish parliaments indicates that the royal government regarded them for all practical purposes as feudal liberties subject to most of the normal features of royal shires.[13] Thus the effective intervention, first of Henry II and later of John, prevented the great Irish lordships from assuming the same constitutional powers and position as obtained in the Welsh marcher lands.[14]

On the death of Earl William's last son, Anselm Marshal, without issue in 1245, the lordship was seized into the king's hands for over a year. Unlike the other Marshal properties, Leinster was only partitioned among William's five daughters and their families in May, 1247. Matilda, dowager countess of Warenne, the eldest daughter, received Carlow, which passed to the heirs of her first husband, Hugh Bigod, earl of Norfolk, who had died in 1225. The second daughter, Isabel, had died in 1240, and her share, the lordship of Kilkenny, passed to Richard de Clare, earl of Gloucester, as the heir of her first husband Gilbert de Clare who had died in 1230. The third and fourth shares were subjected to further complications. Kildare passed to William de Ferrers, earl of Derby, in right of his wife Sibyl. He died in 1254, and the bulk of the property was granted to Walter Marshal's widow, Margaret, countess of Lincoln, as dower. After her death in 1266 it passed to Sibyl's eldest daughter, Agnes, wife of William de Vescy. The fourth heiress, Eva, had married the great marcher lord, William de Braose, who died in 1230. Eva died in 1246, and her extensive holdings were divided among their four daughters, the eldest of whom, Maud, brought the newly created lordship of Dunamase, which was juridically subject to Kildare, to her husband, Roger Mortimer of Wigmore. William Marshal's fifth daughter, Joan, had died in 1234 and her share, Wexford, passed to her son John de Munchensy, and following his death in 1247, to his sister Joan and her husband, William de Valence, Henry III's half brother.[15]

Richard de Clare performed homage to King Henry for Kil-

[13] Statutes and Ordinances and Acts of the Parliaments of Ireland, John–Henry V, ed. H. F. Berry (Dublin: H. M. Stationery Office, 1907), pp. 194–96; Richardson and Sayles, The Irish Parliament in the Middle Ages, pp. 60–61.

[14] This has been convincingly argued by Otway-Ruthven, "Great Lordships of South Wales," pp. 1, 6, 12–13.

[15] PRO, Chancery Miscellanea, C 47/9/20. The Leinster partition is fully discussed in Orpen, Ireland under the Normans, III, 80–107.

kenny on April 30, 1247, and received seisin on May 9.[16] He
probably visited it shortly thereafter, but evidence of an extended
stay dates only from the fall of 1253.[17] Besides the manor, town,
and castle of Kilkenny, which constituted the *caput* of the lordship, the Clares held in demesne the manors of Dunfert, Callan,
Loughmadran, and Brenan. Other properties, not specified in
the partition, included the boroughs of Rosbercon and Jerpoint
and the manors of Offerlane, Palmerston, Thomastown, Coillauch,
Kilmanagh, Ballycallan, Letherdan, and Fermaill. In addition,
the family had advowsonary rights over the churches of Callan
and Offerlane and the priory of St. John's, Kilkenny. The officially
assessed value of the lordship was some £343, and it was held for
the service of 22 knights' fees, although over 36 fees had actually
been created within it.[18]

The Clares visited Kilkenny infrequently. From 1247 to 1262,
Earl Richard seems to have made only one prolonged stay, in
1253. Earl Gilbert the Red received seisin of the liberty in September, 1264, but the first clear evidence that he visited it dates from
June, 1274. Although he undoubtedly was there at frequent inter-
vals for short periods of time, the only evidence of more extended
visits dates from 1279 and 1293–94.[19] Possession of the lordship,
however, was not a liability. It increased the range of family
associations and influence, and added to its material resources.
Moreover, it served a number of useful, if miscellaneous, functions. When the Red Earl captured Gruffydd ap Rhys, lord of
Senghenydd, in 1267, he dispatched him to Kilkenny castle for
safekeeping.[20] Bogo de Clare was rector of Callan from 1256 to
1294, although he never bothered to visit it, and by 1306 Ralph

---

[16] *Cal. Pat. Rolls 1272–81*, pp. 352–53, an *inspeximus* of the Clare portion of
the Leinster partition made for Earl Gilbert the Red in November, 1279, mentions
these dates. Homage to Edward as lord of Ireland was performed in August, 1256.
Cal. Pat. Rolls 1247–58, p. 497.

[17] Tewkesbury, p. 153.

[18] PRO, Chanc. Misc., C 47/9/20; PRO, Min. Accts., SC 6/1239/13; Orpen,
Ireland under the Normans, III, 90–96. The descent of the fees within the liberty
is traced by Eric St. J. Brooks, *Knights' Fees in Counties Wexford, Carlow and
Kilkenny, 13th–15th Centuries* (Irish MSS Commission, 1950). Carlow and Wex-
ford also owed the service of 22 fees to the Crown, but Kildare owed 33. Orpen,
Ireland under the Normans, III, 106–7.

[19] Tewkesbury, p. 153; *Cal. Pat. Rolls 1258–66*, p. 330; *ibid. 1272–81*, pp. 46,
306; *ibid. 1292–1301*, p. 19.

[20] " Chronicle of the Thirteenth Century," p. 282.

de Monthermer's brother John was also rector of the same church.[21] The liberty, in short, could be used to good advantage in a number of ways.

The lordships into which Leinster was divided were commonly regarded as having much the same privileges and powers as the original lordship itself, and their central administrative organization preserved most of the features found under the Marshals. The lordships of Carlow and Kildare have been described elsewhere in detail;[22] the Clare liberty of Kilkenny presents a very similar picture.

The seneschal was the chief administrative officer of the liberty, and had full authority over its affairs in the absence of the earls, in effect, most of the time. Twice a year he presided at the *curia comitatus*, hearing major civil and criminal pleas and the minor Crown pleas, which were not reserved to the king.[23] There is also some evidence that at times he heard the four major pleas of the Crown, although he had to account for the records and profits to the royal exchequer at Dublin.[24] In addition, the seneschal assumed many of the normal functions of a chancellor, who does not appear as such in the lordship despite the fact that Leinster had had a chancery under the Marshals. The seneschal kept the Clare seal and issued the writs in the earl's name to implement the decisions of the court.[25] He had a staff of bailiffs who carried out most of the executive and police work arising out of the court decrees, although on occasion the sheriff was designated to perform these functions.[26] Little can be said about the business enacted at the central court, as very few of its records have survived. It is clear that the court entertained pleas commenced under writ, such as the

[21] *Cal. Papal Letters*, I, 317, II, 20.

[22] W. F. Nugent, "Carlow in the Middle Ages," *Journal of the Royal Society of Antiquaries of Ireland*, LXXXV (1955), 62–76; Otway-Ruthven, "Medieval Kildare," pp. 181–99.

[23] *Calendar of Justiciary Rolls, Ireland, 1295–1303* (Dublin: H. M. Stationery Office, 1906), pp. 88–89, 107. Minor pleas of the Crown in all the liberties remained with the lord. J. Otway-Ruthven, "Anglo–Irish Shire Government in the 13th Century," *Irish Historical Studies*, V (1946–47), 17 note 4.

[24] *Irish Pipe Roll 33 Edward I* (38th D. K. Report, 1906), pp. 96–97, and cf. *Irish Pipe Roll 6 Edward III* (43rd D. K. Report, 1912), p. 44. The seneschal of Kildare heard the major pleas of the Crown in the mid-thirteenth century. *Irish Pipe Roll 45 Henry III* (35th D. K. Report, 1903), p. 38.

[25] *Cal. Docs. Ireland 1252–1284*, no. 1647.

[26] *Cal. Just. Rolls 1295–1303*, pp. 358–59, and for the sheriff, *ibid.*, pp. 88–89.

assize of *novel disseisin*, and that it served as a court of record for the tenants-in-chief of the liberty, who used it to enroll private concords, charters, and deeds.[27]

In addition to his judicial work, the seneschal represented the earls in matters dealing with the royal government at Dublin. Whenever a parliament was called, two " most honest and discreet " knights were to be elected " in plena curia sui libertatis " by the seneschal with the assent of the community of the liberty.[28] Furthermore, the Clares themselves often sent the seneschal in person to the parliaments to present petitions and otherwise act on their behalf.[29] In certain ways, however, the seneschal was as much a royal official as the representative of the Clares. The existence of the liberty excluded the king's ministers, with the exception of the sheriff of Dublin who administered the Church lands;[30] but it did not, unlike the marcher lordships, exclude the king's writ, and in matters concerning the royal government within Kilkenny the seneschal had to execute the writs as if he were a royal agent himself.[31] Whenever the king levied any money from the lands within the liberty, in the form of taxes, aids or scutages, the seneschal collected the sums and accounted for them at the Dublin exchequer. He was also responsible for any other debts the lords of Kilkenny owed the king.[32] In short, the duties of the seneschal of Kilkenny were particularly onerous and important.

[27] *Ibid.*, pp. 88–89; *Cal. Ormond Deeds*, I, nos. 338, 435, and *passim*. A court session of 1344 which heard minor pleas of the Crown and which reproduces Marshal and Clare charters of the thirteenth and early fourteenth centuries is printed in *Liber Primus Kilkenniensis*, ed. Charles McNeill (Irish MSS Commission, 1931), pp. 6–10.

[28] *Statutes of the Parliaments of Ireland*, pp. 194–96.

[29] *Cal. Just. Rolls 1295–1303*, p. 305; *Parliaments and Councils of Medieval Ireland*, eds. H. G. Richardson and G. O. Sayles (Irish MSS Commission, 1947), I, 3.

[30] *Calendar of the Gormanston Register*, eds. James Mills and M. M. McEnery (Royal Society of Antiquaries of Ireland, 1916), p. 123.

[31] See in general Otway-Ruthven, "Anglo–Irish Shire Government," p. 6, and for the use of return of writs in Kilkenny, *Cal. Docs. Ireland 1285–92*, no. 999; *Cal. Just. Rolls 1295–1303*, pp. 72, 211; *ibid. 1305–7* (Dublin: H. M. Stationery Office, 1914), p. 502.

[32] The earliest instances for the seneschal of Leinster date from 1212 and 1232. *Irish Pipe Roll 14 John*, pp. 16–21; *Irish Pipe Roll 16 Henry III* (35th D. K. Report, 1903), p. 33. The accounts of the seneschal of Kilkenny usually appear irregularly and for lengthy periods of time: e. g., *Irish Pipe Roll 25 Edward I* (38th D. K. Report, 1906), p. 26, accounts for 1292–98; *Irish Pipe Roll 3 Edward II* (39th D. K. Report, 1907), p. 31, accounts for 1306–10.

Besides his normal judicial functions he assumed tasks handled elsewhere by other officials, and he served not only as the representative of the Clares in matters concerning the royal government at Dublin, but also as the major official responsible for the general administration of the liberty during the long periods of absence by the lords. In return, however, he was well compensated, and his importance is emphasized by the fact that he received £100 a year, which made him not only the highest paid officer of the lordship, but indeed the highest paid of all the Clare officials.[33]

The duties of the sheriff were more directly concerned with police work. He sat with the seneschal at the central court and aided him in administrative and judicial matters such as executing writs, levying fines, and collecting fees. He also made the tourn of the local manorial and hundredal courts.[34] In the absence of the seneschal, he could hear pleas at the county court and take the necessary actions. He was assisted by a staff of clerks and a serjeant, who did much of the actual routine work.[35] Like the seneschal, he was regarded as a royal agent in matters affecting the king.[36] In general his work seems mainly confined to the routine processes of judicial administration, and he took little part in questions of major importance bearing on the lordship. It is an administrative peculiarity of Kilkenny and the other Anglo–Irish lordships that the functions normally associated with the sheriff were reserved to the seneschal, while the sheriff himself more closely resembled the bailiff of a normal English franchise.[37]

[33] PRO, Min. Accts., SC 6/1239/13. In 1327–29 the single seneschal of the three coparceners of Kilkenny received 100 marks a year. *Irish Pipe Roll 2 Edward III* (43rd D. K. Report, 1912), p. 25. The seneschal of Carlow was regularly paid £100 by the Bigods. Nugent, " Carlow in the Middle Ages," p. 71.

[34] *Cal. Ormond Deeds*, I, nos. 338, 597; *Cal. Just. Rolls 1295–1303*, pp. 88–89.

[35] *Cal. Just. Rolls 1295–1303*, p. 392. There was one serjeant for the entire liberty. When he was called on to levy a debt in some wild Irish backcountry, he had to raise a small army to assist him: *ibid.*, p. 397. Carlow also had only one serjeant, but in Kildare there was a separate one for each cantred: Nugent, " Carlow in the Middle Ages," p. 71 and note.

[36] See *Cal. Just. Rolls 1305–7*, p. 473, where he is found assisting the king's marshal in pursuing an outlaw.

[37] On the whole question, see Otway-Ruthven, " Anglo–Irish Shire Government," pp. 1–28. The sheriff's less important position is reflected in his salary. Under the Clares he received 10 marks yearly: PRO, SC 6/1239/13. Under Elizabeth de Burgh in the 1340's he received £20 per year, but his duties had expanded to include the lands she held in dower in Tipperary and Limerick: PRO, SC 6/1239/16.

The liberty also had a coroner who held the minor Crown pleas in the local courts and made presentments and indictments before the seneschal and the sheriff in eyre.[38] The financial administration of the liberty was under the control of a treasurer. After the partition of Leinster in 1247, each lordship developed its own exchequer.[39] The treasurer collected the revenues from the local manorial reeves and borough officials and audited their accounts. With his staff he made purchases and paid out fees, and he was responsible for delivering the funds he handled to the mainland, possibly by the end of the century to the Clare exchequer at Cardiff.[40] The exchequer seems to have developed no separate jurisdiction of its own, although at times the treasurer is found sitting with the seneschal and sheriff at the central court of the liberty.[41] On at least one occasion he rendered account to the royal exchequer at Dublin in place of the seneschal.[42]

In addition to the major central officials, there was the usual host of minor functionaries, whose activities are less readily discernable. Chief among these were the constables of the major castles, whose primary tasks were to safeguard their strongholds and provide military action when called upon. They were less important under the Clares than they had been under Strongbow and the Marshals. Kilkenny nominally owed 22 and a fraction knights, but there is no evidence of actual service in the thirteenth century, and the Clares were regularly charged with a scutage of £44 8s. 10-1/4d. at the rate of £2 per fee.[43] Scutage was remitted

[38] *Irish Pipe Roll 30 Edward I* (38th D. K. Report, 1906), 62.

[39] *Cal. Docs. Ireland 1252–84*, no. 861; *Cal. Ormond Deeds*, I, no. 435; Otway-Ruthven, " Medieval Kildare," pp. 188–89; Nugent, " Carlow in the Middle Ages," p. 71.

[40] Cf. *Cal. Docs. Ireland 1252–84*, no. 861. The absence of records makes it impossible to say precisely what the final disbursement of the revenues was. There is evidence that close economic relations existed between the Bigod lordships of Carlow and Striguil (PRO, Min. Accts., SC 6/920/7 m. 2d.). There is no mention of any similar connections with Kilkenny in the surviving accounts for Usk or Clare; the family therefore in all probability established such connections with Cardiff, or perhaps with one of the bailiwicks in western England.

[41] *Cal. Ormond Deeds*, I, no. 435; *Calendar of the Gormanston Register*, pp. 124–25.

[42] *Irish Pipe Roll 2 Edward III* (43rd D. K. Report, 1912), p. 25. Under Elizabeth de Burgh, the treasurer was paid £10 per year; Elizabeth established a local receiver at Callan for her Kilkenny properties (PRO, SC 6/1239/16).

[43] *Irish Pipe Roll 46 Henry III* (35th D. K. Report, 1903), p. 44; Mary Bateson, " Irish Exchequer Memoranda of the Reign of Edward I," *English Historical Review*, XVIII (1903), 505.

in 1332 when actual military duty was performed; but the soldiers raised had no relation to the holders of fees in Kilkenny, and they were in the king's pay.[44] There is no indication of the size of the garrisons stationed at the castles, although the constable of Offerlane, which was situated in the midst of a heavy native settlement, had a potentially more vulnerable and dangerous task than the others, and was well recompensed for it.[45]

As the Clares were infrequently in residence at Kilkenny, they made use of attorneys who were sent from the household to Ireland on a periodic basis. There is no evidence that the Clares established an over-all administrative council in Kilkenny, such as existed in the Bigod liberty of Carlow,[46] and the attorneys seem to have assumed this function. They had power to supervise the activities of the seneschal and other officials and to audit the treasurer's accounts, and they undoubtedly provided counsel on questions of vital interest to the earls concerning the liberty. The attorneys were usually men prominent in the administration of the English and Welsh estates. John de Crepping, sheriff of Glamorgan in 1289, 1292, and 1293, served as an attorney in Ireland in 1287–88. On occasion, however, the earls also relied on local officials. John de Clare, who seems to be no relation, served as both sheriff and seneschal of the liberty at various times between 1265 and 1280, and he was an attorney under Earl Gilbert the Red in 1277–79 and 1281.[47]

For the most part, the Clares seem to have relied on local men, largely recruited from prominent families holding mesne fees within the liberty, to staff the major administrative positions of seneschal, sheriff, and treasurer. As the career of John de Clare illustrates, they were often employed in more than one capacity, and some, for example Andrew Avenel in 1279, may have served

[44] *Irish Pipe Roll 6 Edward III* (43rd D. K. Report, 1912), p. 46. Instances of actual service in the 13th century from some other liberties are noted in J. Otway-Ruthven, " Knight–Service in Ireland," *Journal of the Royal Society of Antiquaries of Ireland*, LXXXIX (1959), 4–5.

[45] The constable of Offerlane received £40 in 1314–15, while the constables of Kilkenny and Callan received 10 marks and the constable of Jerpoint £5. PRO, Min. Accts., SC 6/1239/13.

[46] See Nugent, " Carlow in the Middle Ages," p. 70.

[47] For Crepping, see the references cited above, Chapter VIII, note 65, and for John de Clare, *Cal. Ormond Deeds*, I, nos. 233, 348; *Irish Monastic and Episcopal Deeds*, ed. Newport B. White (Irish MSS Commission, 1936), p. 309; *Cal. Docs. Ireland 1254–82*, no. 1412; *Cal. Pat. Rolls 1272–81*, pp. 233, 352.

both the Clares and other Anglo–Irish magnates at the same time.[48] Many of them had wide experience in the royal administration as well. William de Dene, who was Earl Richard's seneschal in 1257–58, became justiciar of Ireland under the Lord Edward in 1260–61.[49] David de Offington, who was the seneschal on three separate occasions from 1283 to 1293, had been a royal official in the 1270's. Finally, John Druhull, seneschal for the last Earl Gilbert in 1307–8, was the royal *custos* of the liberty after the death of the Countess Joan of Acre in April, 1307.[50] In general, the administrative was efficiently organized and run; the clear delimitations of powers and differentiation of functions attest to the growing reliance on trained laymen and clerks, a reliance made more urgent by the long periods of absence of the Clares themselves. The increasing professionalization of the administrative personnel characteristic of England during this period had its counterpart in the liberty of Kilkenny.

Little can be said in detail about the economy. The Clares continued the policy of the Marshals in encouraging the development of fairs and markets, paying special attention to the important ports of Kilkenny and Rosbercon. In 1311 the last earl reconfirmed the charter issued to Kilkenny by William Marshal at the beginning of the thirteenth century.[51] A fair was established at Rosbercon, and when the burgesses complained that Edward I was eroding the liberties of the " franchise de Leyncestre" by imposing arbitrary prises, Earl Gilbert the Red in 1294 issued a charter of liberties on their behalf, modeled on that of Kilkenny.[52] The manorial structure is obscured by the lack of any surviving estate accounts. The only evidence is the account of the royal *custodes* of the liberty from June, 1314, to February, 1316, and

---

[48] See Richardson and Sayles, *The Irish Parliament in the Middle Ages*, p. 296.

[49] *Irish Monastic and Episcopal Deeds*, p. 306; *Cal. Pat. Rolls 1258–66*, pp. 130, 159.

[50] *Cal. Close Rolls 1272–79*, p. 61; *ibid. 1279–88*, p. 229; *Cal. Docs. Ireland 1285–92*, no. 271; *Cal. Just. Rolls 1295–1303*, pp. 88–89; *ibid. 1308–14* (Dublin: Stationery Office, 1932), pp. 43, 104, 111.

[51] The charter is printed in *Liber Primus Kilkenniensis*, pp. 8–9.

[52] *Cal. Chart. Rolls 1257–1300*, p. 337; *Cal. Ormond Deeds*, I, no. 314, which prints the charter from an *inspeximus* of 1 Henry IV. The charter is dated *ca.* 1289 by A. Ballard and J. Tait, *British Borough Charters 1216–1307* (Cambridge, 1923), p. 28. The letter of the burgesses to the earl is in PRO, Ancient Correspondence, SC 1/30/199.

the figures do not necessarily reflect normal conditions. If at all reliable, however, the account indicates that rents were the predominant source of income. In the period June 24, 1314–January 29, 1315, revenue from freehold, burgage, and customary rents came to just under £100, about half the total. The sale of produce from the demesne and pastures and the sale of wood yielded only about 12 per cent, with a similar percentage deriving from assorted seigneurial dues such as fees collected for the use of mills and fisheries, market tolls, prise of ale, pannage, and stallage. Presumably the economy was a straightforward agrarian one, with little or no development of local industry, but the absence of records makes it impossible to assume this with complete certainty. The court profits were high, but this may reflect the government's use of the courts to transact business normally handled by the justiciar at Dublin. In any event, the pleas and perquisites of the central court brought in about one quarter of the total, while the sums collected through the local hundredal and manorial courts were insignificant.

On January 29, 1315, one-third of the properties were delivered to the last Earl Gilbert's widow Maud de Burgh, but the account for the lands still in the king's possession from this date to February 25, 1316, reveals a similar pattern of income. Rents again formed the single largest item of revenue, about 40 per cent. The pleas of the central court at Kilkenny yielded some 30 per cent, with the sale of grain and other produce bringing in 20 per cent and mills, market tolls, and the prise of ale accounting for the remainder. The accounts clearly indicate that rents and court profits were more important in Kilkenny than the sale of demesne produce, but it is impossible to use the actual figures as indicators of normal estate enterprise with much confidence in the absence of other evidence.[53]

The gross income from Kilkenny is also difficult to establish. Total revenue in the period June 24, 1314–January 29, 1315, amounted to just over £205, which for a twelve-month span figures out to some £350. For two-thirds of the properties in the thirteen-month period from January, 1315, to February, 1316, total income came to some £340, but this figure includes £80 " de incremento,"

[53] Both accounts are contained in PRO, Min. Accts., SC 6/1239/13 m. 2. None of Maud de Burgh's own accounts have survived.

which may represent an extraordinary levy exacted by the government for the campaign against Edward Bruce. In this case, normal income would thus be £260, which for the entire liberty for twelve months comes out to some £360.[54] Some other evidence, however, suggests that Kilkenny was worth £400–£500 in the fourteenth century. After the death of Countess Joan in 1307, the lordship was held by the royal escheator. His account for the period April 19, 1307–January 23, 1308, shows an income of £317 5s., which extended over a full year would come to about £425.[55] In 1317 the official valuation of Kilkenny was some £475.[56] Lady Elizabeth de Burgh's share of the lordship from August 21, 1348 to April 12, 1349, was worth over £120. Assuming a constant rate of income, total revenue for a full year would thus amount to about £180, and on this basis, the entire lordship would yield some £540 in the mid-fourteenth century.[57] All that can be said with full certainty is that the value of the lordship had increased since 1247, but the rate of increase and the economic reasons for it must remain unknown. It should be pointed out that Carlow was also valued at some £350 in 1247, but under Roger Bigod was generally worth about £700 gross and £450 net; in the extent made at his death in 1306, however, the official valuation was still given as £350.[58]

Kilkenny was partitioned among the three sisters and coheiresses of the last Earl Gilbert in 1317, and the dower portion of Countess Maud was likewise divided after her death in 1320. The liberty, however, was still treated as a unit, with only one seneschal, sheriff, and treasurer. The seneschal held the county court in the name of all three lords, and each received one-third of the profits of pleas and perquisites. There is little evidence to suggest, however, that any of the descendants, with the exception of Lady

[54] PRO, SC 6/1239/13 m. 2. The account was later entered on the Pipe Roll and is printed in *Irish Pipe Roll 16 Edward II* (42nd D. K. Report, 1911), pp. 50–51. The £80 "de incremento" is not specified as such in the Pipe Roll version, and Orpen (*Ireland under the Normans*, III, 95 note 3) thought the £340 total represented regular annual income. For Edward Bruce, see the references cited above, Chapter VI, note 127.

[55] *Irish Pipe Roll I Edward II* (39th D. K. Report, 1907), p. 23.

[56] PRO, Chanc. Misc., C 47/9/23–25.

[57] PRO, Min. Accts., SC 6/1239/21.

[58] Nugent, "Carlow in the Middle Ages," p. 67; PRO, Chanc. Misc., C 47/9/20, 10/17 no. 14.

Elizabeth and her grandson by marriage, Lionel, duke of Clarence, had any real interest in the liberty's affairs, and the problem of absentee landlordism did much to contribute to the decline of Ireland in the later Middle Ages.[59]

The Anglo–Irish lordships deriving from Leinster constituted an important source of wealth and power for their lords. Administratively they were organized as shires, although the duties and powers normally associated with a sheriff were performed by the seneschal. Each lordship also had its own independent financial organization and permanent exchequer. While Irish villeins were theoretically excluded from English law, the lords had the right to grant common law to them, and William Marshal issued such a charter to the Irish of Leinster in 1209.[60] The holders of these liberties, then, commanded a position far superior to that of the lord of a normal English franchise.

While extensive, however, the legal privileges and powers of the Clares as lords of Kilkenny did not assume the same degree of independence and scope as those they enjoyed in their marcher lordships. The major factor determining this situation was undoubtedly the active intervention of the English kings. Edward I attempted with only partial success to break down the structure of marcher privilege; but this policy had been fully anticipated and largely completed by his predecessors in their dealings with the Anglo–Irish baronage. Henry II and John acted vigorously to prevent Strongbow and the Marshals from exercising an authority in Leinster completely free of royal control and from developing a body of law outside the forms of English common law. After the partition of 1247, both Henry III and Edward I upheld this position. As a dispute between Earl Richard and the master of the Knights Templar of Ireland reveals, Henry insisted on the application of common law in the court of the liberty of Kilkenny and on the right of appeal to Dublin from it.[61] Edward, character-

---

[59] PRO, Chanc. Misc., C 47/88/3 no. 56 m. 2; *Irish Pipe Roll 2 Edward III* (43rd D. K. Report, 1912), p. 25; PRO, Min. Accts., SC 6/1239/16, 21; *Cal. Ormond Deeds*, I, no. 694 (11 Edward III). Orpen's study stops in 1333 with the murder of Elizabeth's son William; for the period down to the Elizabethan reconquest, the best general account is in Edmund Curtis, *History of Medieval Ireland* (Dublin, 1923).

[60] It is cited in a plea before the justiciar in 1299. *Cal. Just. Rolls 1295–1303*, p. 271.

[61] *Close Rolls 1253–54*, p. 113; *ibid.* 1254–56, pp. 158–59, 206.

istically, took advantage of every avenue of royal action to insure his ultimate suzerainty. He subjected Kilkenny and the other Leinster lordships to taxation,[62] and regularly held his parliaments within them.[63] He seized Kilkenny in 1302 after default of justice in its court had been proved, and although he quickly returned it, three years later Countess Joan and Ralph de Monthermer could still complain that the king's ministers were interfering in the affairs of the liberty.[64] Although the lordship enjoyed return of writs, its officials could under certain circumstances be treated as royal agents, and the king's own ministers were not excluded in every instance. Finally, the feudal structure introduced by the Norman conquerors in the twelfth century was closely supervised and controlled by Henry II and was from the beginning subject to the same forms of tenure and service that had slowly crystallized in England during the same period. This meant that local customary law was excluded not only from the courts but also from the holding of fees and the descent of land. Control over feudal incidents such as wardship and marriage were reserved to the king, and such military service as was performed was under royal direction. These conditions effectively prevented feudalism in Ireland from developing in the independent manner of the feudal system in the Welsh marches; it soon became static and remained of value only for certain financial and judicial purposes as the payment of scutages and reliefs and the performance of suit of court.[65] In short, in many important respects Kilkenny, like the other Anglo–Irish liberties, more closely approximated the status of a large English franchise than the marcher lordships from which the original Norman conquerors of Ireland had come.

---

[62] On the taxations of 1290–91 and 1300, see *Cal. Docs. Ireland 1285–92*, no. 974; *Cal. Just. Rolls 1295–1303*, p. 304.

[63] Parliaments were held in Kilkenny in 1277, 1290, 1292, 1295, 1296, and 1302, and under Edward II in 1310, 1315, 1316, and in the 1320's. Richardson and Sayles, *The Irish Parliament in the Middle Ages*, pp. 333–36.

[64] *Cal. Chanc. War.*, p. 158; PRO, Ancient Petitions, SC 8/182/9085.

[65] For a full discussion of the whole question, see the pertinent and illuminating remarks of Miss Otway-Ruthven, "Knight-Service in Ireland," pp. 1–15, especially 13–15.

CHAPTER X

CONCLUSIONS

Despite the incomplete nature of the evidence, it is possible to draw some general conclusions about the over-all economic and administrative structure of the Clare inheritance in the thirteenth and early fourteenth centuries. The sources of revenue may be divided into three broad types:

1) Manorial income, comprising a wide assortment of different kinds of revenue, the most important of which were rents and the sale of demesne produce. Relatively substantial sums were also realized from such items as issues of mills and forests, sale of villein works, lease of pasture, court fines and fees, and miscellaneous seigneurial dues. In general, these subsidiary sources of income were more prominent on the Welsh and Irish estates than in England. The emphasis on direct demesne production, both for consumption by the household and for sale to local markets, was most pronounced on the English manors. In addition, these manors, unlike those on the march or in Ireland, show ample evidence throughout the period of this study of a continual expansion in the amount of land brought under direct cultivation. It should be noted, however, that this expansion was accomplished mainly by the purchase of small properties appurtenant to the already existing demesnes, not by the clearing of waste or forests. There is no evidence to suggest a process of demesne expansion in Ireland, and in Wales it was largely replaced by a politically inspired policy of bringing the outlying commotes under direct control by dispossessing the local chieftains. In view of these disparate tendencies, the normal consequence would be a relatively greater emphasis on nonagricultural sources of revenue in Kilkenny and the marcher lordships than in the English bailiwicks. In all three areas, however, rents and the sale of demesne produce remained the major sources of income. To judge from the very

296

unsatisfactory evidence, rents seem to have been more important in Kilkenny than the sale of agricultural commodities. This reliance on rents would be natural in an area of relative geographical isolation and of relatively marginal interest to the earls. Both in England and Wales, however, grain production, supplemented by the sale of stock and occasionally some other commodities such as wool, was the dominant feature of the economy. In neither area did the Clares exhibit that tendency to a *rentier* status found on some estates by the beginning of the fourteenth century [1] and universal among the great baronial landholders by the end of the century.[2]

2) Income from boroughs, including burgage rents, prise of ale and other dues, and the tolls or farms of markets, mills and fisheries. Again, these items were more lucrative in Wales and presumably in Ireland than in England, reflecting the greater commercial importance of the boroughs in these areas.

3) Income from judicial and feudal resources, including honorial and franchisal courts and feudal incidents such as reliefs and scutages. In all three great land units these items remained of importance, but in large part only for fiscal, not military or political, purposes. In the marcher lordships they were further supplemented by heavy tributary rents and dues not obtaining elsewhere.

Under the last Earl Gilbert gross annual income was close to £6,000, with the English estates supplying some £3,000 to £3,500 of the total, the Welsh estates over £2,000, and Kilkenny about £400 to £500. Unfortunately, the absence of any central financial records in this period makes it impossible to determine how much cash was actually delivered to the earl's wardrobe in any given year, or to determine the amount expended on wages, household necessities such as meat and grain, or costlier items, furs, armor, spices, and wines. Expenditure on these commodities must have been lavish,[3] and a good indication of the amounts involved can be discerned from the fact that Earl Gilbert the Red owed almost

[1] See above, p. 213 and note 40.
[2] For these developments, cf. Holmes, *Estates*, pp. 114–20, and Rees, *South Wales*, *passim*.
[3] The adverse economic consequences of the "noble way of life" have recently been emphasized in Miller, "The English Economy in the Thirteenth Century," pp. 31–32.

£750 to some Flemish merchants in the early 1270's, presumably for the purchase of clothing and luxury goods.[4] The estate profits were probably balanced by household purchases and other expenses such as the munitioning of the Welsh castles, but no precise figures are available from the extant sources.

The administrative organization varied from area to area, and a detailed analysis is only possible for the period after the mid-thirteenth century. The English lands were divided into a number of bailiwicks which did not correspond to the original territorial composition of the honors controlled by the family. The Welsh lordships retained their unity, but while Usk was administered as a separate lordship, with its own seneschal and receiver, Caerleon and Gwynllwg were governed as dependent members of the lordship of Glamorgan. Both Glamorgan and Kilkenny were organized as shires, but there were some important differences between them. Unlike Glamorgan, there was no separate chancery in Kilkenny, and in this liberty the normal functions of the sheriff were assumed by a seneschal, with the sheriff himself performing much the same duties as an estate bailiff or bailiff of fees on the English properties. On the other hand, the Glamorgan exchequer was only established at Cardiff after 1295, while the exchequer at Kilkenny had had a continuous existence since the early thirteenth century. It served all of Leinster under the Marshals, and it remained as the central financial office for the Clare portion of that lordship, with the other liberties deriving from Leinster developing their own exchequers. Finally, the entire administrative structure was controlled by the offices and personnel of the central household, the wardrobe (which superseded the chamber by the mid-thirteenth century), the auditors, attorneys, and the council.

Many of the most important features of the administrative organization do not come into clear focus until the turn of the fourteenth century. For example, the earliest direct mention of the Glamorgan coroner dates from 1299, and the fullest information on the activities of the council and local personnel such as the receivers and the bailiffs of fees dates mainly from the period 1296–1314. The seemingly late appearance of such institutions as the wardrobe and the system of feodaries, however, is largely

[4] *Cal. Close Rolls 1272–79*, p. 338.

due to the chance survival of the records. In all probability, they were well developed under Earl Gilbert the Red, and possibly under Earl Richard as well. Furthermore, the tendency towards the professionalization of the administrative staff, such as that noted for the seneschals of the English bailiwicks, had a continuous development from the time of the first Earl Gilbert, an achievement all the more remarkable in view of the limited supply of trained personnel available in the thirteenth century. On the other hand, certain administrative arrangements, for example the system of dependent wardrobers and the establishment of an exchequer at Cardiff to replace the receivership, date from the years which separated the Red Earl and his son. Both the continuity of the inheritance and the increased efficiency of its organization owed much to Countess Joan and Ralph de Monthermer; but less than a decade later, the entire administrative and territorial structure was permanently shattered.

Landed property was the basis of wealth and political influence in the middle ages. The stability of the family inheritance was the most important matter facing the members of the nobility, and every effort was made to provide for its continuity from generation to generation. But the accidents of birth and death could not be anticipated. Just as the Clares themselves had prospered from favorable marriage connections in the twelfth and thirteenth centuries, the partition of the estates brought about by the sudden death of the last earl, and the events attendant upon that partition, provide a striking example of the importance which royal favor and well-endowed heiresses assumed in the fortunes of the great noble houses. The component lordships and honors into which the Clare estates were divided augmented substantially the wealth and power of the heirs and their descendants and formed an important part of the subsequent inheritances of some of the greatest and most famous families in England in the later Middle Ages.

Appendix I

VALUES OF SOME CLARE ESTATES

The first set of figures records the government valuations of 1262 and 1266/67 (PRO, Rentals and Surveys, General Series, SC 11/610 m. 1 [Wales], mm. 2–7 [England, collated with *Close Rolls 1261–64*, pp. 284–93]); the third the valuation of 1317–20 (PRO, Chancery Miscellanea, C 47/9/23–24–25). The middle set is taken from the surviving estate accounts of the period 1290–1315; references and explanatory material are given in the appropriate footnote. In addition, a few of the most important estates, especially those of the honor of Gloucester, have been included for comparative purposes, although no original accounts have survived to provide a check on the official valuations. Fractions have been omitted.

A: ENGLAND

	1262–67			*ca.* 1300			1317–20		
	£	s.	d.	£	s.	d.	£	s.	d.
Bardfield (Essex)	59	19	0				124	18	9
Bircham [1] (Norfolk)	9	0	0	14 10	6 12	10 3	18	1	6
Bletchingley [2] (Surrey)	52	7	4	72	1	1	55	0	0
Brasted [3] (Kent)				54	1	10	53	10	11
Clare manor [4] (Suffolk)	126	11	9	288	3	0	191	6	6
Clare borough [5] (Suffolk)				16	10	2	20	7	6
Claret [6] (Essex)	14	15	3	18	2	9	18	1	1
Crimplesham [7] (Norfolk)	8	0	5	15	13	7	11	2	8
Dacherst [8] (Kent)				67	17	7	76	19	7
Fairford (Glos)	92	3	0				93	11	9

300

A: ENGLAND

	1262–67			ca. 1300			1317–20		
	£	s.	d.	£	s.	d.	£	s.	d.
Great Marlowe (Bucks)	90	15	9				70	0	0
Hadlow [9] (Kent)				38	2	8	44	16	8
Hanley (Worcs)	53	0	6				42	14	3
Hundon (Suffolk)	103	1	7				139	6	8
Lackenheath [10] (Suffolk)				13	7	8	15	16	6
Rotherfield [11] (Surrey)	75	9	2	82	7	0	73	10	5
Rothwell (N'hants)	130	3	2				160	16	4
Tewkesbury [12] (Glos)	169	2	9				233	12	0
Thornbury [13] (Glos)	131	9	4				233	4	11
Tonbridge [14] (Kent)				10	8	5	13	16	5
Wyke [15] (Dorset)				34	0	0	14	3	7
Yalding [16] (Kent)				79	10	5	66	19	6
				69	18	1			

B: WALES

	1262–67			ca. 1300			1317–20		
	£	s.	d.	£	s.	d.	£	s.	d.
Caerleon [17] (Caerleon)				124	9	0	110	1	5
Caerphilly [18] (Glam)				136	16	3	173	5	10
Cardiff [19] (Glam)	96	1	3	113	1	7	124	3	3
Dowlais [20] (Gwynllwg)	22	2	5	22	5	2	34	18	6
Llanbleddian [21] (Glam)	74	10	5	97	3	9	126	18	10
Llantrissent [22] (Usk)				29	4	9	63	8	9
				89	14	0			

B: WALES

	1262–67			ca. 1300			1317–20		
	£	s.	d.	£	s.	d.	£	s.	d.
Llantwit [23] (Glam)	109	5	1	96	16	4	160	5	0
Newport [24] (Gwynllwg)	40	11	9	38	1	8	48	7	10
Rhymny [25] (Gwynllwg)	63	7	6	61 66	9 16	10 3	85	0	8
Roath [26] (Glam)	26	4	4	14	15	1	45	0	0
Stowe [27] (Gwynllwg)	11	0	4	41	0	9	40	0	0
Trellech [28] (Usk)	57	1	4	54	8	0	54	19	11
Troy [29] (Usk)	20	8	3	48 49	15 11	8 4	58	11	8
Usk [30] (Usk)	150	0	8	280 217 315	5 8 18	5 1 10	289	18	11

NOTES TO APPENDIX I

[1] PRO, Min. Accts., SC 6/930/1–2 (1310–11, 1311–12). All figures exclude arrears collected for the preceding year.

[2] PRO, Exchequer, KR Escheators' Accts., E 136/1/19a m. 4 (1299–1300). Includes both manor and borough.

[3] E 136/1/19a m. 4 (1299–1300).

[4] SC 6/992/8 (1308–9).

[5] SC 6/992/9 (1312–13). Both borough and manor seem to have been valued together in 1262–67.

[6] SC 6/838/9 (1307–8).

[7] SC 6/933/18 (1304–5).

[8] E 136/1/19a m. 1 (1299–1300).

[9] E 136/1/19a m. 1 (1299–1300).

[10] SC 6/1001/5 (1290–91). No separate figure for Lackenheath is given in the 1262–67 valuations.

[11] E 136/1/19a m. 1 (1299–1300).

[12] Includes manor and borough.

[13] Includes manor and borough.

[14] E 136/1/19a m. 1 (1299–1300). Borough only.

[15] SC 6/834/22 (1294–95).

[16] E 136/1/19a m. 1 (1299–1300), SC 6/1247/11 (1307–8).

[17] The 1317 figure includes manor, borough and bedelry, and a lump sum for

all three has been calculated from the early fourteenth century estate accounts, as follows:

manor £63 15s. 10d. (including over £28 "receptiones forinseci"). SC 6/1247/17 (1303–4).

borough £48 1s. 7d. SC 6/920/18 (1309–10).

bedelry £12 11s. 7d. SC 6/920/16 (1304–5).

[18] SC 6/1202/7 mm. 4–5 (Badlesmere's account; 1314–15). Includes Caerphilly castle and manor and its members with Uwch– and Is-Caiach. Figures from this account do not include extraordinary income derived from the sale of grain and stock and then turned over to Badlesmere's successor, Payn de Turberville.

[19] SC 6/1202/7 m. 1 (1314–15). Does not include the actual or estimated value of the *comitatus Glamorganciae*.

[20] SC 6/1202/7 mm. 7–8 (1314–15).

[21] SC 6/1202/7 m. 9 (1314–15). Includes the dependent commote of Talyfan.

[22] SC 6/923/25 (1307–8), 1247/19 (1308–9).

[23] SC 6/1202/7 m. 10 (1314–15). The 1317 figure includes the valuation of Rhuthun *patria*.

[24] SC 6/1202/7 m. 5 (1314–15). Does not include the actual or estimated value of the *comitatus* of Gwynllwg lordship.

[25] SC 6/925/5 (1300–1), 1202/7 m. 7 (1314–15).

[26] SC 6/1202/7 mm. 1–2 (1314–15).

[27] SC 6/1202/7 mm. 6–7 (1314–15).

[28] SC 6/927/9 (1305–6). Includes manor and borough. SC 6/927/9 is the receiver's account for Usk lordship, and the figure for Trellech thus represents net rather than gross income.

[29] SC 6/926/16–17 (1307–8, 1310–11).

[30] SC 927/9 (1305–6), 1247/29 (1308–9), 927/21 (1316–17). Includes manor, borough, and bedelry. The figures are taken from the receivers' accounts for these years, and thus represent net rather than gross income. They also include manorial and burgage rents, which were collected directly by the receiver rather than by the estate officials themselves.

APPENDIX II

LIST OF ESTATES IN THE PARTITION OF 1317–20

The following lists record the shares of the Clare inheritance acquired by the husbands of the last Earl Gilbert's three full sisters. Only demesne estates are included; knights' fees and advowsons are omitted, as are manors held by the earl by virtue of wardship, escheat, or temporary royal grant. Scattered rents, tenements, and courts are not detailed. A "(d)" indicates that the estate was held in dower by the last earl's widow, and reverted to the heir at her death in 1320.

I. HUGH D'AUDLEY (PRO, Chancery Miscellanea, C 47/9/23)

A. England
Buckingham: Little Brickhill.
Gloucestershire: Campden, Rendcombe, Thornbury manor and borough.
Huntingdon: Southoe.
Kent: Brasted (d), Dacherst, Edinbridge, Hadlow, Northfrith forest, Tonbridge castle and borough, Yalding.
Norfolk: Crimplesham, Warham (d), Wells (d), Wiveton.
Northants: Rothwell.
Southants: Clatford, Mapledurham, Petersfield borough.
Suffolk: Disning (d).
Surrey: Bletchingley manor and borough (d), Camberwell, Chipstead, Ockham (d), Tillingdon (d), Titsey.
Wiltshire: Wexcombe (d), Kinwardstone hundred (d).
Bedford, Huntingdon, London, Oxford, Wiltshire: various rents, courts and tenements.

B. Wales
The lordship of Gwynllwg, including the manor and borough of Newport, the *curia comitatus*, Stowe, Rhymny, Dowlais, Dyffryn Ebbw, Machen *patria*.

C. Kilkenny
" Tertia pars placitorum senescalli, vicecomitis et thesaurarii et tertia pars domus placitorum."
Kilkenny borough, Callan [pleas] (d), Coillaugh, Jerpoint manor and borough (d), Thomastown.

304

II. HUGH DESPENSER (PRO, Chancery Miscellanea, C 47/9/24)

A. England

Berkshire: Stanford (d).
Buckingham: Great Marlowe (d).
Gloucestershire: Fairford (d), Tewkesbury manor and borough (d).
Oxford: Caversham (d), Chadlington hundred, Burford vill (d); reversion of Burford and Skipton manors held by Isabella de Clare.
Somerset: courts and tenements.
Surrey: Eridge, Rotherfield manor and hundred.
Worcester: Bushley (d), Hanley manor and castle (d), Malvern chace (d).

B. Wales

The lordship of Glamorgan. For a full list of manors, boroughs, and commotes see above, Chapter VIII and *Cartae de Glamorgan*, III, 1050–56.

C. Kilkenny

One-third of pleas *as above*.
Kilkenny castle and manor, Callan [farms and rents] (d), Dunfert, Rosbercon borough.

III. ROGER DAMORY (PRO, Chancery Miscellanea, C 47/9/25)

A. England (cf. also *Cal. Inq. Post Mortem*, VI, no. 129)

Dorset: Cranbourne manor and hundred, Pimperne manor and half hundred, Portland, Steeple with [Hasilor, Rowbarrow and Rushmore] hundreds, Tarrant Gunville, Wareham borough, Weymouth borough, Wyke.
Essex: Bardfield, Claret.
Hertford: Standon, lands in Popeshall.
Kent: Southfrith forest, Westpeckham.
Norfolk: Bircham, Walsingham.
Somerset: Easton (d) [already held of the Clares by Damory before 1314].
Suffolk: Clare castle, manor and borough, Hundon, Lackenheath, Southwold, Sudbury manor and borough, Woodhall.
Cambridge, Essex, Hertford, Huntingdon, Norfolk, Suffolk: various rents, tenements and courts, along with the pleas and perquisites of the court of the honor of Clare in these counties.

B. Wales

Llangwm [two-thirds of manor].
The lordships of Usk and Caerleon (d), including Usk castle, manor and borough, Cwmcarvan, Llantrissent castle and manor, New Grange, Trellech castle, manor and borough, Troy, with Usk and Trellech bedelries; Caerleon castle, manor and borough, Liswerry, Little Tintern, Tregrug castle and manor, Undy, with Caerleon, Edelegan and Llefnydd bedelries.

C. Kilkenny

One-third of pleas *as above*.
Ballycallan, Callan [borough and manor] (d), Fermaill, Kilmanagh borough (d), Loughmedran, Offerlane, Palmerston.

APPENDIX III

ECCLESIASTICAL OFFICES OF BOGO DE CLARE

This list, with some additions and corrections, is based on A. B. Emden, *Biographical Register of the University of Oxford to 1500* (3 vols.; Oxford, 1957–59), I, *sub nom.* When known, the year of institution, the patron, and the value of the office are stated. Positions are presumed to be held until death unless otherwise specified.

A. Rectorships

1. Callan, Kilkenny (Ossory diocese). Papal dispensation at the request of Richard de Clare, earl of Gloucester, granted May, 1255 (*Cal. Papal Letters*, I, 317).

2. St. Peter's-in-the-East, Oxford (Lincoln diocese). Presented by King Henry III, August, 1259 (*Cal. Pat. Rolls 1258–66*, p. 40). Valued at 30 marks (*Reg. Sutton*, II, 3).

3. Levington, Cambridge (Ely diocese). Held by 1261 (*Reg. Sutton*, II, 3).

4. Chievely, Berkshire (Salisbury diocese). Held by 1261 (*Reg. Sutton*, II, 3).

5. Simonburn, Northumberland (Durham diocese). Held by 1261 (*Reg. Sutton*, II, 3). Valued at 500 marks [*rectius* 50?] (*Reg. Romeyn*, I, 397).

6. Holywell [*Sancta Crucis*], Oxford (Lincoln diocese). Held by 1262 (*Cart. Hospital St. John the Baptist*, II, 364).

7. Adlingfleet, York (York archdiocese). Presented by Maud, dowager countess of Gloucester, January, 1268 (*Reg. Giffard*, p. 20), but not instituted after protracted litigation (above, pp. 183–84).

8. Kilkhampton, Cornwall (Exeter diocese). Held by 1275 (*Register of Walter Bronescombe, 1257–80*, ed. F. L. Hingeston-Randolph [London, 1889], p. 147). Valued at 10 marks (*Reg. Sutton*, II, 3).

9. Rotherfield, Sussex (Chichester diocese). Presented by Richard de Clare, earl of Gloucester, May, 1258, but not instituted until 1280 (*Registrum Roffense*, pp. 591–2, 595). Valued at 30 marks (*Reg. Sutton*, II, 3).

10. Thatcham, Berkshire (Salisbury diocese). Held by 1280 (*Reg. Sutton*, II, 3). Valued at 30 marks (*ibid.*).

11. Eynsford, Kent (Canterbury archdiocese). Held by 1280 (*Reg. Sutton*, II, 3). Valued at 20 marks (*ibid.*).

12. Swanscombe, Kent (Rochester diocese). Held by 1280 (*Reg. Sutton*, II, 3). Valued at 20 marks (*ibid.*).

13. A moiety of Dorking, Surrey (Winchester diocese). Held by 1280 (*Reg. Sutton*, II, 3). Valued at 20 marks (*ibid.*).

14. Dunmow, Essex (London diocese). Presented by Richard or Gilbert de Clare, earls of Gloucester, as it was a family advowson (*Close Rolls 1261–64*, p. 289). Held by 1280 (*Reg. Sutton*, II, 3).

15. Polstead, Suffolk (Norwich diocese). Held by 1280 (*Reg. Sutton*, II, 3). Valued at 30 marks (*ibid.*).

16. Saham Toney, Norfolk (Norwick diocese). Held by 1280 (*Reg. Sutton*, II, 3). Valued at 20 marks (*ibid.*).

17. A moiety of Doncaster, York (York archdiocese). Held by 1280 (*Reg. Sutton*, II, 3). Valued at 25 marks in 1280 (*ibid.*) and at 4 marks in 1291 (*Reg. Romeyn*, I, 397).

18. Llansoy, Usk lordship [now Monmouthshire] (Llandaff diocese). Presented by Maud, dowager countess of Gloucester (cf. PRO, Rentals and Surveys, General Series, SC 11/610 m. 1). Held by 1280 (*Reg. Sutton*, II, 3). Valued at £5 (*ibid.*).

19. Fordingbridge, Southampton (Winchester diocese). Presented by Richard or Gilbert de Clare, earls of Gloucester, as it was a family advowson (*Close Rolls 1261–64*, p. 285). Held by 1280 (*Cal. Pat. Rolls 1272–81*, p. 451). Valued at 40 marks (*Reg. Sutton*, II, 3). See also no. 25 below.

20. Acaster Malbis, York (York archdiocese). Held by 1280 (*Reg. Sutton*, II, 3). Valued at 10 marks in 1280 (*ibid.*) and at 40 marks in 1291 (*Reg. Romeyn*, I, 397).

21. Whiston, Northampton (Lincoln diocese). Presented by Gilbert de Clare, earl of Gloucester, May, 1280, vacated December, 1280 (*Reg. Sutton*, II, 3, 7).

22. Settrington, York (York archdiocese). Presented by Roger Bigod, earl of Norfolk, February, 1283 (*Reg. Wickwane*, p. 114). Valued at £100 (*Reg. Romeyn*, I, 397).

23. Melton Mowbray, Leicester (Lincoln diocese). Presented by Roger de Mowbray, acquired in 1284, vacated by 1286–87 (Giuseppi, Introduction, pp. 13–16).

24. Frant, Sussex (Chichester diocese). Held by 1284 (Giuseppi, p. 19).

25. "Langeford," held by 1284 (Giuseppi, p. 19). Probably another form of Fordingbridge. See no. 19 above.

26. Hemmingbrough, York (York archdiocese). Presented by the prior of Durham, September, 1287 (*Reg. Romeyn*, II, 34). Valued at 250 marks (*ibid.*, I, 397).

27. Colwich, Stafford (Lichfield diocese). Presented by John de Colwich, November, 1288–May, 1289, vacated through lack of sufficient title, November–December, 1289 (*Cal. Papal Letters*, I, 509–10).

28. Pickhill, York (York archdiocese). Held by 1291 (*Reg. Romeyn*, I, 397). Valued at 60 marks (*ibid.*).

29. Tiverton, Devon (Exeter diocese). Presented by Isabella de Fortibus, dowager countess of Devon and Aumale. Held by 1293 (cf. *Cal. Pat. Rolls 1292–1301*, p. 127).

30. Hailsham, Sussex (Chichester diocese). Held by 1294 (*Reg. Winchelsey*, I, 103–4).

31. A moiety of Walpole, Norfolk (Norwich diocese). Held by 1294 (*Cal. Pat. Rolls 1292–1301*, p. 118).

B. Canonries and Prebends

1. Canon and prebendary of Howden, York (York archdiocese). Presented by King Henry III *sede vacante*, September, 1265 (*Cal. Pat. Rolls 1258–66*, p. 449), but failed to obtain admission (*ibid.*, p. 510). Compensated with the office of councilor of Durham Priory Cathedral and a yearly pension of 100 marks in 1272 (*Durham Annals and Documents of the Thirteenth Century*, ed. Frank Barlow [Surtees Society, vol. CLV, 1945], p. 87).

2. Canon of St. Peter's, York, and prebendary of Masham (York archdiocese). Presented by King Henry III *sede vacante*, November, 1265 (*Cal. Pat. Rolls 1258–66*, p. 495). Valued at 250 or 300 marks in 1291 (*York Minster Fasti*, II, 52; *Reg. Romeyn*, I, 397).

3. Canon and prebendary of Exeter (Exeter diocese). Held by 1267 (*Reg. Bronescombe*, p. 137).

4. Canon of Holy Trinity, Chichester, and prebendary of Oving, Sussex (Chichester diocese). Held by 1284–85 (Giuseppi, pp. 19, 31).

5. Canon of Wells (Bath and Wells diocese). Held by 1284 (*Calendar of the Manuscripts of the Dean and Chapter of Wells* [Historical Manuscripts Commission, 1907–14], I, 34).

6. Prebendary of Wilton, York (York archdiocese). See below, "Treasurer of York."

7. Prebendary of Newthorpe, York (York archdiocese). See below, "Treasurer of York."

8. Prebendary of Lichfield (Coventry and Lichfield diocese). Presented by John de Colwich, November, 1288–May, 1289, vacated through lack of sufficient title, November–December, 1289 (*Cal. Papal Letters*, I, 509–10).

C. Other Ecclesiastical Dignities

1. Papal chaplain. Appointed by Pope Alexander IV, May, 1255 (*Cal. Papal Letters*, I, 317).

2. Dean of the royal free chapel of St. Mary's, Stafford. Presented by King Henry III, September, 1259 (*Cal. Pat. Rolls 1258–66*, p. 42).

3. Pensioned councilor of Durham Priory Cathedral. Held by 1272 (see above, "Canon and Prebendary of Howden").

4. Precentor of Chichester. Held by 1283 (*Reg. Epist. Peckham*, III, 1074).

5. Treasurer of York. Presented by King Edward I *sede vacante*, September, 1285 (*Cal. Pat. Rolls 1281–92*, p. 193), vacated by April, 1293 (*ibid. 1292–1301*, p. 9). Valued at 600 marks, with the prebends of Wilton and Newthorpe attached (*Reg. Romeyn*, I, 396–97).

6. Chancellor of Llandaff. Held by 1287 (Browne Willis, *Survey of the Cathedral Church of Llandaff*, pp. 120–24).

BIBLIOGRAPHY

MANUSCRIPT SOURCES

Note on Manuscripts

The bulk of the unpublished documents used in this study are located in the Public Record Office, London. The chancery enrollments, including the Patent, Close, Charter, and Fine Rolls, the Inquisitions Post Mortem, the Inquisitions Miscellaneous and the Welsh Rolls, are well represented by a series of published texts or calendars. The originals of some of the more important documents in these classes were consulted, but reference has usually been made to the printed editions. Important information relating to the Clare family was also found in the still unpublished chancery series, especially the Chancery Miscellanea and the Parliamentary and Council Proceedings. Of particular value were the documents in the Chancery Miscellanea recording the partition of the Marshal estates in 1246–47 and the partition of the Clare inheritance itself in 1317–20.

The exchequer documents were found to contain much useful, if scattered, information. The Memoranda Rolls of both the King's Remembrancer (KR) and Lord Treasurer's Remembrancer (LTR) sides of the exchequer under Henry III, Edward I, and Edward II were examined. Additional material was found in the following classes of documents: Exchequer of Pleas, Plea Rolls; KR Accounts Various; Ecclesiastical Documents; Escheators' Accounts; Ancient Extents; KR and LTR Miscellanea; Originalia Rolls; and the unpublished Pipe Rolls for Henry III and Edward I, especially those dating from the period of Richard de Clare's wardship in 1230–43.

Of great value were the judicial records. Some material was contained in the rolls of the Justices Itinerant, but for the purposes of this study the most important documents were the records of cases heard in the Court of King's Bench. The still unpublished Curia Regis Rolls for Henry III (including *de banco* and *coram rege* rolls) contained useful information. The most important records were the Coram Rege Rolls for the reign of Edward I, which shed much light on a number of topics, particularly on the relation of the Clares as marcher lords to the royal authority. The Coram Rege Rolls for Edward II were found to be of little importance.

The Duchy of Lancaster records contained occasional pieces of information. The following series were used: Ancient Deeds; Ministers' Accounts; Cartae Miscellaneae; and Returns of Knights' Fees.

Of particular importance were those documents classified under the

309

heading of Special Collections. The series of Ancient Correspondence, Court Rolls, and Rentals and Surveys included much valuable material. By far the most important single series of documents, however, was the Ministers' Accounts, comprising both manorial and receivers' accounts. Some of these documents are accounts of royal keepers of the Clare estates, later enrolled on the Pipe Rolls. Most of them, however, are original family accounts, which in one way or another came into the possession of the Crown and have thus been preserved among the government archives. A good series of accounts for the lordships of Usk and Caerleon, dating from the late thirteenth and early fourteenth centuries, shed light on the economy of the estates and the administrative organization. Fewer accounts have survived for the English estates for the period of this study, but those that have survived contained information of great value, especially the receiver's account for the bailiwick of the honor of Clare for 1307–8.

The documents in the Department of Manuscripts of the British Museum, including the collections of Cotton, Harleian, and Stowe Manuscripts, along with the Additional Manuscripts and Charters, were of occasional value. Particular mention should be made of the late fourteenth century Mortimer Cartularies contained in Additional MS 6041 and Harleian MS 1240.

List of Unpublished Documents Cited

1. British Museum

a. Additional MSS
   6041
   6159
   36985

b Cotton MSS
   Cleopatra A VII
   Julius B XII
   Nero A IV
   Vitellius A VIII
   Appendix xxi

c. Harleian MSS
   1240
   4835

d. Stowe MS
   553

e. Additional Charters
   1263–4
   1531
   20039
   20398

2. Public Record Office

a. Chancery

　　C 47 (Chancery Miscellanea) 3/32, 9/20–21, 9/23–25, 9/52, 9/59, 10/17, 14/6, 22/4, 88/3, 88/4
　　C 49 (Parliamentary and Council Proceedings) 1/9, 2/5, 2/13, 4/22, 44/8, 44/9
　　C 60 (Fine Rolls) 59, 63
　　C 72 (Scutage Rolls) 2, 7
　　C 77 (Welsh Rolls) 5
　　C 132 (Inquisitions Post Mortem, Henry III) 27/5
　　C 133 (Inquisitions Post Mortem, Edward I) 77/3
　　C 145 (Inquisitions Miscellaneous) files 25–30

b. Duchy of Lancaster

　　DL 25 (Ancient Deeds, Series L) 2021
　　DL 27 (Ancient Deeds, Series LS) 47
　　DL 29 (Ministers' Accounts) 1/3, 665/10334
　　DL 36 (Cartae Miscellaneae) 1/243
　　DL 40 (Returns of Knights' Fees) 1/4

c. Exchequer

　　E 13 (Exchequer of Pleas, Plea Rolls) 17
　　E 101 (KR Accounts Various) 10/4, 12/17, 13/23, 15/27, 91/9–10, 353/18, 357/28, 360/17
　　E 135 (KR Ecclesiastical Documents) 7/1
　　E 136 (KR Escheators' Accounts) 1/19a, 1/29, 238/23
　　E 142 (KR Ancient Extents) 88
　　E 159 (KR Memoranda Rolls) 1–3, 59, 70, 71, 91, 112
　　E 163 (KR Miscellanea) 1/41, 2/30
　　E 175 (KR Parliamentary and Council Proceedings) 1/8
　　E 368 (LTR Memoranda Rolls) 1, 62
　　E 370 (LTR Miscellanea) 1/14
　　E 371 (LTR Originalia Rolls) 81
　　E 372 (LTR Pipe Rolls) 62, 63, 66, 68, 69, 80, 81, 85, 87, 108, 111, 117, 162

d. Judicial Records

　　JI 1 (Assize Rolls) 59, 1050, 1149
　　KB 26 (Curia Regis Rolls, Henry III) 121, 131, 146, 159, 177, 191
　　KB 27 (Coram Rege Rolls, Edward I–) 11, 21, 24, 41, 57, 62, 64, 65, 67, 94, 118, 122–146, 156, 160, 259

e. Special Collections

　　SC 1 (Ancient Correspondence) 16/40, 30/199, 45/152, 155, 157, 159–63
　　SC 2 (Court Rolls) 213/34–35, 213/112, 214/1–2
　　SC 6 (Ministers' Accounts) bundles 824, 834, 838, 868, 920, 922, 923, 925, 926, 927, 930, 933, 992, 1001, 1028, 1094, 1109, 1117, 1202, 1239, 1247
　　SC 8 (Ancient Petitions) 182/9085
　　SC 11 (Rentals and Surveys, General Series) rolls 22, 610
　　SC 12 (Rentals and Surveys, Portfolio Series) 18/32

PUBLISHED PRIMARY SOURCES

Annales Cambriae. Ed. J. WILLIAMS AP ITHEL. Rolls Series XX, 1860.
Annales de Burton. Ed. H. R. LUARD. *Annales Monastici,* vol. I, Rolls Series XXXVI, 1864.
Annales de Margam. Ed. H. R. LUARD. *Annales Monastici,* vol. I, Rolls Series XXXVI, 1864.
Annales de Theokesberia. Ed. H. R. LUARD. *Annales Monastici,* vol. I, Rolls Series XXXVI, 1864.
Annales Monasterii de Oseneia. Ed. H. R. LUARD. *Annales Monastici,* vol. IV, Rolls Series XXXVI, 1869.
Annales Monasterii de Waverleia. Ed. H. R. LUARD. *Annales Monastici,* vol. II, Rolls Series XXXVI, 1865.
Annales Prioratus de Dunstaplia. Ed. H. R. LUARD. *Annales Monastici,* vol. III, Rolls Series XXXVI, 1866.
Annales Prioratus de Wigornia. Ed. H. R. LUARD. *Annales Monastici,* vol. IV, Rolls Series XXXVI, 1869.
Annals of Innisfallen. Ed. and trans. SEAN MAC AIRT. Dublin: Institute of Advanced Studies, 1951.
Annals of Ireland 1162–1370, in *Chartularies of St. Mary's, Dublin.* Ed. J. T. GILBERT. Rolls Series LXXX, 1884–86.
Annals of Loch Cé. Ed. and trans. W. M. HENNESSY. Rolls Series LIV, 1871.
The Black Book of Limerick. Ed. REV. J. MacCAFFREY. Dublin, 1907.
Brut Y Tywysogyon: Peniarth MS. 20 Version [translation]. Ed. THOMAS JONES. Board of Celtic Studies, History and Law Series, no. XI, Cardiff, 1952.
Brut Y Tywysogyon: Red Book of Hergest Version. Ed. THOMAS JONES. Board of Celtic Studies, History and Law Series, no. XVI, Cardiff, 1955.
Calendar of Ancient Correspondence Concerning Wales. Ed. J. G. EDWARDS. Board of Celtic Studies, History and Law Series, no. II, Cardiff, 1935.
Calendar of Chancery Warrants 1244–1326. H. M. Stationery Office, 1927.
Calendar of Charter Rolls 1226– . H. M. Stationery Office, 1903– .
Calendar of Christ Church [Dublin] *Deeds.* 20th Report of the Deputy Keeper of the Public Records, Ireland, Dublin: H. M. Stationery Office, 1888.
Calendar of Close Rolls 1272– . H. M. Stationery Office, 1900– .
Calendar of Documents relating to Ireland 1171–1307. H. M. Stationery Office. 5 vols., 1875–86.
Calendar of Documents relating to Scotland 1108–1509. Ed. J. BAIN. 4 vols. Edinburgh, 1881–88.
Calendar of Feet of Fines for Bedfordshire. Ed. G. HERBERT FOWLER. Bedford Historical Record Society, vol. XII, 1928.
Calendar of Feet of Fines for Buckingham [1195–1260]. Ed. M. W. HUGHES. Buckinghamshire Record Society, vol. IV, 1940.
Calendar of Feet of Fines for Suffolk. Ed. WALTER RYE. Suffolk Institute of Archaeology and Natural History, 1900.
Calendar of Fine Rolls 1272– . H. M. Stationery Office, 1911– .
Calendar of Inquisitions Miscellaneous. H. M. Stationery Office, 1916– .
Calendar of Inquisitions Post Mortem, Henry III– . H. M. Stationery Office, 1904– .
Calendar of Justiciary Rolls, Ireland, 1295–1307. Dublin: H. M. Stationery Office, 1906–14.

Calendar of Justiciary Rolls, Ireland, 1308–14. Dublin: Stationery Office, 1932.
Calendar of Letter Books of the City of London, Letter Book B. Ed. REGINALD SHARPE. London, 1900.
Calendar of Liberate Rolls 1226– . H. M. Stationery Office, 1917– .
Calendar of Ormond Deeds (1172–1603). Ed. EDMUND CURTIS. 6 vols. Irish MSS Commission, 1933–43.
Calendar of Papal Letters 1198– . H. M. Stationery Office, 1894– .
Calendar of Patent Rolls 1232– . H. M. Stationery Office, 1906– .
Calendar of Plea Rolls of the Exchequer of the Jews. Eds. J. M. RIGG and H. JENKINSON. Jewish Historical Society, 1905–29.
Calendar of the Gormanston Register. Eds. JAMES MILLS and M. J. McENERY. Royal Society of Antiquaries of Ireland, 1916.
Calendar of the Manuscripts of the Dean and Chapter of Wells. Historical MSS Commission, 1907–14.
Calendar of Welsh Rolls [1277–94], in *Calendar of Chancery Rolls, Various, 1277–1326.* H. M. Stationery Office, 1912.
Cartae Antiquae (Rolls 11–20). Ed. J. CONWAY DAVIES. Pipe Roll Society, vol. LXXI, new ser. XXXIII, 1957.
Cartae et alia munimenta quae ad dominium de Glamorgancia pertinent. Ed. G. T. CLARK. 6 vols. 2nd ed.; Cardiff, 1910.
Cartulary of Oseney Abbey, V. Ed. H. E. SALTER. Oxford Historical Series, vol. XCVIII, 1935.
Cartulary of St. Mark's Hospital, Bristol. Ed. C. D. ROSS. Bristol Record Society Publications, vol. XXI, 1959.
Cartulary of St. Mary Clerkenwell. Ed. W. O. HASSALL. Camden Society, 3rd ser., vol. LXXI, 1949.
Cartulary of the Hospital of St. John the Baptist. Ed. H. E. SALTER. Oxford Historical Series, vols. LXVI, LXVIII–LXIX, 1914–16.
Cartulary of the Priory of St. Gregory, Canterbury. Ed. AUDREY M. WOODCOCK. Camden Society, 3rd ser., vol. LXXXVIII, 1956.
Catalogue of Ancient Deeds. H. M. Stationery Office, 1890–1915.
Chancellor's Roll 8 Richard I. Ed. DORIS M. STENTON. Pipe Roll Society, vol. XLV, new ser. VII, 1930.
" Chronica de Wallia," ed. THOMAS JONES, *Bulletin of the Board of Celtic Studies,* vol. XII, 1946–48.
Chronica Maiorum et Vicecomitum Londoniarum. Ed. T. STAPLETON. Camden Society, old ser., vol. XLVI, 1846.
The Chronicle of Bury St. Edmunds 1212–1301. Ed. ANTONIA GRANSDEN. London and Edinburgh, 1964.
" Chronicle of the Thirteenth Century," in *Archaeologia Cambrensis,* 3rd ser., vol. VIII, 1862.
Chronicle of Walter of Guisborough. Ed. HARRY ROTHWELL. Camden Society, 3rd ser., vol. LXXXIX, 1957.
Chronicon de Lanercost. Ed. J. STEVENSON. Bannatyne Club, 1839.
Chronicon Thomae Wykes. Ed. H. R. LUARD. *Annales Monastici,* vol. IV, Rolls Series XXXVI, 1869.
Chroniques de London. Ed. G. AUNGIER. Camden Society, old ser., vol. XXVIII, 1846.
Close Rolls, Henry III [1227–72]. H. M. Stationery Office, 1902–38.
Collectanea Topographica et Genealogica. Vol. IV, London, 1837.
Court Rolls of the Abbey of Ramsey and the Honor of Clare. Ed. WARREN O. AULT. New Haven, 1928.

Curia Regis Rolls, Richard I– . H. M. Stationery Office, 1922– .
Devon Feet of Fines. Eds. O. J. REICHEL, F. B. PRIDEAUX, and H. TAPLEY-SOPER. Devon and Cornwall Record Society, 1912–39.
Domesday-Book. See *Liber Censualis vocatus Domesday-Book.*
Dunstable. See *Annales Prioratus de Dunstaplia.*
Durham Annals and Documents of the Thirteenth Century. Ed. FRANK BARLOW. Surtees Society, vol. CLV, 1945.
EADMER. *Historia Novorum.* Ed. REV. M. RULE. Rolls Series LXXXI, 1884.
Episcopal Acts relating to Welsh Dioceses 1066–1272. Ed. J. CONWAY DAVIES. Historical Society of the Church in Wales, nos. I, III, 1946–48.
Excerpta e Rotulis Finium 1216–72. Ed. CHARLES ROBERTS. Record Commission, 1835–36.
Feet of Fines for the County of Somerset 1196–1307. Ed. E. GREEN. Somerset Record Society, vol. VI, 1892.
Feet of Fines for the County of York, 1246–72. Ed. JOHN PARKER. Yorkshire Archaeological Society, Record Series vol. LXXII, 1932.
Feet of Fines Relating to County Sussex [1249–1307]. Ed. L. F. SALZMANN. Sussex Record Society, vol. VII, 1908.
Feudal Aids. H. M. Stationery Office, 1899–1921.
Final Concords of the County of Lincoln, 1242–1272. Ed. C. W. FOSTER. Lincoln Record Society, vol. XVII, 1920.
Flores Historiarum. Ed. H. R. LUARD. Rolls Series XCV, 1890.
Foedera, Conventiones, Litterae. Ed. THOMAS RYMER. New ed., ed. A. CLARK *et al.* Record Commission, 1816–69.
GERVASE OF CANTERBURY. *Historical Works.* Ed. WILLIAM STUBBS. Rolls Series LXXIII, 1879–80.
The Great Charter of Glastonbury. Ed. DOM AELRED WATKIN. Somerset Record Society, vols. LIX, LXIII–LXIV, 1944–49/50.
GIUSEPPI. See " Wardrobe and Household Accounts of Bogo de Clare, 1284–86."
GUISBOROUGH. See *Chronicle of Walter of Guisborough.*
Historia et Cartularium Monasterii Sancti Petri, Gloucestriae. Ed. W. H. HART. Rolls Series XXXIII, 1863–67.
Irish Monastic and Episcopal Deeds. Ed. NEWPORT B. WHITE. Irish MSS Commission, 1936.
Irish Pipe Roll 14 John. Eds. OLIVER DAVIES and DAVID B. QUINN. *Ulster Journal of Archaeology,* vol. IV, 1941 (Supplement).
Irish Pipe Rolls 16 Henry III–6 Edward III. 35th–43rd Reports of the Deputy Keeper of the Public Records, Ireland. Dublin: H. M. Stationery Office, 1903–12.
Letters from Northern Registers. Ed. J. RAINE. Rolls Series LXI, 1873.
Liber Censualis vocatus Domesday-Book. Eds. A. FARLEY and SIR HENRY ELLIS. Record Commission, 1783–1816.
Liber Primus Kilkenniensis. Ed. CHARLES McNEILL. Irish MSS Commission, 1931.
Liberate Roll 2 John. See *Memoranda Roll 1 John.*
Littere Wallie. Ed. J. G. EDWARDS. Board of Celtic Studies, History and Law Series, no. V, Cardiff, 1940.
The Marcher Lordships of South Wales 1415–1536: Select Documents. Ed. T. B. PUGH. Board of Celtic Studies, History and Law Series, no. XX, Cardiff, 1963.
Memoranda de Parliamento. Ed. F. M. MAITLAND. Rolls Series XCVIII, 1893.
Memoranda Roll 1 John. Ed. H. G. RICHARDSON. Pipe Roll Society, vol. LIX, new. ser. XXI, 1943.
Memoranda Roll 10 John. Ed. R. ALLEN BROWN. Pipe Roll Society, vol. LXIX, new ser. XXXI, 1957.

Ministers' Accounts of the Earldom of Cornwall 1296–1297. Ed. MARGARET MIDG-
LEY. Camden Society, 3rd ser., vols. LXVI, LXVIII, 1942–45.
Monasticon Anglicanum. Ed. WILLIAM DUGDALE. New ed., ed. J. CALEY *et al.*
London, 1817–30.
ORDERIC VITALIS. *Historia Ecclesiastica.* Ed. AUGUSTE LE PRÉVOST. Société de
l'Histoire de France, 1838–55.
PARIS, MATTHEW. *Chronica Majora.* Ed. H. R. LUARD. Rolls Series LVII, 1872–84.
Parliamentary Writs and Writs of Military Summons. Ed. SIR FRANCIS PALGRAVE.
Record Commission, 1827–34.
Parliaments and Councils of Medieval Ireland. Eds. H. G. RICHARDSON and G. O.
SAYLES. Irish MSS Commission, 1947.
Patent Rolls 1216–1232. H. M. Stationery Office, 1901–3.
Pedes Finium or Fines Relating to County Cambridge, 7 Richard I–Richard III.
Ed. WALTER RYE. Cambridge Antiquarian Society, 1891.
Pipe Rolls 2 Richard I–14 Henry III. Eds. DORIS M. STENTON *et al.* Pipe Roll
Society, vols. XXXIX–LII, new ser. I–XIV, 1925–36.
Pipe Roll 26 Henry III. Ed. H. L. CANNON. New Haven, 1927.
Placita de Quo Warranto. Ed. W. ILLINGSWORTH. Record Commission, 1818.
Red Book of the Exchequer. Ed. HUBERT HALL. Roll Series XCIX, 1896.
Register of John le Romeyn, Lord Archbishop of York, 1286–1296. Ed. WILLIAM
BROWN. Surtees Society, vols. CXXIII, CXXVIII, 1913–16.
Register of the Abbey of St. Thomas, Dublin. Ed. JOHN T. GILBERT. Rolls
Series XCIV, 1889.
Register of Walter Bronescombe, 1257–80. Ed. F. L. HINGESTON-RANDOLPH.
London, 1889.
Register of Walter Giffard, Archbishop of York, 1266–1279. Ed. WILLIAM BROWN.
Surtees Society, vol. CIX, 1904.
Register of William Wickwane, Lord Archbishop of York, 1279–1285. Ed.
WILLIAM BROWN. Surtees Society, vol. CXIV, 1907.
Registers of Roger Martival, Bishop of Salisbury, 1315–1330. Eds. KATHLEEN
EDWARDS and C. R. ELRINGTON. Canterbury and York Society, vols. LV, LVII,
1959–63.
Registrum Epistolarum Johannis Peckham. Ed. C. T. MARTIN. Rolls Series LXXVII,
1882–86.
Registrum Henrici Woodlock, diocesis Wintoniensis, 1305–1316. Ed. A. W.
GOODMAN. Canterbury and York Society, vols. XLIII–XLIV, 1940–41.
Registrum Johannis de Pontissara, Episcopi Wintoniensis, 1282–1304. Ed. CECIL
DEEDES. Canterbury and York Society, vols. XIX, XXX, 1915–24.
Registrum Roberti Winchelsey 1294–1313. Ed. ROSE GRAHAM. Canterbury and
York Society, vols. LI–LII, 1952–56.
Registrum Roffense. Ed. J. Thorpe. London, 1769.
Registrum Simonis de Gandavo, diocesis Saresbiriensis, 1297–1315. Eds. C. T.
FLOWER and M. C. B. DAWES. Canterbury and York Society, vols. XL–XLI,
1934.
RISHANGER, WILLIAM DE. *Chronica et Annales.* Ed. H. R. LUARD in *Chronica
Monasterii S. Albani,* vol. II, Rolls Series XXVIII, 1865.
Rolls and Register of Bishop Oliver Sutton (1280–1299). Ed. ROSALIND M. T.
HILL. Lincoln Record Society, vols. XXXIX, XLIII, XLVIII, 1948–54.
Rotuli Chartarum 1199–1216. Ed. THOMAS DUFFY HARDY. Record Commission,
1837.

Rotuli Hugonis de Welles, episcopi Lincolniensis, 1209–1235. Ed. W. PHILLIMORE *et al.* Lincoln Record Society, vols. III, VI, IX, 1912–14.
Rotuli Hundredorum. Record Commission, 1812–18.
Rotuli Litterarum Clausarum 1204–1227. Ed. T. D. HARDY. Record Commission, 1833–44.
Rotuli Parliamentorum. Record Commission, 1783–1832.
Rotuli Ricardi Gravesend, diocesis Lincolniensis. Ed. F. N. DAVIS. Lincoln Record Society, vol. XX, 1925.
Rotuli Roberti Grosseteste, episcopi Lincolniensis, 1235–1253. Ed. F. N. DAVIS. Lincoln Record Society, vol. XI, 1914.
Rotuli Scotiae. Ed. D. MACPHERSON *et al.* Record Commission, 1814–19.
Rotuli Selecti. Ed. JOSEPH HUNTER. Record Commission, 1834.
Rotulorum Originalium in Curia Scaccarii Abbreviatio. Ed. H. PLAYFORD. Record Commission, 1805–10.
Royal Letters, Henry III. Ed. WALTER W. SHIRLEY. Rolls Series XXVII, 1862–66.
SAYLES. *Select Cases.* See *Select Cases in the Court of King's Bench under Edward I.*
Select Cases in the Court of King's Bench under Edward I. Ed. G. O. SAYLES. Selden Society, vols. LV, LVII–LVIII, 1936–39.
Select Cases in the Exchequer of Pleas. Eds. HILARY JENKINSON and BERYL FERMOY. Selden Society, vol. XLVIII, 1931.
Select Cases of Procedure without Writ, Henry III. Eds. H. G. RICHARDSON and G. O. SAYLES. Selden Society, vol. LX, 1941.
Select Charters. Ed. WILLIAM STUBBS. 9th ed., ed. H. W. C. DAVIS. Oxford, 1921.
Select Pleas of the Forest. Ed. G. J. TURNER. Selden Society, vol. XIII, 1899.
Sir Christopher Hatton's Book of Seals. Eds. LEWIS C. LLOYD and DORIS M. STENTON. Northamptonshire Record Society, vol. XV, 1950.
Somerset Pleas. Vols. II–III [41 Henry III–7 Edward I]. Ed. LIONEL LANDON. Somerset Record Society, vols. XXXVI, XLI, 1923–26.
Statutes and Ordinances and Acts of the Parliaments of Ireland, John–Henry V. Ed. H. F. BERRY. Dublin: H. M. Stationery Office, 1907.
Statutes of the Realm. Ed. A. LUDERS *et al.* Record Commission, 1810–28.
Surrey Manorial Accounts. Ed. HELEN BRIGGS. Surrey Record Society, vol. XV, 1935.
Tewkesbury. See *Annales de Theokesberia.*
Vita Edwardi Secundi. Ed. N. DENHOLM-YOUNG. London and Edinburgh, 1957.
"Wardrobe and Household Accounts of Bogo de Clare, 1284–1286." Ed. M. S. GIUSEPPI. *Archaeologia,* vol. LXX, 1918–20.
The Welsh Assize Roll, 1277–84. Ed. J. CONWAY DAVIES. Board of Celtic Studies, History and Law Series, no. VII, Cardiff, 1940.
WYKES. See *Chronicon Thomae Wykes.*
York Minster Fasti. Ed. Sir CHARLES TRAVIS CLAY. Yorkshire Archaeological Society, Record Series, vols. CXXIII–CXXIV, 1958–59.

SECONDARY WORKS

BALLARD, A. and J. TAIT. *British Borough Charters 1216–1307.* Cambridge, 1923.
BARNARDISTON, K. W. *Clare Priory.* Cambridge, 1962.
BARROW, G. W. S. *Robert Bruce.* Berkeley, 1965.
BATESON, MARY. "Irish Exchequer Memoranda of the Reign of Edward I," *English Historical Review,* vol. XVIII, 1903.

BAYLEY, CHARLES C. *The Formation of the German College of Electors in the Mid-Thirteenth Century.* Toronto, 1949.
BEAN, J. M. W. *Estates of the Percy Family 1416–1537.* Oxford, 1958.
BEARDWOOD, ALICE. "The Trial of Walter Langton, Bishop of Lichfield, 1307–1312," *Transactions of the American Philosophical Society,* new ser., LIV (1964), pt. 3.
BÉMONT, CHARLES. *Simon de Montfort.* Paris, 1884. New ed., trans. E. F. JACOB. Oxford, 1930.
BISSON, THOMAS P. "An Early Provincial Assembly: the General Court of Agenais in the Thirteenth Century," *Speculum,* vol. XXXVI, 1961.
BRENTANO, ROBERT. *York Metropolitan Jurisdiction and Papal Judges Delegate 1279–1296.* Berkeley, 1959.
BRIEGER, PETER. *English Art 1216–1307.* Oxford, 1957.
BROOKE, CHRISTOPHER. *The Saxon and Norman Kings.* London, 1963.
BROOKS, ERIC ST. J. "Irish Possessions of St. Thomas of Acre," *Proceedings of the Royal Irish Academy,* vol. LVIII, 1956–57, section C.
——. *Knights' Fees in Counties Wexford, Carlow and Kilkenny, 13th–15th Centuries.* Irish MSS Commission, 1950.
CHURCHILL, IRENE J. *Canterbury Administration.* 2 vols. London, 1933.
C[OKAYNE], G. E. *The Complete Peerage . . . of the United Kingdom. . . .* 12 vols. New ed., ed. VICARY GIBBS et al. London, 1910–59.
CURTIS, EDMUND. *History of Medieval Ireland.* Dublin, 1923.
DAVIES, J. CONWAY. *Baronial Opposition to Edward II.* Cambridge, 1918.
——. "The Despenser War in Glamorgan," *Transactions of the Royal Historical Society,* 3rd ser., vol. IX, 1915.
DENHOIM-YOUNG, N. *Richard of Cornwall.* Oxford, 1947.
——. *Seignorial Administration in England.* Oxford, 1937.
DOUGLAS, DAVID. "The Earliest Norman Counts," *English Historical Review,* vol. LXI, 1946.
EDWARDS, SIR J. GORONWY. "The Normans and the Welsh March," *Proceedings of the British Academy,* vol. XLII, 1956.
EDWARDS, KATHLEEN. *The English Secular Cathedrals in the Middle Ages.* Manchester, 1949.
——. "The Social Origins and Provenance of the English Bishops during the Reign of Edward II," *Transactions of the Royal Historical Society,* 5th ser., vol. IX, 1959.
EHRLICH, L. *Proceedings against the Crown, 1216–1377.* Oxford, 1921.
EMDEN, A. B. *Biographical Register of the University of Oxford to 1500.* 3 vols. Oxford, 1957–59.
FARRER, WILLIAM. *Honors and Knights' Fees.* 3 vols. London, 1923–25.
FRASER, C. M. "Edward I and the Regalian Franchise of Durham," *Speculum,* vol. XXXI, 1956.
G. E. C. See C[OKAYNE], G. E. *The Complete Peerage . . .*
GREENWAY, W. "The Election of John de Monmouth, Bishop of Llandaff, 1287–97," *Morgannwg,* vol. V, 1961.
HOLMES, G. A. *Estates of the Higher Nobility in Fourteenth Century England.* Cambridge, 1957.
——. "A Protest against the Despensers, 1326," *Speculum,* vol. XXX, 1955.
HOLT, J. C. *The Northerners.* Oxford, 1961.
HOWELL, MARGARET. *Regalian Right in Medieval England.* London, 1962.
JACOB, E. F. "The Complaints of Henry III against the Baronial Council in 1261," *English Historical Review,* vol. XLI, 1926.

——. "The Reign of Henry III: Some Suggestions," *Transactions of the Royal Historical Society*, 4th ser., vol. X, 1927.

——. *Studies in the Period of Baronial Reform and Rebellion, 1258–1267.* Oxford, 1925.

JOHNSTONE, HILDA. *Edward of Carnarvon.* Manchester, 1946.

LAWRENCE, C. H. *St. Edmund of Abingdon.* Oxford, 1960.

LEWIS, ALUN. "Roger Leyburn and the Pacification of England, 1265–1267," *English Historical Review*, vol. LIV, 1939.

LEWIS, CERI. "The Treaty of Woodstock, 1247," *Welsh History Review*, vol. II, 1964– .

LEWIS, N. B. "The English Forces in Flanders, August–November 1297," in *Studies in Medieval History presented to Frederick Maurice Powicke.* Oxford, 1948.

LEWIS, RICE. "A Breviat of Glamorgan, 1596–1600." Ed. WILLIAM REES. South Wales and Monmouth Record Society, vol. III, 1954.

LLOYD, SIR JOHN E. *A History of Wales to the Edwardian Conquest.* 2 vols. 3rd ed.; London, 1939.

——. "Llywelyn ap Gruffydd and the Lordship of Glamorgan," *Archaeologia Cambrensis*, 6th ser. vol. XIII, 1913.

LUNT, W. E. *Financial Relations of the Papacy with England to 1327.* Cambridge, Mass., 1939.

LYDON, J. F. "The Bruce Invasion of Ireland," *Historical Studies*, vol. IV, 1963.

McFARLANE, K. B. "Had Edward I a 'policy' towards the earls?," *History*, vol. L, 1965.

McKISACK, MAY. *The Fourteenth Century.* Oxford, 1959.

MILLER, EDWARD. *The Abbey and Bishopric of Ely.* Cambridge, 1951.

——. "The English Economy in the Thirteenth Century," *Past and Present*, no. 28, July, 1964.

MOORMAN, J. H. *Church Life in England in the 13th Century.* Cambridge, 1945.

MORGAN, MARJORIE. *English Lands of the Abbey of Bec.* Oxford, 1946.

MORRIS, JOHN E. *The Welsh Wars of Edward I.* Oxford, 1901.

NUGENT, W. F. "Carlow in the Middle Ages," *Journal of the Royal Society of Antiquaries of Ireland*, vol. LXXXV, 1955.

OMAN, SIR CHARLES. *History of the Art of War in the Middle Ages.* 2 vols. 2nd ed.; London, 1924.

ORPEN, GODDARD H. *Ireland under the Normans 1169–1333.* 4 vols. Oxford, 1911–20.

OTWAY-RUTHVEN, J. "Anglo–Irish Shire Government in the 13th Century," *Irish Historical Studies*, vol. V, 1946–47.

——. "The Constitutional Position of the Great Lordships of South Wales," *Transactions of the Royal Historical Society*, 5th ser., vol. VIII, 1958.

——. "Knight–Service in Ireland," *Journal of the Royal Society of Antiquaries of Ireland*, vol. LXXXIX, 1959.

——. "The Medieval County of Kildare," *Irish Historical Studies*, vol. XI, 1959.

PAINTER, SIDNEY. "The Earl of Clare," in *Feudalism and Liberty.* Ed. FRED A. CAZEL, JR. Baltimore, 1961.

——. "The Family and the Feudal System in Twelfth Century England," *Speculum*, vol. XXXV, 1960.

——. *The Reign of King John.* Baltimore, 1949.

——. *Studies in the History of the English Feudal Barony.* Baltimore, 1943.

——. *William Marshal.* Baltimore, 1933.

PAINTER, SIDNEY, and FRED A. CAZEL, JR. "The Marriage of Isabelle of Angoulême," *English Historical Review*, vols. LXIII, 1948; LXVII, 1952.
PANTIN, W. A. *The English Church in the XIVth Century*. Cambridge, 1955.
PEGUES, FRANK. "Royal Support of Students in the Thirteenth Century," *Speculum*, vol. XXXI, 1956.
PLUCKNETT, T. F. T. *Legislation of Edward I*. Oxford, 1949.
POLLOCK, SIR FREDERICK, and FREDERICK WILLIAM MAITLAND. *History of English Law*. 2 vols. 2nd ed.; Cambridge, 1898.
POOLE, AUSTIN LANE. *Domesday Book to Magna Carta*. 2nd ed.; Oxford, 1955.
POWICKE, F. M. *King Henry III and the Lord Edward*. 2 vols. Oxford, 1947.
――――. *The Loss of Normandy 1189–1204*. 2nd ed.; Manchester, 1961.
――――. "The Oath of Bromholm," *English Historical Review*, vol. LVI, 1941.
――――. "Some Observations on the Baronial Council (1258–1260) and the Provisions of Westminster," in *Essays in Medieval History Presented to Thomas Frederick Tout*. Manchester, 1932.
――――. *The Thirteenth Century*. Oxford, 1953.
POWICKE, MICHAEL. *Military Obligation in Medieval England*. Oxford, 1962.
REES, WILLIAM. *Caerphilly Castle*. Cardiff, 1937.
――――. "The Medieval Lordship of Brecon," *Transactions of the Honourable Society of Cymmrodorion*, 1915–16.
――――. *South Wales and the March 1284–1415*. Oxford, 1924.
RICHARDS, MELVILLE. "The Significance of *Is* and *Uwch* in Welsh Commote and Cantref Names," *Welsh History Review*, vol. II, 1964– .
RICHARDSON, H. G., and G. O. SAYLES. *The Irish Parliament in the Middle Ages*. Philadelphia, 1952.
ROTHWELL, HARRY. "Edward I and the Struggle for the Charters, 1297–1305," in *Studies in Medieval History presented to Frederick Maurice Powicke*. Oxford, 1948.
ROUND, J. HORACE. *Feudal England*. London, 1895.
――――. *Geoffrey de Mandeville*. London, 1892.
――――. *Studies in Peerage and Family History*. Westminster, 1901.
RUNCIMAN, SIR STEVEN. *The Sicilian Vespers*. Cambridge, 1958.
SANDERS, I. J. *English Baronies*. Oxford, 1960.
――――. *Feudal Military Service in England*. Oxford, 1956.
SMITH, J. BEVERLY. "The 'Chronica de Wallia' and the Dynasty of Dinefwr," *Bulletin of the Board of Celtic Studies*, vol. XX, 1962–64.
――――. "The Lordship of Glamorgan," *Morgannwg*, vol. II, 1958.
STENTON, DORIS M. *English Society in the Early Middle Ages (1066–1307)*. Harmondsworth, 1952.
STENTON, SIR FRANK. *Anglo-Saxon England*. 2nd ed.; Oxford, 1947.
――――. *The First Century of English Feudalism 1066–1166*. 2nd ed.; Oxford, 1961.
SUTHERLAND, DONALD W. *Quo Warranto Proceedings in the Reign of Edward I 1278–1294*. Oxford, 1963.
TAYLOR, A. J. "Building at Caerphilly in 1326," *Bulletin of the Board of Celtic Studies*, vol. XIV, 1950–52.
――――. "Military Architecture," in *Medieval England*. New ed., ed. A. L. POOLE. Oxford, 1958.
THOMPSON, A. HAMILTON. *The English Clergy and their Organization in the Later Middle Ages*. Oxford, 1947.
――――. "Pluralism in the Medieval Church," *Associated Architectural Societies' Reports and Papers*, vols. XXXIII, 1915; XXXIV, 1917; XXXV, 1919–20; XXXVI, 1921.

THORNE, S. E. "English Feudalism and Estates in Land," *Cambridge Law Journal,* 1959.

TOMKINSON, A. "Retinues at the Tournament of Dunstable, 1309," *English Historical Review,* vol. LXXIV, 1959.

TOUT, T. F. *Chapters in the Administrative History of Medieval England.* 6 vols. Manchester, 1920–33.

————. "The Earldoms under Edward I," *Transactions of the Royal Historical Society,* new ser., vol. VIII, 1894.

————. *The Place of the Reign of Edward II in English History.* Manchester, 1914. 2nd ed., ed. HILDA JOHNSTONE, 1936.

————. "Wales and the March during the Barons' War," in *Collected Papers of Thomas Frederick Tout.* 3 vols. Manchester, 1934.

TREHARNE, R. F. *The Baronial Plan of Reform 1258–1263.* Manchester, 1932.

WALNE, P. "The Barons' Argument at Amiens, January 1264," *English Historical Review,* vols. LXIX, 1954; LXXIII, 1958.

WATERS, W. H. *The Edwardian Settlement of North Wales.* Cardiff, 1935.

WILKINSON, B. *The Constitutional History of England 1216–1399.* 3 vols. London, 1948–56.

————. *Studies in the Constitutional History of the 13th and 14th Centuries.* Manchester, 1937.

WILLARD, JAMES F. *Parliamentary Taxes on Personal Property 1290 to 1334.* Cambridge, Mass., 1934.

WILLIAMS, GLANMOR. *The Welsh Church from Conquest to Reformation.* Cardiff, 1962.

WILLIAMS, GWYN A. *Medieval London.* London, 1963.

WILLIS, BROWNE. *Survey of the Cathedral Church of Llandaff.* London, 1719.

WOOD, SUSAN. *English Monasteries and their Patrons in the Thirteenth Century.* Oxford, 1955.

INDEX

A

Abethrop, Robert de, 232 and *n*, 236, 237

Adlingfleet (York), church of, 36, 183–84, 306

Alexander IV, pope, 84, 85–86, 90

Amicia, countess of Gloucester and Hertford, wife of Richard de Clare, earl of Hertford (d. 1217), 25, 26, 31

Amiens, Mise of, 101, 103

Attorneys: employment of, by Clares, 238; in Kilkenny, 238–39, 290

Audley, Hugh d'. *See* D'Audley, Hugh

B

Badlesmere, Bartholomew de: marriage to Margaret de Clare, 35, 45, 46, 51, 196; death of, 173; keeper of Glamorgan (1314–15), 247, 250, 303; mentioned, 209, 235*n*, 238*n*, 239*n*

Bailiffs, estate: in England, 229, 230–31; in Wales, 258, 262

Bailiffs of fees, on English estates: duties of, 220, 229–30; origins of, 229, 298–99

Bailiwicks, division of English estates into, 222–25, 298. *See also* Clare estates (England), administration of

Baldwin fitz Gilbert of Brionne, 18

Bannockburn, battle of, 40, 159, 164

Barton-juxta-Bristol (Glos.), 27–28, 131*n*

Bienfaite (Normandy), lordship of, 18, 19, 21

Bigod, Hugh (d. 1225), earl of Norfolk, 48*n*, 284

Bigod, Hugh (mid thirteenth century): and baronial reform movement, 81, 85–91 *passim*, 187

Bigod, Roger (d. 1270), earl of Norfolk, 81, 85, 91, 98, 119*n*

Bigod, Roger (d. 1306), earl of Norfolk, 143*n*, 205, 272–73, 274, 293, 307

Bigod estates: fees on, 27*n*, 77*n*; value of, 205, 293. *See also* Carlow, lordship of; Striguil, castle and lordship of

Bohun, Humphrey de (d. 1265), lord of Brecknock, 48, 97, 99*n*, 110

Bohun, Humphrey de (d. 1275), earl of Hereford and Essex: keeper of Glamorgan (1262), 95, 96, 99, 246; (1266), 117; mentioned, 44, 48, 85, 91, 98, 119*n*

Bohun, Humphrey de (d. 1298), earl of Hereford and Essex: as lord of Brecknock, 132–33, 151–52, 274; and Welsh wars, 140, 144; dispute with Gilbert de Clare (1290–92), 146–53, 272

Bohun, Humphrey de (d. 1322), earl of Hereford and Essex, 162, 163*n*, 169

Bohun estates: fees on, 27*n*; value of, 206; additions to, 213. *See also* Brecknock, lordship of

Boniface of Savoy, archbishop of Canterbury, 85, 208*n*

Borham, Hervey de, 105, 118, 119, 126*n*, 184, 227–28

Boroughs, Clare: English, 207–9, 219; Welsh, 243–44, 249–50, 254–55; Irish, 291; comparative importance of, 297

Braose, William de (d. 1210), son of William (d. 1211): marriage to Matilda de Clare, 29–30, 45, 46, 54

Braose, William de (d. 1211), lord of Brecknock and Gower, 30

Braose, William de (d. 1230), lord of Brecknock, 42, 48*n*, 143*n*, 284

Braose, William de (d. 1287), bishop of Llandaff, 274 and *n*

Braose, William de (d. 1290), lord of Gower, 99*n*, 271–72, 274

321

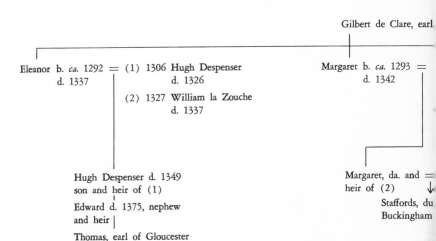

Gilbert de Clare, earl

Eleanor b. *ca.* 1292 = (1) 1306 Hugh Despenser
    d. 1337   d. 1326

            (2) 1327 William la Zouche
                  d. 1337

Margaret b. *ca.* 1293 =
    d. 1342

Hugh Despenser d. 1349
son and heir of (1)
Edward d. 1375, nephew
and heir
Thomas, earl of Gloucester
(forf. 1399) d. 1400
Beauchamps and Nevilles,
earls of Warwick (to 1474)

Margaret, da. and =
heir of (2)
    Staffords, du
    Buckingham

DESCENDANTS

of Gloucester d. 1295

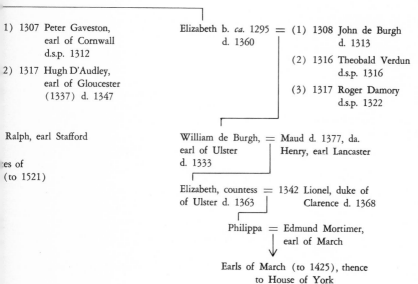

1) 1307 Peter Gaveston,
   earl of Cornwall
   d.s.p. 1312

2) 1317 Hugh D'Audley,
   earl of Gloucester
   (1337) d. 1347

Ralph, earl Stafford

es of
(to 1521)

Elizabeth b. *ca.* 1295 = (1) 1308 John de Burgh
         d. 1360   d. 1313

                         (2) 1316 Theobald Verdun
                             d.s.p. 1316

                         (3) 1317 Roger Damory
                             d.s.p. 1322

William de Burgh, = Maud d. 1377, da.
earl of Ulster   Henry, earl Lancaster
d. 1333

Elizabeth, countess = 1342 Lionel, duke of
of Ulster d. 1363   Clarence d. 1368

         Philippa = Edmund Mortimer,
                    earl of March

         Earls of March (to 1425), thence
              to House of York

THE JOHNS HOPKINS UNIVERSITY
STUDIES IN
HISTORICAL AND POLITICAL SCIENCE

✦ ✦ ✦

EIGHTY–THIRD SERIES (1965)

1. The Right to Vote: Politics and the Passage
   of the Fifteenth Amendment
   BY WILLIAM GILLETTE

2. A Baronial Family in Medieval England: The
   Clares, 1217–1314
   BY MICHAEL ALTSCHUL

✦ ✦ ✦

THE JOHNS HOPKINS PRESS

BALTIMORE

THE JOHNS HOPKINS UNIVERSITY STUDIES IN
HISTORICAL AND POLITICAL SCIENCE

A subscription for the regular annual series is $8.00. Single numbers may be purchased at special prices. A complete list of the series follows. All paperbound unless otherwise indicated.

FIRST SERIES (1883)—Bound Volume.. O. P.
1. Introduction to American Institutional History, An. By E. A. Freeman..... O. P.
2. Germanic Origin of New England Towns. By H. B. Adams.......... O. P.
3. Local Government in Illinois. By Albert Shaw. Local Government in Pennsylvania. By E. R. L. Gould...... O. P.
4. Saxon Tithingmen in America. By H. B. Adams...................... O. P.
5. Local Government in Michigan and the Northwest. By E. W. Bemis... O. P.
6. Parish Institutions of Maryland. By Edward Ingle.................... O. P.
7. Old Maryland Manors. By John Hemsley Johnson .... O. P.
8. Norman Constables in America. By H. B. Adams .... O. P.
9-10. Village Communities of Cape Ann and Salem. By H. B. Adams....... O. P.
11. Genesis of a New England State. By A. Johnston .... O. P.
12. Local Government and Schools in South Carolina. By B. J. Ramage... O. P.

SECOND SERIES (1884)—Bound Volume O. P.
1-2. Method of Historical Study. By H. B. Adams...................... O. P.
3. Past and Present of Political Economy. By R. T. Ely..................... O. P.
4. Samuel Adams, the Man of the Town Meeting. By James K. Hosmer..... O. P.
5-6. Taxation in the United States. By Henry Carter Adams............... O. P.
7. Institutional Beginnings in a Western State. By Jesse Macy............. O. P.
8-9. Indian Money in New England, etc. By William B. Weedon........... O. P.
10. Town and Country Government in the Colonies. By E. Channing........ O. P.
11. Rudimentary Society Among Boys. By J. Hemsley Johnson.............. O. P.
12. Land Laws of Mining Districts. By C. H. Shinn.................... O. P.

THIRD SERIES (1885)—Bound Volume. O.
1. Maryland's Influence Upon Land Cessions to the U. S. By H. B. Adams.. O.
2-3. Virginia Local Institutions. By E. Ingle .... O.
4. Recent American Socialism. By Richard T. Ely..................... O
5-6-7. Maryland Local Institutions. By Lewis W. Wilhelm............... O.
8. Influence of the Proprietors in Founding New Jersey. By A. Scott....... O.
9-10. American Constitutions. By Horace Davis .... O.
11-12. City of Washington. By J. A. Porter .... O.

FOURTH SERIES (1886)—Bound Volume O.
1. Dutch Village Communities on the Hudson River. By I. Elting....... O.
2-3. Town Government in Rhode Island. By W. E. Foster. The Narragansett Planters. By Edward Channing...... O.
4. Pennsylvania Boroughs. By William P. Holcomb .... O.
5. Introduction to Constitutional History of the States. By J. F. Jameson.... O.
6. Puritan Colony at Annapolis, Maryland. By D. R. Randall............ O.
7-8-9. Land Question in the United States. By S. Sato..................... O.
10. Town and City Government of New Haven. By C. H. Levermore....... O.
11-12. Land System of the New England Colonies. By M. Egleston.......... O.

FIFTH SERIES (1887)—$8.00
1-2. City Government of Philadelphia. By E. P. Allinson and B. Penrose....... O.
3. City Government of Boston. By James M. Bugbee..................... O.
4. City Government of St. Louis. By Marshall S. Snow................. O.
5-6. Local Government in Canada. By John George Bourinot............. O.

iii

6-7. White Servitude in the Colony of
Virginia. By J. C. Ballagh........ O. P.
8. Genesis of California's First Constitution. By R. D. Hunt............... O. P.
9. Benjamin Franklin as an Economist.
By W. A. Wetzel................. O. P.
10. Provisional Government of Maryland.
By J. A. Silver.................... O. P.
11-12. Government and Religion of the
Virginia Indians. By S. R. Hendren. O. P.

FOURTEENTH SERIES (1896) — Bound
Volume .... O. P.
1. Constitutional History of Hawaii. By
Henry E. Chambers............... O. P.
2. City Government of Baltimore. By
Thaddeus P. Thomas .... O. P.
3. Colonial Origins of New England
Senates. By F. L. Riley............ O. P.
4-5. Servitude in the Colony of North
Carolina. By J. S. Bassett.......... O. P.
6-7. Representation in Virginia. By J. A.
C. Chandler .... O. P.
8. History of Taxation in Connecticut
(1636-1776). By F. R. Jones....... 1.25
9-10. Study of Slavery in New Jersey, A.
By Henry S. Cooley............... O. P.
11-12. Causes of the Maryland Revolution
of 1689. By F. E. Sparks.......... O. P.

FIFTEENTH SERIES (1897)
1-2. Tobacco Industry in Virginia Since
1860. By B. W. Arnold............ O. P.
3-5. Street Railway System of Philadelphia. By F. W. Speirs............ O. P.
6. Daniel Raymond. By C. P. Neill.... 1.25
7-8. Economic History of B. & O. R. R.
By M. Reizenstein .... O. P.
9. South American Trade of Baltimore.
By F. R. Rutter................... 1.50
10-11. State Tax Commissions in the United
States. By J. W. Chapman.......... 3.00
12. Tendencies in American Economic
Thought. By S. Sherwood........ O. P.

SIXTEENTH SERIES (1898)
1-4. Neutrality of the American Lakes,
etc. By J. M. Callahan............ O. P.
5. West Florida. By H. E. Chambers.. O. P.
6. Anti-Slavery Leaders of North Carolina. By J. S. Bassett............. O. P.
7-9. Life and Administration of Sir Robert
Eden. By B. C. Steiner........... 3.00
10-11. Transition of North Carolina from
a Colony. By E. W. Sikes......... O. P.
12. Jared Sparks and Alexis de Tocque-
ville. By H. B. Adams........... O. P.

SEVENTEENTH SERIES (1899)
1-2-3. History of State Banking in Maryland. By A. C. Bryan.... .... O. P.

4-5. Know-Nothing Party in Maryland.
By L. F. Schmeckebier............. O
6. Labadist Colony in Maryland. By B.
B. James..................... ..... O
7-8. History of Slavery in North Carolina. By J. S. Bassett.............. O
9-10-11. Development of the Chesapeake
and Ohio Canal. By G. W. Ward... O
12. Public Educational Work in Baltimore.
By Herbert B. Adams.............. 1

EIGHTEENTH SERIES (1900)
1-4. Studies in State Taxation. By J. H.
Hollander........Paper 4.00; Cloth 5
5-6. Colonial Executive Prior to the Restoration. By P. L. Kaye........... O
7. Constitution and Admission of Iowa
into the Union. By J. A. James.... O
8-9. Church and Popular Education. By
H. B. Adams..................... O
10-12. Religious Freedom in Virginia:
The Baptists. By W. T. Thom..... O

NINETEENTH SERIES (1901)
1-3. America in the Pacific and the Far
East. By J. M. Callahan........... O
4-5. State Activities in Relation to Labor.
By W. F. Willoughby............._.. O
6-7. History of Suffrage in Virginia. By
J. A. C. Chandler................. O
8-9. Maryland Constitution of 1864. By
W. S. Myers....................... C
10. Life of Commissary James Blair. By
D. E. Motley C
11-12. Governor Hicks of Maryland and
the Civil War. By G. L. Radcliffe.. O

TWENTIETH SERIES (1902) — Bound
Volume .... O
1. Western Maryland in the Revolution.
By B. C. Steiner.................. O
2-3. State Banks Since the National Bank
Act. By G. E. Barnett............ O
4. Early History of Internal Improvements in Alabama. By W. E. Martin. O
5-6. Trust Companies in the United States.
By George Cator.................. O
7-8. Maryland Constitution of 1851. By
J. W. Harry...................... O
9-10. Political Activities of Philip Fre-
neau. By S. E. Forman............ O
11 12. Continental Opinion on a Proposed
Middle European Tariff Union. By
G. M. Fisk...................... 1

TWENTY-FIRST SERIES (1903)—Bound
Volume .... O
1-2. Wabash Trade Route. By E. J.
Benton .... O
3-4. Internal Improvements in North
Carolina. By C. C. Weaver. ...... O

iv

v

vi